Praise for *Even* This *I Get to Experience*

"Lear is one of the great storytellers of our time a̶̶̶̶̶̶̶̶ point home. . . . This book should be required rea̶̶̶̶g ̶̶ ̶ ̶ Hollywood."
—James Patterson

"This is, flat out, one of the best Hollywood memoirs ever written. . . . An absolute treasure."
—*Booklist* (starred review)

"Fantastic stories from one of the wisest, most subversive, and most beautiful human beings the comedy world has ever known. Like the man himself, this book is charming, awe-inspiring, and hilarious."
—Trey Parker

"A TV titan on his memorable life and storied career. Lear, best known as the creative mind behind such classic comedies as *All in the Family*, *Maude*, *The Jeffersons*, and *Good Times*, recounts his extraordinarily eventful life with his signature wit and irreverence. The result is not just a vividly observed and evocative portrait of a long life, but also a fascinating backstage look at the evolution of the American entertainment industry. . . . Lear writes movingly of his service in World War II, his difficult upbringing and subsequent troubled marriages, and his commitment to liberal causes, evidenced by his founding of the advocacy organization People for the American Way and his purchase of an original copy of the Declaration of Independence. That he makes these subjects as engrossing and entertaining as his Hollywood reminiscences speaks to Lear's mastery of storytelling and humor. A big-hearted, richly detailed chronicle of comedy, commitment, and a long life lived fully."
—*Kirkus Reviews* (starred review)

"That Norman Lear can find humor in life's darkest moments is no surprise—it's the reason he's been so successful throughout his more than nine decades on earth, and why Americans have relied on his wit and wisdom for more than six. It's also why *Even* This *I Get to Experience* is such a great read."
—President William J. Clinton

"[A] feisty, thoughtful autobiography . . . Lear pens sharply observed studies of the creative process on his many iconic productions and bares plenty of raucous, someti̶̶̶̶ ̶̶b̶a̶w̶d̶y̶ ̶a̶n̶e̶c̶d̶o̶t̶e̶s̶ ̶ ̶readers get to experience a nude and lewd

Jerry Lewis. . . . In keeping with the bigoted, mouthy, complex, and loveable characters he created, Lear's knack for sizing up a flawed humanity makes for an absorbing read." —*Publishers Weekly*

"Norman Lear is a hero and a friend. . . . He experienced so much in his life . . . sometimes I just want to sit down and ask him questions about life and his perspective. . . . To do it right it would take years of interviews . . . but now that he wrote this book I can experience his journey and wisdom over and over again." —will.i.am

"Many have known the Man behind the stories. Now all of us can know the stories behind the Man. Archie, Edith, Gloria, and Meathead couldn't have told them better!" —Bill Moyers

"An entertaining, penetrating celebration of a richly lived life." —Associated Press

"*Even* This *I Get to Experience* is not just the brilliant, moving story of a man who has lived an amazing number of lives—from making it onto Richard Nixon's 'Enemies List' to changing the face of television—but also a life manual on how to live a life of depth, purpose, and meaning." —Arianna Huffington

"Immensely likeable . . . [Lear] isn't always a mensch in *Even* This *I Get to Experience* (italics, characteristically, his), but at least he can write like one. . . . In this city, Norman Lear and his post-coaxial contemporaries built a mass medium with their bare hands. On good days—as Lear well recalls, and recalls well—they made it sing. If only more with their talent had lived so long; if only more who live so long had his talent." —*Los Angeles Times*

"Norman Lear could never write a more dramatic, touching, or funnier tale of his life than he's done here in *Even* This *I Get to Experience*." —Carl Reiner

PENGUIN BOOKS

EVEN *THIS* I GET TO EXPERIENCE

Norman Lear is the television producer of such groundbreaking sitcoms as *All in the Family, Sanford and Son, One Day at a Time, The Jeffersons, Good Times*, and *Maude*. He has received four Emmy awards, a Peabody, and the National Medal of Arts. As an advocate, Lear founded People for the American Way and supports First Amendment rights and other progressive causes.

Even *This* I Get to Experience

||||||||

Norman Lear

Penguin Books

PENGUIN BOOKS
An imprint of Penguin Random House LLC
375 Hudson Street
New York, New York 10014
penguin.com

First published in the United States of America by The Penguin Press,
a member of Penguin Group (USA) LLC, 2014
Published in Penguin Books 2015

Excerpt from "Try to Remember" (from "The Fantasticks"). Lyrics by Tom Jones,
music by Harvey Schmidt. © 1960 (renewed) by Tom Jones and Harvey Schmidt.
Publication and allied rights assigned to Chappell Co., Inc. All rights reserved.
Used by permission of Alfred Music.
Excerpt from "My Way," words and music by Paul Anka, Jacques Revaux,
Gilles Thibaut and Claude Francois. © 1969 BMG Blue (BMI). All rights administered
by BMG Rights Management (US) LLC. Used by permission. All rights reserved.
"My Way" ("Comme D'Habitude") by Gilles Thibaut, Claude Francois,
Jacques Revaux, and English lyrics by Paul Anka, Architectural Music (BMI),
Jingoro Music (BMI).

Photograph credits
Insert pages 6–7 (top): Mark Sennet Entertainment Inc.
Page 11: Photo by Arnold Turner, reproduced by courtesy of the author
Other photographs courtesy of the author

THE LIBRARY OF CONGRESS HAS CATALOGED THE HARDCOVER EDITION AS FOLLOWS:
Lear, Norman.
Even *this* I get to experience / Norman Lear.
pages cm
ISBN 978-1-59420-572-9 (hc.)
ISBN 978-0-14-312796-3 (pbk.)
1. Lear, Norman. 2. Television producers and directors—United States—Biography. 3. Television
comedy writers—United States—Biography. 4. Screenwriters—United States—Biography. I. Title.
PN1992.4.L365A3 2014
791.4502'3092—dc23 [B] 2014032903

Printed in the United States of America
1 3 5 7 9 10 8 6 4 2

Designed by Marysarah Quinn

For Lyn and my six children,
at whose sweet prodding
I have tried to open my veins

You haven't overcome the fear of death until you delight in your own life, believing it to be the carrying out of the universal purpose.

—George Bernard Shaw

Contents

Preface

WHEN I WAS A BOY I thought that if I could turn a screw in my father's head just a sixteenth of an inch one way or the other, it might help him to tell the difference between right and wrong. I couldn't, of course, and ultimately he—and I—had to pay a serious price for his confusion.

In late June of 1931, just out of third grade and a month away from turning nine, I was eagerly looking forward to my first experience at summer camp. A roll of cloth tape imprinted with "Norman M. Lear, Norman M. Lear, Norman M. Lear . . ." sat on the kitchen counter, waiting for my mother to cut it up and sew my name into the clothes I'd be taking with me in a few weeks.

Meanwhile, my father was about to take a plane to Tulsa. None of my friends in Chelsea, Massachusetts, knew anybody who had ever flown anywhere. It had been only four years since Charles Lindbergh flew thirty-three and a half hours in his single-engine *Spirit of St. Louis* to get from New York to Paris, and the rare plane that was spotted in the sky had us kids chasing around in the street yelling, "Lindy, Lindy!" So Dad flying to Oklahoma was a big deal.

He was traveling on some kind of business—"Monkey business!" said my mother, who sensed that the men he'd fallen in with were not to be trusted—and for my upcoming birthday he was going to bring me back a ten-gallon hat just like the one worn by my favorite film cowboy, Ken Maynard.

"Herman, I don't like this," she told him. "I don't want you to see those men." But Herman, as always, knew better.

"Jeanette!" he screamed, the veins in his neck bulging as he stood over her with his nose all but pressing hers. "Stifle!" And off he went.

Herman Lear, or, as he preferred to be known, "H.K."—the *K* standing for "King," a name he insisted he'd been given and would never admit to having appropriated—was a man of supreme optimism. A predecessor to Arthur Miller's salesman, Willy Loman, H.K. went out into the jungle each day with a shoe shine and a smile, pledging to come home, his fortune made, in ten days to two weeks, tops. And this—whatever he was doing in Oklahoma—was merely the latest scheme that would soon result in our being millionaires.

He was arrested upon his return on July 3 for receiving and trying to sell some phony bonds to the Boston brokerage house E. A. Pierce & Co. High on my list of vivid childhood memories is the photograph of my father on the front page of the next day's newspaper, coming down the steps of the courthouse with one hand holding his hat over his face and the other manacled to a detective. Five weeks later he was convicted and sentenced to three years in Deer Island Prison, off Boston Harbor.

That evening our house was filled with friends and relatives offering comfort as they bought the furniture my mother was selling, she having decided on the spot that we couldn't possibly continue to live in Chelsea in such disgrace. At one point, someone I didn't know (but instantly disliked) offered to buy my father's red leather chair—the throne from which he had controlled the radio dial on our floor model Atwater Kent, just as, forty years later, Archie would control the Bunker family's TV viewing from *his* living room armchair.

As my mother and this scavenger agreed on a price, I was devastated. The loss of my father's chair was like losing him twice in the same week. And, as if that were not bad enough, I would soon learn that my mother planned to take my younger sister to live with her and leave me with various relatives until my father got out of jail and the family could be reunited. I clutched all that remained of my summer dream—that unused roll of "Norman M. Lear" cloth, a piece of silent sadness which I managed to keep with me well into my thirties, perhaps even my forties—and my eyelids bit down hard on the tears I was fighting to hold back. At that point someone—an uncle or cousin or neighbor—placed his hands on my shoulders, looked deep into my eyes, and announced, with that soapy solemnity that so many adults use when they are offering gratuitous counsel to the young, "Remember, Norman, you're the man of the house now."

This had to be the moment when my awareness of the foolishness of the human condition was born. I was just past my ninth birthday, my father had been brought down before my eyes from a ten to a zero, my mother and sister were about to disappear from my daily life, my own identity was no more than a thin bit of fabric in my fist, and I was looking up into the face of this fatuous asshole telling me that I was the man of the house now. And then he added, with a smarmy smile I wanted to rip from his face: "No, no, son! A man of the house *doesn't cry*."

How could I *not* have developed a deep appreciation for the absurdities amid the gravity of our existence?

IN MY NINETY-PLUS YEARS I've lived a multitude of lives. There was that early life with my parents and relatives; a life as a kid with my blood buddies Herbie Lerner and the Schwarz twins; a life in high school zeroing in on the humor in our existence; a life in college cut short by World War II; a life as a crew member in a B-17 bomber flying fifty-two missions over Europe; a life in the world of entertainment, with sublives in television, radio, movies, and music; a life as a political activist; a life in philanthropy; a late-starting life as a spiritual seeker; three lives as a husband, six as a father (with my youngest born forty-eight years after my eldest), and four as a grandfather.

In the course of all these lives, I had a front-row seat at the birth of television; wrote, produced, created, or developed more than a hundred shows; had nine on the air at the same time; finished one season with three of the top four and another with five of the top nine; hosted *Saturday Night Live;* wrote, directed, produced, executive-produced, or financed more than a dozen major films; before normalization, led an entourage of Hollywood writers and producers on a three-week tour of China; founded several cause-oriented national organizations, including the 300,000-member liberal advocacy group People For the American Way; was told by the *New York Times* that I changed the face of television; was labeled the "No. 1 enemy of the American family" by Jerry Falwell; was warned by Pat Robertson that my arms were "too short to box with God"; made it onto Richard Nixon's "Enemies List"; was presented with the National Medal of the Arts by President Clinton; purchased an original copy of the Declaration of Independence and toured it for ten years in all fifty states; was ranked by *Entertainment Weekly* fortieth among the "100 Greatest Entertainers of the Century" (twenty-nine places ahead of the Sex Pistols); ran the Olympic torch in the 2002 Winter Olympics; blew a fortune in a series of bad investments in failing businesses; and reached a point where I was advised that we might even have to sell our home.

Having heard that we'd fallen into such dire straits, my son-in-law phoned me from New York and asked how I was feeling. My answer was, "Terrible, of course," but then I added, "but I must be crazy, Jon, because despite all that's happened, I keep hearing this inner voice saying, 'Even this I get to experience.'"

Early the next morning my son-in-law was on the phone again. He'd heard me say once that I wished to be cremated when I died and he was calling to ask me to please, please change my mind. I asked why. In a voice that choked a bit at the finish, he answered, "Because someday I want to take my children, your grandchildren, to a gravestone that reads, 'Even this I get to experience.'"

THAT CONVERSATION TOOK PLACE IN 1988, and what followed from it was my determination to write this book. Several years later I finally began combing through well over a half century's worth of notes, letters, speeches, articles, interviews, scripts, films, and TV shows in pursuit of my story. I didn't write much manuscript, but I did make notes. Lots of notes. Looking them over a while ago, this one from mid-2000 stopped me cold:

> Write about what I think is the key learning curve in life. How one can grow horizontally by becoming informed in one field, and then informed in many entirely new fields—but that horizontal growth becomes less important as time goes on. The journey that grows more important over time is the vertical journey, the journey into one's self.

Clearly, there was a roadblock on *my* vertical journey. From my first long talks in 1984 with Lyn Davis, who in 1987 became Lyn Davis Lear, she steered me to understanding that my roadblock was an Everest of denial. When she heard that my father had gone off to prison for three years before my tenth birthday, she asked, "So what was that like? How did it feel?" When I told her the whole episode was like a chapter I'd read in someone else's book, she gave me a look that said, "Uh-uh. You just don't want to go there." This conversation recurred periodically over the years. Occasionally things would get heated and I'd wind up crying out something to this effect: "What do you want from me? Look at my life. I've got you, my six kids, three of them yours, all of them in love with each other, a lovely home, a great career—how could my life be better? Leave me alone already!"

I told that story several years ago to a family friend who was also a therapist. She smiled without comment, but later said, "If you ever decide to connect with that kid whose father went to prison, why, to quote one of your expressions, don't you try 'wearing his hat' and ask yourself, what must that boy have gone through?"

That question hung in my head. "What must that boy have gone through?" I began to think about him and to sleep on his story, and then one day I made a connection that informed and expedited the process. As a writer who for so many years had marveled at how often he went to bed with a script that had a second-act problem and awoke with the solution, how could I not have realized that this phenomenon might also occur in the script that was my life? In fact, it did, and soon my head was clearer and my eyes open, enough at least to bring back memories of my youth as a castaway while my dad was serving time. The retrieval of those early memories lit the path to understanding how I got from there to here that you will take with me now.

"Here" is where I am today, a nonagenarian in what the doctors tell me is excellent health, looking down my arm and wondering, as I peck away on my computer, what my father's hand is doing hanging out of my sleeve. My family, nuclear and extended, brings me nothing but joy. I go to sleep each night anticipating and delighting in the great taste of the coffee I will be drinking the next morning—something I have done almost thirty thousand times. And, having looked back with new eyes on all the lives I've been so fortunate to have led, I've learned, as hopefully you now will, who I was as I scrambled to get here from "there."

Even *this* I got to experience.

PART I

Alone in a Going World

Go know.

—MY *BUBBE* LIZZIE

1

EARLY ONE SUNDAY MORNING IN 1983, I got a call from my friend John Mitchell, who was then the president of the Academy of Television Arts & Sciences. He was calling to tell me that the academy was creating a Hall of Fame and that I, along with six others whose illustrious company it astounded me to be included among, was to be one of the first inductees.

I instantly phoned my mother back in Bridgeport, Connecticut. Now, I thought, I would finally get the maternal seal of approval that I was still searching for at age sixty-one. She answered with her usual three syllables, "Hell-*oh-oh*," a sound that always seemed caught between a whine and a cry of pain. In my exultant mood, though, I heard it this time as if she'd exclaimed, at last, in a tone of naked delight, "Norman, sweetheart!"

"Mother," I exploded, "I just got a confidential call from a friend. Nobody knows this yet so you can't tell anyone, but the Television Academy is starting a Hall of Fame, and these will be the first inductees: the man who started NBC, General David Sarnoff; the founder of CBS, William S. Paley; maybe the greatest newscaster of all time, Edward R. Murrow; easily the best writer that ever came out of television, Paddy Chayefsky; the two greatest comedians in television history, Lucille Ball and Milton Berle; and . . . me!"

My mother didn't miss a beat. "Listen," she said, "if that's what they want to do, who am I to say?"

In all the years since, I have rarely spoken publicly without sharing that story and, judging by every audience's reaction, I think that either we all had the same mother or we all can identify with the desperate seeking of a parent's approval.

A phrase leaped out at me once from Annie Dillard's lovely memoir *An American Childhood:* "set down in a going world." Actually, I thought, we are set down in many. Just as we lead lives within lives, and lives end on end, so are we set down in multiple going worlds. There is the going world we all inhabit, of course. But there is also our mother's going world, our father's going world, the world they have attempted to create as a couple, the idiosyncratic worlds of all the other caregivers and influencers in childhood, the worlds that all of us struggle to create in every relationship with another human being, the worlds of our imaginations, and the physical worlds of the bodies we each inhabit. It is a miracle that we mewling and puking little beings, as Shakespeare described us, survive at all.

When I was three months old, according to Lear family lore, my mother dropped me on my head while she was bathing me in the kitchen sink. Frightened, she left me there and ran to a next-door neighbor for help. Over the years this incident seemed increasingly funny to her. It became a kind of set piece in *her* life story, and at every retelling of it in my presence, a version of this conversation followed:

"So, you dropped me in the sink on my head and ran next door?"

"For help," she would respond reassuringly.

"And what was I doing?"

"What could you do? You were three months old. You were screaming."

"That's why you ran for help?"

"Of course. I thought I would die."

"And me?" I'd ask. "Could *I* have died?"

"Of course. Why else would I be running for help?"

Finally, I would cut to the chase. "So, Mother, it was a stranger who pulled me out of the sink?"

"No," she'd say with a sarcasm that could etch glass, "she left you there to drown." Then she'd add, "And besides, she wasn't a stranger. We were neighbors a week already!"

Some guy from a neighborhood that had to have resembled mine once said, "The pessimist sees a pile of horseshit and thinks that's all there is. The optimist thinks that if there is enough horseshit around, there must be a pony someplace." And sometimes the plot in which we find ourselves requires us to become our own pony.

Living from age nine to age twelve at the pleasure of relatives, while your dad's in jail and your mother and sister are residing in another city, just might qualify as such a plot.

MY MOTHER'S FATHER, Shia Sokolovsky, underwent a name trim (to Seicol) when he arrived at Ellis Island from Russia in 1904. He settled in New Haven, and a year later he sent for his wife, Elizabeth, their two sons, Al and Eddie, and their oldest child, Jeanette, age six.

It was Al to whose home I was first shipped after they'd taken my dad. Uncle Al managed the John Irving Shoe Store, a ladies' shoe emporium in downtown Hartford. He had two salesmen working for him, with a third on Saturdays, and a woman at the cash register. He was also a district manager, which called for him to visit and report on two other John Irving stores in the area. In his eyes that made him a master of the universe. At his direction his salesmen dressed to the nines, while Al dressed to the twelves. Damon Runyon would have called him a "swell." To me he was just another relative who didn't seem to know I was there.

Al and his wife, Sadie, had three children: my cousins Elaine, Noel, and Bunny. My way of singing for my supper while I lived with them was to make them laugh a lot. I thought it was my obligation to entertain my cousins because I was the beneficiary of their family's largesse, so I would tell them stories, especially stories taken from films, and I did impressions of the actors. One in particular stands out in my mind. Henry Armetta was a featured player who portrayed combustible Italian characters. In a 1933 comedy starring Wheeler and Woolsey, a classic comedy duo of the time, Armetta played a street cleaner afraid of losing his job because the horses he used to sweep up after were all but lost to the motorcar. At age eleven I thought his rave about the absence of horses, and the consequent lack of manure to engage with his broom, was hilarious. And I was funny—dare I say hilarious?—imitating him.

It was a bifurcated life. There was the reality I was actually living, which I could do nothing about. And then there was the reality that was a product of my need and imagination. That was what I showed to the world, and what I did not yet understand.

I didn't stay that long with Al and his family before being shipped to my maternal grandparents, where I remained until my dad was freed. This meant leaving Hartford, where my mother and sister continued to reside, and moving to New Haven. Many years later, when I finally began to see how hard that had been on me, I confronted my mother about it, and she said dismissively, "What do you mean, you never saw me? You just don't remember."

"Mother," I said, "*why* don't I remember? Help me. Remind me of something we did together."

"We saw each other practically every day," she insisted.

"But how can that be? I was in New Haven, two hours away. I don't remember us being together more than twice a year."

To which she answered, "*Oh, please!*"

If my mother's "Oh, please" reads amusing to you, it does to me, too, *now*. As a child those two syllables made me feel worthless, like an insect she was flicking off her sleeve.

MOTHER'S PARENTS, my *bubbe* and *zayde*, lived in New Haven at 74 York Street, an address and a neighborhood that no longer exists, in a small two-bedroom, fourth-floor walk-up apartment with patterned oilcloth on the kitchen table and on the floor.

My grandfather, tall and slender, wore quiet very well and so was considered learned. Not that he was, but he did make a scholarly figure poring for hours every day over his Yiddish newspaper, which no one else could read, as he sipped tea from a tall glass, a cube of sugar held lightly between his teeth. He had a dress shop, a small lower-middle-class establishment where, on Saturdays, my cousin Elaine and I used to take the black cardboard marked "Seicol's" and fold it into boxes for which we were paid a penny apiece. Ten pennies each got us into a movie—actually, two movies, a double feature. A hot dog or corned beef sandwich cost another nickel. With twenty cents you were rich for the day.

If you knew a little trick, you were even richer. At the Roger Sherman Theater they had two candy machines. In one of them was a great candy bar called Mazuma, and packed with the bar were three play coins called Mazuma Money. What Mr. Roger Sherman evidently didn't know was that the Mazuma coins from the one candy machine worked like the coin of the realm in the other machine. Elaine and I and a few friends sworn to secrecy never ran out of candy through the double features that were preceded by the latest episode of a serial western, the weekly news highlights, and the coming attractions.

A short walk and a trolley car ride away lived my mother's other brother, Eddie, his wife, Ida, and their little girls, Beverly and Myrna. If they'd had a fourth bedroom I might have been sent to live with them, because I spent every weekend at their house babysitting my cousins (who I also happened to adore).

Eddie was a dentist, a sweet but vacant round-faced man with an indiscriminate high tenor laugh that seemed to require no context. Ida, in her late thirties and early forties when I knew her best, was still a little girl, and as uncomplicated as a comma. Never without a smile that said "hug me," Ida was born to serve her Eddie and be thrilled by his attentions to her. Neither had ever dated anyone else and both remained throughout their life together as naïve and unworldly as the day they met. That was not enough, however, to prevent Eddie's father, my *ʒayde*, from accusing Ida—tell me there's not a touch of insanity in *every* family!—of having an affair with my father.

One had a hard enough time imagining Ida in the act of making love with her husband, who probably giggled a lot, let alone with a man who was likely to tell her she was the best lay he'd had since Jean Harlow. But I don't have to imagine the spectacle that took place one day in my grandparents' kitchen when my *ʒayde*, his face twisted in righteous anger and contempt, repeated his allegation about H.K. and Ida. As out of control as I'd ever seen him, H.K. leaped about and hollered back in his own defense. And in the middle of this escalating, vein-popping madness, there was my mother dropping to her knees, her hands clasped prayerlike beneath her chin, knee-walking across the oilcloth from one to the other, begging them to stop. I used to do a mean impersonation of my mother whenever I told that story, which I did often until age put a stop to my crawling about on my knees.

Uncle Eddie took care of my teeth throughout my teens and didn't charge. My mother's obsequiousness toward him for this—and toward everyone in the family who helped us during my father's absence—made me feel even more diminished. I loved my young cousins, but I'm sure the reason that I gave up my weekends to babysit them had everything to do with how beholden I was to their parents. But as grateful to them as I felt I should be for giving me shelter, nothing eased the hurt I felt at how little attention Uncle Eddie paid me, especially in football season.

I was excused from my babysitting duties Friday nights and Saturdays before sundown during the 1932 and 1933 seasons so I could make some money selling souvenirs to the crowds that flooded New Haven on their way to the Yale Bowl. I was so in love with football and the football scene that engulfed the city that thinking about the long-gone romance of it can get me misty-eyed even now.

Late Friday afternoon on a game weekend, I and dozens of other kids my age would be downtown in the commons area. The Green, as it was known to the locals, was already swarming with out-of-towners in their hats and raccoon coats, armed with pocket flasks—the repeal of Prohibition was still a year away—and out for a good time.

Each of us kids carried a board about the size of a large computer screen, to which our wares (pennants, miniature footballs, and other related trinkets) were pinned. I nailed a woolen mitten to my board and put my hand in it to support it, a bit of invention I recall thinking would catch on. It didn't.

Saturday mornings we'd all be at the Yale Bowl with our goodies, awaiting the arrival of the dozens of open-air trolleys, packed to the gills with fur-coated revelers hanging off both sides of the cars. It is an image of such explosive joy and felicity that I'm sure I couldn't forget it if I lived to be a thousand.

There was one Saturday morning, though, which I'd happily forget. Harvard was the visiting team, and the rivalry between the Harvard Crimson and the Yale Bulldogs was and still is one of the longest-running (since 1875) and intense in the history of college football. On top of that, my two greatest football heroes—Clint Frank in the backfield and wide receiver Larry Kelley—were playing for Yale. Heaven for me would have been a seat at that game. I had been dreaming of it for weeks. Uncle Eddie knew how much I loved football, but how much I ached for him to take me to a game never occurred to him. I was hawking my wares and experiencing the ache most keenly on that day of the 1932 Harvard-Yale game, and of course it turned out to be the day I spotted my uncle arriving with a friend of his and the friend's son, just about my age. I wanted to throw up from the hurt I felt, and hid in tears behind my pennants and trinket board as they walked past me into the Bowl.

SOLOMON LEAR, my paternal grandfather, married his half niece Anna in 1890, just before immigrating to New Haven from Russia. I didn't know him very well but I knew that everybody loved him and that his favorite song was "My Blue Heaven." On prominent display in every Lear family home was a photograph of him standing next to a rowboat at the water's edge in Miami, wearing striped pants and a dark jacket and pointing up at the sky. It was an early black-and-white photograph, of course, but so romanced were we all by him and his blue heaven that every time I am reminded of that photo I see it in full color.

I have a fleeting personal memory of him, just a glimpse, really, from when I was six years old. I was sledding down a hill—belly flopping, as we called it—and he popped up, a surprise, to grab and hug me at the bottom of the run. A few months later, while crossing the street in Boston, he was hit by a car, thrown in the path of a second car, and killed. We were living on the second floor of a two-family house, and I can still see my father climbing the stairs to where my mother was waiting, and his reaction at seeing the anguished look on her face, even before she actually told him what had happened. They fell into each other's arms, turning and weeping. Each time I revisit this scene I see them as if on film, with the camera circling 360 degrees around their grief-stricken embrace.

As for my paternal grandmother, she was an indecipherable presence at just a few occasions in my childhood. My father, born on March 19, 1893, was the second of her six children. He had an older brother, Edward, two younger sisters, Fanny and Jenny, and two younger brothers, Jack and Eli. The kindest way I can describe them is to say that they were all a little "bent." My generation of Lears often wondered if that had something to do with our grandparents being niece and uncle.

MY UNCLE ED and aunt Rose had a contested beach cottage in Woodmont, Connecticut. "Contested," I say, because the cottage had been left by my grandfather to his oldest child, but the rest of the clan never ceased to contend that it would have been left to *all of them* had Ed not managed to be the last one to speak to him as he lay dying in the hospital. Many critics have commented about the decibel level on my most popular shows, but no family argument on any of them could have outdone the hysterical squabbles that took place over that beach house.

But that perennial sore subject was hardly the only thing that could provoke an instant Armageddon. We kids were witness to a number of lunatic displays of fury, one of which I inadvertently costarred in with my uncle Ed. (Not to be confused with Eddie Seicol the dentist—no one *ever* called Edward Lear "Eddie.")

Uncle Ed was a glowering figure, stern and stuffy, who relished the tight rein he held over the mountains he made out of molehills. As with my other surrogate fathers, I felt a constant emptiness from his lack of attention. I spent many summer weeks at the Woodmont cottage, and Ed would come home from work every day and whistle for his son, my year-older cousin Harold. We would be somewhere in the area and, at the sound of that familiar whistle, Harold would dart homeward and I would ache for a father to whistle for me. In our thirties, reflecting one day on our childhoods, Harold was stunned to learn how sweet I found that father/son moment and how jealous it made me. And I was stunned to learn how much he hated it. It made him feel like a dog.

If I'd felt like a dog that summer I'd have been feeling better. It was the second year I was alone, my mother and sister were nowhere to be seen, my dad was a hole in my heart, and I think that if I had faced my circumstance squarely I'd have fallen to pieces. Strangely, the closest thing to me in my tenth summer wasn't a relative. It wasn't even a person. It was a gray-and-blue sweatshirt. I don't remember who bought it for me, or how I came to have it. I know only that for one long summer it was the source of my comfort and support. I put it on after showering in the late afternoon, a moment I awaited eagerly all day. My aunt Rose, Harold's mother, came to call it a *schmatta* (Yiddish for "rag") because she saw it on me every day, but how could she know how hugged it made me feel, and maybe slender, and good-looking, too.

Sloppy Joe's was the name of an ice cream shop about a quarter mile down the beach, and I walked it, maybe even strutted it most nights, in my magic vestment. I had no money to spend there but I loved the people and the action and the feeling that I belonged. I felt like I had more in common with them than with my family back at the cottage. Maybe that's because I was among strangers at both places, but at Sloppy Joe's they were content to be strangers and no one saw me as wearing a *schmatta*.

But back to Uncle Ed. One weekend in the summer of 1932, more than a dozen Lears—six to eight adults and as many children—were crowded into the small four-bedroom cottage. At about five in the morning, I woke up with a full bladder. I was peeing sleepily into the center of the bowl when Uncle Ed burst into the bathroom, sending the thin door stuttering loudly against the wall, and yelled—for me, our entire family, and all of Woodmont and perhaps nearby New Haven to hear—that my peeing had just awakened him and that he was going to teach me the lesson of a lifetime. He jerked me aside, pulled out his florid penis (which looked to me as angry as its master), and spurted directly into the bowl as I had been doing.

"You hear that splashing, Norman?" he yelled. "Like Niagara Falls at this hour of the morning, isn't it? Now listen to *this!*" He redirected his stream against the side of the bowl. "What do you hear now? You hear nothing now! *Nothing!*" he shouted triumphantly. "Don't you forget that the longest day you live!" A couple of flicks, a quick tuck-away, and Uncle Ed was gone, slamming the door behind him.

It was indeed a lesson I would never forget, and I did what I could to pass it on to future generations. Ed Simmons (my first writing partner) and I incorporated it into one of the first pieces we sold to an important player, the noted nightclub comedian Joe E. Lewis. In a riff about things that men around the globe and across the centuries agreed upon, we had him conclude, "The most universal truth, an article of faith to men of every race, creed, color, or nationality, is that

Water sprayed on water
Makes a sound that all can hear.

But water schpritzed *on porcelain*
Falls silent to the ear.

The Lear sisters, my aunts Fanny and Jenny, were both *baleboostehs,* a Yiddish word that means "the master caretakers of the house" but also carries connotations of its more explicit English relative, "ballbusters." They were big, tough women with granitelike faces, and they demanded absolute adoration from their husbands, Ben and Joe, who ponied up that adoration like eunuchs. Ben would finish every wretched meal Fanny cooked by pushing away from the table and saying with gusto, "Fanny! You outdid yourself tonight." And Joe, poor Joe, spoke only when spoken to by Jenny. Both husbands died young, which I think of as their means of escape.

Uncle Jack and his wife, Zena, both pudgy, seemed to me more freshly scrubbed—their clothing nattier, their haircuts more defined, their silhouettes just a little more crisp. I remember wondering if they caught more sunlight than the rest of us. Whatever it was, I wanted some of it. Jack was also the only uncle who flipped me a quarter now and then. Since my folks never asked me what I hoped to be when I grew up, all I could think of was to be an uncle who could flip a quarter to a nephew. Jack was a press agent. I had no idea what a press agent did, but it was what I grew up wanting to be.

I DESCRIBED MY DAD and his siblings as "bent." Eli, the youngest, was so bent he was crooked. He was one of the earliest, perhaps the first, of radio's play-by-play basketball announcers. He broadcast on what was then called the Pabst Blue Ribbon Network as Eli "King" Lear. (More family royalty.) Such was his popularity that the first time he was sent to jail for kiting a check, the network put him right back on the air upon his release. He made money so he had no reason to steal, but steal he did. It was like a hobby.

Eli was the center of a mind-blowing incident at a Thanksgiving dinner at our home in Hartford when I was sixteen. Twenty or so of us were gathered around our dining room table, which had been extended with the addition of two bridge tables. The men had been playing Klabiash, a Hungarian card game in which the nine of hearts was called the *manel*. The men loved it. You could tell how long they'd been playing by how low the cloud of cigar and cigarette smoke was hanging over them.

In the late thirties, in small two-story homes like ours with little closet space, guests—especially the ladies—placed their coats and their purses on a bed in an upstairs bedroom. Halfway into our Thanksgiving meal that year, someone commented that Eli, who had left the table for the bathroom, had been gone a long time. Within minutes we kids were treated to the spectacle of our fathers pummeling Eli at the front door, where he was caught before he could escape. It seems he had been upstairs tossing his relatives' handbags and fur coats out the bedroom window to a confederate below. Yes, this actually happened.

Many years later, after the war and my Army discharge, I was working as a press agent, just as I'd always imagined. My first task every morning was to page through the eight daily New York newspapers to see which of our clients' names we'd managed to get into print that day. On April 10, 1946, I picked up that morning's *Daily Mirror* and found this front-page headline: TOY GUN BANDIT NABBED IN PHILLY. It was Uncle Eli. He'd been arrested several times before for robbing hosiery stores. This time he was sentenced to twenty years to life at Leavenworth, then the country's largest maximum security prison. He was fifty-two when he got out, which he did by dying.

I'VE SAVED THE BEST FOR LAST: my maternal grandmother. If Bubbe wasn't the first person to truly love me, she was certainly the first to show me that love, on her face, in her voice, and in every other possible way. She was the most adorable full-grown human I've ever known—short and stout, perpetually moist and tender, with a smile on her round face that assured me instantly that my heart was safe in her care. Her name was Elizabeth, and when we weren't calling her Bubbe we called her Lizzie.

Lizzie, I've realized as I've thought about her over the years, had the only real sense of humor on either side of the family. One rarely saw her when she wasn't in action: cooking, cleaning, sweeping, but always listening. Listening was her strong suit. She didn't speak a lot, but every reaction to what she heard was there to be read on her face and in her smile, the wryest of smiles. Whatever feeling she couldn't contain in a look escaped under her breath.

I picked up on a lot of it, I guess because I knew to wait for it. Most of the others didn't get my *bubbe*. You could eat off her floor. Her fridge was always full. She made the best gefilte fish. They got all that. But there was far more they didn't get. My mother, Lizzie's only daughter, seemed to have no relationship with her. None of her children—or her husband, or my father—got how funny she was, how much of a comment on everything around her flowed from her very being.

Those comments, as I said, were "on everything around her," which means her family and their friends, the pleasures and problems of their lives, and the world that they brought into her kitchen. If something she knew nothing about was mentioned, she had just one question, one concern. The first time I heard it was when I lived with my grandparents and my cousin Noel asked our grandmother, "Did you hear, Bubbe? The Dodgers won the pennant!" Looking up from whatever she was doing and recognizing that here was a subject she'd never understand, she asked her question: "Good for the Jews?"

Despite the vast amount of knowledge Lizzie lacked, she understood her life moment by moment. To do that, I think, you have to be an onstage presence in that life and a member of the audience at the same time. Lizzie had that gift in spades, and it was never better exemplified than the very last time I saw her. I had a speaking engagement in Boston and on the way I stopped in Hartford to see her.

She was in a nursing home, strapped in a wheelchair and slumped so that the waist strap was across her chest, her eyelids gently drawn in the pretty, round, ninety-four-year-old face that was looking more and more like the baby pictures of her first great-granddaughter, my Ellen. She had defecated, judging from the smell probably hours earlier, and had not yet been cleaned. I spoke loudly into the bouquet as I approached her.

"Bubbe, darling, it's Norman. From California."

Her eyelids lifted and her lips parted to become that sanctuary of a smile that had always been a place of comfort for me.

"Norman? Norman from California?"

"How are you, Bubbe?" I asked cheerily.

Her eyes opened a tad wider and played with the fringe of her smile, reaching deep into where my sense of the ridiculous lived, inviting me to take in the totality of her situation. "How *am* I?" she replied.

I laughed, and, oh, how I loved her. "I dressed for you," she added.

"I'm on my way to Boston," I said. "I'm speaking at Harvard. They invited me to talk about America and its problems as I see them. You hear that, Bubbe? They're interested in what I have to say."

Her eyes, a mirthful blue, scanned my face, and she replied, with a line reading no amount of direction could have improved upon, "Go know."

Coming from some—her daughter, for example—that could have been a put-down. But not from my *bubbe*. That was her signature way of expressing her gratitude for the bounty of the universe, for yet another gift she could not have imagined. As life has teased and surprised me over the years, I have taken my grandmother's "go know" with me everywhere. When I've been recognized in restaurants and at airline counters, I have often thought, "Go know."

"I'll see you again soon," I said as I left that afternoon.

"I'll be here," she said. "If I'm here, I'll be here."

2

WHEN MY FATHER completed his sentence in the summer of 1934, he went to the Boston station and boarded the train on the New York, New Haven & Hartford Railroad that was bound for Manhattan. My mother, my sister, Claire, and I were at the station in New Haven, ticketed to go to New York with him, where we were all due to live with another couple and their child, in what turned out to be a smallish three-bedroom apartment, until Dad got a job and we could afford our own.

Standing there waiting for his train to pull in, I was just one small boy, but I was a crowd of emotions. I can't overstate how much Herman Lear—H.K., my father, "Dad!"—affected everything in my life from my earliest memories. He was a flamboyant figure with what appeared to me to be an unrivaled zest for life, and he seemed to fill every room he was in. He leaned into everything that came his way. He bit hard into all of life, and everything in the same measure. He loved my mother, but no more than he loved strawberries, which he ate out of big soup bowls with juice-dripping fingers and which he called "strumberries." I don't think there was any difference between the way he loved *The Lone Ranger* (sacrosanct listening for him) and the way he loved me or my sister. However painful this capacity of his might have been for me, I was so in love with my father that I made a virtue—no, a glory—of it.

As the train pulled into the station and I stood there aching for the sight of him, I remember not being able to shake the warmest yet oddest of memories. Every morning after his first cup of coffee, H.K. would repair to the bathroom with the *Hartford Courant* and a few cigarettes. It had been three years since I'd entered a bathroom and been greeted by the combined aroma of my dad's shit and his Old Golds. It was a ritual we had gone through every morning. By the time he finished his first cup of coffee, he would signal with a couple of high-lows—high-pitched, low-volume farts, like a small child on a trumpet— that he'd be needing the toilet very soon. Thirty or so minutes and a cigarette or two later, he'd vacate the john, sumptuously self-satisfied, like a bear wanting to be tracked to the spoor he'd laid down.

"Tomorrow, maybe," I thought.

The train pulled to a stop in a cloud of steam, and as it thinned, there was my father standing at the end of the car. He was in the same suit he'd worn the morning he left for the airport to fly to Oklahoma, but it was a size and a half too large for him now.

When the train pulled out of the station Claire and I sat together while our parents talked. The three-year difference in our ages, compounded by the infrequency of contact during the years of separation, trumped the brother-sister relationship, reducing us to something close to just having met. After a time my father changed places with my sister, and he and I were sitting together.

There wasn't a word—then or ever—about where he'd been or what he'd been through, nor was there anything more than cursory questions about what those three years had been like for me. We talked about Max Baer, who had just knocked out Primo Carnera to become the first Jewish Heavyweight Champion of the World, and the recent death in a shoot-out of the notorious bank robber John Dillinger. And then he told me something as memorable as anything I've ever heard.

We'd gotten around to talking about my being twelve now, when his face lit up suddenly with the birth of a dream meant for instant sharing.

"Norman," he said, "you're going to be thirteen next year!" Then, despite looking lost in his oversized suit, without the few dollars needed to have it taken in, no job in sight, and on his way to mooch on another family's largesse, my dad told me, "For your Bar Mitzvah I'm going to take you, your mother, and your sister for a trip around the world. We'll be gone a year."

He was dead serious and he was my dad, returned to me at last after a long absence. I believed him totally. "We'll be gone a year" became the mantra of my heart.

When my Bar Mitzvah arrived it was 1935, in the middle of the Great Depression, and we were living in a fourth-floor walk-up apartment on St. Marks Avenue in Brooklyn. It had been exciting to think we were going to make that kind of a trip, but it was just another broken promise. His personality was such, however, that there was always enough of tomorrow's anticipation to drown out today's disappointment. The closest I came to hearing again about a trip around the world was when an older buddy, fifteen or sixteen, said he'd been taken to a hooker who asked him if that's what he wanted. He didn't know what the hell she was talking about and neither did I.

My Bar Mitzvah ceremony was at the Shaari Zedek synagogue. We ordered extra blocks of ICE for the party afterward. I capitalize *ICE* to look like the card my mother put in the window to let the iceman know ICE was needed upstairs. *Way* upstairs when you're climbing four flights with a fifty-pound block on your back, which rested on a leather pad and was gripped by a pair of giant steel tongs in your hands. The home refrigerator was relatively new and expensive at the time, and fewer than a million American families had them. We Lears still lived out of our icebox, and the man who breathed life into it, the iceman, was a welcome fixture in our lives.

On the streets, as he crawled at ten miles per hour so as not to miss window signs, smaller kids scrambled after his truck for the slivers of ice that resulted from his chipping smaller chunks from one of the giant two-hundred-pound blocks he'd picked up at the icehouse earlier. For them the street was their entertainment zone, and when the ice truck made its rounds it drew as much excitement as a roller coaster, as did the fireman who appeared occasionally on the hottest of days to open the hydrant for the express purpose of allowing the kids to frolic in the spray.

The iceman made several trips up those four flights to our apartment on the day of my Bar Mitzvah. The family bathtub was the logical cooler for the beer and soft drinks, and that's where all the ice was chopped and deposited. My parents' friends outnumbered my friends by far, and so our apartment felt like the lobby of a small theater with a hit show. The bathroom, if you could get into it, was like the men's room at intermission.

When I was sure I'd been gifted with my last pen—"Look, Ma, it's a Waterman!"—and had received my last cash handoff, I joined my friends outside. With some thirty-two dollars I'd just earned by turning thirteen and becoming a man (the original Jewish joke!), we decided to go to Coney Island.

A nickel bought a Nathan's hot dog and a frozen mug of root beer in 1935 and the best rides were five to ten cents, so that night we were rich beyond dreams of avarice. We ate everything, rode everything, played everything, and had one hell of a time. The highlight of the evening occurred when my cousin Murray put a penny into a device labeled "How Much Electric Shock Can YOU Take?" and grabbed hold of the two metal handles in front of him. Depending on how widely one could pull those handles apart with an increasing electric charge to each hand, a needle moved from WIMP to REAL GUY. Murray must have been feeling Coney Island brave that night and a little too eager to prove himself a real guy. Instead of slowly pulling apart the metal handles, he jerked them apart, throwing his arms out as wide as he could. In that instant his mouth ripped open, his face contorted to a picture of agony, and, with his arms outstretched like a sixteen-year-old Christ figure, he screamed and cried, "Let me go! I didn't do anything! Please, God, let me go!"

When I got home the crowd had thinned out, a good time was being had by all who remained, and no one, including my parents, asked where I'd been. It took me a full day to realize that I hadn't been missed at my own Bar Mitzvah.

MY FATHER WAS extremely outgoing and affectionate, but the underside of his great good nature was not admirable. Enormously insensitive, he treated absolutely everybody the same way, never taking into consideration that the person he was talking to now might be just a little different from the person he was talking to ten minutes before. Consequently, he would take advantage of people weaker than him, and he wouldn't recognize the strength of people much stronger. He would brag about his ability by saying that he could "sell shit on a stick for lollipops." The problem was that he didn't always know, or particularly care, when it was shit he was selling. And so my mother grew to be frightened when the doorbell rang. Neighbors and family just opened the door and walked in. The sheriffs were more formal.

"Hello, Herman," they'd say. They seemed to know him well. I never knew exactly what brought them there. They stood in the corner and talked in hushed tones about checks (specifically, bad ones), car payments that had not been made, outstanding balances, and some other stuff I didn't understand. When they left, my mother was always crying, and my dad was trying to explain something away.

In *Divorce American Style*, a film I wrote and my partner Bud Yorkin directed in 1967, the sixteen-year-old son of Dick Van Dyke and Debbie Reynolds is seen in his bed with pad and pencil, scoring the fight his parents are having in the kitchen below, under such headers as "WEAK," "STRONG," "LOGICAL," "POOR GRAMMAR," and "OVEREMOTIONAL." I was that kid sitting at the kitchen table in our Brooklyn apartment, scoring any number of my parents' fiercest arguments. It was at that table that I frequently heard: "Jeanette, stifle! Will you stifle yourself?"

My parents, and the Lear clan generally, lived, to use my friend Herbie Gardner's line, "at the ends of their nerves and the tops of their lungs." I thought of inner tubes as I saw the veins in my father's neck bulge as he spat those words—"Jeanette, stifle yourself!"—just above his clenched fists, positioned less to hit my mother, it seemed, than to beat his own chest in frustration.

My dad, like Archie later, was portly. But, unlike Archie, he was natty. He wore a freshly pressed suit, in the corrugated way of portly men, and rarely passed a bootblack without getting a shine. Bootblacks were predominantly older men and, as they were called then, Negro. Relics now, in the thirties they could be found—on street corners, at bus stations, in hotel lobbies and barbershops—in towns large and small across America.

As polished as H.K.'s shoes were, so were his fingernails. He loved his weekly visits to the barbershop and the "great guy" role he played there. As I left the shop with Dad after his haircut and yet another shoe shine, his fingernails freshly manicured and topped off with a colorless high-sheen polish, just right for a man of his big-tipper status, my cup would run over with pride and dazzle.

I never thought to wonder—when money problems were table conversation at every meal—how Dad could afford a weekly haircut and manicure and even more frequent shoe shines, not to mention the fat gold ring with a large onyx stone that he wore on his right pinkie. I hated that ring. It must have symbolized all the other off-kilter things about him of which I was instinctively if not consciously aware.

DESPITE ALL THE HURTS and disappointments, how I loved my father! I wrote love letters to him all my life, many of them in *All in the Family*, in which Archie has so many of my father's characteristics. For example, H.K. believed there were three medications that could cure just about everything—aspirin (only Bayer at the time), bicarbonate of soda, and iodine. If one couldn't fix what ailed you, certainly one of the others could. His belief in bicarbonate of soda was so profound that his face registered pleasure whenever he announced, as he did frequently, that he had "a terrible heartburn." Anticipating instant relief, he'd call for his miracle powder: "Jeanette, the bicarb, please."

In an episode of *All in the Family,* when Edith brought Archie the bicarb he shouted for, Mike said, "Look at him, he's a robot. He swallows the potion, and exactly fourteen seconds later"—finger snap!—"the heartburn's gone." Archie drank and fumed, waving Mike off as he enthusiastically counted the seconds in his face. On fourteen exactly, much to his relief and chagrin, a long, mellifluous belch erupted out of Archie. "Dumb Polack," he said, stomping off.

There was another unforgettable incident involving Dad's miracle prescriptions that wasn't quite fit for prime time. It occurred on a cold winter morning in Boston during the Christmas holiday season. My family was visiting and my uncle Ben Susskind (married to my dad's sister Fanny), his sons, David and Murray, and I were taking one of Ben's daily brisk constitutionals. Ben was a small man with a florid face, a big voice, and an outdoorsy personality who sold insurance door-to-door, unsuccessfully. He was a rarity in that he was able to scratch his crotch through heavy pants and a winter coat, which is what he was vigorously doing as we strode along. Murray was embarrassed by the movement of Ben's hands in the pockets of his coat. He made three syllables of "Dad."

"What would *you* do if your balls itched?" his father sputtered in return.

When we got home my father took over. He shooed the women out of the kitchen and ordered Ben to drop his pants so he could attend to him. How the man managed to be so rough on himself through so many layers of cloth only God knew, but we boys gaped in awe. We'd seen only glimpses of fully mature private parts, never having had the opportunity to soak in the assortment, which would have been a big deal in itself. But even if we had, we wouldn't have been prepared for this human equivalent of a display at a Red Lobster, and we were thunderstruck.

Thinking quickly, H.K. figured that aspirin would take too long, bicarbonate of soda would be too weak—ah, but mixed with iodine!! Murray and I left the room as my father took down a soup bowl and Ben prepared to dunk. My cousin David stayed for Ben's scream, and he was the one who raced him to the emergency room of the nearest hospital.

JEANETTE SEICOL WOULD likely have led a less harried existence had she turned down the romantic overture that presented itself one summer evening in 1921. My mother-to-be was toying with a mound of whipped cream on top of her banana split on a date with a guy named "Pete"—or so my father said each time the tale was told, though my mother insisted each time that she "never knew any Pete"—when one Herman K. Lear stopped by the table to say hello to his buddy and, dazzled by this dark-haired beauty, accidentally on purpose thrust his hand into her dessert. She laughed as the whipped cream gushed between his fingers.

After a whirlwind eight-week courtship, my folks were married in September, and Jeanette Seicol Lear gave birth to me—"Sometime during the day, maybe the night, how am I supposed to remember, it was so long ago!"—at New Haven Hospital on July 27, 1922.

Mother was a world-class narcissist. But my sister and I, as we were growing up, didn't realize that. "Your mother is a saint," our father often said, and we believed him. She certainly played that role to the hilt in their kitchen quarrels. We knew that she had had a serious operation as a child that involved a goiter, whatever that was—we never did find out—followed by other illnesses and procedures. Mom was a poster child for "Fragile," with a need to talk long and often about her doctors and their prescriptions. That's what we knew. It didn't occur to us that a mother might take an interest in her children. She was more concerned with the neighbors—they mattered far more than we did. My father couldn't have cared less, but anytime he raised his voice, it was, "Herman, *the neighbors* . . ." She lived to the age of ninety-one, and to the end she was always her favorite subject, to a fair degree her only subject.

No one could suck the juice out of joy like Jeanette. She was the original *farbissiner,* yet another Yiddish word, which is most easily translated as "sourpuss." But a sourpuss is a *farbissiner* in the face only. A true *farbissiner* is a sour soul. Sour souls stain the company they keep. They wake up to piss on the day, and not just their day. A *farbissiner* doesn't earn the title until she is pissing on your day, too.

Flashing forward to an incident that took place in 1987, I was a sixty-five-year-old man whose mother was coming to California for a visit. I sent a car to pick her up at her apartment in Bridgeport and bring her to the American Airlines terminal at JFK, where I met her with a wheelchair and an attendant. She said she was happy to see me, but before I could reach her cheek to kiss her she began to talk about Dr. Golden, her wonderful new eye doctor, and how could I not remember him, she'd told me about him on the phone a week or so ago.

Before her luggage was out of the car and checked at curbside, she had fished out of her purse the new miracle eyedrops that Dr. Golden, "God bless him," had prescribed for her. All the way up to the gate and onto the plane she talked about how "that scratchy feeling" in her eye was gone; how Dr. Leventhal, Golden's predecessor, had never helped her; how now she was eating better and enjoying life more with her mind off her eye problem; and did she tell me how when she called my sister to rave about her new eye doctor, "It was like she didn't hear a word I said."

We were in the air about an hour, I at the window deep into some reading and she on the aisle, when I noticed her going into her purse again. At the same time a young man was walking up the aisle and my mother pulled at his sleeve.

"Sir, I wonder if you could help me."

"Certainly," he replied.

As I, her quite grown-up, proven stable son looked on, Mother continued, "My new eye doctor gave me this prescription. I have to put three drops, not two, not four, he said, just three drops in each eye every four hours. Would you be good enough . . . ?"

"Of course," he responded, taking the eyedropper firmly between thumb and forefinger, and as I sat there in a state between mind-bending wonder and apoplexy, he squeezed off three drops exactly—not two, not four—into each eye. A moment later he was gone and Mother was putting her drops away, unaware, or so it seemed, that I was staring at her.

In the field of comedy, what she did next would be called a "take." A long, slow take. Very subtly my mother started reacting to something on her left— her son, still staring.

"What?" she said finally. *"What??"*

"Mother," I said. "You asked a complete stranger for help when I'm sitting right here?!"

"I didn't want to bother you," she answered.

"I'm here, Mother," I said through clenched teeth. "The son who takes care of you all year. You think I couldn't have—?"

"Dr. Golden said you have to be very careful."

I was ready to explode. "And did he tell you to ask a *total stranger*, when your son is sitting right next to—?"

"And patient."

"Patient?" I erupted. "Since when can't I be *patient?"*

She had only to look at me. "Some patience!" she said.

BUT, YOU MIGHT WONDER, was there no lightness, no laughter, on St. Marks Avenue? Yes, there was. My father, in a celebratory mood, liked to take us "out for Chinks" (Chinese food) on a Sunday night. Coaxing Mother to go out with him somewhere, he'd say, "Let's get out of here, Jeanette. Let's blow the stink off us." More often we were home, of course, where we relied on Madison Avenue to quench our thirst for entertainment—music and comedy— via the radio. The sponsors ran much of production in those years, and so there were *The Fleischmann's Yeast Hour, Maxwell House Coffee Time, Lucky Strike Hour, The Voice of Firestone, The Chase and Sanborn Hour, Kraft Music Hall, The Johnson Wax Program, The Bell Telephone Hour,* and dozens more. They fielded most of the comedy talent, some of whom went on to become great stars in their own shows, and others who flamed high and flickered out quickly.

We roared at Joe Penner, a flame-out whose "Wanna buy a duck" was a yuk in households everywhere, as was Baron Munchausen's "Vas you there,

Charlie?" (another flame-out). While they lasted, these were retorts audiences knew were sure to come in every sketch. There would be a split-second pause before delivery, and the audience, hushed with anticipation, would explode on the line.

The all-time kingpin of such moments came years later when Jack Benny, whose character was known to be an incredible miser, was being held up at gunpoint, and the robber said, "Your money or your life!" The long pause that followed entered the history books and taught every comic actor and writer alive—and yet unborn—one of the great lessons of comic timing.

Benny led the parade of comics that had their own shows in those years, among them Fred Allen, George Burns and Gracie Allen, Edgar Bergen (and his dummy, Charlie McCarthy), Eddie Cantor, Fibber McGee and Molly, Amos 'n' Andy, and Bob and Ray. If anyone had told my mother that one day her son would know them all, she would probably have laughed harder at that than at anything she heard on the radio, certain they had the wrong Norman.

THE HOMEGROWN MOMENTS of levity in our family, at least those that emanated from my parents, were few but memorable. My folks liked to kid each other about what their lives would be like were they to get divorced. In that event, my dad would always take my sister with him and my mother would take me. Claire and I would hear again and again that she was a Lear, "with Dad's blood in her veins," and I was a Seicol. How gallingly insensitive our parents had to be as they delightedly costarred in these scenes, performed for an audience of two—their devastated children.

The threat of abandonment by a parent, though, is nothing compared to being thoroughly crushed by both, which happened to me when I was twelve. I had only recently discovered—I mean really discovered—my penis. Utterly intoxicated with the ecstasy I derived from causing it to stand erect and bringing it to the point of climax, backing off as the feeling ebbed, and then climbing the magic hill again, I could pleasure myself endlessly this way—until I failed to catch myself and rose to meet heaven as it descended around me. It would be another year before I could ejaculate, but the multiple climbs to climax were as thrilling as they would ever be, as was the climax itself.

I was in the bathtub one evening practicing this craft, climbing slowly up and down my nervous system, when my father, alerted by the sound of water rhythmically splashing for a considerable period of time, did what any father would do—at least any father named Herman Lear. He put his shoulder to the door and ripped the eye hook off the wood as he burst in. A moment later, I was hauled by the ear—naked and dripping wet, trying but failing to wrap a towel around me, my wiener shriveled in shame—to my mother and ordered to apologize to her.

Why would a father do that? What could he have had in mind, demanding that a young adolescent boy apologize to his mother for masturbating? If he had sought help to come up with a way to mortify me, to make me feel damaged, he couldn't have done better. When I ask myself what motivated the weird way H.K. fathered his only son, I come up empty. Was it that we were the two males in the house, and that it was the male's function exclusively in those years to support the family, and that, despite his bravado, his failure rate was eating him up inside? And inchoately, senselessly, he flailed? And I got caught in his flail-ure?

I don't know if boys today are still told that they could go blind if they masturbate, but the notion was alive and well in 1935. Given how into the activity I was and that H.K. had been a witness to it, my heart was in my mouth when I asked him if it could cost me my eyesight. While he didn't suggest I go out and get an eye patch and a tin cup, he didn't exactly disabuse me of the thought, either. I don't remember him ever talking to me about sex after that incident. The only unsolicited bit of advice from H.K. that leaned toward fatherly was when I started dating. He took me aside one day and, recalling a phrase from his Navy days, gravely advised me, "Norman, if you ever find yourself in a group of guys about to bang the same girl"—could there ever have been a father who knew his son less well?—"never take a wet deck."

THE ONE MEMORY I have of my father that was fun, pure fun, was the Notre Dame/Ohio State football game in November 1935, which came to be known as the Game of the Century. I was thirteen and it was one of those occasions where my dad and I bonded so riotously that it blotted out every negative in my life for miles around and years behind. I couldn't have been higher if I were a balloon and H.K. were helium.

My father always said his birthday was on St. Patrick's Day, and on that day he wore a green tie. (It wasn't until he died that we found out through the official records that he was actually born two days later.) He had a great Irish accent—when he worked with Irish guys he'd use it all day—and he could sing Irish lullabies in a sweet untuned voice, so of course we were Fighting Irish fans. Ohio State, the Buckeyes, were rated number one that year, so we turned on the radio in heart-thumping anticipation. Imagining the twenty-two players coursing up and down the field, as we did then while listening to radio, was no less exciting than watching it play-by-play on TV today. But by the end of the third quarter, most of the air was out of our balloons. Notre Dame was losing, 13–0.

William Shakespeare (that was really his name) was in the Notre Dame backfield at the top of the fourth quarter when coach Elmer Layden sent an almost unheard-of member of the team, Andy Pilney, into the game to join Shakespeare. Even as a "What the hell's going on here?" grumble swept the stands, excitement began to build again. With less than twelve minutes left in the game, Notre Dame started to move the ball and the Shakespeare-Pilney combo started to cook. On the couch, and then on the floor, so did the Lear combo. In ten-plus minutes Shakespeare tossed two touchdown passes caught by Pilney, as the Lears, father and son, kicked, screamed, rolled, and hugged on the floor. And then—and *then*—don't ask me what plays led to yet another opportunity to score, but with only forty seconds remaining in the game, Shakespeare threw one last pass deep into the Ohio State end zone. It was intended for Pilney, who couldn't get to it, and was caught instead on a dead run—*YES!*—by Notre Dame's Wayne Millner! The Fighting Irish had won, 18–13, and I'd had the most treasured afternoon of my life with the father of my heart's desire.

When, some fifty years later, a friend who'd heard that story gifted me at Christmas with a 16mm black-and-white film of the game, I felt like I'd been knighted.

3

I N T H O S E B R O O K L Y N years preceding and following my Bar Mitzvah, I
felt less alone when I was by myself in my bedroom than when I was with
my family. My buddies accounted for most of the fun and companionship I
knew. For a time Eddie Pearl, Bernie Fleischer, and I played harmonicas and
called ourselves the Harmonica Rascals, a group that became quite well known
throughout an entire building on St. Marks Avenue. On Halloween I recall our
gang forsaking all treats for the kick of playing tricks. We'd stick pins into
doorbells that buzzed apartments on the upper floors, causing them to ring
until the occupants came down to remove them. We'd let the air out of inner
tubes on cars parked in the streets, leaving as much as half a block of flat tires.
And we were thought to be "good" boys.

Marty Ellen would eat a dead fly for a nickel. We'd chip in to see him do it.
A penny was real money then. It bought a cigarette. Two cents bought a newspaper. Five cents, one each from five of us, bought Marty Ellen popping a fly.
He wanted a dime to do a roach, but with a Uneeda biscuit. A dime was a big
deal, so we wanted him to eat the roach live without a biscuit. Somehow taking
it with a biscuit made it seem doable, although the rest of us wouldn't go near it
for a quarter with two biscuits. I wasn't present the day the deal was finally
negotiated and Marty ate a live roach—*barely* alive, according to Bernie
Fleischer—with a single biscuit for fifteen cents.

Herbie Lerner and the Schwarz twins, Edwin and Elliott, were centerpieces in my life away from home. They've all passed on now but I see them as they were then just as clearly as I picture any current friend today. We all belonged to the Young Israel of Eastern Parkway, where I wrote and we performed *Sir, You Cur, or the Villain Gets It in the End*—Herbie played the villain banker, I the heroine whose house he was foreclosing on—pretty much for our own benefit. If we had a dozen people in the audience, that was more than I recall.

We cooked up a ragtag sandlot football team, too. ACHVA, Hebrew for "brotherhood," was our club at Young Israel, and our colors were maroon and gray. We bought great-looking maroon sweaters with a gray *A* on the chest and two gray stripes on the right sleeve. I was as accomplished at football as I would have been, had I tried, at sumo wrestling. Herbie Lerner was the star runner, passer, and kicker, and my recollections of him doing all that could not be clearer. H.K. would often come to the games, and I ached to be Herbie on those days. I managed to burrow my way to the bottom of a lot of scrimmages, however, so that if he blinked now and then, H.K. might think I was responsible for an occasional tackle. It never worked, but that didn't stop me from trying again two years later when we moved back to Hartford and I entered my sophomore year at Weaver High School.

To please my dad, I tried out for the junior varsity team and made it. It didn't hurt that I appeared to be a two-letter man in my maroon sweater with the gray stripes on the sleeve. When some students asked what school I'd gone to I would say Erasmus High, a well-known school in Brooklyn, but to accommodate the *A* on my sweater, and in Hartford now, I fudged the pronunciation to sound more like Arasmus. A few days into practice, however, I could have been a ten-letter man from anywhere and it wouldn't have mattered. Coach Fred Stone caught on to my pathetic attempts to look like a hard-charging lineman and called me aside. "And what the hell do you think you're doing?" he asked. Minutes later I was pulling my stuff out of my locker and handing back the key.

THE LAST WEEKS of my fourteenth summer, I got myself a job in Coney Island shilling for Paramount Pool and Ocean Bathing, a seedy piece of real estate famous among a group of young male frequenters for the several knotholes through which they could see into the girls' showers. On the sidewalk in front of its crummy turnstile entrance, the management had me calling out to passersby anything that came to mind regarding the wonders of the establishment. And so I barked: "Hey, hey, it's Paramount Pool and Ocean Bathing with your own locker! Only twenty-five cents. Twenty-five cents with your own locker. And shower! Why go home with sand jammed where you just don't want a sand jam? The pool, the locker, the shower—twenty-five cents. You go home just the way you were born, one hundred percent sand-free."

I loved Coney Island. The shotgun marriage of homegrown tackiness to pretensions of glamour and beguilement fascinated me. Everything was the "best." Or the "speediest." Or the most "breathtaking," "heart-pounding," "terrifying," "enchanting," and "thrilling," and all of it "never seen before." Pounding a sledgehammer on a slab hard enough to ring a bell at the top of a wired pole was a "Prove You're a Man!" extravaganza! And so I came back the following year and spent all of my fifteenth summer barking again for Paramount P&O Bathing and shilling for two other attractions, equally eccentric.

There was the thinnest, palest guy I've ever seen, with breath that could peel an onion, who operated a six-for-a-nickel photo booth. I'm not sure whether he spoke English. He hired me off my pool and ocean bathing gig by waving a couple of dollar bills at me. I hoped he meant per hour; he meant per day.

"Hey, hey, it's six for a nickel, five cents, the only place on the island! Looky here, little girl, you ought to be in pictures! Six for a nickel, five cents! A twentieth of a dollar gets you six delicious photos of yourself to last a lifetime! My personal guarantee: If you find a better deal on the island, let me know and I will personally help you spread the word!" In the rain of hyperbole it didn't matter what the hell I said.

My third job at Coney that summer was selling ears of corn out of a steaming barrel for an elderly, sheet-garbed Sikh gentleman who taught me a lesson of the natural world that, like my uncle Ed with the porcelain, he wished me never to forget. "You salt the ear of corn *before* you brush on the butter. Why, you wonder? Because the less expensive salt when applied first will prevent the more expensive butter from running off as quickly, and so that way we use *how much* of the more expensive ingredient? LESS is how much, we use *LESS*!"

I recall thinking that if he had thirty kids selling from thirty barrels for thirty summers, all employing his salt-first strategy, it might have sped up his retirement by thirty minutes. Maybe forty.

THE BEST TIME of year was when my grandparents, Bubbe and Zayde, came to stay with us for the High Holidays. Their arrival was preceded days before by two or three barrels of dishes, carefully wrapped in the Yiddish newspapers Zayde had read to the last word. (The wrapping was to keep the dairy dishes at a remove from the meat dishes and vice versa.) I'm not sure what would have happened had anyone set down a lamb chop on a dairy dish, but the way my grandfather carried on if he saw a hat on the kitchen table or an open umbrella in the house, I'm sure there would have been hell to pay. Granted, the hat and umbrella instances were only superstitions, but they caused him to pound furniture while praying aloud agitatedly between gritted teeth, the Jewish equivalent, I thought, of crossing himself a thousand times. But mixing meat and dairy was a no-no from on high, and I thank God it never occurred in Zayde's presence when I was about.

I loved my grandparents' visits. They provided a reprieve from the four-way stress we lived with daily. And for me there was the oasis of peace, love, and understanding that was my *bubbe*. For several days there was someone in the house who "got" me. My parents and grandfather had one another to stress over, and the difference for us kids was like a month in the country.

IN THE COURSE of our Brooklyn years there was a big stir regarding bonuses that Congress promised to World War I vets in 1922 and finally paid in 1936. My father saw prewar service in the Navy and then joined the Army after the war started. He was stationed in Mexico and did not see active duty, but as a vet he received something like twenty-one hundred dollars, a small fortune at the time. Mother and he ceremoniously placed it in a safe-deposit box, as opposed to an interest-bearing bank account, so that she could visit her cash whenever she felt the urge. No one knew better than her husband that Mother was certain to feel that urge on a regular basis, so it was as meat-headed and irrational as it was deceitful when he raided that box and "borrowed" the cash, all of it, to invest in something that was due to pay off in ten days to two weeks—tops.

My mother cried, beat her chest, and pulled her hair for days. My dad went dumb. I didn't have the stomach for picking up my clipboard. Watching my mother beat herself, I fought hard not to come apart. I thought, "I don't know whether to shit or go blind," an expression I'd heard that conveyed what I was going through and amused me at the same time. It was the amusement I needed.

My sister was in some sort of shock and wouldn't come out of her room. As an older brother, I tried to make her laugh at the goings-on. This was a comedy, I told her, and we should be laughing. That might have worked, but when she looked into my eyes my age and fear showed. There, I was four.

The episode ended with my mother packing to leave and me thinking the time had come when I was going to live with her and Claire with my dad. Given what had gone down between them for so long, that would have been logical. Instead, she was leaving alone and asked me to help her to the subway with the bags. For me it was a three-block death march. She stopped when we reached the entry to the subway and stood there looking down the stairs, then furtively over her shoulder, and then all around, not talking, not descending, and beginning to cry again. A minute or two later, collecting what remained of herself, she turned abruptly and started walking away.

"Where are you going?" I asked, bewildered.

"Home," she responded. "Where else would I be going? Home."

SOME MONTHS AFTER the bonus money fiasco, my folks celebrated their fifteenth wedding anniversary. H.K. took us to his "favorite restaurant in all the world." Not that we had reason to believe he'd eaten in that many fine restaurants, and certainly not across the globe, but whenever he was asked to back up some seemingly questionable declaration, or explain how he happened to be in possession of some arcane statistic that supported his point of view in an argument, he'd say, "Because I've been everywhere the grass grows green and I've seen everything."

Christ Cella on West Forty-sixth Street was famous then for its steak and lobster. The H.K. who walked in with his family that night had very likely had a haircut and manicure that afternoon. Mother enjoyed that H.K. to the hilt, accepting the goods and grandeur, never asking how we could afford it.

Mother, Claire, and I ordered steak, Dad a lobster. "A *female* lobster," he specified. The waiter seemed confused.

"Do you know a female from a male?" Dad asked. It was obvious that the waiter did not.

"The females," Dad informed him, "are more tender." All the waiter could manage was an uneasy smile. My mother to a degree and Claire to the limit were embarrassed. When Dad suggested the waiter bring some live lobsters to the table so he could pick a female, Claire begged him, "Don't!"

Finally, the maître d' interceded and told the waiter to escort Dad to the kitchen so that he might carefully pick out his entrée. Out of his chair in a split second, Dad said, "Come on, kids. I'll show you how to pick a female. Sweet as your mom."

Claire refused to move. I, who'd been hovering between "My dad's being an asshole" and outright awe, was now in the "totally awesome" camp. I followed the waiter and my father into the Christ Cella kitchen. To my surprise, perhaps to my father's also, there were a few tables and people were dining there. They must have looked like the "in" crowd to Dad, because he took me there a few times before I went overseas, and from then on we always ate in the kitchen. As to how you can tell a female lobster from a male? I watched closely with our waiter, the maître d', and a few other fascinated workers as H.K. picked up and poked around the bellies of several clawing lobsters. Finally he said, "Ah, there!" and the others applauded. To this day, you'd have to slip a lobster into tiny panties and a bra before I could identify a female.

On Mother's pillow when we arrived home was a poem Dad had ostensibly written to commemorate the occasion. Actually, he'd confidentially asked me to write it for him. I'd been writing poems for a little while. One of them, nothing one couldn't imagine any young kid writing, received an honorable mention in a New York *Daily Mirror* contest. That gave him the idea and so I wrote, and he presented as his own that night, "TOGETHER":

> *The 15 years I've been with you,*
> *We've shed many a tear, 'tis true.*
> *But life for us has just begun*
> *We've yet to have all our fun,*
> *As long as we're TOGETHER.*
> *And when, my dear, we're old and gray,*
> *And life for us is sunny weather*
> *We'll look back on our lives and say*
> *It has been fun TOGETHER.*

Mother was thrilled with the poem and wept when she read it. Between Christ Cella and "TOGETHER," if their love life was half as hot as she coyly and mischievously maneuvered conversations to suggest when she was in her eighties, they must have had a passionate night.

When we moved to Hartford a year later, Mother framed and hung that poem in the vestibule, where it remained as long as we lived there. To my knowledge she never knew its true author—not even thirty-five years later, when, on the very first episode of *All in the Family*, daughter Gloria buys a gift for her father, Archie Bunker, to give to Edith, his wife, on the occasion of their twenty-second wedding anniversary. Edith takes the little package, tears off the wrapping, and opens the box.

"Oh, my!" she screeches, and, as if picking up the Hope Diamond, adds, "It's a Lady Gillette!" With it came a greeting card that causes Edith to announce delightedly, "I bet it's a Hallmark!" Tearing it open, she adds, without a trace of disappointment, "Well, almost."

And then Edith begins to read "Together." Overcome by just the title, she turns lovingly to Archie, who can't handle affection. "All right, Edith, get on with it, get on with it," he says, and she reads on, with just one change in the first line to accommodate the story line: "The twenty-two years I've been with you . . ."

When Mother called after the show I expected some degree of sentiment, but the poem was never mentioned. She did hope I wouldn't be troubled by what some people might say about Archie's language. And she snickered when she said, "And leave it to that Edith to carry on about a Lady Gillette!"

OUR TIME IN NEW YORK, almost four years, came to an abrupt end one day on the New Jersey Turnpike, near New Brunswick. On April 6, 1938, six men were involved in a two-car collision and only three of them lived to talk about it. One was "Herman K. Lear of Brooklyn, N.Y." The car he was driving was described in a newspaper clipping as "a car full of novelty salesmen."

That clipping was in my pocket days later when the doctors pronounced him out of danger and I was brought to the hospital to see him. Out of danger?

I burst into tears at the sight of him. This, you understand, was before television and before the ERs of that fast-growing world, the hospital dramas. Seeing a body strapped to a hospital bed, especially your own father's—with broken bones wrapped in splints, one leg hoisted, needles stuck into and tubes protruding from every part of him and connected to strange, beeping medical equipment—was horrific, something I could never have imagined. To my nearly sixteen-year-old eyes, he looked more like he was being tortured than cared for.

We never learned what that "car full of novelty salesmen" were peddling that day, but as anguishing as it was to see Dad that way, I still could not help being amused by the presence of "novelties" in the details of the collision that came close to killing him.

4

WE MOVED BACK TO CONNECTICUT—Hartford, to be specific—
when Dad was out of the hospital. His recovery took months. To see
him anytime after that was to know the man had been in a terrible accident. It
left him with a limp for which he often needed a cane. Then there was the facial
scar that came down from his forehead and seemed to go off in several directions. With all of that, I have no recollection of my father complaining. If he
was in pain I never heard it. If he felt the need to slow down, he didn't mention
it to me.

I can recall only exchanges with my dad, never a real conversation. I can see
his fingers feeding strumberries to his mouth. I can see him picking his nose,
thumb-and-forefinger style, as he drove. I can see him in his red leather chair
controlling the radio dial. But for the life of me I cannot recall us sitting together in conversation. Nor can I recall looking at him as he looked at me. Did
we ever look each other in the eyes?

Whatever energy it might have taken to feel sorry for himself, H.K. put it
into building his empire in Hartford. Not that he spoke of building an empire.
That was my presumption as I watched him fail in business after business, but
failing forward and upward, each venture grander than the last.

WE STARTED OUT in Hartford in an apartment on Woodland Avenue, which I remember for three momentous reasons. It was there that I turned sixteen, started to drive, and inhaled my first breaths of freedom. It was there also that I experienced my first love: live theater and vaudeville.

The State Theater in downtown Hartford had no balcony and was said to have had the largest single-floor seating capacity of any theater in the country, some thirty-eight hundred seats. It was built in the early twenties for live theater events only, but made the screening of movies a secondary attraction when the theatergoing tide turned in that direction. When I caught up with the State Theater in 1938 they were showing two films, an A and a B, and a serial western during the week. On Friday, Saturday, and Sunday they intercut a live big band stage show three times daily. I saw Harry James with Betty Hutton there, along with Benny Goodman, Frank Sinatra, Artie Shaw, Tony Bennett, Gene Krupa, Duke Ellington, Peggy Lee, Ella Fitzgerald, and more.

Occasionally there would be comedy on the bill at the State Theater, and one Saturday an act that I adored from their films showed up. They were the Ritz Brothers, my beloved Ritz Brothers. To me, Harry Ritz (the middle guy in the act) was the funniest man alive and his brothers merely appendages. But by the time I reached my early twenties I understood how much Harry needed his brothers Jimmy and Al framing him. Harry was a great clown, and clowns work alone, even in crowds. With his brothers, Harry was a clown encased in an act, and acts play theaters and nightclubs and films.

I began to see, too, how much of Harry's riotous physical comedy erupted out of a deep sadness, a sadness that cloaked every inch of him, with a degree of heartbreak lining his every comic expression. A true clown can make you laugh and, with just a change of expression, can evoke some inner sadness and bring you to tears. Bert Lahr, one of the great clowns in my experience, could do that. Nancy Walker could do that, and Red Skelton, and Redd Foxx. The people I think of as having been great clowns did not necessarily understand their art. They could not talk about it or write about it. They were not, in a conventional sense, intellectual. They were altogether intuitive, comprehending not just the closeness but the oneness of laughter and tears.

I met Harry Ritz at the State Theater when I interviewed the brothers for the weekly *Weaver High Lookout*, where I served as features editor and wrote the humor column. The story appeared with a photograph on the front page, captioned "Leering Lear and the Rollicking Ritzes."

IT WAS IN HARTFORD, too, where I first fell in love, with the lithe and lovely Adrienne Young. Even better, Adrienne was attracted to me. And she was a great kisser. Not that I knew a lot about kissing. Everything before Adrienne was no more than the peck that came during spin the bottle when the bottle stopped and pointed at me—"Oh, my God, what do I do now?"

I must have been quick to learn, however, because in no time at all I could spend hours kissing, or, as we called it then, necking. So much did I enjoy necking, I didn't get to second base until my hand was actually lifted and placed there. As for "a bare one," the only reason I remember the expression is that it was the first question my buddy and confidant Leon Cooperman asked me: "Get a bare one?" When I did say yes, it wasn't from Adrienne. And it was probably a lie, anyway. We guys lied a lot in those years. Eager to be men, we climaxed in our jockey shorts, occasionally from hand jobs, but reported to our buddies that we'd gone all the way.

The girl who would orally copulate a guy was *very* rare in 1938 and was called that three-syllable c-word. As for a man who would do as much for a woman, he was seen as "dining at the Y" and was described with a similar three-syllable c-word. It was an unusual man in those years who ever dared say, let alone bragged, that he'd been there, done that. Oral sex as a topic for discussion was a generation or more from coming out of the closet. We were very naïve in many ways.

Check out the pop songs when my generation was in its teens: "Flat Foot Floogie," "A-Tisket A-Tasket," "Jeepers Creepers," "You Must Have Been a Beautiful Baby," "The Dipsy Doodle," and "Whistle While You Work." In a way, that says it all.

H.K. TOOK A JOB with some builder, canvassing door-to-door in communities of tract homes to sell add-on bedrooms and garages and turn cellars into game rooms. In less than a year he decided he'd learned everything he needed to know and he was a builder himself. One more year and Norclaire Construction, Inc., had six small Cape Cod–style homes being built on Woodstock Street, off of Blue Hills Avenue. We moved into one of them.

Despite all the other addresses we shared, 68 Woodstock Street was always what Claire and I thought of as home. We went to high school there and Dad died there. It couldn't have been more modest—three small bedrooms and a bathroom upstairs; living room, dining room, kitchen, and half bath downstairs. The front door opened to a small vestibule and there hung Dad's ghost-written poem, "TOGETHER."

The furniture was ordinary, but was treated as if it were museum quality. "You could eat off the floor" was an expression spoken ad nauseam at 68 Woodstock, not because it was true but because Mother had a kind of out-of-breath way of eliciting such flattery from friends and neighbors. Spring cleaning was a momentous occasion and every piece was slipcovered throughout the summer months. I never understood that, but the process could not have been treated more seriously if it had been heart surgery, and I never question heart surgery.

I WAS NO MORE THAN a B student at Weaver High, but with an A profile. The A profile part is something I have come to recognize only quite recently in the preparation for these pages; it was not the way I saw myself then.

The paragraph adjacent to my photograph in the 1940 yearbook, *The Weaver High School Portal*, read: "This is Lear, the inimitable Lear—clearing house for ancient, medieval, or risqué jokes, past master of the art of reflex-provoking (sneezing, etc.) and if anyone asks him who Winchell is—he's New York's Lear. An ultra-sophisticate, the 'King' tells a good story, showers before breakfast, writes poetry, likes debating, acting, orating, and is a famous wit (infamous if you must!). We can't seem to do the old boy justice."

I'm addressed as "King" above because, as I said, I wrote the humor column in the weekly *Lookout*, "Notes to You from King Lear." Interesting that I borrowed that appellation then; over the years it was the only time I ever did. I was "Class Prophet," so I also wrote the class play. I did all that writing on a tall, old Remington typewriter. The only space at home that worked to seal off sound was our basement, which my father never got around to turning into a playroom, so the cellar became my study. It was cold and dank, especially at five A.M. before school. Last-minute clutch writer that I was even then, I was there often at that hour, with the sound of my typing occasionally masked by the sound of coal coming down the chute into the five-ton coal bin within twenty feet of my workstation. (This might explain "showers before breakfast" in my *Portal* profile.)

I like the guy in that profile and see now why the writer said he "can't seem to do the old boy justice." Oh, how I wish I'd had that Norman Lear in focus back then. I'd have a different story to tell about myself and Ruthie Glazier, and Hope Sheintop, and maybe a few others at Weaver High.

One spring day in my junior year I decided to organize a hayride. I found a farmer in Wethersfield with a large wagon drawn by two horses, seven of us boys chipped in, and as many couples gathered at six P.M. at 68 Woodstock. I think it was Leon Cooperman who brought Hope, and Mike Kellin who brought Ruth. I can't remember the other guys on the hayride that night. The only reason I remember Mike and Leon in this context is because I hungered to be with either of their dates. But I didn't feel up to either Hope or Ruth. Locked in my gut, shared with no one until I shared it with Hope herself some forty years later, was the feeling that she was too fine for me. I didn't feel like I deserved her.

One day in the late seventies, when I had all those shows on the air, my secretary buzzed me. Hope Sheintop was on the line. She and her husband were in L.A., and the next day they were in my office. Hope looked as lovely as I thought she would. Her husband was a very nice guy, a doctor, as I recall, who seemed to have earned her. I told her in that safe moment how I felt about her in high school and especially on that night of the hayride. Hope smiled, looked tenderly to her husband and back at me. "Such a pity," she said. She'd wanted to be with me, too, and wished all through our junior and senior years that I would call her. We shook our heads and laughed. I was wondering if she didn't respond as she did to make me feel good. And then a moment later, as she and her husband were leaving, she turned and said, "You still shower before breakfast?" as she slipped out the door.

Ruth Glazier was another knockout. I couldn't take my eyes off her, but she seemed to belong with older guys, like Herbie Lerner, who was visiting me from New York the weekend after the hayride. "She's perfect for Herbie," I thought. "He's only a year older, but a great athlete," as if that had anything to do with it. Anyway, I called Ruth but she wasn't home, and her folks didn't know when they might hear from her, so I made another call to a number I had place-marked in the back of my mind. There'd been another great-looking girl on that hayride who seemed like fun—Charlotte Rosen from West Hartford. She answered the phone when I called, and at the sound of my voice she asked, excitedly, "Norman!?" It took my breath away, I was so flattered.

"Listen," I said, "my friend Herbie Lerner, a great guy, is in from New York and . . ."

I didn't get any further. "Call me when *you* want to date me," she said and hung up. Wouldn't you want to spend the rest of your life with a girl, a great-looking girl, who reacted to you that way? That's the way I felt. And, not that many years later, I signed up to do just that. Charlotte Rosen was my first wife.

But Ruth Glazier did call me back and was free on Sunday, so she became

Herbie's date. I made a few more calls, but when Sunday came it was just the three of us—Herbie, Ruthie, and me—who spent the afternoon in Elizabeth Park. Herb developed a quick crush on Ruth, and Ruth was a team player. They hit if off on that basis and, an hour into our afternoon, instead of the three of us it was two of them and one of me.

It began to drizzle and then to rain. They loved the rain, laughed and ran in it, while I grew lonelier and lonelier. At one point I was walking ahead of them. The sounds they were making caused me to turn around. For an instant I saw them as in a wide shot. They were skipping along, holding hands and swinging them wildly, laughing, singing—and then my eyes and heart zoomed into a close-up of Ruth, her drenched jet-black hair matted against her face, cupping her cheeks, framing those drop-dead gorgeous eyes and the lush sliced melon of a smile below them. That face would have been unforgettable had I seen it on a dry afternoon, but in the rain, *wet*, memory wasn't required. Like a billboard occupying a choice spot in Times Square, it has been there in my head ever since.

I saw that face again up close in 1992, more than fifty years later. Ruth was a psychiatrist, had raised a family in Chicago, and was still in practice there. She'd read that People For the American Way, an organization I'd started eleven years earlier—more about that later—was holding a big dinner there, and that I was on the program. If that was so and I had a little time she'd love to see me, she wrote in a note to Art Kropp, then PFAW's president. I was traveling alone, so I asked her to come along as my guest.

As she stepped out of a cab at the hotel, I recognized Ruth easily, expecting her to show her age, of course. And yet, crazily enough, I was disappointed that she was no longer the girl on that billboard. Who knew what Ruth was thinking at the sight of me? Or what the doorman was thinking, for that matter, when he nodded good evening to just another elderly couple entering the hotel.

I did learn what Ruth was thinking that day in the park with Herbie and me. She, too, wished she was with me, not my friend. She'd always hoped I would ask her out. Of course it made me feel good to hear that. But I couldn't help wondering if she'd ask me if I still showered before breakfast.

I STARTED SEEING Charlotte in 1939, my seventeenth summer. She was a year older, had graduated from high school, and was working behind the cosmetics counter at G. Fox & Company, Hartford's premium department store, as I was entering my senior year. We got married in 1943 and, strange as it may seem, we saw each other fewer than a dozen times between our meeting on the hayride and our wedding. There was little about our four-year acquaintance and twelve-year marriage that was not odd. The operative word that found us glomming on to each other had to have been *need*. In that first phone call Charlotte was clearly thrilled that I was calling her. I was excited in turn at her reaction, and for the moment we had answered each other's need.

Charlotte and I had nothing in common, really. I was attracted to the *idea* of a Charlotte long before I met her. I could not have thought of it in these terms then, but it's as if I wanted to be the youngest man with a trophy wife. At sixteen, while we were still living in New York, I cut a picture out of a magazine of a girl in jodhpurs with a face I fancied. I put it in my wallet and flashed it now and again to show off my outdoorsy girlfriend. When I met Charlotte and learned she loved horses, I asked if she had a photo of herself in jodhpurs. She did and I switched the photos in my wallet. As for how Charlotte felt about me, an aunt of my mother's—we knew her as Tante Cookie—once put it this way: "Charlotte would be happiest on a deserted island, with Norman all to herself." How sad for both of us.

Our first date, unlike the rest of our time together, could not have been more eventful. I had a burning love of theater, and the Westport Playhouse, a much-celebrated summer theater in Westport, Connecticut, near the New York border, advertised a production of Ferenc Molnar's *Liliom* starring Tyrone Power, a major motion picture star and matinee idol, and his French wife,

Annabella, a movie star in her own right. I could not imagine a happier, more romantic occasion than this, even if it did include three hours of driving each way—maybe more, depending on the performance of the Model A 1932 four-cylinder Ford my friend Sidney Pasternack and I bought that spring for sixty-five dollars each. (I earned my half working on Saturdays for Uncle Al at the John Irving Shoe Store.)

The morning of my big day my father made it bigger. "I'm coming home early for you," he said. "You can drive my car to Westport." My father was talking about his new 1939 Hudson Terraplane, which would make the drive shorter and absolutely dreamy. I was over the moon with excitement. The family car meant everything in those years; it was a matter of enormous pride, and for a teen to be allowed to take it on a date was extremely rare. He said he'd be home by three o'clock so that I would have time to pick up Charlotte in West Hartford and get to Westport around six, where we'd grab a bite at a diner and get to the theater by eight.

At half past three Dad was still not home. My agonizing increased as the minutes continued to pass, and at ten minutes to four I jumped into the Model A and chugged out to West Hartford, tears running down my cheeks and cursing my father to hell and back. There was no highway or thruway from Hartford to New York then, and so the Little Model A Engine That Could strained and struggled through Berlin and Meriden, around Middletown and Waterbury, skirting New Haven to the county line, and then, finally, mercifully, onto the Merritt Parkway, the expressway to Westport (and beyond to New York City). Relieved and cooling off as we tooled along on a road that seemed made for this day and this event, Charlotte and I suddenly heard a horn. "Honk! Honk, honk!" In my rearview mirror, there was my father in his new Hudson Terraplane. Unable to reach me otherwise, he had chased me from 68 Woodstock to West Hartford, through half of Connecticut, to the Merritt Parkway, less than half an hour from Westport, so as to let me have his Terraplane and drive back to Hartford himself in my Model A. The grandstand play of my life.

I might have seen Charlotte a time or two more that summer, but left to its own devices the relationship was destined to peter out. I had a full-time summer job driving a Good Humor truck, ringing those familiar bells through neighborhoods during the day and parked at night on the Boston Post Road, where local families out for an evening drive would stop by for their summer evening treat.

MY SENIOR YEAR at Weaver High was like a well-planned picnic. We seniors were the kings and queens of the roost; the school year was set to play out in a mounting series of highlighted events, culminating with class night, our senior prom, and the graduation itself. But the senior residing at 68 Woodstock Street was obsessed with one concern. What college could I get into, assuming my folks could afford to send me at all? My mother often moaned that it didn't look likely, while my father just needed ten days to two weeks and everything would be looking different.

I liked what I'd heard about Northwestern University, which was reputed to have a wonderful theater program. And, if reported correctly, it had a liberal Jewish quota system. That even such exalted institutions as Harvard, Princeton, and Yale limited the number of Jews they would accept each year was a fact of American life when our class was graduating. My friends with Jewish-sounding names must have felt like italicized beings as they filled out admission forms. Those with Gentile-sounding names, like mine, were spared the feeling until we came across the inevitable request to disclose our religious affiliation.

The news that to be a Jew in America was to be "different" had come to me shockingly when I was nine years old, just before they sent my dad away. He had bought me a crystal radio kit. It consisted of a spool of thin wire, the crystal itself (like a small stone), and another little wire my dad called a cat's whisker, with a tiny handle you maneuvered between your thumb and forefinger, lightly scratching the crystal until you picked up a radio signal, which you could then hear on the headset that came with the kit. We applied our crystal radio components to an empty oatmeal box, and to this day I can see my dad and me tickling that crystal with the cat's whisker for many minutes until, suddenly, we caught a spine-tingling AM signal! And what was it? Amazingly, it was the unforgettable theme that introduced *The Lone Ranger*, H.K.'s favorite radio show.

One night I was alone in bed poking around on my crystal set when I stumbled upon a man's voice so overwrought that he could have been a member of our family. But this was not a voice ranting about someone who came late to Sophie's wedding eight years ago, or a family member screeching that Burt should have known better than to recommend that butcher Dr. Pickman to Dorothy, who looks like a squirrel now—"You heard me, a squirrel. She looks like a squirrel now!" No, this voice, a strong high-pitched male voice, as I remember it, was carrying on about people who were calling him "an anti-Seemite" (as he pronounced it) when all he was doing was warning the 40 million working people who belonged to unions that some of their leaders were representatives of the devil. They were Communists, this voice went on, American-hating, anti-Christian Communists with Jew-sounding names— not that they necessarily *were* Jewish names, but they sure sounded like it—and that did not make him, Father Charles Coughlin, anybody's anti-Seemite!

Coughlin, often called the Father of Hate Radio, broadcast for an hour weekly from Detroit. He despised Franklin Roosevelt, fulminated endlessly about the New Deal as a betrayal of American values, and attached prominent Jews to everything he was railing against. Coughlin repulsed me thoroughly, but I listened to him enough and was so chilled by his polarizing and divisive rhetoric as to be reminded of him throughout my life whenever I've run into an irrational, self-serving mix of politics and religion. This was my introduction to the fact that there were people who disliked, mistrusted, even hated me because I was born a Jew. If I didn't have a nose for the slightest whiff of anti-Semitism before, I had it from that moment on.

IN THE WINTER of my senior year at Weaver, as my parents wrestled with the question of what college they could afford to send me to, the American Legion announced the inauguration of its first National Oratorical Contest. The first competition would be between the three high schools in Hartford, followed by the county, state, and regional competitions. Each entrant was to prepare an eight-minute speech about the United States Constitution and then speak extemporaneously for three to four minutes on a related subject that would be slipped to them as they approached the lectern for the second time. The first prize for winning the county competition was a scholarship to Emerson College in Boston.

The title of my prepared speech was "The Constitution and Me." Fueled by the idea of a quota for Jews seeking admission to certain colleges, my memory of Father Coughlin, and now the word out of Europe—where Hitler had marched into Austria, and Benito Mussolini, emulating Hitler, began enacting the first anti-Jewish legislation in Italy—I chose to speak to the specialness of being a member of a minority for whom the constitutional guarantees of equal rights and liberties just might have a more precious meaning. I won both the city and county contests and the scholarship to Emerson, but a "funny" thing happened on the way to that second competition.

On the morning of the event that would take place that evening in the civic auditorium, I woke up with a case of the shivers and a bout of extreme nausea. No temperature. No aches or pains. Just the feeling of death warmed over. I was competing against three other high school champions, I was scared, and I knew it. As I sought to "Straighten Up and Fly Right"—the title of a popular song of that era—it was clear to me that all I needed was comfort and support. My father was who-knew-where—I doubt that he was even aware of the event—so of course I turned to my mother. I see her now, coming into my room.

"Darling, are you all right? You look terrible."

"I'll be fine, Mother," I muttered stoically. All I needed—ached for, actually—was a little maternal encouragement.

Instead, I got, "There will always be another contest, darling. Stay home, you're coming down with something."

It didn't take long for my parents to forget that they'd ever worried about not being able to send me to college. Now they boasted of my acceptance to the class of '44 by that prestigious Back Bay Boston institution Emerson College, right there on Beacon Street, along the Charles River. The source of the scholarship that made it possible somehow never came up.

5

THERE WAS A LOT going on in America during the summer of 1940, just before my freshman year at Emerson was to begin. Having struggled to deny the growing sense that war was inevitable, Congress was now close to establishing its first peacetime draft; Charlie Chaplin brilliantly satirized Adolf Hitler as *The Great Dictator;* President Franklin Roosevelt began his run for an unprecedented third term, against Indiana Republican Wendell Willkie; and in August my friend Sidney Pasternack and I decided we would spend the last weeks before college driving leisurely up through New England in our spiffy Model A. To make our expenses, we arranged to sell Roosevelt and Willkie pennants, buttons, and trinkets door-to-door.

We sold some merchandise, more Willkie than Roosevelt in New England; it didn't take much to satisfy our needs. Compared to the frenzy and vitriol of the election process today, the entire populace was sleepwalking. The Democratic and Republican conventions (in Chicago and Philadelphia, respectively) were raucous, at times rancorous, but the thousands of delegates from around the country, most from small towns, left no doubt that whatever was on their minds politically, they were also out for a good time. It was rare for most people to be that far away from home and shackle-free, and there was a palpable sense of joyous abandon and conviviality we don't see at conventions today. The word *gentler* comes to mind when comparing that time to now. Even at the tail end of a depression and with a war brewing, we were living in a gentler time. Day after day Sidney and I lay on neighborhood lawns under giant oaks, talking for hours and napping. I haven't napped in as blissful a state in any circumstance since.

I FELL IN LOVE with Emerson College and with Boston. Both felt absolutely right for me. Emerson had been known since its founding in 1880 as the Emerson College of Oratory. Just a few years before my arrival, the "Oratory" was dropped and the Emerson College that today specializes in the dramatic arts and communication—with campuses on both coasts—was born.

Since my ambition was to be a press agent, I enrolled with the intention of majoring in journalism, a new program that was being offered as a junior-year option. The student body was around two hundred (today it's four thousand) and overwhelmingly female, which presented no problem for the dozen or so of us who were male. We were there to study the "spoken arts"—voice, theater, radio announcing, and radio as theater. Talk of communications as a field of study was in the air, enhanced by speculation about this thing called television, though its realization was extremely remote. (A few scientists were on record saying it would never happen at all.)

I lived at 270 Clarendon Street with four other Emerson freshmen, all male, and a handful of women in their thirties who worked for one of the many insurance companies headquartered in Boston. The Back Bay rooming house was owned and run like a dormitory by an Irish couple in their forties known to us as Ma and Pa Lawless. Except for me, everyone at 270 was Christian, and despite my lack of direct connection to my religion, I couldn't have been more conscious of myself as a Jew if Hitler had been in the room pointing at me. Not that my being Jewish mattered to anyone else there—I never got a hint of that.

But that didn't stop me from being extremely conscious of my circumcised penis. In those years, whether it was or not, circumcision seemed to be a particularly Jewish thing, so for weeks I scheduled my shower times to be sure I was alone in there. One day, off by a few minutes one way or the other, I found Stewart McGreggor entering the shower just as I was stepping out. There we stood, each of us stark naked, and I was stunned to see that he had been circumcised also and that his penis had a strong resemblance to my own. I couldn't have felt more like a winner and a regular guy if I'd been awarded the Heisman Trophy.

THERE ISN'T A LOT TO SAY about my academic work at Emerson. I was not a serious student, there was no pressure from my parents to be one, so I aimlessly peeked into every nook and cranny of the Emerson curriculum. I did as much with the city of Boston, fell more and more in love with them both, and made some wonderful lifelong friends. But I never lost the sense of being outside looking in. I could be, and often was, at the very center of things and still felt like an outsider.

In the South Boston of that time Scully Square had a reputation for being a naughty neighborhood, which is why I quickly began to explore it. What kept me coming back was my discovery of the Old Howard, a historic theater established in the 1880s as a home for Shakespeare and other classic theater. By 1940 it had suffered two fires and a downturn in the number and class of people who were attracted to it. Now it was a well-known burlesque house featuring the most celebrated strippers of the day, along with some of the bawdiest comics, a few of whom would, years later, make big reputations on television.

I saw every new bill at the Old Howard during my two years at Emerson, soaking up the comics and the sketches and delighting in the bump-and-grind grand dames of strip. I think I learned as much about comedy from those queens of burlesque as I did from the comedians. Strutting the stage imperiously, and so teasingly taking it off, were, among others, Sherry Britton, Ann Corio, Georgia Sothern, Rose La Rose, Lili St. Cyr, Sally Rand, and Gypsy Rose Lee. And performing a handful of sketches that would outlast all of them—"Meet Me 'Round the Corner," "Pay the Two Dollars," "Slowly I

Turned," to name a few—were the likes of Red Buttons, Rags Ragland, Jack Albertson, B. S. Pulley, Bobby Clark, Phil Silvers, Bert Lahr, Joey Faye, and Red Skelton.

Burlesque and its practitioners touched me to the marrow as they mirrored the foolishness of the human condition. Absent all depth, absent all subtlety, but falling-down funny, these comics hung humanity out to dry. Their imperious counterparts, the statuesque strippers, did it their own way. They put us all on. It was our response that made us the ones who'd been had. Gypsy, Georgia, Lili—they all paraded, peeled, and undulated with a bump here and a grind there that were about as erotic as a stewardess pouring hot fudge on a ball of ice cream. But generic to the moment were those mostly middle-aged and older men in the first rows, whooping and hollering "Take it off" while a stripper was taking endless time to seductively roll a long sleeve from a naked shoulder and down a bare arm as if she were approaching climax.

I loved every second of it and, without being aware of this at the time, used it as a course of study. You could call it my major. Burlesque and its audience were my acting, producing, directing, and casting school. I think back on my TV shows and the lead characters they spawned and couldn't be more grateful to the Old Howard. And as the world has turned for me, small wonder that years later, long after burlesque was gone, several of its practitioners would turn up in my life again, a few rather importantly.

IN MY SECOND SEMESTER at Emerson I played Uncle Stanley in a production of *George Washington Slept Here,* a trifle of a play, but a hit, by George S. Kaufman and Moss Hart. As it turned out, at the very beginning of my career I would have a rather significant influence on the life of Mr. Hart. Leaping ahead for a moment:

It was after the war and I had become the press agent I'd always wished to be. I was working for a Broadway publicity firm, and it was my job to get our clients' names in the news or in one of the several well-known gossip columns.

There were eight major daily newspapers in New York at the time: the *Times*, the *Herald Tribune*, the *Daily News*, the *Daily Mirror*, the *Post*, the *Journal-American*, the *World-Telegram*, and *PM*, the only outspoken leftist daily I can ever recall. No paper today would dare lay claim to being left leaning; at the same time we witness an entire media empire, Fox, leaning decidedly rightward and denying it under the preposterous rubric "fair and balanced."

Two of the clients represented by the company I worked for were Moss Hart and actress, singer, and future game show panelist Kitty Carlisle. Dorothy Kilgallen, famed showbiz columnist for the New York *Journal-American*, printed this squib concocted by me out of thin air in my first month on that first job: "Kitty Carlisle gifted friend Moss Hart with a pocket flask measured to his hip while he napped." Moss and Kitty met for the first time when he phoned her to laughingly thank her. Within a year they married and were together until Hart died in 1961.

I WAS IN MY THIRD SEMESTER at Emerson when all hell broke loose for America. It was a Sunday and we were rehearsing an old play called *The Two Orphans* in the small theater behind 130 Beacon, under the direction of Gertrude Binley Kay, a tall, effusive Back Bay Brahmin of a woman who headed the theater department and directed most of its productions. GBK spoke in a loud, hilly coloratura that seemed to bounce off whichever colorful, large-brimmed hat she happened to be wearing. She was carrying on at the top of her powers when a woman from the front office staggered in weeping, barely able to choke out something she'd heard on the radio about the Japanese and an attack on our sleeping forces in Hawaii. Before she could get it all out coherently, two separate phones were ringing and someone remembered there was a radio in a cupboard backstage. Within minutes the rehearsal was over, we were gathering all the facts about the Japanese attack on Pearl Harbor, and Gertrude Binley Kay was bellowing an invitation to join her and "march right down to that Japanese store on Commonwealth Avenue and throw a brick through the window!" The next day a more sensible, though no less passionate, President Roosevelt declared December 7, 1941, "a date which will live in infamy" and Congress took a vote. America was at war.

SOME WEEKS LATER I phoned my grandfather to tell him I was thinking of enlisting. I called him first because I'd always loved the way he talked about *his* enlistment as a boy in Russia. "Oh, when I went for a soldier . . ." was the way his remembrance would begin, and I was enraptured. As I think about it, those words pretty much bookended our life together. They were among the last words that passed between us just a day before he died at ninety-two. He was in New Haven Hospital and I was told he hadn't spoken or reacted to anything for a day or more. I, too, got no reaction from him, not even to my big hello, or to the mention of my name, or that I'd come from California—nothing, until I said, "Zayde, tell me about when you joined the army." A beat and then, as if the sun were rising inside him, he beamed and murmured, "Ohhh, when I went for a soldier . . ." I must have relived that moment a thousand times since.

So when I called my *zayde* to discuss the idea of my going for a soldier, perhaps I should not have been so surprised at his response. He didn't say "Go," he didn't say "Don't." He simply wept. My mother cried, too, when I phoned her: "But you're in college! *Nobody* enlists in college." Then, calling for my father: "Herman!" As he came to the phone I heard her add, "I need *this* now!"

Dad played it cool. Obviously, I hadn't thought it through. I should wait for the emotion of Pearl Harbor to settle down. In six months we'd talk about it again. And by then, as only H.K. could reason, "Who knows, with a little more education you could enlist as an officer."

My enlistment was on hold but service was on my mind when my closest friend, Nick Stantley, and I were talking one day behind the little stand we'd set up to sell school supplies at Emerson. How we might help the defense effort was the topic, and it occurred to me that we might sell Defense Stamps and Bonds for the Treasury Department. Defense Stamps sold for twenty-five cents each. With the first purchase you got a booklet to put them in, and it held $17.50 worth of stamps. You then turned that in and it bought you a Defense Bond, which matured in ten years and paid $25.

Word in the family had it that my uncle Jack, the press agent, was now working with the government as a dollar-a-year man. These were men and women who had some expertise in their line of work that could be of value to the war effort. They volunteered that expertise for a dollar a year. Uncle Jack signed on to market "Unusual Non-Military War Efforts" by the folks at home. Our idea was right up his alley, and he phoned the guy he reported to. A few days later I got a long-distance call—"long distance" being a big deal then, automatically anointing a phone call as, at the very least, important, and quite possibly urgent—from one Millburn McCarthy Jr. in Washington, DC.

Millburn McCarthy Jr. Holy shit! Talk about your stirring, rock-ribbed American names. This was a name that suggested real class and power, and a family history that didn't begin within a thousand miles of a shtetl. Such thoughts occurred to me then, and do to this day, because that kid poking around on his crystal set, spooked by a Jew hater, still lives in me. In 1982, for example, at age sixty, I walked into the office of Andrew Heiskell, the longtime chairman and CEO of *Time* magazine, six feet four, crisp, iron-jawed, gorgeous, and quintessentially Gentile. I was there to tell him about People For the American Way and ask if he would care to join the newly formed board, but the subtext in my mind throughout our meeting was "This is the tallest, most spectacular goy I have ever seen." Andrew, a Republican, by the way, until his death in 2003, was one of our strongest board members and a great friend, but—and I said this in my eulogy for him—the Jewish kid in me never spent a minute with Andrew Heiskell when he wasn't conscious of feeling special, "chosen," if you will, to be close to this man.

It was the same part of me that in 1942 needed not just to enlist but to see action. Imagining the war coming up conversationally later in life, I simply *had* to have served and seen serious action in it. Would I have felt this special need had I not been Jewish? I'll never know for sure, but my sense of it is that nothing much had changed in me since the American Legion National Oratorical Contest, when I wondered if my appreciation of the Constitution didn't run deeper because I was a Jew.

Millburn McCarthy Jr.'s response to the idea of selling Defense Stamps at Emerson was phenomenal. Emerson would be home to the nation's first Collegiate Defense Stamp Bureau, and the idea would then be marketed to colleges across the country. I don't recall McCarthy's notion spreading nationwide, as he had hoped, but for Nick and me it became a one-act bonanza of excitement. The Associated Press did a story, it was printed in the *Boston Globe*, and a few days later we received an invitation to appear on national radio. It was a CBS program called *The March of Time*, which featured, along with the news of the day, stories of ordinary folks who created, invented, or performed extraordinary things. It was hosted by a series of announcers who were stars in their own right then, such as Harry von Zell and Westbrook Van Voorhis. This was, of course, my first dip into show business, the human dynamics of which remain so unchanged that it could have occurred last week. We got a call from a breathless young "producer" from *The March of Time*, who made it sound like he had discovered us and our story, but whose real job was simply to locate us for the real producer and book our appearance.

In a matter of weeks a date had been selected, and Nick and I were in a parlor car on a train to New York, heart-pumpingly out of our league but attempting to appear casual to the porters. In New York we were put up in a stately two-bedroom suite at the Roosevelt, one of the top hotels in the city at the time. The Guy Lombardo Orchestra famously played for dinner dancing at the Roosevelt. For two nights we were pigs in heaven in our hotel suite. To Nick and me, *Room Service* was a film starring the Marx Brothers. Suddenly it was a wheeled table, draped in an elegant white cloth, tended by a pair of waiters who brought the food we'd just ordered on plates and with cutlery fit only for aristocrats.

That night we slept in the kind of lush bedding we associated with movie queens and matinee idols. And when I woke up the next morning, staring up at the ceiling was a spiritual experience. It was, by many feet, higher than any of the eight-foot ceilings I had looked at from any bed I'd slept in before. Gone were the white stucco and the round air vent with the ring of brownish stain around it, at that point all I had ever opened my eyes to among the ceilings of my life.

Room service breakfast was even better than the previous night's dinner, and we were far more laid back in the way we received it. Before we were finished, a script arrived from *The March of Time* for the Stantley and Lear segment that we were to rehearse starting at midday for the live broadcast at eight P.M. that night. It called for Mr. Van Voorhis to announce that the Treasury Department had just discovered the work of two young patriotic students whose brilliant concept to help the war effort at Emerson College was about to go nationwide to colleges everywhere. At which point music was to swell, then come down to hear the two students, Nick Stantley and Norman Lear, speculating as they walked along Boylston Street in Boston about what they might do to aid their brothers fighting abroad, until one of them, in a "Eureka!" moment, erupts with the haunting and unforgettable "Hey, that's it! We start the first Collegiate Defense Stamp Bureau!"

Nick and I read our lines together fifty times and had them memorized before we got to the CBS studio, met our producer and director, shook hands with Mr. Van Voorhis, and learned, to our dismay, that professional actors were going to play the parts of Nick and Norman. Following that, a ninety-second slug of time was allotted for Mr. Van Voorhis, known to conduct one hell of an interview, to chat with the real Nick and Norman.

The show was in full rehearsal from the top, and just as they were getting to the "CDSB STORY," as it was listed in the rundown, we became aware of some bustling in the control room. Before we could hear ourselves played by actors, someone came out waving a copy of one of the afternoon papers, which featured a front-page photograph of an adorable little boy in leg braces, a victim of polio, kissing President Franklin Roosevelt, himself a later-in-life victim of the disease. Further, word came down from the powers that be that the boy had been located at Campobello, Roosevelt's home, not far away, and would be on his way to CBS shortly to be spontaneously interviewed on *The March of Time* in place of the "CDSB STORY."

In an instant it was as if Nick and I were standing on the sidewalk watching *The March of Time* march on. And no one found a moment to apologize. If our friends at Emerson who tuned in heard anything at all about us, it flew past at the very end of the show as fast and unintelligible as the disclaimers we hear today after every commercial for a medicinal product. "People taking this drug have been known to develop worms, or suffer heart attacks and strokes; do not take this drug if you have liver problems or a history of forgetting your keys; call your doctor if you have ever sneezed or coughed or scratched an itch anywhere on your body or the body of a family member, especially anyone named Helen."

6

As a result of my generation's response to Pearl Harbor and a war for which we were totally unprepared—yet, with our allies, managed to win—Tom Brokaw titled his book about us *The Greatest Generation*. There was indeed an instant and phenomenal coming together of Americans everywhere, men, women, and children alike. The votes to declare war—82–0 in the Senate, 388–1 in the House—were a perfect reflection of the overnight solidarity Pearl Harbor generated. And "the war effort," as it was termed, was an extraordinarily modest title for what followed. From a standing start we had to conscript and train our troops; ship them to two theaters of war, Europe and the Pacific; and clothe, feed, and supply them with the firearms, ammunition, trucks, tanks, boats, submarines, and planes to do battle on the ground, on and beneath the water, and in the air—an altogether impossible task but for the backbreaking, mind-bending effort of all those at home, including men who for whatever reason could not serve in the military, women who had never worked in factories before, and mothers who historically never worked anywhere before. This greatest generation, almost to a person, quickly became a round-the-clock workforce as able, revved up, and dedicated as our fathers, brothers, and sons on the battlefield.

But as part of that greatest generation, I have to acknowledge how much more we had going for us that contributed to our Pearl Harbor response as compared to, say, this generation's burst of patriotic fervor at 9/11, which petered out when a war that couldn't be adequately explained—and has been overwhelmingly regretted—suddenly enveloped us. Soon, too, we were drowning in cheesy rhetoric aimed at restoring our feelings for the old red, white, and blue, but as soulless as the flag pins that bloomed on DC lapels.

I won't argue that we Americans loved our country more in 1941, or that we love our country less today. But I will say that we were far more *in* love with America and far more connected to the *idea* of America than we are now. The good ship USA had not foundered as often and as publicly then and so we were surer of our country, believing more in its propensity to do good in the world. We had frequent reminders of our history and our values. In some junior high schools and in virtually all high schools we were taught civics. The news that came to us by way of radio was unrushed and in context. News departments were not pressed to be profit centers, and that held true when television came along just a few years later. And so rape, murder, and other horrors did not lead the news; our senses were not assaulted across the dial by an unholy array of shouters hurling social and political invective at one another, and the news was not offered up in opinionated bumper sticker sound bites.

We saluted the flag and recited the Pledge of Allegiance every morning (before the words "under God" were gratuitously added to it). There were lots of parades, too: celebrations of America on Independence Day, Armistice Day, Memorial Day, and Washington's and Lincoln's birthdays (observed independently then, jointly now as the generic Presidents' Day). Those parades, most of them small but no less proud, were replete with college and high school bands, military bands when available, World War I veterans in full force, a diminishing group of Spanish-American War vets, and, of course, the flag. Vivid in my mind are memories of my *zayde* standing with me at the curb, holding my hand and squeezing it tightly as the flag passed by and the martial music played—"Stars and Stripes Forever" was his favorite. When I looked up at him, there'd be that inevitable tear running down his cheek.

I TALKED TO MY FOLKS about enlisting a half dozen times over the next several months, each time bowing to my mother's pleas not to. The country didn't really need me. It needed college graduates more, needed lawyers more. Oops, so she forgot I didn't want to be a lawyer. Well, then, they needed *whatever* I wanted to be more. Couldn't I see how this upset her? She had to get off the phone. Her stomach was acting up again from all the aggravation. "Here, talk to your father."

H.K. by then was himself a part of the war effort, scouring the Connecticut countryside to locate tool-and-die makers, metalworkers, and small factories in the hinterlands and bringing them small-parts work from major Midwest plants with federal contracts to make heavy equipment for the military. Aircraft manufacturers, for example, needing hundreds of small parts they couldn't spare the time or the specialists to produce themselves, contracted out to factories that would be brought to their attention. These middlemen were known as ten-percenters, that being their commission on the deals they brought in. Herman K. Lear was their man in Connecticut, and he was doing well. And by then he knew some retired generals who were working for the War Department (renamed the Department of Defense in 1947). So, not to worry, H.K. assured me, one phone call to General So-and-so and he'd get me a desk job right here in the States.

After nine months I stopped talking about it and enlisted without telling anyone. They learned of it a week later. You may wonder how I could have taken so long to enlist, given what I described as my need to serve my country, but, then, how amorphous and faceless was "my country" as compared to the beseeching face of the woman who gave birth to me, was extolled by my father as a saint, and had once suffered a goiter? When she heard of my enlistment she went straight to bed. It was like I'd stabbed her in the heart, she said. She couldn't even find the strength to ask into what branch of the military I had enlisted. It was the Army Air Forces. That pleased my father, because he knew just who to call to assure me of that desk job in the States, now "maybe even close to home." It didn't occur to me that his ability to secure this "desk job" was just another of his pipe dreams, and I begged him not to make that phone call as strongly as my mother had begged me to stay in college.

HAVING ENLISTED IN SEPTEMBER, I was called up for service in early November 1942 and sent to Atlantic City for basic training. Thousands of us were stationed in the ocean-side hotels along the boardwalk. Gambling and casinos didn't come to AC until 1978, so we passed our time watching training films, taking instruction, and working out in the various hotel ballrooms. We drilled and marched on the boardwalk.

Despite my new uniform with its Army Air Forces shoulder patch, I still felt like a pretend soldier, drilling above the beach, the ocean on one side and the other side flush with stores and entertainment emporiums now courting tens of thousands of GIs. Coursing up and down from my room on the sixteenth floor and trotting as instructed through a hotel lobby to join my platoon, I felt as silly as I thought I must look. When I tried to put a positive spin on this choice of unmilitary surroundings, I saw it as a measure of how thoroughly every segment of our society was mobilized to participate in World War II.

Before long I was sent to Scott Field in Illinois (an hour's ride from St. Louis, Missouri) to be trained as a radio operator. I had enlisted to become a pilot—it was right there in my papers—so I spoke to every high-ranking officer I could find about this mistake. I was told that my next stop would be Laredo, Texas, for in-flight gunnery training.

My memories of Scott Field include learning Morse code and meeting two fellow GIs: Wally Kuflick, who had no eyelashes because he pulled them out in class, often as we watched him; and another private from somewhere in the South whose name I've mercifully forgotten, who in one fell swoop alerted me like nothing I'd ever read or heard before to the issue of race in America. I was on line to get into the mess hall when I heard this jovial, pleasant-looking guy, five or six men behind me, say something about having played "Nigger baseball" back home. There wasn't a chance that a black guy might have overheard this, since the military wasn't desegregated until 1948. I couldn't have been the only GI to be startled by the expression, but no one could have been more sickened by it, especially as described. The game was played by a few white boys in a car with the rear right window open, driving through a black neighborhood, looking for a man or boy on a bicycle. When they sighted one, the car would come from behind to pass him on the left, and a baseball bat would shoot out of the open window to clip the rider on the back of his head. Nigger baseball.

I'd give anything to add that I belted the private, or at the least chewed his ass off. Instead, I held back and just felt nauseated.

When our radio training concluded we boarded a troop train to Laredo. Most of the men traveled in regular seats, but a dozen or so of us were lucky enough to draw berths. At about three A.M. I was lying down, dressed and reading, when we stopped at Texarkana, bordering Arkansas and Texas. The train emptied in a flash when we saw a group of women wearing USO aprons serving coffee and doughnuts on the station platform. I can't be sure we GIs fully appreciated the support, affection, and respect we were being shown at every turn wherever we were stationed or transported. It was just an everyday manifestation of the 360-degree, wall-to-wall war effort. I haven't known anything like it since and it warms me more than I can say to remember it now.

This stopover in Texarkana is memorable for another reason—in a phrase extremely popular at the time, it was a "Lucky Strike Extra." One of the USO women had a daughter helping her, nineteen or so and delicious. She had never seen a troop train, and with my lower berth twinkling like a star in the corner of my mind, I offered to take her aboard for a peek. The entire stopover could not have been more than half an hour, but that was enough time, coffee and doughnuts aside, for that young woman to contribute to the war effort.

Note: This lickety-split assignment was not all my doing. I was not—never have been—a lickety-split man with the ladies. The girl, caught up as much as her mother in the how-can-I-serve emotion of the moment, was simply doing *her* part as a patriot.

WHILE I CONTINUED to talk to the top brass in Laredo about my stated intention when I enlisted, I learned to handle a 50-caliber machine gun. From a seat behind the pilot of a single-engine plane I fired at a plastic target trailing some hundred feet behind another small plane. I passed muster and went from radio operator to radio operator–gunner, and I made sergeant. It was only when I received the orders for my next post that I learned someone had finally heard me. I was being transferred to the University of Buffalo—where the Air Force had set up a College Training Department (CTD) on the campus—for pilot training.

Before we take leave of Laredo, there is one brief, repulsive memory that I haven't managed to expunge. A bunch of us GIs heard that there was a tent show in Nuevo Laredo, the town across the border. I don't specifically recall, but I'm sure I knew what I was going to see and—for shame—went anyway. The tent was the size of a two-car garage, it was a blisteringly hot summer day, and there must have been fifty or more GIs in attendance, pressing and jostling to get a better view. The show consisted of two women and a small horse, and whatever you can imagine taking place with that cast of characters. Yes, *whatever* you can imagine.

IN BUFFALO we learned to fly in an AT-6 single-engine trainer aircraft, one of the most highly regarded worker planes in the history of aviation. While the Air Force thought us too green to solo, we did get to do it all with an instructor at the end of our term, an afternoon I will never forget.

One of the two best friends I made in the service was Jimmy Gorman, a great-looking, singularly Irish lad with blue eyes and jet-black hair. I had a full head of black hair and blue eyes also, and when we were together most people thought my mother could have come from Ireland, too. That, of course, pleased the gnawing sliver of me that persisted in feeling himself an outsider.

One night toward the end of our training, Jimmy and I were double-dating at the Circus Bar, a rotating merry-go-round cocktail lounge atop the Statler Hotel in Buffalo. Jimmy had fixed me up on a blind date with an Irish lass by the name of Helen O'Leary. Of course the joke of the evening was that if Helen and I were to marry, she would become Helen O'Leary Lear. In our dress uniforms Jimmy and I were a striking pair, the girls we were with were extremely pretty, and this could have been the very first time I thought of myself as good looking. Fit and slender, too, because the Air Force had us running five to six miles each morning wherever we were stationed. No memory in my long past is clearer than that of the four of us sitting at the edge of the Circus Bar as it slowly turned above the city, sipping our Southern Comfort and basking in one another's presence. I have tried all my life since to understand what I did next.

In a pause between laughs, I got up and walked to a pay phone visible from our table. Although I hadn't talked to her in well over a year, I remembered Charlotte Rosen's number and phoned her, person-to-person collect, in West Hartford, Connecticut. She picked up and, just as happened the first time I called her, the delight in her voice was unmistakable when the operator asked if she would accept a collect call from Norman Lear in Buffalo, New York.

"Yes, of course," she exclaimed.

It took no more than a few minutes to tell her what I was doing in Buffalo and to learn that she and her folks were contemplating moving to Florida. Then, with tear-filled eyes and a misty view of Jimmy and the two girls on the merry-go-round bar oh so slowly coming into view, I heard myself ask, "Want to come up to Buffalo and get married?"

There wasn't so much as an "Oh, my God," not even a "Really?" Her response was instantaneous: "Yes!" If I were writing fiction here, I might describe the moment as dreamlike. But it wasn't. I knew what I had done. I just had—and to this day have—no idea why.

A few more phone calls following the historic one, and plans for the wedding were set. Her folks and mine—who had never met—would drive up to Buffalo in two weeks. I would hire the rabbi, make the other necessary arrangements, and the ceremony would take place on a Saturday night at the Statler, in a private room adjacent to the Circus Bar. When that day arrived—October 21, 1943—the only guests were a handful of cadet friends. The wedding party consisted of bride and groom; the bride's parents, Al and Rhoda Rosen; the groom's parents, Herman K. and Jeanette Lear; the groom's intended best man, Jimmy Gorman; no bridesmaid, because Charlotte didn't want one; and, to my surprise, my father's best friend at the time, Sidney Fineman, who was brought along by H.K. to serve as my best man.

The Yiddish word *plotz*, which means "so stricken as to burst," was invented for me for that moment.

"But, Dad," I stuttered, "Jimmy Gorman is my best man."

"Norman, Sidney isn't well, but still he came all the way from Hartford, look at him, how can I tell him you don't want him?" my father said, while my mother raised her eyebrows over his shoulder in her patented "What can you do?" way.

My best man was Sidney Fineman, in the deadest of wedding ceremonies. Somewhere between ashamed and destroyed, I got shit-faced with my buddies and waved my bride off when she went to bed. For the newlyweds, our first week together was every bit as unromantic as the wedding and the marriage proposal. Charlotte and I were strangers when we made love and, if possible, knew each other even less well when we had concluded.

A WEEK AFTER our wedding Charlotte went home and I was sent to what was called a staging area in Nashville, where we were given thorough physicals and took a number of written tests, largely mechanical and mathematical. When they were over I was told I had "failed the physical," and was "disqualified for aircrew training." Not only couldn't I be a pilot, I couldn't fly altogether. But wait. I had already been trained as an airborne radio operator and gunner, and now I wasn't fit to fly?

I was to ship out in two days, but to where and in what capacity? All I knew for sure was that I was grounded, but why? I thought it might be my sinuses because some doctor somewhere had once questioned them. In any event, when I was handed my orders I was astonished. I was being transferred to Avon Park, Florida, where I was to be assigned as a radio operator and gunner on either a B-24, known as the Liberator bomber, or a Flying Fortress, more often called the B-17.

Double-checking my military record recently, I found that tests concerning my "reflexes, gait, coordination, musculature, tension, tremor, and other pertinent tests were: NORMAL." I was physically fit to fly, but based on written math tests, I was not. "Estimated adaptability for military aeronautics: LOW" was the way they put "too stupid to be a pilot."

A HUNDRED OR SO of us were billeted underneath the stands at a ball field in Avon Park. Hundreds more were scattered about in local hotels and motels, as well as at MacDill Field, an Army Air Forces base. We were shipped there from units across the country to be assigned to aircrews in our individual specialties, though it would be about two weeks before we got those assignments. After a couple of days of being run aimlessly around the field and ordered to attend lectures we'd already heard—with titles such as "Why Condoms," "She Could Be a Carrier," and "What You Need to Know About Venereal Disease"— I responded to a notice on the bulletin board about a plant "important to the war effort" that needed some help the next week. I grabbed the opportunity for a change of pace and scenery.

The plant I signed up to work in made fertilizer. It was not as unpleasant a place to work as its product might suggest. I would describe the air as heavy and musty and the task I was assigned as arduous and boring. I steered a huge wooden wheelbarrow under a wide metal chute that opened just long enough to fill it with some five hundred pounds of fertilizer, which I then wheeled down a long wooden gutter to a spot where the contents were emptied and shoveled into a waiting truck. I then pushed my empty wheelbarrow back up the wooden gutter to pick up another load and repeat the task.

There were maybe eight guys doing the work I've described, all but me black. The gutters were side by side, so when I was wheeling down one track, I'd pass several of the men coming up. And vice versa. In the week I spent there I must have passed each face a hundred times. At first their curious expressions marked me as an oddity, but by day two there was an occasional wink with the hint of an "Okay?" My return wink signifying "Okay, indeed!" resulted in welcoming nods and grunts until a gentle layer of amusement began to grow, too, out of our unorthodox situation.

It was in this atmosphere that I was suddenly—how I love this expression!—tickled silly. There was one guy in his fifties—"as black as the ace of spades," as my father would have described him—large, and with eyes and a smile that a child could have carved into a pumpkin and lit from the inside. I don't know how many times we passed each other, but each time we did he would turn that face to me, his eyes twinkling, and say: "Gator gonna get you, white boy!"

"Gator gonna get you, white boy!" I never learned his name, but I know I was sipping the milk of human kindness each time he smiled and said it, and every one of the thousand times he and that line have come back to me since. I have also read volumes of understanding into it at various, usually difficult, moments in my life. Now, in my nineties, I find it the most delightful way of expressing what is approaching all of us, and likely me before most of you.

THE DAY OF ASSIGNMENT finally arrived and I was told to report to the crew of a B-17 led by Captain Albert Brown (Brownie) and copilot Bill Binzen. We all fell in, liked one another quickly, and took to our brand-new B-17 like fraternity brothers to a new frat house. We named our plane Umbriago ("old chum") after our favorite comedian, Jimmy Durante, who closed his radio show each week with that word. For some days we practiced teamwork in the air, flying day and night training missions, and by the fall of 1944, when we took off to join a bomb group already in battle, we were a proud and sharp Flying Fortress B-17 crew.

Brownie was handed our orders just before takeoff and instructed not to open them until we had reached our flying altitude. There were two theaters of operations in World War II, the European and the Pacific. Leaving from the East Coast, it seemed most likely that we'd be directed to the European Theater, but we could not have been sure. In the European Theater the 8th Air Force flew out of London, the 15th out of Italy. The crew, with no knowledge as to where we were heading, gathered behind the captain as he opened the brown envelope. With stops in Gander, Newfoundland, and the Azore islands, we were to continue to southern Italy, where we would be joining the 772nd Bomb Squadron of the 463rd Bomb Group, a wing of the 15th Air Force, at an air base outside a town called Foggia. We knew from the press that one of the storied targets of the 15th Air Force was the Ploiesti oil fields in Romania. Ploiesti, which supplied a third of the oil that fueled the Axis forces, was one of the most difficult and best-protected low-altitude targets in Europe, and the 15th Air Force had been suffering major losses there.

When we took off from Avon Park we were eager to join our brothers in battle overseas. By the time we experienced two nights in Gander—the coldest, most godforsaken spot any of us had ever been to—the freshness of the experience was wearing off, the learning curve somewhat flattened, and with the new reality of the Ploiesti oil fields in our future, the appeal of flying into battle was somewhat more of a stretch.

I drew guard duty the first night. Why our planes had to be guarded on the tarmac in the dead of night when we were all American servicemen on our own military base on an island one hundred miles from nowhere I'll never know, but between midnight and three A.M., in the freezing cold, my gloved hand shouldering a shotgun, I walked at attention in front of the plane from wingtip to wingtip for three bullshit hours. Or was I arrogantly overlooking some dark possibility? Had the Germans been training B-17 crews to be dropped on Gander in the dead of night to steal unguarded planes? And those wily Japanese, might they have put something in our food supplies that would cause us not to hear plane engines start up at night, especially when the pilots were Germans? Wait! Was that a "Heil"?

My agitated imagination carried me for a while, until a measure of fear and loneliness began to overtake it. Into my second hour, the loneliness was met with tears and I was singing at the top of my voice, "We'll meet again, don't know where, don't know when . . ." And "I'll walk alone because to tell you the truth I'll be lonely, / I don't mind being lonely when my heart tells me you are lonely too . . ." I knew at least a dozen heartbreaking love songs and, bleary-eyed, sang every one of them into the cold and the wind. My kids are amazed at how many of those songs I recall to this day.

That night in Gander I learned this about love songs: if there is a relationship and a face to which you connect the lyric, the song can break your heart. Without that, it's not so much heartbreak as heart*ache*. My heart ached that night for the safety and the comfort of the familiar: my bed, my closet, the things on my wall, certain foods, my shower curtain ("Go know!" as Bubbe would say), and friends and family, which now included Charlotte. I could connect no one person to the "love" in those love songs as I marched wingtip to wingtip in the blackness, alone.

7

WE ARRIVED IN FOGGIA in the late afternoon on November 1, 1944, just as a group of B-24s were returning from a mission. The boxy 24s, less sleek than the B-17s, were from a different squadron, landing at a field nearby. That was when we learned that the 772nd Bomb Squadron, to which we were attached, was the only squadron of B-17s in the 15th Air Force. A bit faster and more maneuverable, our plane proved by a slight percentage to be the safer of the two. Slight as that percentage might have been, throughout my life it has made the list every time I have counted my blessings.

The 463rd Bomb Group air base in Foggia consisted of a couple of hundred tents and a few stone buildings on a desolate open field, a short ride by jeep from the planes and runways. It would be two weeks before we flew our first mission, and we used that time to improve our accommodations. The tents were tents only, no reinforcement on the sides, no lights, no stove, and no floor, just dirt and grass. In 1986, when we were all in our sixties, our tail gunner, Danny Carroll—with the help of other members of the crew—wrote a book, *Crew Umbriago*, about our tour of duty. Reading it many years later, I learned that I had been key to achieving those improvements.

"There was no such thing as normal supply channels to get what we had been taught in civilization were necessities," Danny wrote. "These had to be obtained by begging, scrounging, midnight requisitioning, politicking, or you did without. We were fortunate to have as a member of our crew, Negotiator Par Excellence Norman Lear, who could accomplish the near impossible." I was pleased to read that our tent had the only brick floor because "our 'Norm' had a pile of bricks delivered to our billet by an Italian guy who lived outside the Air Base." He also described our having just one lightbulb in the center of the tent until "as if by magic six bomb bay lights were obtained, one was installed over each cot and we had the best quarters of any flight crew in the squadron. But our magician, Norm, was still at work," Danny continued. "He took a ride to a Fighter Group and acquired two P-51 wing tanks which held about seventy-five gallons each. They became our new and improved fuel and water tanks. But the icing on the cake was the headsets over each of our bunks, which were tapped into the Armed Forces Radio Network."

While I didn't remember the specifics of *what* I got done for my Umbriago crew, I do recall that even as a boy I was never good at taking no for an answer. As I think about it, that probably came from my constant struggle to get through to my parents. Trying one tack after another to gain their attention—occasionally to be listened to and, even more rarely, heard—I developed reasoning and presenting skills, along with a talent for herding ideas and selling them.

JIMMY EDWARDS VIES with Jimmy Gorman as the buddy I felt closest to in the service. Like me, Edwards was a radio operator and gunner, a member of Captain Guy Del Signore's crew. In formation they flew off our right wing as we trained in Florida, and as we made our way to the European Theater of Operations. We met earlier at Scott Field, where we learned Morse code and became radio operators, talking and sharing a great deal, and playing a lot of bridge. I think of bridge today only in the context of remembering Jimmy Edwards. It comes to me as a kind of sense memory. I'm playing bridge with Jimmy as my partner and I feel a quiet calm settle over me.

Jimmy was himself a quiet calm. Tall, thoughtful, bookish, he came across to me as if he sat on a fountain of secrets that amused the hell out of him. Suffice it to say I found Jimmy Edwards deeply interesting—a very new experience for me at the time. To this day he is a wisp of a presence in my life, like a poem I used to know by heart.

Ironically, our two crews were posted to fly four times before we actually completed that first mission. Four times we took off and headed to target, only to have the mission scrubbed because of bad weather. With orders not to land with a full fuel tank and a full bomb bay, twice we dropped our bombs in the Adriatic and returned to base early and twice we flew the requisite hours to use up our fuel before landing with the bombs intact.

The first day we were posted to fly, Jimmy and I had breakfast together, after which we went to the john, sitting side by side on a long line of wooden pot holes. The next time, one of us didn't have to go to the john but we both went anyway. The following times, whether or not either of us had to go, we went there and at least touched down. A superstition had set in and we eagerly obliged it. The fifth day our crews were posted to fly, either we took too long to eat or the officer who ordered us into a jeep despite our pleas must have had, in Army parlance, a hair across his ass.

"No way," he said, pointing to the jeep as, with our entire bodies, we demonstrated our need.

"Ten seconds," we pleaded. "We'll just touch down. It won't take longer than crossing ourselves, sir. Ten seconds!"

Nothing helped. We were whisked off to the flight line, Jimmy to his plane, I to mine, and the 772nd Bomb Squadron of the 463rd Bomb Group took off.

The target, we learned at altitude when Brownie opened our orders, was an aircraft plant in Regensburg, Germany. Our squadron consisted of eighteen planes flying in what was called wing formation. As radio men, Jimmy and I reported back regularly by Morse code to Central Command, informing them as to our condition and location. The radio position and accompanying top gun being closest to the bomb bay, it was also our job to check the bomb bay after we'd heard "Bombs away!" from the cockpit, to be sure all the bombs had been released and the doors could be shut. After some four hours, within thirty minutes of the target, we rendezvoused with the 8th Air Force out of London and started on our first bomb run.

As we neared the target we were suddenly hit by German fighters soaring in from every angle and spitting three hundred rounds at us in three-second bursts. We radio men were now at our 50-caliber gun posts spitting back. Our vision was limited to what was coming at us from high angles at the side and from above, so I didn't see it happen—I just heard another crewman say "Del Signore's been hit." My heart thumping, I strained to see for myself, but my vision was blurred by heavy flak and angry puffs of black bursting everywhere, a kind of deadly Rorschach in the sky. As we fought our way out of there, Del fell behind. Soon he was out of sight and my heart sank. But about twenty-five minutes after the rest of us had landed, Del—with only two engines firing—managed to get his crippled plane back to base.

I was racing to greet them when I learned that two crewmen, the ball turret gunner and radio man Jimmy Edwards, were dead. Thick-headed and choking back a scream, I *had* to say good-bye to Jimmy, but by the time I got to the plane they had already removed the bodies. Sometime later, still in a stupor, the horror of something I'd witnessed at the plane returned to me. It was a member of the ground crew stoically hosing out the ball turret, and I could no longer stifle that scream. Two days afterward I accompanied Jimmy's body to Bari, Italy, where he was buried in a GI cemetery.

I've thought long and hard, especially after that first mission and Jimmy's death, about how they could get me, just a few days later, and so many times after that, to board a plane and fly long hours only to be shot at from the ground by hundreds of antiaircraft installations and attacked in the air from every angle by dozens of swastika-emblazoned fighter planes. Yes, I loved my country and offered to risk my life in its defense. Yes, the Jewish part of the American in me made me especially eager to kill those who would eliminate us. But to enter a space at thirty thousand feet, in what could be a metal coffin for nine, carrying up to eighty-five hundred pounds of bombs in its belly, which, if hit by one of the missiles now exploding in the air nearby could lead me to such madness as wondering how many B-17 smithereens it would take to fill my closet at 68 Woodstock—no, no, that's not me.

Unless! Unless we humans come equipped with an unconscious or subconscious something that convinces us, no matter what the evidence to the contrary, that we will not die now. We lead numbers of lives—lives end on end and lives within lives. By the time I flew my first mission I had already lived so many—a life in grade school, another in high school, one in the dramatic club, another on the debate team, the one with my family, the many in my imagination, and on and on. So as we approached the bomb run and I manned the radio and top gun, I was scared, of course, but at the core of me, having already lived so many lives, I was by then wired to believe that this was simply another one, and that even as I lived *it*, the next life was on its way.

AROUND EIGHT P.M. a few days after Jimmy's death, we learned our crew was posted to fly the next morning. A light breeze of fear began wafting through my chest, a mixture of apprehension and excitement. Since childhood, the culture had instructed us to believe that being male and facing danger came with good cheer and a touch of bravura. Add a little peer pressure and there we were, having rushed to the board to learn with cheers and yelps that we were posted to fly. It wasn't until I was under my bedcovers, alone in my thoughts, that apprehension began to gain ground on excitement.

By morning and our wake-up call—no bugle, just a shout-out at about four-thirty—the apprehension had turned into fear. It seemed palpable in everyone. There was little chatter as we dressed, which, given the fact that we were preparing for temperatures that could reach thirty to forty below, was an ordeal in itself. Over our own underwear we wore a set of heated long johns, heavy outer pants and jacket, a "Mae West" life preserver, a parachute harness to which a parachute would clip if needed, and, over all that, a flak jacket and helmet. On our way to the flight line some guys dipped into Bibles they were carrying; some touched crosses to their lips; I looked heavenward, touched my right buttock and then my heart, my way of praying for God—whatever God there was—to save my ass.

From Foggia the average airtime to target was four to six hours at a minimum. (Our crew had the distinction of flying the longest single mission in the European Theater, some thirteen hours, to Berlin.) I would cheat at my radio desk and steal time listening to Armed Forces Radio play the music of the moment: "Don't sit under the apple tree with anyone else but me," "When Johnny comes marching home," and "There'll be bluebirds over the white cliffs of Dover . . . When the world is free." On one otherwise unmemorable mission, the one song I can recall my mother going mad over popped up.

One Sunday night in the 1930s, on *The Jack Benny Program*, she heard the tenor Frank Parker sing "Isle of Capri," and instantly it was as if that were the only song ever written. She never sang a note of it herself, never even hummed it, but as long as she lived, when music came up in conversation, or someone referred to a new song, my mother would brighten as if she had just awakened and ask if anyone knew "Isle of Capri," and if so, would they please sing it? Occasionally someone would start to grant her request, only to be interrupted before they got eight bars into it. "Oh," she'd say, "you should have heard Frank Parker sing it."

That day on the mission when I heard Frank Parker sing her song, I started to weep. At an altitude more than ten thousand feet I was sobbing into my oxygen mask, an activity not encouraged by Air Force medics, who favored the ability to breathe. After the war my mother showed me a letter I had written her describing the incident. It was a love letter.

AS I FLEW OUT OF FOGGIA, bombing German factories, airfields, and troop installations while listening to Armed Forces Radio, I was making notes for a variety show I planned to produce and stage between missions, titled *Hol-*

iday Hangovers. The holiday referred to was Thanksgiving 1944. Our copilot, Bill Binzen, once showed me a letter he'd written to his folks, dated November 26, 1944, describing the show I'd put together and performed in: "Last night the boys put on a show at the EM (Enlisted Men) Club. The place was sufficiently intimate and smoky, the gags kidding the commanders raw enough for anyone, and everyone had a good time. Norman Lear, our radio man, was emcee and really carried the show. He's got a wit that can cope with most any situation. The thing started off with an awkward silence when Lear feigned drunk as a member of the audience, and was very obnoxious. The CO got mad, Lear continued his remarks, and everybody was getting very tensed up. I'd been tipped off, but still couldn't help feeling a little uneasy until the gag was exposed as such."

What made Binzen uneasy was my ability to fake outrage and fury, which I'd learned and honed in my relationship with my pal Nick Stantley at Emerson College. Nick was a master at extreme behavior with a straight face. If he told you in advance that he was going to fake going nuts, he would proceed to a point where you believed him to be great at it; and to a point beyond that, where you could not believe *how* great he was at it; and past that to a point where you started to wonder, then worry, that maybe he had been sucked into the quicksand of his own madness; and then to a place where you had bought that possibility and were scared shitless.

Nick and I staged fights in front of friends and strangers everywhere. Carrying on one day in Filene's Basement in Boston over who reached first for a particular shirt for sale, we cut ourselves short when we saw the color drain from a salesperson's face as she struggled soundlessly to call for help. I carried the shtick forward for many years without Nick and that is what I was up to at the top of *Holiday Hangovers.*

Several years later, when I was writing on the Dean Martin and Jerry Lewis radio show for NBC, Jerry and I would do the routine as part of the audience warm-up. Jerry, faking anger about a bad joke his writer had written for him, carried it to such a fevered pitch, while I, the writer, cried and begged his forgiveness, that we brought the audience to a giant wince, their discomfort obvious until we let them off the hook and they laughed explosively.

PERHAPS THE BIGGEST, certainly the most celebrated, American entertainer in 1945 was Frank Sinatra. He'd already had some two dozen top ten hits by then and his appearances at the Paramount Theater in New York in those years were known to cause riots. As many as thirty thousand fans, largely female, jammed the streets in front of the theater. *Time* magazine said of him in that period, "Not since the days of Valentino has American womanhood made such unabashed public love to an entertainer."

Overseas, the average American soldier had a difficult time with this. Never having seen the man, all they knew was that Sinatra had been classified 4-F, disqualified to serve in the military because of something laughably (it seemed to us) labeled a punctured eardrum, and that back home all their girlfriends, sweethearts, and wives were carrying on over him like loony tunes and throwing themselves at his feet. The only way I can aptly express their feelings for Sinatra is to say they hated his fucking guts! And then one day, to our antipathetic delight, we read in the GI publication *Yank* that the USO was bringing the skinny little prick to Foggia. I couldn't have guessed that hot spring day—with some twenty thousand of us GIs all prepared to hiss and boo, many carrying excess vegetables the cooks and KPs had been saving for us to toss at the stage—that later in life I'd make a film with him (*Come Blow Your Horn*), fall in love with the guy, and enjoy a long, slight but storied relationship with Ol' Blue Eyes. Another thing I could not have guessed was the showbiz lesson I would be taught that afternoon, a lesson I found applicable from then on in situations of all kinds.

Crackling in anticipation and giddy with the grudge we were about to adjudicate, we sat on the field before the wooden stage that had been built that morning, we baby men of the 15th Air Force. As some canned music played loudly over speakers, three khaki-clad GIs finished setting up and fine-tuning the equipment. Suddenly, the music scratched to a halt and a big voice blared over the speakers that the USO was proud to present, as a big surprise to the troops, "One of America's most beautiful women . . ." (TWENTY THOUSAND GI HEARTS SKIP A BEAT) "As a top model, her face and figure are well known to all of you . . ." (YELLS, WHISTLES, AND CHEERS) "Fresh from the Hollywood Canteen—for you guys and your eyes only . . ." (HOW DO YOU FORGET *THAT* LINE?) "Here, on her very first visit to Foggia . . ." (AS IF THERE'D EVER BE A SECOND) "is the lovely and talented Jinx Falkenburg!"

If there had been a vote to select the Body of the Year in 1945, it could have been Jinx Falkenburg. She just might have known that, too, because she walked out in tennis shorts and heels. The boys went ape shit, of course, and she said something that strained to be amusing about having just run over from the Beverly Hills Tennis Club. She picked up a racquet and a bucket of balls up-stage and proceeded to hit autographed tennis balls into the crowd. That was her entire act, but from the reaction of the troops at the sight of her in shorts, and the escalating frenzy when she complained of the heat and whipped them off to reveal more skin in a bathing suit, Ms. Falkenburg had every right to feel she gave her all for the war effort. And, for the rest of her career, to rest well on her laurels for having "entertained the troops abroad in World War II."

Now, we thought, the moment we were really there for. The three GI stage-hands were back onstage tidying up after Jinx, and more music was blaring, when the big voice cut through again and an expectant rumble rolled across the field. This crowd was READY. When it heard that some comic was being in-troduced, not Francis Albert, the expectation turned to annoyance, as if to say, "Okay, we played along with that chick and the tennis balls, but let's not take advantage—we want what we came for!" Instead, we got Phil Silvers.

At that time, I might have been the only GI on the field who'd ever seen or heard of Phil Silvers. He had played the Old Howard burlesque theater in Bos-ton when I was at Emerson, one of those funnymen I learned so much from.

Silvers didn't do jokes. He played a character—a glad-hander and hustler, armed always with an ear-to-ear smile and a tall story. Just his "Glad to see you" earned a laugh. In the 1950s Silvers would become a household name when he starred as Sergeant Bilko in a show created around his character by the man I thought to be the best of the TV comedy writers, Nat Hiken. That afternoon in Italy, totally unknown, Silvers's job as an entertainer was to secure—in his case, hustle—a warm welcome for Frank Sinatra from the twenty thousand pent-up airmen gathered there. It was the equivalent of wringing blood from a turnip.

Wearing a kitschy houndstooth jacket, and flashing his come-one-come-all salesman's smile, Phil said something by way of hello and, noticing the GI stagehands about to walk off, called out: "How about these guys? Let's hear it for three of your own, Curly, Moe, and Jack." A small laugh was accompanied by big applause and cheers. Then: "Hey, you, Moe, come here." The GI didn't seem to like being called "Moe" and just stood there. Silvers turned to us: "What's he afraid of? I'm not gonna bite him. Don't tell me you guys in the Fifteenth are all scaredy-cats!" Putty in deft hands now, like any people throughout history (a phenomenon that is as good an explanation as any, I suppose, for the war that brought us together that afternoon in Italy), in an instant we joined forces with Phil Silvers and shouted and hooted the GI to Silvers's side. He stood there embarrassed and nonplussed. Silvers asked his name. Giving up, the GI shrugged and said, "Moe." We howled.

"What're you, a wise guy?" Silvers shouted into his face. Then, turning back to us: "You know this guy. Is he a wise guy?" Some shouted no, some yes, but pretty much everyone was caught up in the web Silvers was spinning. He turned to Moe again. "You wouldn't be here to stop me from introducing Sinatra, would you?"

"God, no," the guy all but cried.

"Maybe you think you can do better than him. Let me hear you sing. Three notes, give me three notes. *Do re mi*. Do it!"

A low, timid *do* issued from Moe.

"You call that a *do*? A note, even a single note, comes from here"—a poke in the chest—"to here"—a slap under the chin to indicate the throat—"and away." He squeezed Moe's open mouth roughly several times. We howled at all of this. "Try it again," Silvers said. "And again." Dissatisfied each time with what he heard, he insisted it be repeated. The jabs became slaps to both cheeks, a palm of the hand to the forehead, and a full body shake following the squeezed mouth.

It reached a point of total hilarity, but then, as funny as Silvers was, a rumble of empathy began to overtake the sound of mirth. At a point when the empathy threatened to take over, Silvers suddenly said, "I give up," pushed Moe away, and stormed off the stage. That was the cue for an offstage hand to place a needle on a recording, and over the speakers came Sinatra's music, a full orchestra playing one of his big hits, "I'll Be Seeing You." Twenty thousand men in uniform didn't know what hit them when Phil Silvers's bedraggled victim reached for a microphone and started singing a lyric that would cut to the heart of every man present, no matter who was singing. And here was Frank Sinatra, who would come to be considered peerless at mining the meaning of a lyric:

> *I'll be seeing you*
> *In all the old familiar places*
> *That this heart of mine embraces*
> *All day through . . .*

As unpopular with this crowd as Sinatra was at the beginning, he survived by emerging in a cloak of empathy that had been masterfully woven for him before his arrival. The characters of Archie, Maude, and George Jefferson all benefited from that lesson I was taught, wet-eyed, on the grass in Foggia.

ON THE SUBJECT OF TEARS, some minutes after we were awakened to fly a mission on April 12, 1945, a second face representing the command poked its head into the tent and announced that word had just been received: President Roosevelt was dead. Everyone was devastated. At mess most eyes were red, some couldn't stop carrying on about him, and some of us had to sit alone in our grief. I was one of the latter.

Roosevelt was our family's only full-out hero, and I don't recall knowing a family who felt differently. The fact of his election for a fourth term says everything about his popularity, but you have to get to the American heart at that time to understand the degree of the love and trust we of the middle class had for Franklin Roosevelt. He filled the singularly most important role I feel we need from our president. He was a father to us. His "fireside chats" on radio had us sitting at his knees feeling like we were part of the American portrait.

It would be many years until *elite* would become a bad word and Americans were coached to despise and mistrust anyone who appeared to be one. The Roosevelts were irrefutably among the elite, socially, intellectually, and every other way. Even when chatting, FDR's sound had a cathedral tone. With his rakish trademark fedora atop his head, a cigarette in a holder clenched at a jaunty angle between his teeth, wearing a cape he seemed born with, in a wheelchair he made his throne, he was royalty, American style.

We didn't know Eleanor the way we thought we knew Franklin, but among the first ladies of my time, Eleanor Roosevelt appears to me to have been the best casting. None of the others—Bess, Mamie, Jackie, Lady Bird, Pat, Betty, Rosalynn, Nancy, Barbara, Hillary, Laura, or Michelle—seemed as inherently "elite" as Eleanor. She reminded me of Mrs. Pie, a music teacher I had in fourth grade who had a speaking voice that raked the music scale on every syllable. I can see her now, hand cranking her floor-model Victrola and playing a 78-rpm recording of a soprano singing Dvorak's "Songs My Mother Taught Me." Throughout the twelve-plus years of Eleanor's term, there, too, was Mrs. Pie. And that song.

Just before takeoff, the mission that had been announced moments before we learned of the president's death was canceled. By ten A.M. dozens of us were already in beautiful downtown Foggia, and by noon the narrow streets and three bars were full of sad-eyed, wine-sluicing GIs drinking to the fallen president. The warm surprise was that we were not drinking alone. The townsfolk, largely middle-aged and older, cried and drank with us.

I was drunk out of my gourd by noon. The scene plays in my head like an old, flickering black-and-white film: I am standing in front of the municipal building, atop a flight of concrete stairs, looking out at fifty or sixty Foggia townspeople gathered there, and I am speaking to them in Italian and English about the death of Franklin Roosevelt. A boy who spoke English about as well as I spoke Italian interpreted for me when necessary, and three things stand out in my memory: Italian faces, tears streaming down their cheeks, their mouths running with prayers as they stretched to understand me; the unstrung feeling everywhere in me from the way I was pressing, with every ounce of me, to reach them; and the trip back to base that saw Danny Carroll and waist gunner Bob Oswald holding one leg each while I, reborn as a wheelbarrow, "rolled" home hand over hand.

I fell in love with Italy and its people during my time there, and that has not changed since. In World War II a joke described the Italian people best: "What is the thinnest book ever published? *Italian War Heroes.*" Benito Mussolini, Il Duce, was that joke incarnate. Italians are about music and great food and making love—the antithesis of making war. On furlough in Rome and Naples I was often taken for Italian in romantic situations and I did nothing to convince anyone otherwise. Today, among all my friends who travel extensively, I am not sure I know anyone whose favorite country is not Italy.

8

ONE SPRING DAY IN 1945, when the war in Europe had just been won and my tour of duty was coming to an end, I went into Foggia and found myself a print shop. It was a tiny place with a single operator behind an ancient linotype machine, so ancient that the operator had to fingerpick the letters one at a time to typeset them. I stood over him and pointed to every letter until I'd created a one-page announcement:

> One Norman M. Lear, having survived VE Day, and realizing the prox-
> imity of DD Day (date of discharge), is now able to lend active consid-
> eration to his heretofore neglected future. Somewhere there exists a
> Publicity Department or Public Relations Office which, if acquainted
> with the facts, might take interest in said future. This is an effort to link
> the two. Norman Lear has spent the greater part of his twenty-four
> years dreaming of, and preparing himself for a career in the field of
> PUBLICITY! . . . Lear was born to do for others—find them, mould
> them, publicize them—BUILD them!!! Rather than BE "IT," he is BE-
> HIND "IT." . . . On his ocean of ideas it is always high tide . . .

As soon as this one-pager had been printed, I sent it to my uncle Jack, the quarter chucker, with the instruction that it be disseminated to publicity houses in New York, Chicago, and Los Angeles. At the bottom there was a small square box and, squeezed into it, this epigram, headlined ON MODESTY: "Whilst there be no one to do it for you, tootest thou thine own horn." Attributed to Frustratees, 1050 B.C.

Through Uncle Jack my announcement went out to sixteen publicity firms. I heard back from two. One response was from George Evans, possibly the most celebrated press agent of the moment because he handled Frank Sinatra. The other response was from George and Dorothy Ross, a firm that handled Broadway shows as well as personalities. Evans offered me a job interview. George Ross, sight unseen, offered me a job.

THE GERMANS SURRENDERED in May 1945, the Japanese in August, and it would be October before the crew of Umbriago was sent home to be mustered out of the armed services. While we were waiting and the U.S. military was reconfiguring its postwar presence in Europe, a notice was posted looking for volunteers to ferry men and supplies about. It occurred to me that I could be called up to be sent home and miss the opportunity because I was away. But the lure of cities like Paris, Cairo, and Athens was headier than that of Herman, Jeanette, and Charlotte, and I signed on.

Flying over Europe on a clear day and, for the first time in hundreds of hours, with no body armor, no deadly puffs of black exploding around us, no enemy planes streaking toward us, no chance of being shot out of the sky, I was experiencing PEACE—in capital letters, underlined, and in neon. I lay on my belly in the glass nose of our plane, drunk on the sensation of the universe in my embrace. Four decades later, the time or three I took Ecstasy, I would think, "Hell, I was higher than this in the nose of that plane."

On October 5 we were finally on our way back to the States. Sitting alone in my radio room, I raked over all the experiences of the past few years. This might have been the first time I called to mind the terrifying moments experienced in combat. I had wanted to remember just the good things, but now everything came flooding back: Jimmy Edwards's death; the time we came away from the target on two engines, the other two having been shot up; watching an injured plane out of formation, set upon by a half dozen Messerschmitt fighters and spiraling to the ground; several planes, ours among them, bouncing about like popcorn in reaction to a German missile exploding nearby—truly terrifying moments.

There were also moments of exaltation on those missions and I love being reminded of them—moments of exaltation that dissolved the hate of war and replaced it with something akin to love, certainly brotherly love. The sight of a P-51 fighter plane coming to escort us to our target triggered that. There were two groups of fighter planes that came from wherever they were stationed to fly escort as we approached target: the P-38 Lightning and the P-51 Mustang. I thought the twin-engine P-38 the handsomest plane in the sky. But it was the sight of the more ordinary single-engine P-51, flown by the only black squadron in the force, that triggered the exaltation and warm feelings.

Hailing from Tuskegee, Alabama, these pilots came to be known as the Tuskegee Airmen. Their tails were painted red, and as escorts their role was to protect us from enemy aircraft. The nearer we drew to target, the more antiaircraft fire we could expect from the ground and the more enemy fighter planes in the air attempting to shoot us down. And so the longer and closer our escort stayed with us, the safer we were. From the time they rendezvoused with us—say, twenty minutes before we reached our target—they would fly so close to our wing we could see their faces. That's how I knew they were black.

When we encountered enemy fighters, our fighter escorts, whichever squadron happened to have been assigned that day, went into action. We B-17 crew members were also firing at the enemy from our bottom ball turret, left and right waists, the tail gun, and top turret, but it was our fighter escorts that accounted for most of the swastikas that were shot out of the sky. And the most welcome among them were the Tuskegee Airmen in their red-tailed P-51s. They seemed to plunge and soar, swerve in and peel away, with a bravura and grace unique to them.

Exaltation and that brotherly feeling also ran high on the long trip home from a mission when, sufficiently out of danger, we crewmen would gather in the waist section to talk about what we'd just been through, reverently and with enormous gratitude. As the missions piled up and we could compare earlier experiences, the bond between us grew tighter and stronger. At war's end it seemed we would know one another forever. Bob Oswald tried throughout the years to keep us all in touch. His effort was pretty much in vain, but for one occasion in 1988 when he succeeded in getting all but one of us to attend a reunion of the 463rd Bomb Group in Tucson, Arizona.

Our crew, all in civvies now, sat up all night with our wives, attempting to retrieve a spark of that bond we shared so long ago when we were young, endangered, and responsible to one another for our very lives. Basically, the conversation we had as sexagenarians in Tucson was pretty much the conversation we'd had on that flight home from our service abroad. Of course we'd all been living lives worth reporting on in the forty-three intervening years, but we shared far less of that than we did of our wartime memories. For six hours or so we sat there, life-tested men recalling the almost unimaginable fact that once upon a time we were prepared, or at the least offered ourselves as prepared, to die together. If anyone were to tell me at any time that I could benefit from a nice cry, I might drag out two photographs of crew Umbriago, the one taken in Florida when we were assigned our plane and the other forty-odd years later at our Arizona reunion.

WHEN WE TOUCHED DOWN on American soil for the first time since we'd left for combat duty, it was Florida again, this time Palm Beach. Getting off the plane, we all fell to the ground and kissed America. As I did that I thought, "After what I've been through, how can I ever be afraid again?" A couple of hours later, all checked in, freshly showered, and feeling every bit the returning hero everyone on base was treating me like, I was bused off the field and deposited on a highway to hitchhike my way to Miami, where Charlotte and my in-laws, who lived there, were waiting. Why weren't they in Palm Beach to greet their loved one just returned from battle? I had a pretty good guess.

Charlotte's father, Al Rosen, was a peerless tightwad. When she was a teenager he checked the mileage on the family car each time Charlotte drove it, insisted the car got far fewer miles per gallon than it did, and billed her allowance for every thimble of gas it consumed. Since Umbriago's exact arrival time could not be determined, if it landed later than expected they would have had to spend the night in Palm Beach, which would have entailed the expense of two hotel rooms. Enough said.

Everyone in the area was aware that GIs returning from abroad were landing daily at the local airfield. Talk about being treated like a hero! When I was on the road hitchhiking, my medals and citations firmly planted, drivers pulled up to me before I could raise a thumb. "Hey, soldier, bless you for your service. Can I buy you a beer?" "Can I buy you a dinner?" "When'd you last have a good steak, Sergeant?" It was thrilling and I was sky-high without a plane.

When I arrived in Miami at my in-laws' apartment, all that changed. My mother-in-law did not cook that evening because they thought that to *really* celebrate we'd all go out to dinner. Hooray! We left the apartment and walked several blocks to a commercial area with numerous restaurants and cafés, where Al checked the menus posted in their windows. We walked past those that had no postings. Ostensibly he was looking for great dishes, food fit for a kid just returned from fighting for his country, who hadn't eaten anything but GI food—meals prepared for hundreds at a time, ladled onto a metal tray by some phlegmatic nineteen-year-old in a space appropriately named a *mess* hall—for almost two years. Tough order; no wonder Al was having a difficult time. And then suddenly, eureka! What an idea, why didn't he think of it earlier? There are no delis in Italy. And we're in Miami, for Christ's sake! "Look at the grin on that boy," Al said.

I have to admit it was a fine delicatessen he took us to. They had takeout, of course, and a table area where, given that it was well past nine by now, only a few people were dawdling. As we walked to a table, we passed one that hadn't been cleared yet, and several dollars, obviously a tip, sat among the dishes and flatware. Just as I noticed it I heard my father-in-law again. "Hey, whadda we need with these bright lights and strangers, anyway?"

Twenty minutes later we were sitting at a kitchen table in the Rosens' extremely efficient apartment, making our own salami sandwiches. "They make them there, you eat them there, and you pay twice as much, you know," Al instructed. "Tricks of the trade," he added with the wink that usually concludes lessons from assholes. And, should you be wondering why salami and not corned beef for the returning vet, well, the beef wasn't up to speed that night. "Too fatty," said Al.

You have to be wondering what Charlotte and I said to each other that night. Very little that wasn't perfunctory, halfhearted, and forced, I'm sure. We barely knew each other at all, well enough to go to a movie together—a matinee—but that was about as far as it went. She was a stranger to me, as I must have been to her. We had practically nothing in common. I was trying to build a marriage, a life, on the foundation of one moment of delight in a phone conversation. The only thing that kept us together, once she arrived, was our daughter, Ellen.

JUST A FEW WEEKS AFTER arriving home, landing in Palm Beach, kissing the earth and telling myself I could never be afraid again, there I was sitting in the anteroom of George and Dorothy Ross Associates in New York, waiting to be interviewed for the job Mr. Ross had promised two months earlier, and scared shitless. Inside my head I was screaming at myself, "It hasn't been a month since you came home from a fucking war, what do you mean you're afraid *now?*" When Mr. Ross came out of his office to bid me come in, I must have slipped into some hidden reservoir of self-confidence, just as I did at seventeen when I won that oratorical contest instead of staying in bed with a nervous stomach, as my mother had advised.

George Ross was a natty professorial type who radiated Harvard despite having graduated from Brooklyn College. George was a far cry from the Damon Runyon types, like his wife, Dorothy, who inhabited the Broadway scene. I remember the Rosses, their two associates—Michael Frank, a woman, and Bunny Simon, a man—better than people I worked with longer and far more recently. I was there to innovate, to write witticisms, to make up stories and attention-getting comments that would be put into the mouths of a long client list of actors, playwrights, producers, designers, and others, for the many columnists—Dorothy Kilgallen, Leonard Lyons, Walter Winchell, Frank Kingdon, Earl Wilson, Ed Sullivan, Danton Walker—who held forth in the eight daily New York papers, each of them as powerful in their own way as the talking heads or commentators on television and cable news today. And, as advertised in my announcement from Foggia, I wished to be the person *behind* the curtain, the shadow promoting someone else from his anonymous, well-worn Remington.

Ross told me that I could start on Monday and that my pay would be thirty-five dollars a week, which by inflection he made to sound like an important sum. Then, because I'd foolishly told him up front that this appointment with him was the first of two, he added, "And I have to know now that you want to be here." As he awaited a reply, I was thinking about George Evans. This was a job in hand, Evans only a possibility. But with Evans came "The Voice," as by now Sinatra had been labeled. I was in no position to walk out on a job in hand, but fortunately Mr. Ross misinterpreted my pause. "Forty dollars," he said.

A year or so before I started to work at Ross Associates, my father had turned over a new leaf also. His work as a ten-percenter in the war effort having concluded, H.K. decided that, with the contacts he'd made among small manufacturing plants around Connecticut, he would go into the manufacturing business himself. During the war, the big companies—General Electric, Westinghouse, and Whirlpool—cut way back on the manufacture of home appliances in order to serve the product needs of the military. At war's end the pent-up demand for new stoves, refrigerators, and washing machines had those major manufacturers working at warp speed to answer it. While they concentrated on major appliances, there was, as H.K. perceived it, a window of opportunity for a new company to make a line of small appliances—toasters, hot plates, waffle irons, and tea kettles. And so my dad's Lear, Incorporated, was born.

There was another, earlier and far more established, Lear, Incorporated, in Michigan, founded by Bill Lear, inventor of the car radio. H.K. knew that, of course, and that was the whole point of naming his company Lear, Incorporated. H.K. was confident that Bill Lear would not want the identity of his firm confused with another and would pay him a million dollars to change the name of the company that was producing the coveted Lear Two-Burner Hot Plate and the soon-to-come Lear Whistling Tea Kettle. Bill Lear, unfortunately oblivious to the advent of either product, went on instead to design and manufacture the Learjet.

My work as a fledgling press agent didn't last a year, but it was packed with incident and seasoning. Getting along with George, Dorothy, Michael, Bunny, and the other Broadway types I had to deal with was a high-wire act. The tightrope was a line of communication that one walked balancing bluster and wit with a full imagination and a touch of veracity. Ironic that my strengths on that tightrope were exactly what got me fired.

My job was to get our clients' names in print. When the *Journal-American*'s Dorothy Kilgallen ran that bit of bluster I mentioned earlier about Kitty Carlisle gifting Moss Hart with a pocket flask measured to his hip while he napped, it was a rare twofer, two clients in a single item, and I was king for a day in the office. Kilgallen called George to say she was embarrassed she'd printed it, but said it was indeed cute. "But tell that kid to tone it down," she said. "I won't think it cute the next time."

Some weeks later one of our clients, a hit Broadway musical revue, *Are You With It?*, needed some attention. It starred some favorites of the time, Johnny Downs, Lew Parker, and Dolores Gray. In the cast, too, was a major vaudeville act, Buster Shaver and His Midgets. The midgets were Olive and George. I hit another double with Kilgallen when she, or some daft associate, as evidenced by Ms. K's later reaction, okayed this item for her column: "Buster Shaver and his midget, Olive, stars of *Are You With It?*, seen shopping Fifth Avenue, he on foot, she on a St. Bernard."

Evidently, someone had challenged her with something like, "Come on, Dorothy, how could you print such bullshit?" At which point Ms. Kilgallen had a fit, phoned George Ross, and demanded that my ass be fired. Begging for his forgiveness, I offered to take a cut in pay to the original thirty-five dollars per week, but it was a no-go. I was summarily dismissed, and without severance.

A few days later we learned that Charlotte was pregnant, which prompted a decision to move back to Hartford. My father had been asking me to join him in Lear, Incorporated, which he believed could be the next GE. "It took two world wars to open up this big an opportunity," he said. "Give me two years, just two years, and you can *buy* the company that fired you!" Despite every previous disappointment and the manic claim that we'd build a giant company in two years, this was my dad, and I went with him.

9

IN THE SUMMER OF 1946 Charlotte and I found a little two-bedroom house with a convertible den for sale in Windsor, a few miles outside Hartford. We didn't have the $1,500 down payment on the $11,500 purchase price until H.K., in another of the grandstand plays for which I adored him, hocked his hotshot pinkie ring. (It was on his pinkie again within a month, most likely while he was being dunned for the money he'd borrowed to get it out of hock, or to cover the check he'd written for the same purpose.) This was something like my tenth residence in twenty-four years. I had very little space to call my own in any of them, yet I can't recall having a bad day for that reason. That could be because wherever I was living there was so much else to do just to save my ass.

My father lived every other day saving his ass because on the surrounding days he was busy doing something to get his ass in trouble. No one knew that better than his attorney William J. Burke, a former judge who was mesmerized by Herman K. Lear, handled all the legal work putting Lear, Incorporated, together, and even loaned him half of the forty thousand dollars H.K. raised to get started. Bill Burke was a round, life-loving Irishman. I've always divided people between wets and drys. Dry people are cold, brittle, and very certain; they don't hug well, and if you should hug one you could cut yourself on his body. Wet people are warm and tender, and when they hug they melt in your arms. Bill Burke was sopping wet. H.K. was a sopping wet personality with a bone-dry conscience.

Lear, Incorporated, was turning out about one hundred fifty two-burner electric hot plates per week, and George Thompson, its designer, had Lear's electric tea kettle ready to go when I entered the scene. I never knew what his qualifications were as the designer and inventor he held himself out to be, but George looked the part—tall, gray, and sloped, as if he'd spent a lot of time poring over important stuff. I could see why my father was excited about the "one-cubic-foot nonelectric refrigerator especially designed for the trunk of your car" that Mr. Thompson had invented, and for which he would have the prototype very soon.

Lester Gowin was the owner of a tool-and-die factory in Middletown, Connecticut, that stamped out the aluminum bodies for the Lear hot plate. Lester was a low-key, serious, and amusing fellow with a mustache that could have passed for an eyebrow. I liked him immediately. The burners and wiring were installed at a plant in Wallingford owned by Izzy Wolfson. Izzy, a pleasant, portly fellow, sat behind a big desk all day but was never really there. He was a ruminator seeking a topic. "How's the missus, Izzy?" could get him ruminating for minutes. "She's fine, she tells me, but sometimes I think women only tell the truth to other women, and I wonder if it was women only on the planet . . ." Izzy would get so lost in reflection that a person could have a heart attack in front of him and he'd incorporate it. "So the thought of it pains you, too, every man on earth disappearing . . . ?"

There were three other factories involved in the hot plate process—the frames were painted in Meriden, the switches made in Waterbury, and the nameplates made in Bridgeport. There was a lot of hauling to be done, and there were some weeks when our deal with the trucker lapsed and I did the trucking. Any deal, as a matter of fact, could lapse at any time, so slipshod was Lear, Incorporated's paperwork. H.K. did not have a bookkeeper or a secretary. His office was his hat, and his desk was the band at its brim, into which he stuck bills and receipts, bank notices and purchase orders, and—as many days as not—a list of food items or dry cleaning to pick up for my mother on the way home.

On September 15, Charlotte and I welcomed our beautiful daughter, Ellen, into the world. This was before Hartford Hospital invited fathers to be present at the birth, so the closest I could get was to have her held up to me on the other side of a glass wall. I recall looking at this tiny, squished-up face and not knowing what to feel. Was I not guy enough to have that proud "fruit of my loins" kind of feeling? Or was I standing there more like a boy with a "see my new puppy" kind of feeling? Did I love this little person? If so, was that because I was expected to? Shouldn't I have been less aware of my sterile surroundings—the lip marks on the glass separating me and my child, that disinfectant antiseptic hospital smell, the young black nurse with the old-looking hands holding the baby up for me? Shouldn't I have been more caught up with the miracle of birth, the wonder of it all, and the God-given blessing that was about to change my life forever? But the fact is that, at age twenty-four, I was spectacularly unready to become a father.

I DIDN'T ACTUALLY report to anyone at Lear, Incorporated. I just saw what I had to do and did it. With an old Army jeep pulling a small trailer, I crisscrossed the state, hauling metal and parts from one place to another as needed and making excuses and apologies for everything that was constantly falling through the cracks. It all wound down to how much more H.K. promised every step along the manufacturing way than he could actually deliver.

Orkil, Incorporated, in Hartford, was the GE distributor for Connecticut. Because GE wasn't making small appliances at the time, they agreed to distribute the Lear hot plate and electric tea kettle, which stuttered into production late in 1947. They took a big interest, too, in Lear, Incorporated's forthcoming one-cubic-foot nonelectric refrigerator that worked on some new cooling principle and could be kept in the trunk of an automobile. But H.K. didn't encourage Orkil's interest.

During the war, as a ten-percent man, he'd done business with several top people in the War Department who were now retired from the military and running the Ohio companies they worked with during the war. Orkil was okay for his hot plate and tea kettle, but with the Lear, Incorporated, first-ever one-cubic-foot nonelectric refrigerator close at hand, here, H.K. thought, was his chance to play with the big boys again. And so he plucked a couple of business cards out of his hat.

One morning my dad and I picked up George Thompson in Greenwich, along with the prototype of his one-cubic-foot refrigerator that would work in the trunk of a car, and drove on to New York, where we were to present it. I emphasize that the unit would work in the trunk of a car because that was a big selling point. In the 1940s people took a drive not just to go someplace but for the joy of taking a drive. Our relationship to the car we drove was a romance, and the thought of pulling over to the side of the road for a cold drink right out of our own trunks heightened that romance. As a nation we took enormous pride in the American motorcar. To see a world leader stepping out of an automobile, on the front page of our newspapers or in the newsreels, was to see that leader stepping out of a Lincoln, a Packard, or a Cadillac. The American motorcar was a symbol of America's class and power, and the most visible source of its self-esteem. Its slow erosion from being the standard of the world tore the first hole in the fabric of the American Dream.

Dad's presentation to an eager group of manufacturing executives from major companies in the Akron and Toledo areas was set for four P.M. in a suite he'd reserved at the Waldorf Astoria. I learned on the drive to pick up George that he'd reported a few days earlier that he had the temperature down to a perfect thirty-two degrees, but just couldn't be sure how long it would hold.

"He's not sure how long the temperature will hold?" I asked in alarm. "What does that mean?"

"You know George, he's a perfectionist." And then, even more nonchalantly, "And, anyway, he's had three more days." I recalled Dad bragging once about his prowess as a salesman—"I can sell refrigerators to Eskimos"—and gritted my teeth.

Four very impressive executive types—dark-suited, square-jawed, and extremely Gentile—showed up in the suite at the Waldorf Astoria for the presentation. We had been there since noon, when we'd put a few bottles of beer in the prototype, allowing them four hours to be refrigerated. In all that time neither George nor my father checked to see what was going on inside. George, I think, was too busy praying. My father didn't want to let any of the cold out.

When the time came, everyone sat around a low coffee table on which rested the prototype, while George Thompson explained his new refrigeration system, a speech so indecipherable to me it bid fair to make my eyes cross. But I do remember "propane" and maybe "kerosene" being a part of it. Dad smiled and nodded with deep understanding at everything George said, and when he felt the timing right he interjected suddenly, "By the way, anyone thirsty? How about a beer?"

Flipping open the fridge door, he turned to the most senior-looking executive. "General?" The general reached in, grabbed a bottle, and his expression twitched in multiple directions. H.K. took the bottle from him. It was as warm as spit.

To my astonishment, my father didn't see this as a disaster. George Thompson looked as if he expected, perhaps even wished, to be whipped. Our guests, stunned and bewildered, were stopped dead for a moment, like robots waiting for someone to throw a switch. But H.K., running at the mouth in a kind of "These things happen and who would know that better than you guys?" mode, persuaded his guests—to his satisfaction, though, as time would prove, not to theirs—that this was just a glitch. The general and his cohorts got up, stuffed whatever they were feeling into a few tight-jawed exit lines, and fled.

Lear, Incorporated, staggered through 1947 and 1948, its hot plate output limited by one problem or another, but still managing to eke out its electric tea kettle. Of course, forcing the kettle into production when Lear, Incorporated, still had problems getting its hot plate out the door only added to the overall stress the company was dealing with. Everyone working for or dealing with Lear, Incorporated, could see that—except, of course, Mr. Lear.

I'M NOT SURE when I came upon the notion of a mountain climber and his grappling hook as a metaphor for living. Until he reaches the very peak, the climber tosses that grappling hook over and over into the space ahead of him and pulls himself toward it. Whatever I may be engaged in at the moment, I see myself as needing something more, maybe several things that I am pulling myself toward at the same time. While working with my dad, I had a grappling hook out there in a new manufacturing enterprise that I started with Lester Gowin, whose tool-and-die plant was stamping out the hot plate frames.

Lester and I became good friends. Since I was in and out of his plant several times a week anyway, we talked up the possibility of doing something else together. Most of us were smokers in those years. I, along with every other GI, had been encouraged to smoke by the armed services. A little brightly colored pack of three cigarettes, donated oh so generously by the tobacco companies themselves, was placed in every prepackaged meal, known as K rations. By the time I met Lester I was smoking two packs a day.

One day I came up with an idea that addressed an annoyance—a trivial, silly piffle of an annoyance—related to after-dinner smoking, particularly in the home. When coffee was served at dessert, guests who smoked were inclined, to the distress of their hostesses, to flick their ashes into the saucer. To relieve those poor women, I dreamed up a small ashtray that would clip to the rim of the saucer and be delivered to the smoker with his beverage. Lester thought it a nifty, easy-to-produce gift item. We named it the Demi-Tray, made a pilot set of four in copper, and boxed it as fancily as we were able to.

I knew I had to find a distributor with a truly enterprising spirit. A good sense of humor couldn't hurt also. My first stop was a prominent high-end gift shop on Madison Avenue, Carole Stupell Ltd., and it was Ms. Stupell herself, a large, garrulous woman, often credited with the first bridal registry—enterprising indeed—who greeted me.

Ms. Stupell and I hit it off immediately. She took one look at our simple set of copper Demi-Trays that Lester Gowin thought we could retail at $4.95, smiled, and asked, "Can I have these in silver plate to retail at $12.95, and sterling silver at, say, $35.95? And can I have them in the shop for the holiday season just before Thanksgiving?" A phone call to Lester revealed that we could make the date and the prices, but the sterling silver would require a substantial down payment. Ms. Stupell did not need to be talked into it. I felt like the million dollars H.K. was to have received from Bill Lear by now as I made my way to Penn Station with a purchase order and the promise of a check when production began.

Carole Stupell had a big Christmas in 1947 and did very well with her expensive novelty item. "A practical measure for smoking pleasure," read the copy line. Lester and I did very well also, and with Carole Stupell's encouragement we decided to develop a line of small silver and silver plate products for the 1948 holiday season. Lester designed a small line of products to follow the Demi-Tray, and we used every penny of our current profits to invest in the tools, dies, and metals needed to make them.

Since we'd gotten lucky manufacturing with the smoker in mind, and the more expensive product seemed to sell best, Lester created a bed of four small sterling silver ashtrays and, in sterling and silver plate, a handsome silent butler. (The silent butler was a larger ashtray with a lid that a maid or the hostess herself would empty smaller ashtrays into during the evening.) Then, thinking of the candles on most fine dinner tables, Lester added a candle snuffer to the line, also in sterling. Carole Stupell agreed to carry these items, but she shortordered at first to see how they sold. They didn't.

We had made a classic mistake. My Demi-Tray was an original—a cutesy trifle, but an original. Nobody had ever seen one before. Price it high enough and it's a "How darling!" for one season only. And so Ms. Stupell ordered it in sterling silver. What Lester and I did with the silent butler, the ashtrays, and the candle snuffer was totally unoriginal. Yes, Lester effected some design change, but these products were still known in the trade as knockoffs. We had violated the First Commandment of retailing: *Thou shalt not mark up when knocking off.* And in no time at all we were out of business.

WHEN CHARLOTTE and I moved to Windsor I tossed out a second grappling hook, this one in search of a social life. We joined a young theater group, the Hartford Players Guild, a company that staged four plays a year at the Avery Memorial Theater. I remember it, among other things, for Tom and Gladys Conroy, veterans of the Players Guild and members of a middle-class union family.

I loved hearing the Conroys talk politics. My family's discussions couldn't get past a headline or subhead before they ran out of information on whatever the subject. The Conroys held sharp and distinct points of view and had the subtext to back it up. I learned the importance of subtext and context from my time with them. And as clear, too, in my head is a moment of Gladys's performance in a Noel Coward play, the unforgettable sound of her British accent, playing a haughty socialite referring to a trip she took. I shall never forget the way Gladys held her head, the pitch of her neck, the little trills in her voice as they rose and fell and finally ripened and climaxed over her trip's destination: ". . . and we disembark finally at *Kuala Lumpur.*"

I ask myself again and again why that bite-sized memory of Gladys's reading of "Kuala Lumpur" should stick with me all these years, as if under glass, while several weeks in a Players Guild production that by all odds was sure to have affected me quite traumatically has gone totally unremembered. There is a framed, yellowing newspaper photograph of me, cut out of the *New Britain Sunday Herald* and dated March 1949, on the wall just a few feet from me as I write. It has hung there for the quarter century we have been in this house, and in other homes that preceded this. Despite the proof positive of that photograph, I have absolutely no recollection of having played a starring role in a major Players Guild production, let alone that of the son, Chris, in Arthur Miller's *All My Sons*.

No doubt this clipping has caught my eye thousands of times. I've paused over it often when visitors to my study have taken notice of it and asked me questions that I have absently answered. It is only now, as I get to this part of my life, that I am forced to make sense of it, and it stupefies me that I am unable to dig up one memory of the entire production. How could I not remember having been cast in a leading role in a play by Arthur Miller that just two years earlier had won a Tony for Best Play and for its director, Elia Kazan? How could I have submitted to an intense rehearsal schedule, forged the uniquely emotional on- and offstage relationships that go with the territory, taken a ton of direction, experienced the inevitable stage fright as house lights dimmed and a curtain parted, and then played a highly dramatic character in front of a live audience, and remember not a minute of it? It is a puzzlement that had me staring at these words for hours. And then I made a connection that, unbelievably, I had never made until it stopped me dead in my tracks.

In the aged photograph I am standing, fists clenched, ready to strike the actor playing my father, Joe Keller. Chris Keller has just learned that the father he loves so much manufactured some defective aircraft parts in World War II that resulted in the deaths of twenty-one American airmen serving in Asia, and that he knew they might be defective when he okayed their shipment. As many times as I have looked at that dramatic *Sunday Herald* photo of me as Chris Keller, ready to strike my father, Joe, I might as well have been looking at a shot of two nameless actors in a theatrical archive somewhere. Only now, despite the several productions I have seen of *All My Sons*, am I realizing how deeply this father-son story affected me. So deeply that the photograph, just a few feet from the desk I have worked at for twenty-five years, had not stirred a single recollection of the production in which I apparently played a lead.

"In which I apparently played a lead" is the way that sentence just fell out of me. I found it all so hard to believe that I could not write past it without having to learn more about a Hartford Players Guild production of *All My Sons* in

March 1949, and I asked a researcher to check the morgues of other local newspapers of that date. Two days later she received from the microfilm files of the *Hartford Courant* a review of the Players Guild's March 13, 1949, production of *All My Sons* bearing this headline: VIGOROUS PRODUCTION OF ARTHUR MILLER DRAMA OFFERED AT AVERY MEMORIAL. In the middle of a fairly long and positive review it says of my performance: "Norman Lear is giving a stalwart portrait of the son who manages to keep faith with the truth he has learned in war. Taking it simply and quietly at the outset, he builds the part up to an impassioned interpretation at the play's second act close."

Strange how I can't recall a moment of that, but I can see the suit H.K. was wearing when they took him away. According to a worn news clip, H.K. wasn't, as he'd testified, trying to flip some bonds that he didn't know were phony. The bonds were stolen, and swearing to the authorities that he couldn't remember the names of the men who'd told him they'd sell like hotcakes was not viewed as exculpatory.

My high school buddy Bob Krechevsky, who became chief judge of the Connecticut Bankruptcy Court, also knew my father very well. "I'd passed the bar and just opened my law office," he once told me, "and Herman came to see me, saying he was in terrible straits, and I remember he was sweating profusely. I was in a very small office, and he needed a couple of hundred dollars, so I gave him the money and he said he would get it back to me immediately. Well, it was a few days, but he did come back and he gave me a check. I guess I waited a day or so before I deposited it and the check bounced. It bounced twice. But then he finally brought me the cash—didn't send it, brought it because he wanted to see me and give me some advice. He sounded like a judge lecturing from the bench. 'Robert,' he said, 'when someone gives you a check, you don't know how many checks that person wrote that day and maybe only a couple of them will clear—so you don't wait, you get to the bank soon as you can and cash that check.'"

I remember laughing when I first heard that and thinking, "What a character!" I see clearly today what a shoddy tale that is. Earlier, I avoided naming what he was doing when I described his attempt to sell the one-cubic-foot re-frigerator that he knew in his heart didn't work, and the word *fraud* was missing when I told of the stolen bonds he'd tried to sell when they put him away. All my life, thinking or talking, and now writing, about my dad, I have tweaked the language or angled the story to make him seem less a liar and a fraud, and more like a rascal and a rogue. He was *all* of those things.

10

I N T H E E A R L Y S P R I N G O F 1949, with Lear, Incorporated, having been statutorily dissolved by the state of Connecticut for operating for two consecutive years without filing an annual report, I talked to Charlotte about restarting my career in publicity, but this time in California. In short order we put our house up for sale and disclosed our plans. No one thought it a good idea, especially my mother.

"Hollywood's not for you, dear," she said, reinforcing this with a look that went with smelling something rancid. Mother never had a bad thing to say about California when my father would promise it to us, and it was a verbal evergreen in our home even before he was sent away: "One day, Jeanette, I'm moving the family to California. We're going to buy a ranch house"—he could have been invoking Monticello with the words "ranch house"—"all on one floor, no stairs, and we're going to lie in bed with the window open and pick oranges from our tree."

It was late May when Charlotte, Ellen (then two and a half), and I set out for California. The *Hartford Courant* covered our leaving this way in a column called "City Briefs": "Mr. and Mrs. Norman Lear and their daughter, Ellen, formerly of 55 Plymouth Street, Windsor, are en route by automobile to Los Angeles, California, where they will make their home."

My father having assured me—incorrectly, as it turned out—that if I bought a late-model convertible in Connecticut and sold it in California I'd make enough to cover the cost of the trip, we were en route in a green 1946 Olds 98. The drive cross-country was pretty much without incident, but for a few flat tires. Today I can't recall my last flat tire, but they occurred regularly back then and are memorable because changing them was, along with shoveling snow to clear walks and driveways, the heaviest manual labor I'd been called on to perform since wheeling fertilizer in Florida.

We arrived in L.A. late on a Saturday afternoon. I parked us at a cheap motel on Sunset Boulevard near Western Avenue. My cousin Elaine, the only person I knew west of New York City, had moved there some months before with her husband, Ed Simmons, who wanted to become a comedy writer, and had written to warn me that finding a rental was extremely difficult. So, despite these being our very first minutes in a strange land, and in a room that would have been ashamed of itself if rooms had feelings, Charlotte and I decided that I would go out and pick up an early edition of the Sunday *Los Angeles Times* to check the classifieds for a lead on the next day's offerings. If I came across a possibility while it was still daylight, I had license to check it out. "But get back here as soon as you can" were the last words I heard as I walked out the door.

It was a lovely June evening on Sunset Boulevard, street of dreams to this wide-eyed New Englander. No longer exhausted by the eight days I'd spent driving in this same vehicle, I cruised with the top down, smoking a Fatima cigarette, which had recently gone "extra long," passing landmarks like Schwab's Pharmacy, Ciro's, the Trocadero, and Earl Carroll's Vanities, by then just a shell and a sign, but no less romantic to me. I was enraptured. I never imagined myself as anything other than a publicist, the figure *behind* the talent, but it was the broad field of entertainment that was seducing me now. "Who *is* that young man in the stylish convertible? I know I've seen him before," I fantasized coming from gawkers I imagined on the sidewalk.

Returning to reality, I bought a copy of the Sunday *Times* and headed back toward the motel, venturing off Sunset onto side streets along the way. My heart all but stopped as I drove onto El Centro, a residential block in mid-

Hollywood, and came across a small building called the Circle Theatre, sporting a handmade marquee that read: OPENING TONIGHT—SHAW'S MAJOR BARBARA. The Circle had been a grocery store but was now fashioned into a ninety-nine-seat theater-in-the-round. I had never been to a theater-in-the-round and was fascinated by the idea. George Bernard Shaw was my favorite playwright, and *Major Barbara* my favorite of his works. Oh, my God!

Suddenly, rejoining my family was off to the side. All I could think of was the play. It contains a colloquy between Barbara, a major in the Salvation Army, and her father, Andrew Undershaft, one of the world's largest munitions makers. Undershaft, for his own good reasons, offers to make a large donation to the Salvation Army and Barbara refuses it on moral grounds. Undershaft, she feels, made that money by selling munitions and, as a consequence, death. The major will not accept a donation from such a source. Undershaft insists she would be doing a greater good were she to accept. They parry and thrust brilliantly and at considerable length, the audience thinking at every thrust that the line just rendered could not be parried. And of course it is. Shaw comes down on Undershaft's side eventually, or at least that's my reading. In any event, I view it as one of the greatest exchanges in all of the English-speaking theater. It's a high-wire act with only words to maintain balance, and its impact on me was very direct.

There was a fellow sweeping the sidewalk in front as I drove up. Noticing me sitting there, he asked, "You new here?"

"Yes, I am," I answered. "Matter of fact, I just got here a few hours ago from Connecticut."

The man with the broom was George Boroff, who ran the Circle Theatre. He got a kick out of my having just driven cross-country with a wife and kid who were now stashed in a motel while I shot the breeze with him. I told him I had come to Hollywood to be a publicist. The theater had a publicist who could probably use help, Boroff said, and, intrigued by my story, he offered to let me hang with him until I learned enough to move on. At my grateful reaction, he sweetened the deal, offering me a seat he had been holding for tonight's opening, lights down in thirty minutes. I couldn't say no. It was too much. And it was certainly too much for Charlotte.

How hard would it be to get your wife to accept that you couldn't resist a burger and a few beers with your buddies before you came home to the birthday dinner she'd spent all day preparing for you? That would be a little nothing compared to the phone call I had to make. "Our first minutes in California, and you're going to leave your wife and daughter in this hellhole to see some goddamn play in a round theater?" she cried out in furious disbelief. *"On our first night?"*

"I have to," I said, in the spirit of "One day you'll understand." There was no way in this lifetime that could happen, or, from her viewpoint, had any right to.

My seat was in the second row, and in front of me there were three seats taped off. As the house lights dimmed and the stage lights were coming up—a moment when I have always been moved to whisper to my seatmate, "Magic time!"—three people entered and approached the empty seats. As they drew close I recognized the great character actor Alan Mowbray, multiple Academy Award nominee Dame Gladys Cooper, and—it could not be, but it was!—the best-known face and silhouette in the world, Charlie Chaplin. His son Sidney, it turned out, was in the play, along with Strother Martin, William Schallert, and Diana Douglas (Michael Douglas's mother).

It was easily the best production of *Major Barbara* I'm ever likely to see. Mr. Chaplin, we soon learned, was equally impressed. When the show ended and the house lights came up, all eyes were on him as he remained seated. No one moved. There being no backstage, the cast began to slip into the theater and sit on the floor facing him.

When they were all there, he rose. Expressing his deepest respect for the production, his all-out praise for the cast and direction, and his gratitude for being so well entertained, he concluded with something to this effect: "I rarely feel words can convey what I feel when I've had *such* a good time, and the best way I've found to handle that is to attempt to pay you back in kind." At which point, just a few feet from me, within a few hours of my arrival in California, Charlie Chaplin proceeded to perform a pantomime of a man, a bit tipsy, a letter in hand, trying to reach a mailbox in a high wind.

When I got back to the motel, well beyond enchanted now, Charlotte wouldn't talk to me. I'm not sure she would ever have cared to hear about my experience at the Circle Theatre that night. I had no idea what interested Charlotte. We lived in two different worlds, separated by infinity.

I left the motel soon after dawn, *L.A. Times* in hand, to check out apartment rentals. My eyes searched each neighborhood as I raced through them to the one promising listing I found, which turned out to have been rented. Driving glumly away, just two blocks over, on Kenmore Street, a block off Beverly Boulevard, I spotted a woman, still in a robe and nightgown, approaching a spot on her lawn with a FOR RENT sign in one hand and a hammer in the other. I swerved to a stop and leaped out of the car, shouting, "Hold that hammer!" She laughed and held. Her rental was a small one-bedroom cottage behind her house. I took it in an instant and the Lear family moved into their first Los Angeles residence the next day.

WHILE I SOUGHT A JOB in publicity, I decided to join my cousin Elaine's husband, Ed Simmons, who, while trying to find a gig as a comedy writer, had just begun selling home furnishings door-to-door for the Gans Brothers. Elaine, who had worked with me on Saturdays at our grandfather's dress shop, could not have been closer to me. In her eighties she would still repeat (and laugh as joyously as ever at) the title of a story she insisted I wrote at age nine: "Hachoo Blow Nose, My Blue Honey Maid."

The Gans Brothers operated out of an untidy combination of storefront and warehouse, and it was there that we door-to-door salesmen gathered each morning. Ed and I had only one clunker per family, so our wives drove us to the brothers Gans, one of whom would drive us "to territory"—single-home suburban neighborhoods—to ply our trade. I loved that expression, "to territory," and it still amuses the hell out of me. Territory was where the American Dream of owning your own home was being lived. It was where those simple tract homes began to sprout second garages, and where a number of their driveways began to sport RVs and trailers hauling boats.

The dream was seen as so pure that the signs of its certain long-term disintegration—poor zoning, insufficient planning, too few parks, too much asphalt, sensible cars morphing into gas-guzzling, vision-blocking vans—were overlooked altogether. Companies like the Gans Brothers flocked to these neighborhoods as if welcomed by a giant neon sign: CONSUMERS LIVE HERE.

Each morning before heading out to territory, we salesmen were given the choice of a gift item with which to entice the unsuspecting housewives we were calling on. We could carry either the "large lamp," pretty much what it sounds like, or the "ship clock," a piece of crockery in the shape of a ship with a timepiece in the middle. By ten-thirty each morning there we were, facile-tongued and hungry to score, with our lamps and clocks in tow, knocking on doors in search of our prey. I would step or lean as far inside as possible when the door was opened by the lady of the house, scan the room for the condition of the furniture, and introduce myself.

My job was to leave the lamp in exchange for setting a time for our Mr. Simmons to meet with the lady. He was the "closer" and his job was to sell her a seven-piece dining room set or an upholstered chair, ottoman, and end table, for which she had already received a lamp. Of course, if she bought nothing, he took the lamp with him on his way out, making a liar out of the man who'd given it to her. I did mention how much I hated this, didn't I? With the hope that we might do better selling a different product, Ed and I switched to taking and selling family photos door-to-door. We traded in our bait, the clocks and lamps, for an album of family pictures only a mother could envy.

As we perused the neighborhoods, we favored homes with tricycles, scooters, and carriages strewn about, looking for those young mothers with a tendency to believe that every shot of their precious children captured an instant of priceless memory. When I found one, I would announce with as dazzling a smile as I could manage, and in a "how lucky can you get?" tone of voice, that our photographer, Mr. Simmons, would be in the neighborhood that afternoon and the coupon I was about to hand her would entitle her to a free photograph, an eight-by-ten, no less, "that is, unless you would prefer a five-by-seven, which an occasional mom does, you understand, because her shelf can accommodate more pictures that way, but no matter, you can have your choice when our award-winning photographer, Mr. Simmons—you can't believe how great he is with children—gets here around three o'clock."

So I would make appointments for our Mr. Simmons one day, and he would make appointments for our Mr. Lear the next. The free photo, chosen from the dozen or more proofs, was never the best shot of the child. "May I see those other proofs?" the young mother would invariably inquire after a quick glance at her disappointing gift. A smile of relief followed her flipping through the far more worthy photos, and the skids were greased for ordering a number of prints. What a lovely surprise for Dad! But, then, shouldn't the beaming mother of those adorable children be thinking of the grandparents? Both sets? Not to mention aunts and uncles, we all have our favorites, and don't overlook the wallet size.

CHARLOTTE AND ELAINE, young mothers themselves, became friendly, and the four of us spent a good deal of time together after Ed and I returned from territory. Neither of our families could afford a television set, so we visited Uncle Al and Aunt Sadie, Elaine's parents, religiously on Tuesday nights to see *Texaco Star Theater*, also known as *The Milton Berle Show*. At eight P.M. on those Tuesdays, neighbors everywhere descended on the houses on their block that boasted a TV set. Berle, also known as "Mr. Television," was an outrageous funnyman. Loud and hilariously vulgar, he personified the guy who'll do anything for a laugh. A lot of his humor could be described as "early homosexual." He swished and puckered and spoke with a gay inflection before gay became a topic or an issue in the media.

Ed and I tried to schedule our job-hunting interviews and other efforts on the same days. I'm not sure what Eddie was doing to become a comedy writer, but I started knocking on the door of every publicity firm I could locate and tried to get an interview with the press department at every studio. While this effort was gestating, I threw out a couple of grappling hooks far afield from the career I was seeking, both quintessentially misguided.

The 1950s was known as the Golden Age of Wrestling, and the order of the day for a star wrestler was, as the Stephen Sondheim song goes, "You Gotta Have a Gimmick." The gimmick consisted of a move or a hold, unique to that wrestler, that put his opponent away. Argentina Rocca, for example, had an elaborate, pretty much trademarked kick to the lower back that rendered the other guy "absolutely helpless." He'd drop like a stone.

We met a guy who'd been captain of his college wrestling team who was also a baritone capable of reaching a single high tenor note. The gimmick we conceived for him was built around that note. Fans would cheerfully go along, we felt sure, with our guy wrestling his way to a position that saw his mouth within an inch or so of the other guy's ear. Once there he would let out just two notes, going from a low-register baritone to a piercing high tenor, ostensibly shattering the other fellow's eardrum and causing him to fold like a towel and fall to the mat.

The second grappling hook occurred to me one day driving along Sunset Boulevard in Bel Air. Every half mile there seemed to be another car pulled over on a side street, the driver on the boulevard holding a sign that read, MAP OF STAR HOMES. For five bucks you could have the addresses so you could drive to the homes of your favorite TV and movie stars. It hit me like the proverbial ton of bricks. What, I wondered, about all the fans who couldn't afford a trip to Hollywood and must settle for *writing* to their favorite stars? Wouldn't they relish the opportunity to reach them directly at home? A little research and we learned that three hundred dollars would buy an inch-and-a-half classified ad in Sunday newspapers around the country whose combined circulation would reach more than 25 million readers. We were off and running. Our ad offered six addresses—"you name the stars"—for one dollar.

A Master Clark Lee of Bowling Green, Ohio, was our one and only respondent. In westerns of the day, the lead always had a Mexican sidekick, whose girlfriend was usually played by the actress Estrellita Rodriguez. Master Lee's request was for her address only, and he was happy to pay the full dollar for it. That was one dollar more than we made with our Singing Wrestler, on whose behalf it took some serious muscle just to make it into a room with a promoter.

OUR LUCK CHANGED one night when the Simmonses and the Lears had an early meal, and the girls, as we referred to our wives then, decided to go out to a movie, leaving the men to babysit the kids. I had a book to read and Eddie was working on a parody of some popular tune. At some point we started to talk about what he was writing and wound up finishing it together. When the girls came home we sang it to them and they laughed. It was amazing, one of them said, that we hadn't thought of writing together before.

I saw Eddie putting the song in a folder and asked what he intended to do with it. He didn't have much of an answer; he was building a library for when he got a job writing for some comic. I suggested we go out right then and find a comic to sell it to. It was only eleven or so, and there were a number of nightclubs featuring live entertainment back then, several of them well known, like Billy Gray's Band Box, Eddie Foy's, and the Bar of Music, among others. Charlotte and Elaine encouraged us.

Our first stop was the Bar of Music, and when we walked in there was a woman at a piano doing insult humor, interspersed with an occasional song and story. Her name was Carole Abbott, and we sold our parody to her on the spot for forty bucks. Since I didn't make more than fifty in a good week and I'd just made twenty in a couple of hours, it became clear to me, and to Eddie also, that we should continue writing together. The idea of earning a living by sitting around making each other laugh was clearly preferable to trudging about with clocks and lamps and photo albums trying to separate innocent housewives from their money.

Eddie and I rented a little office above a delicatessen on Beverly Boulevard for six bucks a month, worked in territory during the day, had dinner with our families, then wrote or whiled away the hours above the deli attempting to write, until one of us dropped. One day we came up with an idea for a routine for Danny Thomas. In nightclubs Danny was as big as you could get, a magnificent raconteur. The next day, browsing a copy of *Daily Variety*, we noted that Thomas's agent was Phil Kellogg at the William Morris Agency.

At one P.M., it being 98 percent likely that Mr. Kellogg was at lunch, I phoned his office. Speaking as fast as I could, I identified myself as a reporter for the *New York Times*. "I've been out here for two days interviewing Danny Thomas," I told his secretary breathlessly. "I'm at the airport now, writing this piece on the plane, filing it as soon as we land, and I have two last questions for Mr. Thomas. Quick, please, they're calling my flight."

I had his number in an instant, dialed it, and Danny Thomas picked up the phone. He was working with his piano player, Wally Popp, but was curious to learn how I'd gotten his home phone number. When I told him the truth, he laughed and was intrigued with what I wanted to pitch him.

"I've got a date tomorrow night at Ciro's, a Friars' Frolic," he said. "They know my routines, but I have no time to learn something new. I'm looking through my stuff for something old enough to seem fresh," he said.

"This is short and will learn easily," I responded.

"Tell me in two sentences," he ordered.

"Three Yiddish words," I spoke quickly. "They have no counterpart in English and would take a paragraph to express in any other language . . ."

"Get over here right away," he said, and gave me his address in Beverly Hills.

"I can't get over there now, but my partner and I will be there by six. How's that?" I asked prayerfully.

"But you said you're in Hollywood. You're twenty minutes away."

"Yes," I said, "but I've got other things to do."

"You've got something more important to do than sell me a piece of material you've been killing yourself to get to me?" he yelled incredulously.

The truth was that we hadn't yet set a word to paper. But I finessed his question with, "Well, you gotta admit, we're off to a funny start!"

Amused despite himself, he said, "All right, but if you're not here by six sharp, forget it."

Simmons and I got there with no time to spare with our finished piece, "Tsemisht, Fardrayt, and Farblonjet"—three Yiddish words describing escalating degrees of confusion.

Thomas was perhaps the greatest storyteller of his time, and we'd written him a story about each of the words. One described a waitress at a diner who had to fill a take-out order for eight cups of coffee—one with two sugars, no cream; one with one cream, no sugar; one with two sugars, two creams; etc. (And this was back when the lids and the paper cups came together much less securely.) She was *tsemisht*. Another woman—nine months pregnant, with an infant crawling on the floor, a cake in the oven, the phone and doorbell ringing, and her water bursting—was *fardrayt*. Finally, we had a guy driving a huge flatbed rig in a pouring rainstorm with a two-story home on the back, turning mistakenly into a dead-end street. He was *farblonjet*.

The next night Ed and I stood in the kitchen at Ciro's, peering into the club and listening to the laughs Danny Thomas was getting with his inimitable rendition of the routine we'd written for him. He was a smash. He gave us five hundred dollars for the piece when he first read it, and said if it worked he'd pay us another thousand. He performed that piece for years, but we never saw the extra grand. I teased him about it every time I saw him, and he'd always say, "Bless you, my son. The money's doing more good at St. Jude," a children's hospital Thomas raised money for tirelessly throughout his career.

The morning after the Friars' Frolic, I got a call from David Susskind, my first cousin and son of the uncle Ben who, along with H.K., taught their sons conclusively that iodine was not the cure for an itchy scrotum. David was a young agent with Music Corporation of America, a Goliath in every area of entertainment. He had been at Ciro's when Danny Thomas "killed, but I mean *killed*, Norman." When he asked Thomas who wrote the new piece and heard it was "some kids from out of nowhere, Simmons and Lear," he wasn't even sure the Lear was me, but he had heard something about my moving to California and couldn't wait to make the call.

David was the MCA rep for a new network variety show going into production and he asked me if Simmons and Lear had written for television. I said, "Yes, of course," feeling comfortable with the lie since we had never written for a nightclub comic before, yet our success there was why he'd called us in the first place.

"I'm flying back east tomorrow," he said. "Can you get me a couple of sketches I can show to Jack Haley in New York?" Haley was a low-key song-and-dance man and a light comic, famous for playing the Tin Man in *The Wizard of Oz*. The Ford Motor Car Company had just hired him to host a new NBC musical comedy show, the *Ford Star Revue*, and David was helping to assemble the elements.

The woman whose bungalow we were renting lived with Ted Stanhope, a bit player in films who'd also done some TV, and he had a few scripts lying around. TV scripts were formatted differently in those early days, the page divided down the middle, with the actors' words on the right side, and what the audience would be seeing on the left. In that format Eddie and I wrote two sketches, "School for Comics" and "Blind Date," which David Susskind took with him to New York. Three days later he phoned us. Haley loved the sketches and wanted to do one of them on the first show. We would be paid seven hundred dollars per show for the team, and he wanted to know how quickly we could get to New York. Seven hundred dollars! Three hundred fifty dollars each! It seemed like as much money as there was in the world. A quick confab with Charlotte and Elaine and we called back to say we could be there the day after tomorrow.

The night before our early-morning flight we decided to dine together at the Simmonses' apartment. On the way, Charlotte and I picked up a pint of Fleischmann's gin, all we could afford, to toast ourselves with. Giddily, we did. Then there was the toast to Jack Haley: "May he be the Second Coming." The First, of course, was Danny Thomas.

Having driven cross-country when Charlotte, Ellen, and I came to L.A. a year before, this trip with Eddie—American Airlines, Los Angeles to New York—was my first cross-country flight, a very big deal at the time, and the beginning of my professional life in entertainment. On top of that, NBC flew us first class. Eddie and I were flying high before we got off the ground.

At LaGuardia Airport there was a car waiting for us, and the uniformed driver at baggage claim was holding up a little sign. It was the first time we'd seen it in print: SIMMONS AND LEAR. My God, we felt important!

I hadn't called my folks long distance from California to tell them the good news for the same reason we'd bought a pint of Fleischmann's to celebrate with. In those days transcontinental phone calls were expensive, so the way I would communicate all's well was to place a person-to-person call to Norman Lear. They would say I was out, I'd ask when Norman would be back (so that they would hear my voice), they'd say they weren't sure, I'd thank the operator and say I'd call back, and the message was delivered. No charge for that in those years.

Now, while waiting for our luggage at LaGuardia Airport, I phoned Woodstock Street and my father answered. He was surprised at how close I sounded.

"Yeah, Dad," I said, my child's heart racing to share the news while the adult in me hoped it didn't show. "I just landed at LaGuardia."

"You're in New York? What're you doing in New York?"

"It's a long story, Dad," I answered in an uncontrollable rush. "Eddie and I wrote a routine for Danny Thomas and last week he did it at Ciro's, you know, *Ciro's*, and the audience, all big shots, laughed their heads off, and Ed and I have been hired to write a new show for Jack Haley, the *Ford Star Revue,* can you believe it, on NBC, and Dad, listen to this, they are paying us seven hundred dollars for the team. I will be making *three hundred and fifty dollars a week!*"

"When you make a thousand dollars a week," H.K. replied, "*that's* a lot of money."

PART 2

Those Were the Days

At the moment of commitment the entire
universe conspires to assure your success.

—JOHANN WOLFGANG GOETHE

1

FROM LAGUARDIA AIRPORT we were taken to the Hotel Wellington in Midtown Manhattan, where a small one-bedroom suite with twin beds had been reserved for us. It was a Wednesday night, and we had four days to write a one-hour show—two big sketches, a monologue, and some incidental dialogue—to go into rehearsal Monday morning. The show had been on for a few weeks, and Eddie and I were replacing the original writers.

Our job that first week was eased by the fact that Mr. Haley wanted to do one of our audition sketches, "School for Comics." That sketch was the first thing we wrote that was cast, captured by a TV camera, and available live to East Coast viewers. For the rest of the country, the shows were recorded on kinescope—placing a camera in front of a video monitor, filming the broadcast, then shipping it to other time zones for showing days later. Hal Kanter, one of the earliest and funniest comedy writers, famously said of the kinescope, "It was like viewing pea soup well enough to see the croutons."

If the top of the fifties wasn't quite the birth of television, it certainly qualified as the medium's infancy. Most of the writers attracted to it came over from radio, so those of us who wrote exclusively for television were seen as a new breed. Eddie and I were looked upon as avant-garde members of the new medium and that lent us a special cachet. Yes, our personalities and abilities lived up to the buzz, but it was the dawning of a new era in entertainment that made us hot from the get-go.

We learned much of what we needed to know by paying close attention to the multicamera directors of the earliest TV variety shows, the Jack Haley show among them. Our director, Kingman Moore, was a god to all of us, and the director's booth—with its multiple screens, mysterious panels of buttons, and the low hum of engineers and assistant directors who worked them—was holy space. One entered it in those early days as one might enter a shrine.

But back to "School for Comics." It remains unforgettable for reasons beyond marking the start of my career in television. Jack Haley played the school's teacher, real comics were cast as the students, and there we were, Simmons and Lear, our first days in the biz, working with a group of the best funnymen around early in their careers: Jackie Gleason, Jerry Lester, "Fat Jack" Leonard, Jack Carter, Joey Faye, and a few others. Haley was teaching his class a category of comedy known as insult humor. The students were lined up facing something like a statue with a blanket thrown over it. One by one the student-comics were to approach the statue, pull back the blanket to make the reveal, say something funny about it, and toss the blanket back over it. Of course, under the blanket—thought to be hilarious in 1950—was an unattractive woman.

In rehearsals Jackie Gleason, two years away from his giant success as star of the show named for him, never used a line we wrote for him and never said the same thing twice. This frustrated me, because I wanted him to do a line I felt we could depend on, and some of his ad-libs in rehearsal made no sense at all. It was Gleason who taught me, that very first week, that a truly funny man can make anything he says seem funny. Unable to pin him down, I had no idea what he would say when it was his turn in the live broadcast to pull the blanket off the homely girl. When it happened, with that inimitable Gleason delivery, he said, "You've heard of nose drops? Well, hers did." The audience howled.

"Live. Up at eight o'clock, off at nine," is the way we described the physical broadcast. The experience of putting your week's creation—comedy, song, and dance—before the pitiless eye of a camera to be shared with an unseen audience of millions is indescribable. It was a fraught, vulnerable high, akin in a way to flying a mission. After all the preparation, you were out on a limb and a prayer, and it would play out as planned, or not.

Our first show played out as planned. The audience loved it, Jack Haley was pleased, but no one I knew saw it. My folks didn't have a TV—why they didn't go next door to their friends who did, I'll never know—and it would be a week before they ran a kinnie (kinescope) in L.A. But a certain stranger did see it and phoned before noon the next day. He introduced himself as Adolf Wenland, said he'd enjoyed the show last night, and asked if we'd been surprised by anything that morning. It was a strange question and I said we'd been here only a week and it was still a surprise waking up in New York, but that wasn't what he wanted to hear. He cut to the chase and asked if we had yet left our suite that day. When I said we hadn't, he said cheerily, "Well, then, open that front door, why don't you?" We did, and there sat a case of Cutty Sark scotch. Indeed surprised, I reported it to Wenland and he said, "The Lamb Association of America wants you to know it is grateful for Mr. Haley's mention of the word *lamb* in his monologue last night."

Ten days earlier I was stretching to buy a pint of Fleischmann's and now I was being given—*given!*—a case of Cutty Sark, twelve bottles, not pints but fifths, free. A bit of undisputed street wisdom leaped up at me: them what has, gets.

ED AND I had a small budget for another writer on the Haley show, and an itinerant TV scribe named Danny Simon was recommended to us. He arrived for a meeting with his kid brother Doc, whom he was mentoring. Our budget for one writer covered what the brothers, Danny and Doc Simon, asked for as a team. Doc eventually dropped his nickname, and Neil Simon became the most celebrated writer of hit comedies in the American theater, most of them equally successful as films. His first, *Come Blow Your Horn*, was produced by

Bud Yorkin and Norman Lear, directed by Yorkin, the screenplay written by Lear, and starred Frank Sinatra. More about that coming up, but another point of connection was that years later, after both Neil and I had become well known, our mothers, both widowed, lived for a time in the same building in Bridgeport, Connecticut.

Danny Simon came to have an early dinner with his mother one day. The women in the building enjoyed sitting together in the lobby in the late afternoon on an ad hoc basis, and on this day Mrs. Simon was one of them. Danny was making a good living in TV at the time, he always did, but Neil was a rock star, play after Broadway play of his going through the roof. Mrs. Simon saw Danny come in, and as she motioned to him, she said to the women nearest her, "Oh, girls, I want you to meet Danny, my son's brother."

THE SECOND AUDITION sketch we wrote for Jack Haley was called "Blind Date." I hardly recognize the guy who could cowrite, be content with, and reap the reward for such a piece. "Blind Date" was about an extremely nearsighted guy whose buddy escorts him to the front door of a girl he has been fixed up with. When the camera cuts to the girl inside the apartment, we see that she, too, is nearsighted, and a girlfriend is preparing her for her blind date.

In those years, as a matter of vanity, men and women were less inclined to be seen wearing glasses, and the soft contact lens was not yet an option, so it seemed normal for their friends to suggest that the daters would make better first impressions without their glasses. And so the audience was treated to the spectacle of two near-blind people with their glasses removed, pretending to be well sighted while they stumbled, mistook things, and groped for other things, including each other.

Jack Haley did well with the sketch, but can you imagine what Jerry Lewis, with his genius for outrageous physical comedy, could have done with it? Well, that's what Jerry Lewis himself wondered when he saw it on TV. Just a few weeks away from his own debut with Dean Martin on *The Colgate Comedy*

Hour, Jerry phoned his agent at MCA and lowered the ramp for the next move on Simmons and Lear's upward climb: "I just saw the Jack Haley show. Get me those writers!"

Since the *Ford Star Revue* and *The Colgate Comedy Hour* were both represented by Music Corporation of America, or, as it had been nicknamed, The Octopus (with its tentacles into every corner of show business), it was a simple matter to move Simmons and Lear from one show to the other (with a raise to $750 a week). In its giant roster of stars at that moment, none was hotter than the team of Dean Martin and Jerry Lewis. They'd already established a big reputation in supper clubs and, in 1949, took moviegoers by storm as featured performers in the film *My Friend Irma.* Their forthcoming hosting—in rotation with three other comics—of NBC's competition to CBS's Sunday night Ed Sullivan show, *Toast of the Town,* was the most anticipated event of the 1950–51 TV season.

The head writer whom we would be working under was older than us, with a long history in radio, and was renowned for being funny not just as a writer but as a persona. Harry Crane more than lived up to his reputation. Ten minutes with him, and Simmons and Lear doubted who they were and why they were there. The man was hilarious. He could tell you your mother had an ear infection and make you laugh. He could add that she got the infection from sneezing near a plate of pitted olives and make you roar. The problem working with and under Harry was that after days of laughing together there was nothing laughable to write down. It required Harry's delivery.

Two days before rehearsals were to begin we were told to expect a visit from NBC executives Pete Barnum, Sam Fuller, and Pat Weaver, the celebrated head of programming at NBC. They were looking for a heads-up on the material we'd been developing, which was hopefully on paper by now.

As we greeted the NBC giants, Eddie and I, without a word on paper, were struck dumb, but Harry Crane feasted on the moment. Pat Weaver and company, who held our careers in their hands, were eating out of Harry's within minutes. He told them we were working on two sketches that were "so funny you could die, like dead, like drop dead, like when the boys read them they'll die, too, and the audience, forget about it altogether, they will rock so hard with laughing, the whole building could shake, until the mezzanine falls into the orchestra, with the whole balcony on top of that, you can hear the sirens now, the ambulances, with the National Guard, the Red Cross with the blankets for the injured, and who knows, maybe doughnuts, all from the laughing, belly laughing, hysteria like you've never heard it. Tell them, Norman."

I could not have uttered a syllable with a gun to my head. I didn't have to. Harry Crane went on to describe a sketch with Dean Martin and Jerry Lewis trying to rehearse in a tiny dressing room, with a fat woman in red sneakers holding on to a small boy with a kite, and wherever the hell it went from there, and the NBC execs were finessed and laughed their heads off. When they left it was to grab a drink at Toots Shor's. With a wink and a "See you in the A.M.," Harry went with them.

If Harry only wrote as funny as he delivered, he'd have been the most sought-after talent in the field. He was perfectly suited for Jerry Lewis—much more so, I came to realize, than Simmons and Lear were—but ironically he went on to something else after the first show and we stayed with M&L for three seasons.

The first Martin and Lewis episode of *The Colgate Comedy Hour* aired on September 17, 1950. We encouraged Harry Crane to write some version of the dressing room scene he had sold so brilliantly while we tackled another idea, "Movies Are Better Than Ever." It was a send-up of the PR campaign by that name on behalf of the Theater Owners Alliance and the Motion Picture Association. Scared that they might be losing audience to the new medium, they were spending a fortune on ads in all media to downplay the advent of television. As it turned out, it was also my introduction to controversy.

In our sketch Dean was the manager of a movie theater and Marilyn Maxwell, a starlet of the time, played a ticket seller. So desperate were they to sell tickets that Dean was marking down admission prices and Maxwell was using all her feminine wiles to lure passersby into the empty theater. When Jerry, as Melvin, an innocent youth bouncing a basketball, wanders by, Marilyn applies every ounce of sex appeal to stop him and Dean hustles him with fast talk. But Melvin wants to go home instead because there's something he wants to see on television. Every time Melvin says the word "television," he's clobbered over the head by Dean. Punchy from Dean's attack and slathering over Maxwell, Melvin finally buys a ticket and goes inside, where the dark, the emptiness of the theater, and the loud echo of his voice frighten him and make him want even more to go home and "watch television," at the mention of which he is of course clobbered once more.

A side note about the name Melvin. Somehow "Melvin," with a rising whine in its middle, fell out of Jerry's mouth funnier than any other name he tried. So Dean made a point of asking Jerry his name in every sketch, and his response, with the audience by now anticipating it, was always "Melvin." It grew funnier each time. In another scene in which Jerry said his name, Dean went on to ask if he had a last name.

"Yes," Jerry replied. "Melvin." Dean's incredulous "Melvin *Melvin?*" was hilarious, topped only by Melvin's proud delivery of his full name, "Melvin M. Melvin." Then, after the laugh: "I suppose you're wondering what the *M* stands for."

As that first broadcast ended, I was dissatisfied. Even with the Melvin business, I thought we'd written a scene that had some real bite; funny, yes, but satirically edgy. Jerry played it 100 percent slapstick. "But did you hear those laughs?" asked David Susskind. "That's all they'll be talking about around the watercooler tomorrow morning."

Of course David was right. When television was young and not everyone owned a set, it was the office watercooler they all gathered around to discuss what some had seen and others had missed the night before. Fresh on the scene, their comic sensibilities pricelessly matched, Dean and Jerry could do no wrong, and sure enough, on the Monday morning following that first show, they were all the watercooler talk in offices everywhere. And a day later I learned that, despite my concern, Jerry's clowning did not destroy the meaning of our sketch. On the contrary, the sketch had enormous impact. In his biography of Jerry Lewis, Shawn Levy wrote, "The nation's movie theater owners and film producers were outraged by this savage parody of their fight against the onslaught of television." The skit created so much of a hullabaloo among the studios and theater owners that Hal Wallis, the boys' movie producer, urged them to take out full-page ads in *Variety* and *The Hollywood Reporter* apologizing for their assault on the industry. Martin and Lewis did further penance by offering to perform at the next convention of the Theater Owners Alliance.

THE FORMAT OF ROTATING HOSTS—among them Donald O'Connor, Abbott and Costello, and Eddie Cantor, each with their own set of writers— meant that our Martin and Lewis hour ran every four weeks. But Dean and Jerry were also playing nightclubs and doing a radio show for Liggett & Myers on behalf of Chesterfield cigarettes ("Chesterfields smoke milder, it's *my* cigarette," said Dean), which we would be writing soon. When our second show was due, they had a commitment at the Chez Paree in Chicago, which, along with Ciro's in L.A. and New York's Copacabana, was one of the nation's top three supper clubs.

We were all staying at the Ambassador East Hotel, as fancy and classy a hotel as there was in the country, which the Martin and Lewis contingent treated like a frat house. Between the food fights in the hallways and the fire hose on the wall to rinse off with, Abby Greschler, Dean and Jerry's manager, had to write a very large check for damages before we got out of there. But that isn't what I first think of when I recall that time in Chicago.

One night Ed and I walked down the hall to pick up Jerry to go to dinner. When we knocked on his door he called out, "Come on in!"

We opened the door and entered. The room was pitch-black. As our eyes grew accustomed to the dark, we heard the scratch of a match, and suddenly we were greeted with this hilarious sight. The irrepressible man-boy, Jerry Lewis, alone on the sofa, with an erection. As the lit match in his hand came down toward his penis—of which, let me tell you, he was very proud—we could make out one of those tiny birthday candles sprouting from it. And as the fire met the wick, Jerry began to sing, "Happy birthday to you, / Happy birthday to you, / Happy birthday, dear closest friend I have in the world, / Happy birthday to you." Go forget *that*!

As a comic figure, I thought Jerry Lewis possessed a touch of genius. Months later, in California, alone in his playroom, Eddie and I would throw ideas at him and he'd laugh us breathless. "You're a bartender. A bartender with a bad limp. With a limp and a lisp. And your ass itches. Did we mention you're Irish? But grew up in Spain. Oh, no, your aunt's calling, you hate the bitch. But you're afraid of her . . ." And on and on. He would incorporate it all and absolutely kill us.

There is no doubt in my mind that Jerry Lewis added time to my life. As did Dean Martin, who was gorgeous, crooned deliciously, and was funnier than any straight man had a right to be. You may question how something can kill you *and* add time to your life. Hey, we're talking comedy here.

Did I mention that Dean had funny knuckles? I thought he did. They amused me every time he held a drink or lifted a cigarette. When he made a funny aside in the middle of a song, they provided the accent. There were times when Dean was too funny for Jerry's good. We rehearsed for several days before we went into the studio, in a space in the West Forties. Some days Dean would come to work in a particularly amusing mood. His attitude, his view of the world and himself, and you—*everything* was funny.

Often enough, when Dean was in one of those moods and the center of attention, we'd find Jerry lying on the floor in the corner, complaining of a stomachache. On a few of those occasions, Jerry's doctor, Marvin "Miv" Levy, flew in from L.A. to treat him. Levy was an internist, but he played psychologist and confidant long enough to confirm to me that the pain in Jerry's belly was just what we thought it was—nothing.

WE FINISHED OUT that first season with a few more shows from New York. By then the transcontinental coaxial cable had been laid, making coast-to-coast live broadcasts possible from both New York and Los Angeles. Considering M&L's moviemaking schedule and the stress of flying cross-country in the pre-jet era, NBC chief Pat Weaver decided to let us broadcast from the West Coast. The decision to bring all of NBC's comedies to Hollywood soon followed.

As the time grew close to leave New York, we all became very sentimental. New York and television production went together, and we would miss it. We would miss the Stage Deli and Lindy's cheesecake and the pharmacy at the corner of Seventh Avenue and Fifty-eighth Street, adjacent to the Alwyn Court apartment building where the brilliant comedian Fred Allen lived for many years. The Alwyn Pharmacy was particularly important to many of us who wrote for live television in those chaotic early years. Ed Simmons and I, for example, lived on Seconal and Dexedrine, the first for sleeping, the second for staying awake, and they were over-the-counter items, at least for those of us known to the people behind the Alwyn counter.

Bud Yorkin, later to become my partner, was one of the show's four stage managers, the others being Jack Smight, John Rich, and Arthur Penn, all of whom went on to become important directors, Penn (*Bonnie and Clyde*) foremost among them. We all threw a farewell party at Bud's apartment the night before we were to leave for California. In the course of that halcyon evening a bunch of us stood around the piano and made up a parody to commemorate the event that had us all heeding Horace Greeley's advice to—on NBC's orders— "Go west, young man."

"When the transcontinental coaxial cable is laid, is laid," we wrote and sang our hearts out to an old tune, "we'll be on the run to the land of sun and swimming pools / the dramatic shows will be static shows if they stay, those fools . . ." I can see Pat Weaver, the man who invented the *Today* and *Tonight* shows, the most creative network president in television history, singing along with us and then, as the party ended, bidding us good-bye. We could have been his sons.

2

UPON OUR RETURN, Charlotte and I rented the bottom floor of a Hollywood duplex on North Orange Drive near Beverly Boulevard, a far cry from the ten-floor apartment building we'd been living in on West End Avenue in New York. It was owned, the leasing agent informed us, by Buster Crabbe, an Olympic gold medalist in 1932 and the only man to play three comic book heroes in films: Tarzan, Flash Gordon, and Buck Rogers. It was there that I began to feel like a family man for the first time. The cottage on Kenmore had never felt like a home, and the effort to get a toehold in something concrete enough to provide a future left very little headspace for unencumbered creativity. But now our first-floor duplex made me feel cushy and safe, even a bit upscale, and as Martin and Lewis's popularity grew, so, in our corner of the universe, did the awareness of Simmons and Lear.

On top of all that, Ellen was six now, and her lifelong love of horses had begun. Anyone who knows L.A. but wasn't here in the 1950s will find it hard to believe that at the corner of Beverly Boulevard and La Cienega there was a small amusement park with a pony ring. I took Ellen to her horses every Sunday and can still see my little girl coming around the far turn at a gallop, her little legs splayed wide like the smile on her face. And how I loved that face!

Charlotte's parents followed us out to Los Angeles and took an apartment around the corner from our duplex. Ellen didn't have to cross any streets to get there, so on Sunday—Charlotte's and my day to sleep late—she would walk to her grandparents, have breakfast with them, and be back in time to go to Ponyland.

Early one Sunday morning, when she was usually with her grandparents, I was awakened by her loud voice outside our bedroom window. I pulled up the shade to see her standing there talking to the most underfed, sorriest, and scariest excuse for a German shepherd I could imagine. I cracked the window open to tell Ellen to get the hell away from that creature when she looked up at me and took me completely off guard.

"Oh, hi, Daddy," she said. "This is Ginger, a dog I know."

My friend Maurice Zolotow—the biographer of, among others, Marilyn Monroe and Billy Wilder—often talked about what a great title that would make for a children's book: *This Is Ginger, a Dog I Know.*

AROUND THIS TIME, my mother began pleading with me to come to Hartford the next time I was in New York. "All right, so you don't have a weekend, but you have a Friday night. Who doesn't have a Friday night?" Mother reasoned.

So one Friday night I showed up to a packed house at 68 Woodstock. Every chair in the house was jammed into the living room, occupied by family, friends, and neighbors. The prodigal son was the center of attention, the only one in the room who had been to California, let alone Hollywood, and had flown cross-country in both directions. After a dozen or more questions, including "So they really serve hot food on those planes?" and "How many toilets do they have?" there was a long pause. Into the silence my mother's best friend, Jeanette Aaron, asked, "So what's with Spencer Tracy and Katharine Hepburn?"

They were monumental stars, of course, but that was all the information I had.

"I don't know anything about them, Jeanette," I said.

"Sure," she said caustically.

"Norman," my mother implored, "who is she going to tell? Answer Jeanette."

"Mother, I'm only there a few months, I never met Spencer Tracy or Katharine Hepburn."

"Tell her," my mother repeated.

"There's nothing to tell," I said.

"Big shot!" Jeanette Aaron fired back. I'd have thrown Mrs. Aaron a bone that night had I understood the moment better. Something like: "I was right there, Jeanette. Spence let Kate drive off in his Rolls-Royce. Don't tell anybody, but I think he's *shtupping* her."

BECAUSE WE FOUND ourselves working all hours, Eddie and I took an apartment on North Flores Drive to write in. Several other writers rented apartments there to use as offices, and it was a rare moment of any day when there wasn't a gin rummy or poker game going on somewhere in the building. And still, scripts for *The Ed Wynn Show, Four Star Playhouse, Our Miss Brooks,* and *The Colgate Comedy Hour* poured out of there.

In addition to their TV hour, Ed and I were asked to write the weekly Martin and Lewis radio show. Writing for radio was a special treat for the imagination. Where else could you do a takeoff on *A Streetcar Named Desire,* having Dean Martin play the conductor, Dinah Shore a passenger, and Jerry Lewis the streetcar? The show was broadcast from the NBC studios on the corner of Hollywood and Vine streets, and there wasn't a hotter ticket in town. We wrote for such guests as Bing Crosby, Jane Russell, Boris Karloff, Jane Wyman, William Holden, Anne Sheridan, Arlene Dahl, George Raft, and a host of others. Riding high on the Martin and Lewis carousel was great fun, but the occasional life lesson was the brass ring. Thankfully I caught one now and then, and one of them influenced my career profoundly.

In January 1952 a guest on the radio show was the great Welsh actor Hugh

Griffith, who is best known for his roles in *Ben-Hur* and *Tom Jones*. In the fifties Griffith was a bit of a tippler, and he was already high when we started the table read just after lunch. The half-hour show consisted of two comedy segments interspersed with two songs from Dean and some chitchat with the guest. Evidently Dean's interludes gave Mr. Griffith all the time he needed to continue tippling, because within twenty minutes of the doors opening to let the audience in, it was clear that he was roaring drunk.

Dick Mack, our veteran producer and director, who had a nervous tick that caused his head to shake slowly from side to side, was thinking about canceling the show. Dean—who had to face away from the booth when he sang because no matter how well he was sounding, his director's tick seemed to be telling him, "No, uh-uh, no way"—just wanted to finish up and get the hell out of there.

As Dick Mack decided there was no way he could work with a loaded Hugh Griffith, I recalled having seen the well-known character actor Hans Conried in the building performing in an earlier taping of another radio show, *Fibber McGee and Molly*. I felt sure that Hans, a man and an actor for all seasons, all accents, and all roles, could read the Hugh Griffith part over once and play it with ease. With Dick's permission, I ran down the hall, found Conried, and asked him to come by our studio. An hour later we had taped our show as scheduled and were toasting Mr. Conried for saving the day.

Alone with him for a moment, I said, "You're a major talent with a big reputation. Why do you agree to substitute for another actor without a single question, not about billing, or even money?" His response became a marker along my career path. "I work to work, Norman, and the rest follows," he said, adding, "When it isn't about the money, it's funny how much seems to come your way."

EDDIE AND I WROTE for Dean and Jerry for three years, bracketed by a full-page ad they took out in *Variety* after we'd written three or four shows—

"Writers have always been the unsung heroes of our business. This is to tell you publicly how grateful we are for all the wonderful sketches you've written for us, and to sing songs of praise for two great guys, as well as great talents"—and our abrupt exit from their world after a November 1953 article in *TV Guide* reported that we'd been given an "unprecedented" raise to $10,400 per show, making us, the article bragged, "the highest-priced writers in television." One month later, inexplicably, Jerry picked up the phone and fired us. From that day to this, in dozens of interviews and a couple of books, he has never acknowledged that he had writers, let alone mentioned our names.

If it seems to you that it was Jerry making all the decisions for Martin and Lewis, that's because he was. Dean didn't seem to know or care. Simmons and I loved Dean. And early in our relationship we were *in* love with Jerry. Out of his great need for that quality of love, Jerry could not have been more seductive. For the time he focused on you, he required *all* of you, and for a while we were happy to give all.

We loved spending time with him. Shopping with him, for example. Long before we saw it as megalomaniacal we thought it irrational, but not without its beguiling boyish charm, to see him walk into Sy Devore's on Vine Street and order two dozen made-to-order suits of a certain style in as many fabrics, and all the accoutrements—shirts, socks, ties, etc.—to go with them. There was a lot of that. But over time this behavior became less beguiling, especially as it began to intrude on our work together and, most particularly, on the quality of his comedy.

There are seeds in every great comedian from which, depending on how he responds to his worshipful fans, he grows either to become a pure clown or to assume the papacy. When we laugh together we are one. The ability to elicit that feeling of oneness from a huge crowd, and at a whim, is an enormous power, a power that can humble one entertainer and make a pope of another. The pope/comic, not unlike the world's understanding of the real pope, is all-knowing and all-controlling. Nothing tends to destroy comedy like certainty.

Certainty is the realm of the straight man. I will leave it to the readers who have observed Jerry Lewis throughout his career—especially, for example, Jerry as himself, hosting the muscular dystrophy telethons over the years. That person we all watched Jerry Lewis grow into brought with him what remained of the clown, appearing over time more and more like an abused child, senselessly kicking and screaming along the way.

Nowhere was Jerry's route to the all-knowing more pronounced than in the ceremonious way he gave and received gifts. He was very generous, but his gifts came with a price: his full name or initials embroidered, imprinted, or otherwise permanently attached to just about every gift item. Ernie Glucksman, a comedy veteran from the Catskills (also known as the borscht belt) and producer of the Martin and Lewis TV show, was once gifted at Christmas with a floor-model television set. I visited Ernie sometime later and there it was. Large, elegant, costly, with a signed brass plate bolted to the top reading: "Thank you, Dean and Jerry." I still have my "Thank you, Dean and Jerry" cuff links.

Behind the Lewises' house on Amalfi Drive in the Pacific Palisades, there was the Garron Playhouse, named after Jerry and wife Patti's sons, Gary and Ron. Regulars on weekends included Sammy Davis Jr., Tony Curtis and Janet Leigh, Danny Arnold, and Ed and me. We must have made a dozen wild and crazy short films and celebrated everyone's birthday there, one of which, Jerry's twenty-seventh, in March 1953, is particularly memorable.

In addition to his close friends, Jerry had developed an entourage who sought to outdo one another, presenting him with costly tokens of their affection—from an expensive hunting rifle (because he once joked about being the only Jew who hunted) to a three-thousand-dollar tennis racquet that once belonged to Wimbledon champ Jack Kramer. Not wishing to compete in this game, we racked our brains to come up with something funny, preferably relevant and funny.

On Jerry's birthday the landlord of the apartment building where we had our office sent us a carpenter to fix a window that was stuck. He was a rugged little man in his sixties or seventies, a Popeye look-alike if ever there was one. Suddenly I had an idea, then a quick talk with Eddie, and together we asked him if he'd like to work that night. He said yes, but it would cost us fifty dollars, which in the fifties was a handsome fee for an evening's work.

We took him down to a gift-wrapping establishment on Melrose near Fairfax and had him measured for a box he could fit into so that we could give Jerry Lewis the gift of a lifetime, his very own human being. The gift card accompanying it read: "You have a lease on a few of these already, Jerry, but here now is 100% of one—your very own, full-time human being, lock, stock and barrel. Happy birthday."

When they finished it, the box, with a tube through which our squatting little man could breathe, looked like it contained a tabletop television set. It was gift-wrapped so that the ribbon would fall into place when the top was put on, and the gift itself didn't have to get in the box until the last minute.

We drove out to Jerry's house and left Popeye in the car. When Jerry was getting to the end of the present-opening ceremony, we ran out, put our little guy in the box, placed the cover on so that the ribbon fell neatly in line, and said, "Remember, you want to look serious. We'll make it a hundred dollars if you don't smile." He said okay and we carried the box inside.

As soon as the door opened someone yelled, "Hey, Simmons and Lear got him a television!" We brought it in and set it on the large coffee table where Jerry and Patti were opening the last of the gifts. It was Patti Lewis who got to ours, removed the top, and peeked in. She gasped and her eyes popped in horror. I looked quickly into the box to see Popeye's eyes closed and his face contorted in an effort to hold back a laugh. I yelled at him, "It's okay, you can smile now!" Thinking that this was part of the game and determined not to blow his hundred-dollar fee, the little guy paid me no mind and held. At which point, positioned at the perimeter of the crowd around the gift table, the aforementioned Dr. Marvin "Miv" Levy stepped up on a chair so as to see over their heads. Viewing what Patti had gasped at, and reminded of his days as a frat boy and med student, the only MD in the room shouted, *"Simmons and Lear gave him a cadaver!"*

In the long history of human screams, could there ever have been heard a shriek like the one that issued from Patti Lewis, followed by a flurry of supportive outrage and contempt on all sides? If looks could kill, Eddie and I would have been dead and buried, and this birthday party our wake. The only people who appeared more delighted than upset, I suppose because their relationship with Jerry gave them the license, were the producer of the Martin and Lewis films at Paramount Pictures, Hal Wallis, and his wife, Louise Fazenda, the star of some three hundred silent comedy films and shorts. Dean, who held an even more exclusive license, didn't feel the need to be in attendance at all.

Plied with drinks and treated like "that poor thing" by guests who believed he'd been in the box for hours on a cold March night, the Popeye of all cadavers had the time of his life. He was still partying when Ed and I left, so we never got to take him home. Sammy Davis Jr. did that honor.

DEAN AND JERRY led separate and distinct lives, and held very separate and distinct views of their relationship. For Dean there was no love lost, it was a business. Not that Jerry didn't see that, too, but he couldn't live with it. Despite the polarization and simmering unease, for Jerry there had to be a love there, an affection between two strong men. Paraphrasing Jerry now on a rare intimate occasion, it was a love "so deep and so profound that Dean and I can't talk about it so we don't, but you see it there in our work, and it wouldn't work without it, not at the heights Dean and I reach, it's us and the audience, that bond, that three-way bond, is all about love, and it all starts with our love, Dean's and mine, it couldn't happen any other way, not without that unbreakable, shatterproof love between us, and that is what makes us Dean and Jerry."

What made this so memorable was the absence of tears. The words and the moment called for tears. I know that not just as a professional but as a human being. But Jerry was dry-eyed. I believe he meant every word of his story. But it was only one of the stories he needed to sustain him, one he could lean into in the telling, and rub and polish to a high gloss, a gloss in which he might find himself.

I wonder, as I focus here on Dean, how well I knew him. My friend the writer Nick Pileggi worked for nearly two years with director Martin Scorsese to develop a film based on Nick Tosches's biography of him. Fascinated by what Tosches had to say about Dean's life and the world he lived in, Pileggi felt they had a story, but not the man. To learn more about Dean from the inside, Nick started interviewing just about everyone who knew and worked with him, me among them.

"Dino" everyone called him growing up in Steubenville, Ohio, and again after he'd become, with Frank Sinatra, a founding member of the Rat Pack, which grew to include Sammy Davis Jr., Peter Lawford, and Joey Bishop. Dean was the guy who seemed to have wandered in, seemed to not give a shit about anything, but seemed to like everything—especially, it seemed to all, the drink in his hand. The operative words here are "seemed to." All everyone knew about Dean was who and what he seemed to be. So what Nick Pileggi and Martin Scorsese saw from afar was pretty much what those who knew him best saw up close. How to explain that?

We all loved Dean. Like his every performance, Dean was easy, light and easy. It cost nothing to be his friend—not your time, your concern, or your affection. He was the ultimate loner. And inscrutable. You could be with him at the height of some happy occasion, enjoying him, his friendship, the closeness, in a way that occurs only when you are partnered in those feelings. Then suddenly, where'd that partner go? Dean was still there. But the close friend, where was he?

Better make that good friend. On second thought, what do you mean by "good"? Nothing had changed in Dean. He remained exactly who he was. What had changed was how *you* saw the relationship. So "inscrutable" is not about the inscrutable one, it's about the one who sees him that way. At one point we suddenly realize we don't really know who this person—this new friend, old friend, good friend—is. He's not really a person then. He's not even a pronoun. He's an adjective. Inscrutable.

Hanging with Dean and Jerry was my first encounter with the power of celebrity. As hot as they had become in films and on TV, they were instantly recognizable by the multitudes, magnetic draws to everyone who could hold a camera. Fans, mostly women, waited endlessly in the hope they'd emerge from wherever, squealed with delight at the sight of them, rushed everywhere after them, and were driven silly by a moment's conversation with them. And more.

NBC held a yearly weekend convention at a hotel in Boca Raton, Florida, for its top executives and affiliate station honchos across the country, and in 1952 Dean Martin and Jerry Lewis were the main attraction at the Saturday night dinner where I was witness to "more" at the extreme. Of course the convention included meetings to discuss the next season, to review schedules, to exchange ideas and address problems, with a few speakers discussing the general state of media, etc. But the desire to attend the business of the convention had strong competition from an array of other needs of its participants, i.e., to "get the fuck away," "let my hair down," "drink as much as I fucking want," and, with a wink, "who knows what else?"

A pair of well-known agents at the time decided to suck up to the network by helping to satisfy the "who knows what else?" part of those needs. From Miami, some forty-five miles away, there arrived a busload of attractive young women, showgirl types dressed to kill. About ten P.M., as dinner and the M&L performance were ending and many of the execs were deciding to have one more drink, a nightcap, these women waltzed in. Before you could sing a chorus of "There'll Be a Hot Time in the Old Town Tonight," there were parties in the lounge and bar, followed by couples here and there wandering off, almost all winding up later at two or three swinging parties in upstairs suites.

I participated in none of that. Not that my loveless marriage was in the way, but I was concentrating on one specific girl. I remember her only as Esther, because the instant I saw her I thought that, whoever she was, wherever she'd grown up, she had to have played Esther in the Purim play. It turned out she never played the role and didn't even know that Purim was a Jewish holiday, though she was Jewish. I thought she looked like an angel. To me at that time an angel was a very pretty girl who had no problem letting me know early on that she desired me. I was sure that was true of my Esther. And that was even before she spent an hour with me radiating charm, all of it directed at recognizing the miracle of our meeting and how clearly we were meant for each other. At about twelve-thirty it was clear she was hot to trot, so I slipped her my room number and, heart high, went upstairs to shower.

By one-thirty, I had torn orchid petals from a large bouquet and spread them everywhere she might sit and look, including the toilet bowl and bidet; lightly dabbed myself here and there, especially there, with Aphrodisia by Fabergé (the cologne Jerry used); and had a chilled bottle of Dom Perignon and some canapés at the ready. I, too, was ready. The room, the moment, the mood, and the man, all ready. At about two-thirty I lay down to wait, fell asleep quickly for a man about to have his hard (no typo) broken, and was awakened by the doorbell at four-thirty A.M. It was my angel, my Esther, still exquisite, but looking like she'd been through hell. She was crying. And as if she'd never met me, not to mention having been wooed by me, she gushed this story.

She'd agreed to make the bus trip all the way to Boca Raton to meet Jerry Lewis, who is so special to her that her pulse starts going crazy when she merely reads about him. And then, finally, she met him here for the first time and knew right away she was meant for him. Then I came along and she sat with me, never taking her eyes off Jerry. She was sure I saw that, and it made her feel so safe, me sitting with her all that time knowing that in her heart she was all Jerry's—and remind her later to kiss me for that—but right now, do I know what room Jerry is in? The desk wouldn't tell her and no one else is around, and she can't believe she came all this way, and has been with so many of the others, but not Jerry. She knows how late it is and he's probably sleeping, but if she only had Jerry Lewis's room number, she just knows he wouldn't mind letting her, at the least, blow him.

That's right. That's what she said, my little angel, my sweet Esther. This was my biggest encounter until then with the power of celebrity.

FRED ALLEN—comedian, writer, and most sardonic of wits—was possibly the single biggest influence on my own writing and sense of the comedic. I was twelve when I first heard him on the radio, and I followed him so faithfully that I hear his voice in my head to this day. It was a pinched nasal sound perfectly suited to the droll, biting humor that issued from him. Typical of Fred was his attitude toward television. "It is called a medium," he said, "because it is neither rare nor well-done." As to "the minds that control it," he said, "you could put them in the navel of a flea and still have room enough beside them for the heart of a network vice president."

Fred had been asked to join the rotation of Colgate comics, and Ed and I had a meeting with him to discuss our producing his show. As it happened the show never came together, but we were determined to maintain contact with him. At Christmas we sent him holiday greetings. In January he wrote us in response.

"You can enjoy a tidy feeling after the Xmas holiday," he said, "if you receive a card from every person to whom you have sent a card." And if they had not sent a card, the least they can do, he went on, "is to mail you a receipt for the card you sent them. I am all even now," he concluded.

We wrote again to say, "Just as you like to feel you've come out even, we like to stay ahead." To that note we added, from out of nowhere, this postscript: "P.S. Ran into Harry Saminow the other day. Flo is fine but she hasn't gotten the crib yet. Sol is due in next Tuesday for a week and will let you know about the andirons."

Within days we heard back from Fred Allen, who wrote only in lowercase. Addressed to ed simmons—norman lear, he wrote: "if you run into harry saminow again will you ask him to tell sol not to bother about the andirons. we had three andirons in the old house, one at each side of the fireplace and to balance the room mrs. saminow suggested the third andiron be placed in the fireplace. the winter was unusually cold that year. when we moved to the duplex we had two andirons and a large ingot. if sol can match the ingot we will be ready to give him the andirons. regards—fred allen."

And thus began a two-year correspondence between Fred Allen, Simmons and Lear, and Harry Saminow, who wrote and invoiced on his own stationery, of course. It read: "HARRY SAMINOW—ANDIRONS AND INGOTS. My Bell If You Ring It, I'll Sell You an Ingot."

When Ed and I were in New York we held dinners to discuss what was happening. They became known as Saminow Seminars. For a good deal of the time at each seminar, no one broke character and the conversation went everywhere our crafty minds could take us in the continuing saga of Harry and Moe Saminow and their ANDIRONS and INGOTS, not to mention their BALLED WINCHES, REAMED BRAZIERS, AND BRASS COUPLINGS.

The recollection here all but brings a tear to my eye, not for the specifics of the fun we had but for that time, when life seemed to hum rather than chase, and such sweet playfulness was accommodated.

3

WE WERE OUT OF WORK just a few short weeks toward the end of 1953 when an offer arrived for us to replace writer-producer Nat Hiken on *The Martha Raye Show*. Martha was the Carol Burnett of her moment, and Hiken—in my opinion the cream of our crop of writers—had worked wonders, creating an original book-musical format for TV. The book (script), with roles for guest stars and a dance chorus, was original, but the songs were standards woven into the story line. That first year Hiken and Martha had done six of them, with the boxer and middleweight champ Rocky Graziano as her "goombah," her friend and protector.

Simmons and I loved Martha, were crazy about the book-musical format, and felt challenged by the idea of replacing Nat Hiken. The offer was sweetened for me when whoever they'd asked to direct the show stepped aside and I was asked to replace him. I was over the moon, but with one big problem. Though my wife and daughter had joined me in New York when I started working for Dean and Jerry, now Charlotte did not want to leave Los Angeles. With four days to go before I had to give NBC a decision, I flew back to L.A. to talk it over with her.

At stake for me was the question of separating from Ellen. At stake for Charlotte, I learned, was separation from her psychiatrist, Dr. Henry Luster, and their five-times-weekly visits. I met with him at Charlotte's suggestion and in our forty-five-minute acquaintance he seemed a pleasant and reasonable fellow. He understood when I explained that, from a long-range career standpoint, I had to take the job in New York, but he didn't accept that I *had* to take my family with me. Shouldn't we think of Ellen first, I asked, and wouldn't she fare better with both rather than one of us? In a perfect world, yes, he replied. But (a) if I agreed that her mother's emotional health was important to Ellen, this was no time to pull her out of therapy, and (b) because at Ellen's age girls require their mothers more than ever, he recommended that I let well enough alone for now, a proposition I didn't feel up to challenging.

I did just that, and there is much to tell regarding the year that followed. But while we're in his office, let me skip ahead to the second and final meeting with Henry Luster. It took place almost a year to the day after the first one. In the intervening year I talked with Ellen daily, flew out to L.A. to be with her every other weekend, and talked with Charlotte regularly about our being together in New York the following year, should *The Martha Raye Show* be picked up and our contract renewed. Charlotte never gave me the satisfaction of directly accepting that supposition, but neither did she directly reject it—until the day she told me she'd set an appointment for me to see Dr. Luster again.

I'd arrived in L.A. the evening before, and in the morning was excitedly describing the perfect apartment I'd located, within walking distance of a good private school for Ellen, when I noticed something in Charlotte's expression. Nothing. I could have been telling her the taxi driver found her scarf in the backseat. Was she trying to tell me I faced another year of cross-country separation from my daughter? She was. Why? Her therapy was critical. Still? Yes. More critical than her marriage? "You need to hear it from Dr. Luster." Dr. Luster again? I went bat shit.

Meeting for the second time, Henry Luster seemed a little more distant, bordering on cold. As I entered his office and moved to assume a chair opposite him, he motioned me to look at something on his side of the desk first. As I came around to do that, he said in a cautionary tone that he didn't know my mood, but he wasn't a stranger to enraged husbands. This office had seen its share of them, and perhaps we should start with my knowing *this*, he said, opening a drawer and nodding for me to take a look. In it there lay a pistol. Nothing else. He closed the drawer quickly. Mad fucking man.

Well into a third year of five visits per week, Henry Luster was still advising Charlotte that she would do herself great harm by stopping therapy at this point. I asked him if he would still feel that way knowing that her staying in L.A. could result in a divorce. But how could he know that? "Only the decision maker could know that," he replied, smiling at me with what I read as pity. Now I was enraged, and imagined picking up that pistol! And divorce proceedings followed.

THE APARTMENT I'D FOUND in vain for our family was lovely. But the apartment Eddie and I had been living in that first year working on *The Martha Raye Show* was spectacular. It was a three-story penthouse at 25 Tudor City Place at the end of Forty-first Street, overlooking the East River. The living room was three stories high, with a ground-floor bedroom off it, and a winding staircase that led to another bedroom on the second floor, and past that to a door on what would be the third floor, but that opened instead onto a large roof garden.

It was a showplace, fit more for a sheikh than for a pair of comedy writers, and it was also rent-controlled, which made it a palace and a steal at the same time. I saw an ad for it late one Saturday afternoon in the next morning's *New York Times*, but as fast as I was to call the woman renting it, someone else had gotten there first. The woman had just shown the apartment for the first time to someone who grabbed at it, and she was still there in a pleasant state of shock with a check in hand for the first and last months' rent. I had no idea, really, that I could get her to tear up the check, but I told her that before I killed myself I just had to see the apartment I'd lost by a whisker. But that would only make me feel worse, she said, so coming over to see the apartment made no sense at all. Just the opposite, I returned, when you consider that a man should at least see what he's about to take his life over. I knew I had her when she laughed.

I CAN'T IMAGINE A CRAZIER, more inept work schedule than Ed and I maintained writing, and in my case also directing, *The Martha Raye Show*. It's possible that Ed Simmons was a clutch writer for neurotic reasons of his own, but I believe it was I who brought clutch to the party. I could not and did not write *with* Eddie. We never sat in a room together and wrote. Nor did I ever work that way in my long history of collaborations. I could sit for days and talk through stories and scenes and dialogues. All the later work with multiple writers was recorded and transcribed, and much of that material still exists. After we agreed on a story, Ed, the only writer I worked with in partnership, would write the first or second half of a show, while I tackled the other half. Then each of us would rewrite or touch up the half we hadn't worked on. After that, compulsively, I had to spend time alone with every script.

We would broadcast live every other Tuesday from eight to nine P.M. and have a table reading of the script for the next show, on Wednesday eight days later. Depending on how well that went, we then either started to rehearse or went home to rewrite and start rehearsals the next morning. We'd rehearse dry—that is, without cameras—through Friday and, in an emergency, some of Saturday, move into the theater Monday, and rehearse our way to a stop-and-go dress rehearsal with songs and dances by Monday evening. Tuesday, after an early start, we camera-rehearsed until three-thirty P.M., had a complete dress rehearsal before an audience at five, broke for notes and dinner, and broadcast live before a second audience at eight o'clock. On average the show broke down to three or four major scenes, out of which grew three or four songs, a couple of full dance numbers choreographed by Herb Ross (who went on to direct, among dozens of films, *Footloose*, *The Turning Point*, and *Play It Again, Sam*) and a handful of interstitials. It all had to serve Martha; her goombah, Rocky Graziano; and guest stars such as Cesar Romero, Tallulah Bankhead, and Paulette Goddard.

All of that was hard enough. What complicated it even more was how Simmons and I approached the writing of each script. Wednesday and Thursday following the broadcast we took off altogether. It was our weekend. When we sat down to talk script on Friday we had five days to write the show for Wednesday's table reading. Don't ask me where the next three days went. I know we tended to wake early, have breakfast, and start talking. I see flashes of us now, sprawled in a variety of positions on couches and on the floor and at a table in the living room. In the evening we'd have some food delivered or walk over to The Palm, a steak house on Second Avenue, return to the apartment, and scratch our heads some more.

By day two I was starting to feel what I described, when I sought therapy years later, as "shit in the head"—"S.I.T.H." My God, it's an anagram!—a mental state that tied ideas and concepts into knots; saw them banging smack into one another; had them brawling, begging individually for consideration; and at the same time battling collectively against the intrusion of disconnected ideas, recollections, contemplations, problems, and fears having nothing to do with the subject at hand, all making for a giant jumble of mind-blowing shit. I must have been eating at my desk many years ago in just such a mood when I wrote this:

THOUGHTS WHILE LUNCHING ON A BOWL
OF CHICKEN SOUP WITH RICE
How long dead the chicken from whose minimal residue
This soup was made and named, killed by whom?
Who fed this fowl, penned it, and what did it see
Before it lent itself to soup and me?
Isn't it interesting that such thoughts lurk
Only when I sit down to work?

While my S.I.T.H. was clogging my synapses, several departments were waiting to see what the next script would require. Set construction, wardrobe, music, and choreography all had to get to work days before the table reading. Ed and I were always late to get words on paper, and several times so late that it was early Monday morning, the table reading just two days away, before we could meet with the department heads and tell them what they needed to know. When the meeting ended the set designer knew we were opening in Martha's home, the choreographer and designer knew it would be a street corner next and a park following, the wardrobe people had a sense of what everyone would be wearing scene by scene, and the music people knew that Martha needed a happy song here, a heartbreaker there, etc.

Once they all left, Ed and I would sit in separate rooms and start writing. With two days to turn out a full script, enter the Alwyn Pharmacy and those much-needed writers' assistants Dexedrine and Seconal. Tuesday evening we'd finish working on the script and try to get a few hours of sleep before I'd run it over to the mimeograph people, whose smelly purple ink-drenched runoffs preceded the Xerox machine, so that copies would be ready for me to take to the table reading Wednesday morning at eleven.

In the days we had relatively free between shows, Eddie and I held some great parties at our showplace of an apartment. The winding staircase served as a stage, and I can still see the likes of Gordon MacRae, Imogene Coca, Red Buttons, Jack E. Leonard, Henny Youngman, and Martha herself, singing or clowning from a perch on that staircase some feet above us. One party stands out in my mind. The crowd had thinned out and a handful remained, including Martha and a couple of the singers who backed her up. As a performer, Martha was a cartoon character, loud and vulgar and physically outrageous, with a mouth that looked like a large rip in her face. When called upon, however, she could also evoke enough sadness and compassion to tear your heart out. It was that Martha, sitting on the floor now, more than a bit high, singing everything in her repertoire from a heart soaked in tears. Not that there was no joy to be had. But it, too, was soaked in tears. Martha Raye at her best was a clown.

IT HAD BEEN almost ten years since I'd last seen him in Foggia, Italy, when I got a call from my 772nd Bomb Squadron buddy Leonard Sosna. He was in town from Chicago with a friend, they were visiting a girl they knew, and he somehow got my phone number through NBC. Could we get together? Of course, I told him.

"Great," he said, "we are in a town house on Thirty-eighth Street near Fifth Avenue."

"I'm on Forty-first," I said, "ten minutes away."

How could I have known this was the lead-in to my second marriage, the beginning of a thirty-year chapter of my life, when Frances Loeb opened the door to her second-floor flat?

"So you're Norman Lear," she exclaimed, as if thrilled by a name she'd known all her life. She hadn't, of course—she'd probably never seen or heard of it before that evening—but that didn't stop her. "I never watch television, but I certainly know of you," she continued warmly. That was Frances. What I didn't know as we met that night was that in another mood she could meet someone who said, "Hello, I'm Cindy Crawford," respond crisply, "Of course you are," and move on without another word.

Frances Loeb, thirty-two and twice divorced, was excitement personified, effusive, combustible, and striking. She had great flair and a great figure, a combination that leaned as much toward elegance as it did toward sex appeal. When she walked into a room, an air of danger and a touch of class came with her. And that was true whichever of her bipolar moods she was in. (She wouldn't be formally diagnosed as manic-depressive until eighteen years later, shortly after turning fifty.)

I didn't think I'd see Frances again after that evening with Leonard and friend. As it turned out, it was Leonard I didn't see again. Frances phoned me a few weeks later, said she was unhappy making the call because she fully expected me to phone her, but promised to get over it if I accompanied her to a dinner party Saturday night. The conversation was great fun, and as it was ending I asked what time she would be picking me up on Saturday. She laughed and said, "See you here at seven-thirty."

"Uh-uh, see you here," I replied.

"I'm not that hard up," she chirped. "See you here!"

Now, I've never been as indifferent to the prospect of being with a beautiful woman as this could make me sound, but I was a clutch writer who felt he needed every second at his Remington. Then, too, I suspect a bigger need was to prove something to myself, so I stood firm. Following some minutes of strain and a few laughs, Frances swallowed her pride. When she called from the lobby on the night of our date, I said I'd be a few minutes and asked her to come up.

"Why don't I lie down under a steamroller first so I can slip myself under your door?" was her response. I met her in the lobby.

This prompts a confession about me and the women in my life. I've bragged to myself for years that my advances were never spurned by a woman I fancied. It wasn't until sometime recently that I recognized the reason behind that reality. I was never spurned because it was never I who made the first move. I needed a sign, a hard-and-fast signal that my move would be welcome, before I came on to anyone. Charlotte, at the very beginning of our relationship, and again at the lead-up to our marriage, was enthusiastic at just the sound of my voice on the phone. Frances was similarly inviting. In every relationship I might have behaved like I was cocksure that I was wanted, but I never moved on it before the woman involved signaled me to come and get it.

Frances Loeb was a big deal at Lord & Taylor, which was a very big deal then for fashionable women. She was the sportswear buyer. Sportswear occupied the entire fourth floor, and that was her domain. Imperious and impeccable, a pencil in her prematurely gray hair, she crisscrossed her floor, weaving between the racks and tables, her perfect body astride—in playwright Larry Gelbart's words—"legs so long they looked like they would go on forever if there wasn't a floor to stop them."

I was altogether taken with the dramatic figure Frances cut, and when I learned the childhood she came out of I marveled at the distance she'd come. In a nutshell, she was in an orphanage until she was six, when she was adopted by a couple who were split as to whether they wanted a child. He very much did. She did not. He committed suicide when Frances was ten. Her mother remarried when she was twelve and her stepfather began making nocturnal visits to her bedroom when she was thirteen. The mother, who knew what was going on, died when Frances was nineteen and left a note to be sure her daughter knew how "terribly disappointed" she was in her.

Everything I knew about her difficult and colorful life before I appeared at her front door fascinated me and caused me to admire her more. She'd made it, and made it so well, in a man's world, through that horrendous childhood, two failed marriages, a half dozen relationships worthy of discussion over long dinners and packs of cigarettes, among them one or two that began, admittedly, as career builders (but she *did* care for the men), and several attractions that never made it to a relationship. And when, soon after we met, she was flying off to Paris on her first buying trip, everything I found strong and admirable about Frances's past became a threat.

A Parisian named Claude, a figure in the fashion world, weaved in and out of Frances's relationships. Their affair had ended years before but they remained good friends. I liked what I knew of Claude. Amazing how abruptly that feeling was reversed when Frances so matter-of-factly told me that her old friend Claude had found her a lovely suite at a charming little hotel and was taking the time out of his busy schedule to show her Paris. In an instant I became obsessively jealous. I hated and feared Claude and loathed the words *lovely* and *charming* as applied to a hotel room. I asked the William Morris Agency to find me a super suite in the finest hotel in Paris. Frances checked it out at my request, granted me it was lavish, but garish, too, and asked me to understand if, in Paris, she chose "lovely and charming" over "lavish and garish." Manfully I said I did, and shriveled boyishly inside.

The following day I made an appointment with Frances's psychiatrist. I didn't understand at the time that seeing me without his patient's knowledge was a violation of her trust, a violation he compounded by asking me to keep our meeting confidential.

Her psychiatrist was Nathaniel Breckir, like Frances a striking figure. Because he'd had polio as a child, one leg was shorter than the other. He walked with a singular limp and an antique cane, and he wore an evening cape, usually off the shoulder, and a homburg hat. At the sight of him you felt it was the early 1900s and there had to be an opera house nearby. As befitted his appearance, he spoke softly, struck poses during pauses, and seemed to be a very wise man. He assured me that Frances and Claude were friends only and that Frances wouldn't be unfaithful under any circumstance. Then he spoke of Frances as a person and as a patient, and I heard something that touched me to the core.

He described Frances as "the most alone person" he had ever met. He didn't say she was lonely. She was alone, the most alone person he had ever met. I cannot overemphasize the effect on me of those words. I knew what it was like to feel completely alone in the world.

WHILE LIVING IN NEW YORK, I flew out to Los Angeles to see Ellen as often as I could, and on her school breaks she visited me. Since it was three hours earlier in L.A., I was able to touch base with her just about every morning before she went to school, often before she was out of bed. The divorce consumed more cross-country telephone time, endless conference calls in various combinations between me, my accountant, my attorney, Charlotte's accountant and attorney, and, of course, Dr. Luster, whose job it was to interpret Charlotte's feelings and reactions. While necessary, these long-distance calls were expensive as hell and were of mounting concern, until suddenly the impossible occurred and I might as well have owned the phone company.

One day I'd just hung up after a conference call when the phone rang again. It was the conference operator, inquiring in a working-class Boston Irish accent as to whether my call had been properly completed. I said it was and thanked her for her courtesy. She assured me I was welcome and then stunned me by asking if I had talked with my daughter in Los Angeles that day. It seemed that she'd heard me talk about Ellen on a conference call a day or two earlier and was touched by the idea that we talked daily. And then she wondered if I would like her to get Ellen on the phone for me tomorrow. Thus began a four-year relationship that saw Mary—she would never reveal her last name—become an integral member of the extended Lear clan, placing just about all of their long-distance phone calls from that point on, gratis.

Over time I teased out Mary's story. She was a girl from a poor South Boston family who'd gotten a job with the phone company. She was in her early twenties when, reporting to work one winter's day, she fell on the ice in front of the building and sustained a serious spinal cord injury that confined her to a wheelchair. The settlement her family negotiated was not a payoff but lifetime employment as a conference call operator. With the latitude that accompanied her special circumstance, Mary sat unsupervised with the means to connect people anywhere to people everywhere, while also allowing her to listen in on—and live vicariously through—a lot of lives.

She certainly seemed to revel in mine as it unfolded in front of her. Whether it was the attorney-client discussions that shaped my career, family matters and crises across the board, every aspect of my divorce, the fresh relationships that came from my meeting Frances Loeb, or the courtship that led to our marriage, Mary was involved in all of it. It never troubled any of us that Mary was eavesdropping, or that we were using the company's goods and services without paying for them. But that's no worse than declaring a social lunch a tax-deductible business expense, an early accounting lesson taught to us by the very best and brightest. Far more sophisticated today, thousands of high-paid attorneys, accountants, and number crunchers have found sufficient twists, turns, and loopholes in the law to sell us all—we consumers and our political, social, and business leaders alike—the kind of bull that someone I knew well used to merchandise as lollipops.

IN THE SUMMER OF 1955 *The Martha Raye Show* had been renewed, my divorce was moving forward but with great difficulty, the relationship with Frances was building furiously, and my father was hit by a train in a truck he claimed had stalled at a railroad crossing. There were no witnesses and he lay near death for a week before recovering, so his claim to his truck having stalled went uncontested. My mother thought differently, however, and I learned piecemeal over the next year how H.K. had worked himself into more trouble than he'd ever known, enough for him to consider suicide many times over.

There were numbers of farmers of fairly recent Scandinavian origin throughout Connecticut in the 1950s, and Herman K. Lear, president and chief executive officer of Norclaire Builders, combed the countryside to sell them that add-on garage, new kitchen, or playroom they desperately needed. Wary of New World banking practices, these Old Worlders preferred to pay cash, and that was perfectly fine with Mr. Lear. He'd sell the addition for, say, $795, take the money, and then have the farmer sign something to confirm the deal. That "something" was actually a promissory note that Mr. Lear promptly discharged at his bank for a second payment of $795. Of course the promissory note had to be paid back. All that was required in order to raise the money was the sale of another attachment. What complicated that for Mr. Lear, however, was that the bank expected the payback from the farmer, and was in the habit of sending out monthly notices regarding the payments. Those notices went out around the first of the month. Now all H.K. had to do was to pilfer some rural mailboxes of those notices and see personally that the bank got its money.

When he wasn't frantically trying to sell that new garage or playroom to catch up, H.K. had four mailboxes he had to get to on time each month and two more such situations developing. In my mind's eye I forever see Dad's truck on a railroad track, just the other side of a sharp bend. Stalled? Or parked there?

THAT SUMMER I rented a cottage on Fire Island, two doors away from Carl and Estelle Reiner. Ellen, nine years old now, spent a month with me. The four Reiner kids meant a lot to her that summer, especially Rob, who was within a few months of her age. He was playing with Ellen one day, showing her how to play jacks, when I first thought, "That kid is funny."

By nine years of age Rob had already spent scores, if not hundreds, of hours in the company of Jewish comics and writers. He never attempted to imitate them, he simply sounded like one of them. He intonated, cocked his head, and used his hands like one of them. So when he sat on the floor with jacks in one hand and the ball in the other, telling Ellen how to toss the ball ("Not too high, you don't get points for how high") or how to pick up the jacks ("You don't grab, you scoop. No one ever taught you how to scoop?"), he was hilarious. Sixteen years later, watching him rehearse with Carroll O'Connor, I would be reminded daily of Rob on the floor with Ellen, teaching her jacks that summer on Fire Island.

Frances drove out from Manhattan every Friday night, usually bringing a friend or two with her. When we were planning the summer, before Ellen ever heard of Frances, I thought it would all go down best if Ellen met some of Dad's friends, one of whom was Frances Loeb. Of course Ellen went to bed first, so there was no problem with Frances sleeping with me—until morning, that is. I handled that brilliantly, I thought. I woke Ellen every morning for a father-daughter breakfast date, and by the time we returned, Frances and friend would be up and having their breakfast. It was many months later, after Ellen and Frances had become close, that I asked my daughter if she had known what had been going on that summer. Summoning up every ounce of the pity youth takes on their elders' blindness, she gave me that roll of the eyes for parents only and said, "Are you kidding??"

———

ONE NIGHT THAT SUMMER the Reiners had a group of us over and Carl, playing the host of a TV talk show, started to interview several of us on a portable tape recorder. When he got to Mel Brooks he got to a man who seemed to know everything. Somewhere in the interview Carl asked Mel how he could have known about something that took place centuries before, and Mel said he was there when it occurred. Carl had to ask, "How the hell old are you, anyway?" Came the answer, "I'm two thousand," and what had been a routine that amused Sid Caesar and his writers on *Your Show of Shows* started to go wide. By the end of that summer the entire island was gathering at one house or another to hear Carl Reiner interview the 2,000 Year Old Man.

AS HARD AS ED AND I WORKED, as little as we slept, and as much Dexedrine and Seconal as it took to keep us on our toes and our backs, our time in New York doing those one-hour book-musicals with Martha Raye was a gas. In 1955 television was still a baby, and among its babysitters, Simmons and Lear were on the A list. We lived in a showcase apartment. We were invited to many but had no time to join more than a few of the three- to four-martini lunches at Toots Shor's, *the* place to be seen during the fifties, named after its big, bear-hugging, backslapping host. From Mickey Mantle to the chief justice, you weren't as "in" as you thought if your entrance didn't earn a big welcome by Toots.

I've often wondered if the casual male hug wasn't born and raised at Toots's place, from which it matriculated to the late-night TV talk show, where the male guest always made his entrance to the thundering sound of the house band, into the waiting arms of his host, and hugging became an accepted male ritual nationwide. To me, Toots Shor's place and the multiple-martini lunch best reflected the Madison Avenue mood of that time—what, as a result of the hit show, the current generation looks back on as the *Mad Men* years.

Early in the 1955–56 TV season the writing was on the wall regarding the demise of *The Martha Raye Show*. Two back-to-back shows did us in with the sponsor, Revlon, and specifically with its boss and creator of the brand, Charles Revson. I liked Mr. Revson. He had a reputation for being gruff but I found him direct and agreeable. Revson wasn't the biggest fan of Martha Raye personally, but he appreciated her popularity and the ratings the show delivered. When the shit hit the fan, however, he let us know in no uncertain manner. And soon thereafter let us go.

In September 1955 *The $64,000 Question* was a phenomenal hit CBS quiz show. It was one of the highest-rated shows on television, hosted by a man who later became a good friend, Hal March, and who still later starred on Broadway in the Neil Simon play that became Bud Yorkin's and my first film, *Come Blow Your Horn*.

One week, twelve-year-old spelling whiz kid Gloria Lockerman won the $64,000 prize and, as *Jet* magazine described her, "emerged as the brightest Negro juvenile entertainer since the heyday of boogie woogie pianist Sugar Chile Robinson." In the heat of that moment, Eddie and I booked young Gloria to appear on our show and wrote a story about a little girl's fantasy in which Martha played her Good Fairy and that week's guest, the great and fierce stage star Tallulah Bankhead, played her Bad Fairy.

The show was hilarious, the studio audience fell in love with the girl (as did Martha and Tallulah), and during the final bows both women showed it by hugging and kissing her. A number of viewers in this pre–civil rights era were disturbed, and it was reported that letters of protest "flooded" the Revlon ad agency. As I would learn in the seventies, a dozen protest letters from among millions of viewers were considered a "flood" to an advertising agency, also referred to as shit hitting a fan. In the fifties, however, the shows were produced by the ad agencies representing the sponsors, not the networks, and so the Young & Rubicams, BBDOs, and J. Walter Thompsons of the time had far more power regarding content than they do now. Charles Revson and his team insisted that they did not take personal exception to the tenderness expressed so publicly by Martha, Tallulah, and Gloria Lockerman, but they had a product to protect and were obligated to take *corporate* exception to the incident. "I'm sure [Martha] can be entertaining without being so physical and unwomanly," was Mr. Revson's carefully worded admonishment.

Our guest star on the next show was the distinguished actor and motion picture star Douglas Fairbanks Jr. In the course of the story we developed for him and Martha, we based one scene on an old vaudeville and burlesque sketch known as "Guzzler's Gin." Our rewrite had Martha trying to make a very special tropical drink for Fairbanks's character. While the drink was supposed to be without alcohol, Martha was unknowingly using a mislabeled bottle of fruit juice that contained an appreciable amount of whiskey. Not satisfied with what she was preparing after tasting it, and tasting it again, she tossed it down rather than offering it to Fairbanks, and started over. She was, of course, getting soused.

In rehearsal I asked Martha not to play drunk, but rather to play tipsy. And to play tipsy as one of the great cinema queens, like Irene Dunne, Loretta Young, or Myrna Loy, would play it. Martha Raye, elegantly tipsy à la Myrna Loy, mincing about on her tippy toes, was an outrageously funny Martha Raye. I was overjoyed and proud of her performance and told her after dress rehearsal not to change a hair for me. But as luck would have it, as I went on to give production notes to others, Martha's husband, Nick Condos (a former dancer and Mob favorite) visited her after watching the dress rehearsal from the back of the theater.

"What the fuck are you doing, woman?" he asked her. When she told him how I directed her to play it, he blew his top altogether.

"Myrna fucking Loy?" I was later told he had screamed. "What is this Myrna Loy shit? You're Martha Raye! You're *funny*, for Christ's sake!"

At eight P.M. we were on the air live. Martha, able to please only one boss at a time, chose her husband. When the scene came up, I, her clueless director, stood by helplessly as tipsy swiftly gave way to sloppy drunk, and as Charles Revson's words "physical and unwomanly" flashed in neon before my eyes, there was Martha sluicing from the bottle, pouring it into her cleavage, tossing it up into her armpits, and finally spraying it from her aforementioned unusually large mouth directly into the face of Douglas Fairbanks Jr. As swaths of makeup ran down Mr. Fairbanks's face, Mrs. Fairbanks was standing nearby in the wings looking at a TV monitor and roaring with laughter.

Martha brought the house down. A live audience will always howl over such chaos. They know that something unscripted has happened and they're thrilled to have been there to see it because it happens so rarely. To everyone who's not part of that "in" group, though, it feels like they don't care about you and they're just carrying on for their own amusement. To the viewers at home—for example, at Charles Revson's home—it just seems self-indulgent and unprofessional.

With that, *The Martha Raye Show* was canceled with just a few shows left to deliver. One of the last guest-starred Errol Flynn, Captain Blood himself, the only swashbuckler since Douglas Fairbanks Sr. who also made it to matinee idol. Mr. Flynn's swashbuckling wasn't limited to the silver screen. So celebrated by the press were his predilections for booze and young women, some underage, that any man who was scoring with a woman in those years was described as "in like Flynn." We of *The Martha Raye Show* caught up with Mr. Flynn after thirty-some years of swashing and buckling, three years before he died of a heart attack. He looked worn, his in-like-Flynn persona still in play but on automatic. So was his appetite for sex. Our dancers knew that. He hit on them because it was expected of him. He had no other investment.

THE END OF MAY saw the end of *The Martha Raye Show*. Meanwhile, my divorce settlement talks were still going on. Charlotte's attorney, as my father would say, was "a pip, a real pip." I was awed by the fact that the man had nine children. It moved me to listen to him more than I might have otherwise, and he came up with a very unusual proposal. He said he had represented several women whose magnanimous divorce settlements provided them a way of life that, in most cases, they would have to give up were they to fall in love and wish to marry again. As a divorcée Charlotte could easily be in that category, and this was his recommendation: Should she remarry, all alimony would expectedly cease immediately. If, however, within two years of that marriage she left her husband, the alimony would return in full. By allowing her room for a mistake, I would be encouraging Charlotte to feel far less at risk should she wish to enter a relationship that might result in marriage. It made no business sense to my attorney, who flatly rejected the idea, but it appealed to me as sane and commonsensical. Overriding the advice of others who were more numbers oriented, I accepted it. (Mary liked it, too.)

With the agreement finally in place, I left for Las Vegas in late October to set up temporary residence. Divorces were granted in Vegas in six weeks, as long as one partner in the proceedings had been a resident for that amount of time. Proof of that residency was a witness who charged "no more than the daily rate for a good hotel room"—an exceptionally good hotel room, it turned out—who would testify to having seen me every day during that period. My witness, like the many I'd heard about, had a vivid imagination, sufficient to have imagined seeing me all the days I wasn't there—likely about half the time—because I was in Los Angeles. After months without a paycheck, with my alimony and child support choking me, and within weeks of getting married again, money was a big concern, and the stolen time in L.A. was spent writing original material at night and looking for assignments during the day.

My six-week Las Vegas residency was up and I was a free man on December 7—the fifteenth anniversary of the bombing of Pearl Harbor. Frances, having left Lord & Taylor and closed her apartment, arrived in Las Vegas on the sixth. I had arranged for a rabbi to marry us in his home the next day, as soon as my divorce was final and I had the decree in my hands. The rabbi cautioned me to be sure we got to him before sundown, as the seventh was a Friday and of course he couldn't work on the Sabbath.

The decree wasn't in my hands, however, until midafternoon; we were due to fly back to L.A. that night, and with everything else there was to do, the sun was setting as the three of us—Ed having flown up to be my best man—finally set out for the rabbi's house. On the way there, as the sky darkened, I imagined the rabbi turning us away and our having to get married at one of the ever-ready chapels that dotted the landscape. But as we drove up his street I reflected on his being a rabbi in a resort town, Las Vegas, no less, so I had two hundred-dollar bills in my right hand as I stepped out of the car in the twilight. When he opened the door his look said "So sorry," but it quickly became a bright "Come in" as he shook my hand. Half an hour later, courtesy of the Resort Rabbi, Frances and Norman Lear were at the start of their nearly thirty-year marital journey together.

Ed peeled off after the ceremony so the bride and groom could have dinner together. Frances chose the dinner show at Caesars Palace, where Milton Berle was playing. She had never seen Mr. Television in person and he cracked her up totally that night. But it wasn't the laughs she remembered through the years, it was what took place when we went backstage to see him. With a full line of chorus girls and other acts, the star's dressing room was kind of small. Milton was sitting down, bathrobe open, in his boxers, when he yelled his "Come in!" Even if he hadn't been touching himself, his package had not been exaggerated. Still, his bathrobe remained open as we chatted and we had all we could do to look Uncle Miltie in the face as we talked. At one point Milton asked me, "You smoke cigars, don't you? Somebody just gave me some great ones." When I said yes, he shouted to the closed door, "Schvartz! Hey, Schvartz!" Yiddish for "black one," Berle's incantation saw the door open and his black valet enter. He wore a smile that looked like it had been stamped there. "Schvartz, Mr. Lear likes a good cigar, get him one." Immediately next to where Miltie sat, there hung his suit jacket. It all but grazed his face. The valet reached into an inside pocket, maybe a foot and a half from his boss's left arm, and withdrew a cigar for me. If Berle thought that was funny, I was grateful that Frances did not.

4

I FOUND A COZY BUNGALOW on Mulholland Drive with a master bedroom that had an unobstructed view overlooking the San Fernando Valley. Our king-sized bed had a headboard with a cutout that allowed us to lie on our stomachs with the valley spread out like a city planner's model in front of us. At night, in the distance, the twinkling model met the twinkling sky and I felt a great peaceful oneness. Three months later Frances was pregnant and Ed and I were still out of work. Though the situation was serious, we did turn down a few jobs that offered too little money. We had been very highly paid, and an equivalent salary was simply not available to us. Close but no cigar was an opportunity to be head writers of *The Perry Como Show,* a musical-variety hour on NBC. The show came out of New York so we couldn't push hard in person. We relied on our agent—nameless here to spare any of his descendants who might be reading this any discomfort—at MCA, The Octopus. It was MCA that had put the show together in the first place and we had an outstanding reputation in New York, so overall we felt very good about our chances.

Our agent said he had pitched us on the phone and had written a very strong letter singing our praises. Only a day after his letter was due to have arrived, we learned that another team had been hired. He said he was sorry and reassured me he had done his best, but I couldn't shake the feeling that he hadn't. The writers who got the job happened to be MCA clients also. I went to see him and, "just for the heck of it," asked to see the letter he'd written on our behalf. He didn't take the request as casually as I intended, and asked why. I couldn't add more than that I was interested to see it.

"You don't believe me," he said.

"It isn't that," I fumbled.

"What is it, then?" he asked directly. Feeling him to be as threatened by the situation as he likely was, I tried to tell him it was simply my curiosity as to what he'd written.

"Norman," he interrupted, "I can't sit here and let you imply I lied. I wrote the letter. It went."

"Then show it to me," I choked. It was clear that, whatever the outcome, our relationship would not recover from this. He picked up the phone and asked his secretary to bring him that Simmons and Lear letter he'd written to the Como show, then turned to me, told me she'd gone to the file room to get it, and, too hurt to spend another moment with me, asked me to wait in the empty office adjacent to his. Too restless and upset to sit, I paced that office and then ventured out into the hallway. His secretary was in a cubicle outside his office, with a telephone at her ear, typing something. I strolled over to her desk and saw that, from behind his closed door, he was dictating the letter she was typing. This was his last act as our agent, and we avoided each other from that moment on.

WITH A BABY ON THE WAY, I was just about broke when my friend Bud Yorkin threw me a lifesaver. Actually the lifesaver was meant for both Ed and me, but Ed had a problem with it. Bud, who had been a stage manager on *The Colgate Comedy Hour* in New York, became its director sometime after we moved to L.A. and was now producing and directing Tennessee Ernie Ford's weekly hour on NBC. He offered us a job on the writing staff, headed by a writer named Roland Kibbee, but the show couldn't pay more than $1,500 for the slot we were being invited to fill. We were almost back to our beginnings,

$750 each, and Ed categorically refused it. We'd last earned more than $10,000 for the team and he wouldn't accept the full $1,500 if it were offered to him alone.

We were sitting at the counter at Schwab's Pharmacy on Sunset Boulevard, where Lana Turner was famously discovered, when I told Ed that I just might have to accept the offer. There were a couple of possibilities at much higher salaries still out there, and Ed thought it would be a mistake not to give it a few more months. But we'd seen a number of those possibilities vanish in the past year, and I had Charlotte, Ellen, and Frances to support, with a baby due in December. Hans Conried's words about the importance of working for work's sake were ringing in my head, too, as I told Ed, finally, that I was going to take the job. Our lives, just like Lana Turner's, took a huge turn on the stools at Schwab's.

We went off in different directions and consequently didn't have much contact during the years that followed. He and my cousin Elaine divorced, so that connection, too, was ended. After helping Dean Martin craft his nonchalantly drunk persona, Eddie went on to write for Red Skelton, Carol Burnett, and Vicki Lawrence. He also wrote a delicious little book of poetry, *I'm Okay and Neither Are You.* In the nineties he was a big hit lecturing about comedy at OASIS, a center for senior citizens, and called one day to ask if I would be a guest lecturer. One spring afternoon, Simmons and Lear, in their seventies now and drenched in nostalgia, were a heartwarming success with a few of their peers and a number of their elders. Eddie passed away the next year, in 1998.

I'M OFTEN STRUCK by the consistency of the themes that run through my life, so there is something satisfying and appropriate about my first solo job as a TV writer having been for country singer Tennessee Ernie Ford, who crossed over to the top of the charts in 1955 with the biggest of the midcentury protest songs, "Sixteen Tons." It was a dark ballad about the life of a coal miner, with an unforgettable chorus:

You load sixteen tons, what do you get
Another day older and deeper in debt
Saint Peter don't you call me 'cause I can't go
I owe my soul to the company store

Not that Ernie Ford was any man's rebel. His catchphrase was "Bless your little pea-pickin' hearts," and he recorded enough religious music over the course of his career to wind up in the Gospel Hall of Fame. It was I, I guess, who heard it as one of the early protest songs, nurturing my equal opportunity and fairness sensibilities, and my respect for those the establishment labeled "the blue-collar class."

When I worked with Ed Simmons it was I who steered. If what made sense to Ed didn't make sense to me, we worked until it did. If I didn't find it satisfying, we worked until I did. And so it was throughout my career, except for the man I came to work for on the Ernie Ford show, the head writer, Roland Kibbee. There were times working with Kibbee when the jokes were good and made sense to me, but they had to make a more refined kind of sense to him, and he would not settle for less.

I learned from Kib that just about anything can be improved, and that reaching for perfection, not necessarily achieving it, was worth the effort. He couldn't tolerate a false note, not in the slightest of sketches or among the jokes in a monologue. The monologue had to have structure, or, as Kibbee put it, "a spine." It seemed to me from then on that everything, from a relationship to a simple dinner conversation, benefited from a structure, a spine.

The need for things to ring true grew in me because of my experience with Kib, and I can't think of anything anyone ever taught me about writing that was more important. I couldn't have had this career without having taken this to heart and mind.

Just as I can't overstate Kibbee's influence on me, neither can I overstate the torture I put myself through when it came to writing my portion of the show. I was light and funny when I sat with the writers and we pitched ideas for the sketches, the guest star, and the subject of Ernie's monologue. The monologue was my beat. It was to be three to four minutes long, and I had two days to write it. I'd sit at my typewriter for those days, starting and stopping, firing and misfiring, mountains of crunched paper building in the wastebasket beside me.

By nightfall I'd clocked six to eight hours at the typewriter, smoked a couple of packs of Old Gold cigarettes, and spoken to my shrink several times, until the shit in my head bid fair to explode. And then, at, say, two A.M., the very last minute, the shit inexplicably drained, my head cleared, and I wrote, rewrote, and tweaked the monologue. I finished, a happy man, around five A.M., got a few hours' sleep, and arose in time to shower and drive to the studio, eager to hear Ernie read my words and confident of the laughs he was going to get.

Guests on the Ernie Ford show included Jane Wyman, Charles Laughton, José Ferrer, Ronald Reagan, Rosemary Clooney, and Lee Marvin, among many others who brought a good deal of attention to the show—and to us writers. So much attention that after just one season I was asked if I'd like to write and produce *The George Gobel Show*, a giant half-hour hit that was expanding to an hour early in 1958 on NBC. My salary was equal to what I was making when Simmons and Lear were riding high.

IN OCTOBER 1957, Frances and I moved into a larger and more expensive home, nursery included, also off Mulholland. On December 13, my darling daughter Kate came into the world. On December 23, Herman K. Lear left it.

It was difficult to leave my newborn daughter to face the reality of my father's death across the country. Talking to my mother on the phone, I felt the pain begin. Not that she phoned me herself to tell me Dad had died. My sister gave me the news and added that there was to be a funeral in a few days. I was surprised because H.K. had spoken often about wanting to be cremated when he died, with no funeral. H.K. hated funerals. When I phoned my mother and reminded her of that, her answer, of course, was, "Oh, please."

I got to Hartford and the funeral home as they were about to transport the body to the synagogue. When several men arrived to pick up the casket, I asked them to hold it open a moment longer. It was then that I learned that, according to Mrs. Lear's instructions, this was to be an open-casket funeral service, something H.K. particularly despised. I could have slapped my mother. This wasn't just adding insult to injury, I thought, this was the crown jewel of her narcissism. And of course it played out just that way. After the service, led by a dreary rabbi who knew nothing about my father but never met a corpse for whom he couldn't find some empty rhetoric to indifferently intone, they had a hard time pulling the weeping widow away from her beloved. It was one of her better performances.

As she carried on, I had that moment I'd asked for in the funeral parlor. Dad lay there, so calm and serene in his velvet-lined coffin, looking for all the world like he'd just left the barbershop, tipped munificently for his haircut and shoe shine, and was ready now for his lunch date with a lady lobster at Christ Cella.

The official cause of death was coronary thrombosis, but the H.K. we all knew was never the same after the train hit him. The old H.K. passed away two years before his actual death. Cleaning up after him took several visits to Hartford and, between the bank and the several farmers he bilked and still owed money to, something like $100,000. Earlier I labeled my father's activities as "shoddy." That was as far as I allowed myself to go to avoid calling him a thief.

I knew him. I knew his fingers and his strumberries and his bathroom fragrance. I saw him leap over a bush once when I was five. I saw him sing "Ol' Man River" in some show the temple put on when I was little and he was ten feet tall. I saw him tip a shoe shine boy a whole five-dollar bill once. I saw him order female lobsters, and listen to *The Lone Ranger,* and nap on the living room floor, and roll around there with me when Notre Dame beat Ohio State. I saw him in my rearview mirror, chasing me across Connecticut so I could take my date to the theater in his new car. I saw him come home in the evening, worn, so worn, but carrying the dry cleaning and groceries my mother had him pick up, and I saw him the following morning, as bright as a penny—or was that a slug he was calling a penny?—then off with a smile and a shoe shine to take on the world. And, it tears at me to say it, I saw him, more than once, found out. My dad, "found out."

If H.K. was a marvel of sorts, so were Archie Bunker, George Jefferson, and Maude Findlay, among others. They were all entertaining marvels, examples of what I think of now as the H.K. genre. Larger than life, they were all repositories of that need to be seen and heard and understood, even as they showcased themselves, and dealt with in others, the foolishness of the human condition. That foolishness, it occurs to me, includes a fellow in his tenth decade as he writes this, still seeking to create a dependable full-blown father figure out of two letters of the alphabet.

THE GEORGE GOBEL SHOW was as strong and joyful a building block as I could have wished for at this transition in my career. Lonesome George, as he called himself, started as a country singer who gained more favor talking to his audience than singing. He was a sharp, witty, and astringent commentator, but his look and personality were his most unique features. Stated simply, George Gobel was adorable. At a time when TV variety shows opened with big music and big sound, the Gobel show would open cold. Lonesome George, in black and white, was standing there talking, alone and endearing. No one else at the time could have pulled that off.

As before with Martha Raye and Nat Hiken, I inherited *The George Gobel Show* from another great comedy writer, Hal Kanter. It was a half-hour show at first, Saturday night at ten on NBC. Wherever you were, whatever you were doing, as long as you were near a TV set everything stopped for George Gobel on Saturday night. No less than Milton Berle or Martin and Lewis or Ed Sullivan before him, George Gobel was "it" when NBC decided to expand his show to an hour and hired me to write, produce, and shape it.

A character in George's monologue was his wife, Alice, previously played by Jeff Donnell. I delivered Alice in the person of Phyllis Avery, a piquant actress who innately shared George's innocence. And, having spent years scouring the Off- and Off-Off-Broadway scene when I lived in and visited New York, I brought out, for their first time in Hollywood, Rue McClanahan, Carl Reiner, Tony Randall, Bea Arthur, and Paul Lynde, among others. Our guest actors from then on featured dozens of New York theater people, including Dabney Coleman, Conrad Bain, Bill Macy, Jean Stapleton, Bob Balaban, John Amos, Sherman Hemsley, and Barnard Hughes.

Ron Meyer and Mike Ovitz, two of the founders of Creative Artists Agency, the largest talent agency in the world today, have said that when they started out in the seventies and we had multiple TV shows on the air, they would hang out at our rehearsals to meet our stage-trained East Coast talent and seek to become their West Coast representatives.

BUD YORKIN AND HIS WIFE, Peggy, and Frances and I became close friends in this period. The Yorkins had two children, Nicole and David, who were the same ages as our Kate and Maggie (who was born April 16, 1959), and nothing can bring two families closer than having kids who are growing up together. We were inseparable, especially after we Lears moved into a home in Encino, just a few blocks away from the Yorkins. Until Kate and Maggie were ten or so we spent virtually every weekend around our pools. I carried a large attaché case, I recall, filled with water guns of various shapes and sizes. Half the time Bud had a kid on his shoulders trying to rip a kid off my shoulders. The Kibbees, with slightly older kids, came over in the late afternoon in time for a quick swim and a barbecue. Or we would all trek down for ribs at Monty's Steak House, where the kids crawling around beneath the table were literally underfoot.

When Ellen turned fourteen the law allowed her to decide which parent she wished to live with, and she chose us. She'd asked, even pleaded, to make the move several years before. Charlotte, however, insisted it would be wrong for Ellen because she needed her mother, and Henry Luster agreed. I offered to pay for a child psychiatrist the two sides would agree on and let him or her help with the decision. With the aid of doctor friends we came up with six local child psychiatrists for Luster and Charlotte to choose from. Luster tossed our list aside, offering to agree on one name and one name only. His choice was a nationally recognized child psychologist whose practice was located at the Austen Riggs Center in Stockbridge, Massachusetts.

I didn't trouble to ask Dr. Luster if he expected the Stockbridge doc to move to California to spend time with Ellen and the two homes and lifestyles she was to choose between, or whether Charlotte, Frances, Ellen, and I should move to Stockbridge. Instead, I told Ellen that any day she felt she had to be with us, she should take a taxi to Encino and there would always be someone at home to pay for it. She did that a number of times. It drove Charlotte nuts, but Ellen persisted, and she celebrated her fourteenth birthday by moving in with Frances, her sisters, and me.

IN OCTOBER 1958 Bud Yorkin caught the brass ring and it turned out to be gold. He produced and directed *An Evening with Fred Astaire*, a one-hour musical special on NBC, and the very first to be shot "in living color." It attracted enormous attention, was well conceived and produced, and earned nine Emmys, two of them Bud's. Already a known commodity, he became an overnight sensation in the musical-variety arena. Shortly after that the Yorkins and Lears met for a meal in Beverly Hills. We were walking to our cars afterward, Bud and Frances walking ahead of Peg and me, when Peg asked if I'd ever thought of teaming up with Bud—me writing, him directing, and producing jointly. We stopped for a nightcap to discuss it.

Some weeks later Bud and I formed Tandem Productions. The paperwork was handled by Bud's attorney, Greg Bautzer, the best-known, best-dressed, best-looking celebrity lawyer in the business. Greg was married to Dana Wynter, as ravishing a screen presence as ever there was. I've never thought of Dana

My first white hat.

My fourteenth summer,
working on Coney Island.

My maternal grandparents,
Lizzie and Shia Seicol.

My parents, Herman K.
and Jeanette Lear.

In uniform, with my sister,
Claire, and our parents.

I looked like this for ten minutes
in Rome one day.

Marrying Charlotte in Buffalo, New York.

Bomb crew Umbriago, 1944
(I'm standing on the right).

Our same crew, fifty years later.

With Ellen and
"Ginger, a dog I know."

With Dean Martin and Jerry Lewis.

Taking notes with Ed Simmons, Vincent Price,
Martha Raye, Hedda Hopper.

With (clockwise) Ellen, Frances, Maggie, Kate.

On the
Come Blow Your Horn
set with Bud Yorkin
and Frank Sinatra.

Maude.

All in the Family.

On the *Good Times* set.

The Jeffersons.

One Day at a Time.

Mary Hartman, Mary Hartman.

With Mary
and Tom Hartman.

With Martin Mull
(*Fernwood 2 Night*).

With Alex Haley and
our ten-year-old alter egos
(*Palmerstown, U.S.A.*).

With my TV families.

The original Fab 5: Frances and me with
(left to right) Ellen, Maggie, and Kate.

Yenem Veldt, our "other world" get-away group. Clockwise from top left: Carl Reiner,
Anne Bancroft, Frances, Pat Gelbart, Carol DeLuise, Dom DeLuise, Estelle Reiner, me,
Mel Brooks, Larry Gelbart.

Television Academy Hall of Fame induction: Milton Berle, me, Mrs. Edward R. Murrow (accepting for her husband), Robert Sarnoff (accepting for his father, David), Lucille Ball, Bill Paley, Bob Fosse (accepting for Paddy Chayefsky).

With Jerry Perenchio and Alan Horn.

With Hal Gaba, Howard Schultz, and
Concord's first CD for Starbucks.

Cartman and gang.

Declaration of Independence road trip.

Eightieth birthday.

Declare Yourself.

People For the American Way.

At long last,
with Lyn Davis Lear.

The second Fab 5:
Lyn and me with Brianna, Madeline, and Ben.

Godmother Maya Angelou with
Madeline, Ben, and Brianna.

Lyn and Ben
in the Lincoln Bedroom.

MY FAMILY OF FAMILIES

Me and my kids at The Gulley. Left to right:
Ben, Kate, Madeline, Brianna, Maggie, and Ellen.

Celebrating my eighty-fifth in Majorca: (back row) Jon LaPook, Daniel
LaPook, Ben; (middle row) Kate, Noah LaPook, Lyn, Brianna, me,
Madeline, Maggie, Dan Katz; (in front) Griffin Katz, Zoe Katz. Unable to
attend: my dearest darling Ellen.

without seeing her dazzling, bikinied body, and face to match, coming ever so slowly out of the surf in front of their beach home in Acapulco, Mexico.

Within the month, Bautzer made a development deal for Tandem at Paramount Pictures to do six TV pilots over a three-year period while allowing us to produce specials and develop films at the same time. The day we moved the company to Paramount, Bud and I could not have been more excited or confident. Peg and Frances surprised us with a tandem bicycle that was waiting for us on the lot.

Magic words, "on the lot." To be there was a dream come true. There were the five acres of New York sets and streets where *Breakfast at Tiffany's* and dozens more movies were shot; the Western Street that was home to *Bonanza;* the huge outdoor tank for close-ups of action at sea in a ton of movies; the European village where *Star Trek* and *Hogan's Heroes* would be filmed; two dozen soundstages for interiors; and, in the center of it all, a row of town houses that served as on-lot "homes" for Paramount's major stars. Dean and Jerry had houses there, as did Bing Crosby, Bob Hope, Danny Kaye, and Frank Sinatra. The sight of those guys tossing a football around of an afternoon was not unfamiliar.

Our deal at Paramount called for the development of TV series as well as films, so we hatched a few ideas and started working on them. One of them, *Band of Gold,* was in essence a small repertory company with the same actors playing different characters every week in a series of love stories. Those stories were to take place in or out of marriage, set in any time or location, requiring talents capable of playing a wide range of characters in tales symbolized by the *Band of Gold.* Happily, we found talents of extraordinary range who also made for a most handsome couple, James Franciscus and Suzanne Pleshette. The pilot episode, shot in black and white and directed by Bud from my script, turned out well. To sell the idea of the series and illustrate the versatility of our players we had to show our stars in a full half-hour story, and in several other scenes, playing a totally different couple each time.

In the full half hour, Jimmy played a European count and Suzanne a New York shopgirl. Then, combing through the standing sets on the Paramount lot, I found a fire escape on a New York tenement building that inspired me to write a Paddy Chayefsky–like love scene. On another stage there was a seventeenth-century ballroom, and I wrote a John Barry–like scene for a princess and a footman. Our pilot for the series consisted of four such scenes calling for different, contrasting characters played by Franciscus and Pleshette, tacked on to our complete half-hour episode.

That was what we sent over to Jim Aubrey, president and head of programming for CBS. Aubrey had a reputation for being tough and hard to deal with, and so it was a giant surprise when he called us that very day to rave about the show. He invited us over to tell us exactly when he was going to program it: Tuesday nights at eight-thirty. When we told him we were thinking of taking our wives to Acapulco for a long weekend of celebration, he wished us Godspeed and sent us off with an uncharacteristic hug.

I don't remember whether the industry had as yet tagged Jim Aubrey "The Smiling Cobra," but we had no trouble seeing him in exactly that light when we returned from Acapulco and learned that *Band of Gold* would not be airing after all, and that what we'd been told was to be our time slot had been passed to Keefe Brasselle, a now-and-then actor who was the cunning Cobra's closest friend.

A YEAR INTO OUR DEAL at Paramount, Neil Simon, who had worked for Ed Simmons and me on the Jack Haley show, heard that I had a studio deal and sent me a copy of the very first play he wrote, *Come Blow Your Horn*, which he believed was going to Broadway. We loved it, and I started working on the screenplay. The other projects in the hopper at the same time were a TV special with Bobby Darin, the young talent who had become a star overnight with a song called "Splish Splash" and an instant classic, "Mack the Knife"; another special, starring the multitalented Danny Kaye; yet another, starring Carol

Channing, the inimitable originator of Dolly Levi in *Hello, Dolly!*, and one starring Dick Cavett. Additionally, Bud and I made a pilot episode of a series, *Three to Get Ready*, about two pilots and a stewardess on international flights. We also did a most unusual special we called *Henry Fonda and the Family*—cowritten by me and Tom Koch, the driest comedy mind I knew—which used that year's census figures to hold a mirror up to the state of the American family; and we conceived of and executive-produced a one-hour musical-variety series for Andy Williams. Last in that period, Hugh Hefner and Tony Curtis, who were friends at the time, decided to do a film together—*Playboy*, with Tony to play Hef—and asked me to write an original screenplay. Except for *Playboy*, all these projects were completed and found their audiences in the two years before February 1963.

DAN SEYMOUR WAS the executive vice president of the J. Walter Thompson advertising agency in 1962, and he called on Bud and me to ask what we thought of doing a weekly variety series with Andy Williams. Andy had done a series on CBS and Seymour thought he was a terrific singer. He wondered, however, if he wasn't "too uptown," meaning too unfolksy for the products J. Walter Thompson had in mind to sponsor the show. We thought it funny, because Andy was from Wall Lake, Iowa, as folksy a town as one might find in America. But that gave us an idea. We sat down with Dan Seymour again and told him how we would bring Andy Williams "downtown" if we were given the opportunity. We would feature Andy as coming from Wall Lake, create some funny Wall Lake characters to interact with him, put him in a sweater, seat him close to the audience, and have him sing a set of down-home songs. Dan Seymour liked what he heard, as did Andy, and we got the order.

Busy as we were with other projects, our deal called for us to bring on a first-rate producer of musical variety for the day-to-day work, and for Bud and me to serve as executive producers. We hired Bob Finkel, long a highly re-garded producer of the genre. I had conceived of a pair of characters from Wall

Lake to fit the talents of a comedy team that I remembered from the days I was scouring Off-Broadway clubs and theaters. They were Marian Mercer and R. J. Brown, known as "The Prickly Pair."

Of course, for it to work, our producer, Bob Finkel, had to see what we saw in them, so we had them audition for him. He didn't get them. I decided to go over Bob's head and have Mercer and Brown audition directly for Andy, not in a cold rehearsal hall but in a crowded nightclub. I asked our former agents, MCA, for help, and a young agent, A. Jerrold Perenchio, was assigned to book the act into a club, which he did expeditiously and without fanfare—no small feat in Hollywood. Andy Williams liked Mercer and Brown, and the Wall Lake characters became part of the show.

The Andy Williams Show on NBC was a smash and ran for nine years. One of the talents responsible for its success, it pleases me to recall, was George Wyle, who came up with all the special material, arrangements, and medleys Andy did with his guests. Their product suggests to me that there was an entirely different individual work ethic at play back then. The bar was set higher. It just might be that they loved what they were doing more than their counterparts do today.

5

THROUGHOUT THIS PERIOD Bud and I had been shopping a film of the play *Come Blow Your Horn* that Neil Simon sent me. From the day we read it the only actor we could see in the lead was Frank Sinatra, and Paramount agreed to finance and distribute the film if we could get him. Getting Frank to read my script over the next year was equal to the wildest, craziest chase scene I could imagine. Howard Koch, who later went on to run Paramount Pictures, as dear a man as I knew in the business, was Frank's producer. He liked the script, thought Frank would be perfect in the leading role, and did all he could on his end to call Frank's attention to it. Nothing worked. I went on a mad campaign.

Come Blow Your Horn concerned an older brother, a bit of a rogue and a lothario played by Sinatra, who is tutoring a shy, introverted younger brother awakening to the ways of the world, especially the ladies. And so we changed the title to *Cock-a-Doodle-Do* to reflect that awakening more directly. Over many months, script in hand, I hunted down Mr. Sinatra all over town—at restaurants, hotel bars, a few recording studios, a men's shop, and once when I wormed my way into a secured soundstage where he was rehearsing with Judy Garland for a special they were doing.

They were at a microphone together when he saw me from across the stage some fifty feet away. I was as bald as I am today, but the hair I had was darker and cut very close. By then he'd seen me time and again over several months and knew my look well enough to have given it a name, because he stopped the music and yelled, "Is that The Helmet? How the fuck did The Helmet get in here?" And a big burly guy eased me out.

My gut told me that my actions had triggered something in Sinatra and he was getting a kick out of what he was putting me through. Not because he was a sadist, but maybe because he picked up on the hint of fun I was having and wanted to see how far I would take it. If so, he had to enjoy the cage of roosters we delivered to his home one morning along with another copy of *Cock-a-Doodle-Do,* and the box of toy trumpets we had at his front door on another morning after we changed the title back to *Come Blow Your Horn.*

I was close to losing hope of nailing Sinatra when I came up with an idea that I thought irresistible. No way could he deny me a look at the script after this. I would send him a reading nook, the corner of a room perfect for sitting down with our script. The "Reading Kit" consisted of a rug, an easy chair and ottoman, an end table, an ashtray and a pipe, a smoking jacket, a floor-model reading lamp, a record player with an album of Jackie Gleason's *Music to Read By,* and, of course, another copy of the script.

The Paramount prop department set up our Reading Kit in the back of a truck, where it looked ideal, the corner of a lush den waiting for the lucky reader. Howard Koch had assured us that the house was empty. Frank was flying in from New York that night with his valet and it was the other help's day off. Perfect. I made sure there was a long cord on the lamp and record player, and told the driver, since no one was home, to set up the delivery on the lawn, and be sure the light was on and the music was playing when he drove away.

It delighted me to imagine the look on Frank's face when he drove up his driveway that night and saw a lit lamp in the distance, heard music as he drew closer, and came upon this cozy reading alcove on the lawn near his front door. But it didn't work quite that way. Koch was wrong about there being no help on hand for Mr. Sinatra's arrival late that night. They showed up after the delivery of our Reading Kit but before their boss's arrival. Joke killers and tidy housekeepers that they were, they put the delivery away. All Sinatra knew about any of this for several days was that he had a smoking jacket in his closet that he couldn't recall buying. I, on the other hand, certain that Frank had found our delivery and, alas, did not appreciate it, was furious and wrote him off. His agent was informed that Frank wouldn't be troubled by me again. The agent, who hadn't heard about the latest stunt, called me and laughed when I described it. There was no way, he said, that Frank could have seen this and not reacted to it big-time. He simply did not know.

"Well, too late now," I said. A few days later I found myself joyously eating my words. Frank learned about the Reading Kit, loved the energy and creativity that went into it, and—this is the important part—had as good a time reading the script. I knew that for sure when he phoned me and, tongue in cheek, bawled the shit out of me for not getting it to him sooner.

The day *Variety* announced that we were making the film I got a call from Leo McCarey, one of the top movie directors of the forties and fifties. Mr. McCarey had just met with a recent graduate of his alma mater, Notre Dame, and was very impressed with him. His name was Tony Bill, he'd appeared in several productions at Notre Dame, and McCarey had a hunch he could be just what we were looking for to play Frank Sinatra's younger brother in our film. A meeting within an hour of the phone call resulted in a screen test the following morning, and a day later Tony had the role.

Tony, a gentleman and a scholar—his subject, the human species—is the only actor I have ever heard of who, after enjoying a brief brush with movie stardom, playing opposite Frank Sinatra in his first film and on his way to leading-man status, walked out on it all. Within a month of the film's opening at Radio City Music Hall, Tony was in my office to ask for some advice. He didn't like the nature of the attention he was getting, 90 percent of it having to do with his good looks. He thought himself far more serious than that and wondered if he shouldn't produce and direct rather than continue to perform. I advised Tony that, given these feelings, he should drop acting and follow his heart. He did, and most successfully.

For the mother I cast a great star of the Yiddish theater in New York, Molly Picon. The role of the father was written for the great character actor Lee J. Cobb, who played it on Broadway. Lee, a longtime friend of Roland Kibbee's, became a fixture in my life until his death in 1976.

Lee Cobb was regarded as one of the greatest actors of his day, notably remembered for his roles in *On the Waterfront* and *Twelve Angry Men,* and for creating the iconic Willy Loman in the Broadway production of Arthur Miller's *Death of a Salesman.* He was blacklisted in the fifties because of his "involvement in left-wing political causes and his support of political and charitable organizations alleged to be communist fronts." The blacklist hurt him so much that when *Salesman* went to film, despite the aura of greatness that followed him for the rest of his life as a result of his Willy Loman portrayal, Cobb was not offered the role. It was performed by Fredric March.

A year or more later, his family's needs unfilled, Lee had reached a point of desperation. As he asked himself when interviewed then by *The Nation:* "Why am I subjecting my loved ones to this? I am just as idealistic as the next fellow, but I just had to be employable again." He submitted to an interview with the House Un-American Activities Committee and pandered to them by naming names of some people he'd seen at events he'd attended that the committee held suspect. Every name he gave them had been mentioned before, so no one new suffered from Lee's testimony, but elements on the Left never forgave him for caving in.

One night Frances and I had a party and I mistakenly invited the director Marty Ritt (*Norma Rae, Hud*) and his wife, Adele, along with Lee and Mary Cobb. Marty had been blacklisted, too, refused to testify, and hadn't forgiven Lee, so he didn't go near him that evening. Adele Ritt chose to show her disdain for Cobb flagrantly. She sat in a folding chair facing a wall in the living room. It couldn't have been a stranger sight and every one of the sixty or so guests who came by had to know what was going on. That was what Adele wanted, of course, and she conducted her one-woman protest against Lee Cobb all evening. Her husband could have left early and taken his wife home, or Lee could have left early to spare his hosts, but there are no more stubborn, intransigent people than dyed-in-the-wool lefties, and neither Lee nor Marty would give the other that satisfaction.

ALSO IN THE CAST of *Come Blow Your Horn* was Phyllis McGuire, the youngest sister and the beauty in the famous singing trio the McGuire Sisters. Phyllis had a visitor on the set the day we were shooting the first of her two scenes. He was called to the phone a number of times and answered every "Call for Dr. Stern" in a strange, guttural voice with a "Yeah, Dr. Stern, ovah here." But for his phone calls, the good doctor seemed uninterested in what was going on to the point of napping on the set, until wardrobe brought a couple of leopard coats for Phyllis to choose between. She would be wearing one of them in an upcoming scene.

Phyllis was pleased with one of them but Dr. Stern asked to see a few more. To his chagrin, he was told that there were no other leopard coats in Beverly Hills at the time. My script called for a leopard coat for no reason that any snazzy coat wouldn't cover as well, and I told Dr. Stern as much. If looks could kill, I'd have been dead in a week.

"She looks good in leopard," Dr. Stern growled. "I like it." Two days later two racks of leopard coats were delivered to the set, one from Chicago and one from New York. They were sent overnight, courtesy of the notorious Mob boss Sam Giancana, longtime beau of Ms. McGuire's and a.k.a. our own Dr. Stern.

WE HAD A GOOD TIME on the set of *Come Blow Your Horn*. We'd heard Sinatra wasn't easy to work with, but by the same token we knew what to expect, so there were no surprises. Well, there was one. Frank was notorious for not doing retakes, and late one day I was on the set and suggested to Bud and Frank that they do another take of a scene they'd just shot. He refused.

"No retake, no way," he said.

To ease the moment I muttered something to the effect that I might agree with him after I'd seen the dailies. The first thing the next morning I looked at the scene in question and was even more certain that it needed to be reshot. I picked up the phone. Frank, whose day didn't start until eleven A.M., was in a makeup chair.

"Frank, I just looked at that scene and we really have to do it again," I began. He asked why, and I told him.

"My mother in New Jersey ain't going to notice that," he said.

"But, Frank—"

"Did you hear me, pally, there is no fucking way I'm doing that again."

"But we have to, Frank," I said earnestly.

"You give me one reason why," he fumed.

"Because I fucking said so," I exploded.

"Okay," he said. And *I* was frightened by what he perceived as my rage.

FRANCES AND I had been married six years when, one Monday morning in 1963, I was watching the previous Friday's *Come Blow Your Horn* dailies and someone ran into the dark screening room giddily calling out for me with a message from my attorney. Over the weekend Charlotte had gotten married! A bet I'd made years earlier had finally paid off.

Five years into that sledgehammer of a settlement, Frances and I had been discussing money matters and bemoaning the fact that Charlotte hadn't remarried as yet, when Ellen said, "Mom will never get married, Dad. She never meets anyone, she doesn't leave the house." That's how I learned that Charlotte wasn't working. I asked my attorney to call hers and ask why.

"She doesn't have to," came the answer.

I told my attorney to get the word to her that I'd give her a dollar for every dollar she earned if she went to work.

"On top of what she gets now?" the attorney gasped.

With an approving nod from my daughter I said, "Yes." While she didn't have to work, Charlotte liked money, and even though it took two more years, on the job she did finally meet the man she'd marry. That marriage didn't last two years, but before it ended she met the man she knew she would spend the rest of her life with. And she met him on the job also.

IN MAY 1963 the world premiere of *Come Blow Your Horn* was held in Palm Springs, home to Barbara Marx, then married to the fourth but least known Marx brother, Zeppo. It was there that Barbara met Frank Sinatra, whom she later married. I can't remember why Palm Springs was chosen for the premiere. The reason it's of any significance at all is that Barbara, still married to Frank when he died, thanked me several times over the years for staging the event, without which she and the Chairman of the Board, as he was also known, might never have met.

The opening of the film a few weeks later at New York's Radio City Music Hall felt more like a world premiere. Bud and I were beside ourselves. Radio City! Our film playing that most fabled of film palaces and music halls! And onstage, the Rockettes! We're talking long ago, when the sight of a line of twenty-four pairs of legs, bare from the hip, high-kicking in unison, could tear the house down. It was heady stuff for a forty-one-year-old teenager.

We had a party after the screening for friends and family, to which I invited Sinatra. Between us Bud and I invited about fifty people, more relatives than friends. There was no way I thought Frank would show up, but he did, and he hung in a while. I told my mother that Mr. Sinatra didn't like to be touched, and cautioned her to remember that when she met him. So of course when I introduced her she screamed, "Oh, Frankie, my Frankie!" and threw out her hands to bear-hug him. Good-naturedly he went along with it, but over her shoulder he muttered, "I think I banged this broad thirty-six years ago."

Since Sinatra died there have been a dozen books written about him, and it has pissed me off that no one ever sought to interview me. I have two stories about a side of him that has rarely been reported on, his respect for talent and his capacity for friendship. Both stories concern Lee J. Cobb, whom Frank idolized from the moment he saw him create the role of Willy Loman.

A few years after that, Cobb suffered a severe heart attack. Sinatra, who'd made a point of keeping up with his idol's welfare, learned of this and of the date Lee was to be released from the hospital. A day or two before, a registered nurse appeared at Lee J. Cobb's bedside on behalf of Mr. Sinatra, whom Cobb had never met. Mr. Sinatra, the nurse informed Cobb, was going on tour for the better part of a year and his home in Palm Springs, fully staffed, would be available for Mr. Cobb's recuperation and recovery. And some more years later, *Come Blow Your Horn* finally brought them together. Had I known this story when I was trying to get Frank to read the *Come Blow Your Horn* script and told him I wanted Lee to play his father, I might have saved myself months of outrageous begging.

Several years after the film, Sinatra came through for Lee Cobb once again. I got a call early one morning from Lee's wife, Mary. She was in tears. Lee, whose penchant for gambling was a family concern, was in Las Vegas and in serious trouble. Mary had just spoken to him and could tell from his voice that he'd been up all night. The fact that he wanted ten thousand dollars wired to him right away—ten thousand dollars the Cobbs could not spare—told the rest of the story. The only thing I could think to do was to call Frank. I left word in several places that Lee J. Cobb needed help and to call me as soon as possible. Within an hour I heard from Frank directly, and soon thereafter Sinatra's plane landed at McCarran Field in Las Vegas. Two weighty pilots, with the Sinatra imprimatur and the help of security, hauled Cobb out of the casino at the Sahara Hotel and flew him back to L.A.

AT ABOUT THE TIME *Come Blow Your Horn* opened, I finished my first draft of *Playboy*—to star Tony Curtis as Hugh Hefner—for Columbia Pictures. The film never came to pass. Tony and Hef had had a falling-out before my script was finished and the project was a no-go. But I spent some interesting time with Hef in Chicago and he visited me on the Paramount lot as we began the project.

He arrived late one afternoon in a chauffeured stretch limousine. We talked about the story I was working on, and when he was ready to leave I asked if he'd like to come home with me to have dinner with the family.

"Thank you, but I have very important work to do tonight," he said, pulling a few five-by-seven photos out of his pocket. The girl couldn't even have been twenty and, with or without clothes, was drop-dead gorgeous.

"Our March Playmate," he said. "I'm sending the car to pick her up in Encino."

"Encino? I live in Encino," I offered absently.

"She lives with her parents," Hef added.

"She lives with her parents?" I exclaimed, altogether shocked.

As someone who lived for years with his family in a modest house in an Encino cul-de-sac where a dozen couples and their thirty kids would hold holiday barbecues, take weeks to prepare for Halloween, and stay in touch for years after moving away, I held the photos up to Hef's face and rasped in astonishment, "You mean to tell me there's a family in Encino with an eighteen- or nineteen-year-old daughter that looks like this who's going to watch that daughter step into a block-long limo in front of their very own Encino home, to be carted off and delivered to Hugh Fucking Hefner?"

"Don't you know *anything* about this culture we live in?" he said. Who did I think those naked photographs of beautiful young women came from? They came from fathers and husbands. From brothers and boyfriends. From mothers and sisters, too.

Hef looked at me as one might look at a twelve-year-old on life support.

6

IN 1964, AT FORTY-TWO, I was fairly young as producers went then. As a result of my years in New York combing through the theater and night-club scene, often with my friends Jack Rollins and Charlie Joffe—manager/ mentors to Harry Belafonte, Mike Nichols and Elaine May, and Woody Allen—I was aware of theater talent in the East of which the insular Holly-wood cognoscenti were totally oblivious. My friend Howard Koch, who had become president of the Film Producers Guild, asked me to join that board, and at a meeting to discuss entertainment for an upcoming Lewis Milestone Awards dinner, I suggested Woody Allen to emcee, or at the least do a comic turn. I'd seen Woody in small Village nightclubs, "yearning to go back to the womb—anybody's," and found him unique and hilarious. Actually, I had already talked to Jack Rollins and knew that Woody would come out if invited. None of the illustrious names around the table, from Roger Corman to Stanley Kramer, had ever heard of Woody Allen at that point and they turned down the idea of invit-ing him. A year later, *What's New Pussycat?* was released and overnight made a household name of Woody Allen. He never accepted an invitation to perform at another such event.

Also in 1964, Bud and I were asked by Warner Bros. to produce and direct the film of Sumner Arthur Long's Broadway hit *Never Too Late*, for which he'd already written the screenplay. Ready to go, starring Paul Ford, Maureen

O'Sullivan, Connie Stevens, and Jim Hutton, it fit into a relatively short pocket of time, so we were able to take it on. The most memorable thing about that experience was coming to know Jack Warner. Jack emerged from among the four siblings to rule over the Warner Bros. studio and its output for forty-five years. He was Hollywood royalty, and was also a loudmouth and a vulgarian. To make matters worse, he thought he was funny, and he read as amusement the discomfort his antics caused in others. The choicest story of Jack Warner at his obnoxious peak was repeated so often over the years as to have become legend.

One day at lunch in his private dining room, his special guest of honor was Madame Chiang Kai-shek. It was one of those days when Jack's warped sense of humor was at the peak of its power to humiliate. Mr. Warner entered a minute or two after Madame Chiang, whom he had seated next to him at the head of the table. Everyone else was already sitting, among them Mervyn LeRoy, Ann Sheridan, and Farley Granger, along with several Chinese who were obviously accompanying the first lady of China. As Jack walked along the table to his seat he was introduced to the other Chinese guests and finally to Madame Chiang. He bowed courteously to her and then, looking down the table to the others in her party, smiled his version of winningly and said, "They will have my laundry by four P.M., won't they?"

My personal memories of Jack are two moments that occurred while watching our *Never Too Late* dailies with him. The film was about an older couple— she's fiftysomething, he's sixty—having a child. I had a scene where the husband has just learned that his wife is pregnant and he's going to sleep, and he's lying there in bed with his eyes wide open. She says good night, he says good night, she rolls over, and we fade slowly to black. We stay on black for an eternity, maybe twenty or thirty seconds with the screen totally dark, and then the dawn comes up ever so slowly, and we see him lying there with his eyes wide open in the same position. It was a great, great laugh. Jack Warner watched it and said, "What the fuck is that? There's nothing going on in that scene." To his credit, he didn't ask me to change it.

And, in his own abrasive way, he taught me a lesson I never forgot. After viewing a half dozen scenes and some terrific performances, he got up to leave and snarled, "That tie your star was wearing could catch flies. You want them listening to him or applauding his neckwear?"

WHEN PARAMOUNT BOUGHT the rights for Tandem Productions to make the film of *Come Blow Your Horn,* it also secured the rights for us to Neil Simon's next two plays, which turned out to be *Barefoot in the Park* and *The Odd Couple,* two of his biggest hits. They became hit films, too, but Yorkin and Lear had nothing to do with them. Foolishly and unintentionally I gave away our rights to those plays.

You could call what I did a crime of passion, with Bud and me the victims. My passion was for the story of a blacklisted radio performer who'd just won the largest judgment ever awarded in a libel case and had written a book about it, *Fear on Trial.*

Wisconsin senator Joseph McCarthy and the House Un-American Activities Committee were running rampant in the cold war era of the fifties, accusing dozens of prominent Americans of having Communist affiliations. The committee's favorite targets were high-profile people in the arts, and a for-profit corporation inspired by the committee, AWARE, Inc., became the leading tool for sniffing out the low-lying Commies. In 1955 they developed a nose for radio folk humorist and civil libertarian John Henry Faulk, who was fighting blacklisting. Having made the blacklist he was fighting against, by 1957 John Henry (as he was known) couldn't find work anywhere. With the support of such people as Edward R. Murrow and Walter Cronkite, the fabled New York attorney Louis Nizer took the case for a song and brought the suit that resulted in that record $3.5 million libel judgment. An appeals court later reduced it to $500,000, and accumulated legal fees took most of that, but the original figure remained for some time the symbol in the public mind of the court's rejection of blacklisting.

Fear on Trial and John Henry Faulk fanned the civil liberties embers in me that were present when I stood with my grandfather at parades and looked up to see him cry; when, alone in my bed with my crystal set, I learned with dismay that there were people who hated Jews; when I entered the American Legion National Oratorical Contest; when I started the Collegiate Defense Stamp Bureau; and when I enlisted in World War II. But I was pretty much alone in those instances. With John Henry Faulk I found a partner and mentor in those beliefs and stirrings, and one who had been articulating them long before he met me.

Then there was John Henry's inimitable sound. He informed and entertained our world in a nasal, syllable-stretching East Texas twang that sounded to this northeastern Jew how deep-down "Amurican" was supposed to sound and turned up every patriotic ember in me into a four-alarm fire. That fire in the belly for *Fear on Trial* made me neglect Tandem's option to bring Neil Simon's *Barefoot in the Park* and *The Odd Couple* to the screen. Fires in the belly can often melt minds.

Robert Redford and Elizabeth Ashley starred in the pre-Broadway summer theater production of *Barefoot* at the Totem Pole Playhouse in Bucks County, Pennsylvania. Since we were due to make the film, Bud and I flew east for a weekend on behalf of Paramount and Tandem to attend the opening. Only days before we were to leave for New York I read and fell in love with *Fear on Trial*, published in 1963, two years earlier. An inquiry into the film rights revealed they were still available and that John Henry was in New York discussing that very matter with his publisher. Before we boarded our plane on Friday I had reached him, gushed over his book, and we agreed to have an early breakfast Saturday morning. On the trip east Bud read the book and was as excited as I was about it.

Our Saturday meeting with John Henry, from early morning until midafternoon, when Bud and I had to leave for Bucks County, was a love-in. How do you not love a man who, in that East Texas drawl, says of some fatuous asshole in the news, "I'd like t'buy the somunabitch for what he's worth and sell'm for what he thinks he's worth!" After six hours of conversation about him and the blacklist and what turned out to be the incipient beginnings of the Moral Majority and the proliferation of evangelical TV ministries, we had a clear path to *John Henry and the Do-Right People*, a title—and what it implied—that I went mad for. The "do-right people" was an expression of John's reflecting the generous Christian angle from which he always approached individuals on the Religious Right. He chose to see them as people no different from everyone else, and no matter that they insisted you lost all standing as a Christian and would never make it to heaven and to Jesus if you did not see it their fundamentalist way.

On the way to Bucks County that's all we could talk about. We were excited about seeing *Barefoot*, the play, and elated to be the team charged with making the film. We knew we had to come clean about wishing to do another film first. We knew, too, that Paramount wanted to get started on *Barefoot* right away, however early in its Broadway run. But if Bob Redford, Neil Simon, and Mike Nichols, the director, didn't mind the film coming out later in the run, we thought the studio would go along.

Because it was a rain-filled weekend, Bud and I expensed a limousine to take us to and from Bucks County. In my early forties, and despite having earned some good money, I was still relatively broke and did not take being in a limo for granted. It was a big deal. And I knew it would be a big deal to Mike, Neil, and Bob, too. We were all pretty much at the beginning of our careers, and a limo from New York, no matter the pouring rain, screamed "Hollywood!" at the Totem Pole Playhouse in Pennsylvania. Bud and I were grateful that no one saw us as we arrived.

Barefoot in the Park was a hilarious piece of work, this production was excellent, and Robert Redford emerged into all of our lives and has maintained a presence there for fifty years. Bud and I knew it would be a big hit on Broadway, and it did indeed become the longest-running play by Neil Simon, winning three Tony Awards. But we knew, too, that we had to come clean about the John Henry project while we were together after the opening.

The audience was on its feet before the curtain fell and it was bedlam backstage. With all the celebratory hugging and kissing, the popping of corks from champagne bottles, and the explosive release of the anxiety that had been riding herd on cast and crew for months, it was impossible to broach the subject. And so we hugged, kissed, and extolled, too, but less as the participants we had every claim to be and more as the defectors that guilt made of us.

Mike and Neil walked us to the stage door, where the limo was so close that the overhang covered us to the backseat door. Surely they were expecting to hear something about how excited we were to be making the film of the crowd-pleasing play they'd just shown us. But even as we continued to laugh and pay them more compliments, we choked on the commitment we'd just made to John Henry to film his story next, and raved on about the great time we'd just had. We did that all the way through the handshakes, hugs, pats on the back, and into the limo with a cheery "Talk to you soon" before the door slammed.

Convinced we had hurt them to the quick, and worried that we'd made the mistake of our lives in terms of our own careers, Bud and I didn't say two words to each other on the way back to our hotel.

WHEN WE RETURNED to California I took the John Henry project to studio head Jack Karp, and told him that we'd like to make it our next film and how eager I was to start on the screenplay. I pointed out that there was no rush to film *Barefoot*, since it would surely run on Broadway for years. When Jack told me that Neil hoped he could write his own screenplay this time, I thought that strengthened our case. While Neil was working on his screenplay, I would be writing mine, and Bud and I would produce, and he direct, whichever film was ready first. Somehow, though, in the exchange of personal and informal inter-office memos that followed, my request was interpreted as a willingness—worse, a request—to drop Tandem's option to produce, in conjunction with Paramount, Neil Simon's second and third films so that we were clear to proceed with *John Henry and the Do-Right People*.

Although the film never got to production, my passion for it never waned.

John Henry the man and his one-in-a-million Southern Baptist liberalism had an enormous influence on my developing political activism. From my ninth year on the planet and my introduction to Father Coughlin, I was a kid version of a political junkie. In New York, around the time of my Bar Mitzvah, I discovered *The Nation*, a liberal journal that is part of my life to this day. The writer George Seldes rocketed to my attention from those pages. Seldes was an investigative journalist and a muckraker, a term attributed to Theodore Roosevelt to describe a journalist who indulged in "the relentless exposure of every evil practice, whether in politics, in business, or in social life." Seldes exposed everything from homegrown red-baiting to the truth of Benito Mussolini's Fascistic nature (for which Seldes was run out of Italy) to one of the earliest exposés of the relationship of cancer to smoking tobacco. He went on to publish his own periodical, *In Fact*, a four-page weekly compendium of "the news other newspapers wouldn't print." It became my behind-the-headlines bible. George Seldes was a hero to me, and, as my luck would have it yet again, a great many years later I was flying up to White River Junction, Vermont, with his niece, the actress Marian Seldes, Senator Patrick Leahy, and Abigail Van Buren to spend an afternoon with him on the occasion of his ninety-eighth birthday.

I. F. Stone, whose *Weekly* for many years followed in the Seldes mold, was another hero of mine. As was Thomas Paine, the original American muckraker, and as are the biggest muckrakers of this moment, Bill Moyers on PBS, Christopher Hedges on *Truthdig*, and Thom Hartmann, author and dynamic radio host. Even more than my boxing hero, Max Baer; my football hero, Knute Rockne; or my movie hero, Clark Gable, they were and are the kind of men I wished my father to have been.

Reflecting further on this, I've wondered why the political activist in me took four decades to fully surface. I think it had something to do with money. Not dollars per se, but the feeling of comfort and safety that flows from acquiring enough of them. As a young married man I was focused on becoming a success and taking care of my family. As a kid of the Depression I heard the term "He's a good provider"—from the lips of my grandparents and other

Yiddish-speaking ancients—so often that to this day it sounds to me like a much-beloved Yiddish expression.

At the time, "He's a good provider" could be said of very few men—one of whom used to flick me that quarter, you may recall—so to be a good provider became the holy grail to me. No story lines in all the shows we did in the seventies touched me more deeply than those that dealt with Archie's worries about making a living. A scene with Edith and Archie in bed comes to mind. She, seeking to comfort him at such a moment, is turned away by Archie, whose pained "Aw, Edith, not now, huh?" is excruciating still.

I recall exactly when it dawned on me that perhaps I'd reached that lofty place where my ancient aunts Cookie, Hannah, Rachel, and others would consider me a good provider. When Bill Moyers interviewed me in 1982 for a series he called *Creativity,* he asked what that expression meant to me.

"Well," I said, "every once in a while, after a party at the house . . . I've seen the last guest out and I turn around . . . the lights are still on, the house is nice and bright, and we have provided the ambiance for all those people . . . and I hear the chorus of my grandparents, aunts and uncles, dozens of them out of the past in my head's version of a Tabernacle Choir, singing, 'He's a good provider.'"

It occurred to me in a dollars-and-cents way when I awoke one morning and started to pack for a trip. I had been flying cross-country quite often and thought it necessary to get to the airport forty-five minutes early. Not for searches and pat-downs—we Americans were all good guys then—but to take out extra flight insurance. In some airports there were coin machines, in others salespeople at card tables, and ten bucks bought you ten thousand dollars' worth of added insurance—for the one flight only. I was up early one morning and dressing for such a flight when I realized that someone else was handling that concern for me now, an insurance broker. Not an insurance salesman like my door-to-door uncle Ben, but a real broker, with an office that had his name on the door and others in his employ, a broker who wasn't just selling me a policy but "fulfilling all my insurance needs." Hot damn, was I a good provider! And from that moment on I added the role of a social and political activist as well.

My activism began in December 1962 with a letter to Chief Justice Earl Warren about a speech he'd made suggesting the need for advisers on ethics in business, education, and government. This was followed by a letter to President John F. Kennedy suggesting that this might be the time in our history to create a new cabinet post, minister of ethics. I was committed to the idea, convinced that this was the president who would do it, and I started talking to others about a letter-writing campaign on its behalf.

Then the phone rang just past ten-thirty one November morning and a friend told us to turn on the TV. President Kennedy had just been shot in Dallas. From that moment until three days later when his body was transported to his grave in a horse-drawn carriage, a lone empty-saddled horse behind it, I can't remember moving an inch from my television set, caught in a time capsule of helplessness.

I've always been attracted to the values that derive from the Left in our culture, but it was John Fitzgerald Kennedy who sold me on the language that defines those values: "I believe in human dignity as the source of national purpose, in human liberty as the source of national action, in the human heart as the source of national compassion . . . for liberalism is not so much a party creed as it is an attitude of mind and heart, a faith in man's ability through the experiences of his reason and judgment to increase for himself and his fellow men the amount of justice and freedom and brotherhood which all human life deserves."

On the plane back from the Dallas assassination, Lyndon Baines Johnson was sworn in as our thirty-sixth president. This telegram to him during the next year's election was typical of me and of my voice.

DEAR MR. PRESIDENT:

IT HAS BEEN REPORTED THAT THE GOP IS GOING TO
WRITE OFF THE STATE OF NEW YORK IN NOVEMBER STOP
AND IT HAS BEEN SUGGESTED THAT THE DEMOCRATIC

PARTY WRITE OFF THE STATES OF MISSISSIPPI AND
ALABAMA STOP TELL US PLEASE THAT THE DEMOCRATIC
PARTY AND LYNDON B. JOHNSON AREN'T ABOUT TO
WRITE OFF ANY UNDERLINE ANY STATE IN NOVEMBER
STOP THERE ARE FIFTY STATES IN THIS UNION AND YOU
INTEND TO GO AFTER EVERY ONE OF THEM STOP IF THE
GOP INTENDS TO WRITE OFF A STATE OR TWO THAT'S
THEIR BUSINESS STOP BUT TO COIN A PHRASE DOESN'T
THAT REPRESENT A NO WIN POLICY? STOP PARENTHESIS
LAUGHTER AND APPLAUSE CLOSE PARENTHESIS
    NORMAN LEAR

That wire to LBJ was found in storage among twenty-some boxes of my
correspondence with senators, congressmen, governors, and the Departments
of State and Justice on issues running from my concern over the sale of eavesdropping devices to the separation of church and state to urging a Democratic
Party rebuke of Barry Goldwater for not disowning the support of the KKK.
Once begun, it never stopped.

7

A RELATIVELY NEW FILM COMPANY, National General Corporation, agreed to finance the John Henry film as part of a two-picture deal we made with them, and I went to work on the screenplay. The story National General bought for our second film was sparked by the title of a 1961 Italian film, *Divorce Italian Style*, and based on what I had gone through in my divorce from Charlotte. I brought in a fine comedy writer, Robert Kaufman, to work on the outline of the *Divorce American Style* story while I was writing about John Henry and the Do-Right People.

And somewhere, somehow, I also found time to fall in love with a book by Rowland Barber, *The Night They Raided Minsky's*. The name Minsky and burlesque were synonymous when burlesque, to my everlasting enrichment, reigned over my parade. Barber's story was about the attempt by the "Society for Decency" to outlaw burlesque (which had its origins in Italy of the 1500s as commedia dell'arte) after the accidental invention of what became one of its key components: the striptease. National General passed on it but my friend David Picker, one of the most effective of the studio heads I have known, liked it. David is one of a handful of people I have thought of as "congenitally secure." He was running United Artists at the time. We agreed to make two films for UA, *The Night They Raided Minsky's* and *Cold Turkey*, the only film I wrote and also directed, about a small town in Iowa that attempts to stop smoking to win a $25 million prize.

Ironically, I wrote the screenplay for *Cold Turkey* in a small study off our living room, smoking three-plus packs a day and an occasional cigar, a statistic that amazes and startles me to this day. As someone who now can sniff out the one smoker in a crowd from the smell of that person's coif, no matter the density of hair spray, I can't imagine what our house smelled like and how we lived with it. When I recall that my daughters were raised in that smokehouse, I feel mortified at my unconsciousness.

I wished to be there for my kids at all times, and for the most part conned myself into believing I was. They knew they could call me at work at any time and my office would put them through to me. They could be sure that a "Daddy, make me laugh" would cause me to perform, on the spot, until something— now and again bright, but more often a mental or physical distortion for pre-teens only—earned the laugh that was called for. The only place I could be counted on to be totally present, though, was at work. The Lear household got shorter shrift from their dissociated Dad than did his TV families.

I'D LIKE TO SAY that what my girls missed from their dad they received from their mom, but Frances, unfortunately, was far more occupied with her as-yet-undetected bipolar self and the escalating war that was our marriage. Frances's jealousy simmered through my early successes and came to a boil one night in May 1972, when *All in the Family* and *Sanford and Son* were creating a stir. Johnny Carson was hosting the annual Emmy Awards and came back after a commercial with "Welcome back to an evening with Norman Lear."

The impact of that moment on Frances was monumental. She described how she felt this way: "The disease of lost identity had been forming slowly in me, and became acute when fame moved its goods through the front door. . . . I walked down the street with the man I was the wife of and I was recognized and greeted. I walked down the street alone and I was not recognized, nor was I acknowledged. We had become he."

In 1992, six years after we divorced, Frances wrote her book, *The Second Seduction,* and in it, four lines, a quatrain, make the point like a stiletto:

> *My life is like an epic poem*
> *With lines that rhyme with he and she.*
> *He is what I might have been*
> *And she is only me.*

I can't imagine a subconscious love-hate relationship expressed more exquisitely. Frances adored the me she wished to be, but then could not bear that me in contrast to what she thought of herself. And so the marriage went downhill and the pain uphill in direct proportion to my rising star. We fought a great deal, I know, because I've heard about it every time I've asked those who were there. And because I do remember such surreal moments as overturned tables of food, baked fish and sauce slipping down a wall, and the time I was driving down Melrose Avenue with a boiling Frances beside me and my great friend Herb Gardner trapped in the backseat and wondering if he'd ever see *his* family again. Frances and I were carrying on to such a degree that I, having lost all control, stopped in the middle of the street, in traffic, no light or stop sign, jumped out of the car, dodged vehicles to get to the sidewalk, and ran blocks before Frances could make it to the wheel, drive to catch up with me, and beg me to get back in the car.

Many of our male friends who suffered her inverse chauvinism also recall laughing with her. For me, laughing with Frances ran parallel to quarreling with her. Our daughters remember us laughing a lot together, and talking. "You never stopped talking," Maggie has said. "We always marveled at how much you had to say to each other." Much of what Maggie remembers as talk early in her life and our marriage were disagreements that didn't make it to the category of a fight. The laughter was nonetheless real. One of my fondest memories is of handing Frances something I'd written and hearing her laugh all the way from our bedroom to my study.

Frances shared in my early success. She loved my being a writer, had a keen intelligence and a wicked wit, and early on, as she read and gave feedback, she felt she was a part of the process. That was not to last, however, and would never be enough in any case. When it all began, although we were as much in love as we could be, the life we were building together was a struggle. It is easy enough to write here that Frances and I, with two children in two years, had to live on less income than did Charlotte with her settlement, but living it was a big struggle for us both. In that struggle we were equals. We were no less equals the evening *All in the Family* debuted and the career that had been launched years before we met now reached the stratosphere. Frances and I were relieved of our common struggle, but she inherited another in the same instant. And the new struggle hit her right in her sweet spot.

Evidently I had an inkling of that when we married and begged her not to stop working, but to continue on her career path. I convinced her to at least see if there wasn't a great job opportunity for her in Los Angeles, building on her career in New York. Frances confirms this in her book when she writes of moving to L.A. and visiting with the merchandising head of the May Company, who invited her to take over the sportswear department at a salary "higher than I had ever expected to earn in this life." As she went on, I could not imagine her being more successful at screwing herself if she had a doctorate in it:

"I was afraid for my marriage, for myself, afraid that buying for the May Company would keep work as the focus of my life. I had a new focus now: a home, a husband. His career was my security. I would have children. I would live as women were supposed to live, sheltered and adored. In the swiftest and deepest and most lasting misstep of my life, I turned down the job. One person, a man, told me I was making a mistake. But I was too caught up in my new role to listen to Norman Lear."

Frances's attitude to being a woman was as bipolar as her chemistry and mood swings. Betty Friedan's book *The Feminine Mystique* came out in 1963.

The Frances who turned down the May Company hated that book and sat down to write her own book, *A Critique of the Mystique*. She struggled with that for two years, but she couldn't finish it. It all but tore her apart. By the time she had come through that period, Frances had done a 180-degree turn and embraced the mystique, feminism, and Betty Friedan wholeheartedly. From then on there was no more vocal and ardent feminist anywhere.

There was no better illustration of Frances's rabid feminist persona than one evening on Mooncrest Drive when she tangled with a genuine movie star who also happened to be spectacularly male. Roland Kibbee, Lee J. Cobb, and their wives and kids were over for a weenie roast one evening when Burt Lancaster, a great friend of Kibbee's, dropped by. Kibbee and Burt had made the fabled film *The Crimson Pirate* together. I got to know him well years later when I became an officer of the ACLU and he was our spokesperson, as flamboyant as the roles he played, more flamboyant even than Frances, on the world stage, no less, and certain to grab column inches on any issue with which he cared to be identified.

On this night the Lears were meeting Lancaster for the first time. Typical of Mrs. Lear, when the conversation turned political, she took an opposing view to something someone, in this case, Burt, had just espoused. He took the bait. We onlookers were at once concerned for where this could be heading and excited by every twist and turn. It was clear that the two flamboyancies had met their match. Until—as their complexions reddened and their volumes rose—this unforgettable moment took place.

Burt was seated in an easy chair on one side of the room when it began and Frances was standing over him, in his face, telling him he didn't know what he was talking about and relishing it. The rest of us sat there mouths agape. Lancaster, looking up at Frances, astonished at first, started to respond, quietly to begin with, and then, also no slouch at taking umbrage, growing charismatically lustier as he rose out of his chair. Totally into his role and more the master of his argument than was Frances, he backed her across the room, where she plopped on the sofa next to a shaken Mary Cobb and Louise Kibbee, silent now in the face of his well-practiced fury. Clearly the scene—and the combatants, too, perhaps—had climaxed. In the manner of delivering a curtain line, Burt issued his final words to Frances, strode to the front door, and exited, slamming it behind him.

There is a postscript to this story. On page 104 of her book, Frances wrote just two lines. "I married three times in front of a judge and not one photo or one marriage remains." The second line reads, "I hungered after Burt Lancaster for most of my life."

MOST PEOPLE SAW the Frances Lear you meet here as volatile and unstable but fiercely intelligent and exceedingly interesting to boot. Marilyn Bergman, who, with her husband, Alan, wrote some of Barbra Streisand's biggest hit songs, including "The Way We Were," "You Don't Bring Me Flowers," and the score of *Yentl*, was close to Frances, loved her dearly, and tells a story that best combines all of the above, along with her capacity for ending relationships. Frances had the foresight to start a Hollywood women's feminist support group, ten to twelve high-powered women—writers, actresses, attorneys—who met monthly at our house to discuss what each of them was going through at work, at home, and in their dreams and aspirations. As Marilyn described it, "It was as if we were all lying on a couch opening up to each other, totally vulnerable, and taking turns in the psychiatrist's chair, too, when we thought we could be helpful."

Frances, while smart and intuitive, had a tendency to be too helpful, to the point where the other person's vulnerability seemed a turn-on to her. Before a sister's problem could be fully articulated, she was commenting on it and had the cure. The others, unable to slow Frances down, found her harsh and hurtful, and voted to banish her from the group. Frances, believing the group came to their decision because they needed time to catch up with her psychoanalytically, agreed to step down, in her mind temporarily, and nobly insisted they continue to meet in our home. Unaware of her reason for exiting so genially, and in the spirit of not wishing to hurt her feelings more, they accepted her invitation. And so the meetings continued, absent Frances, at chez Lear.

Living with Frances day in and day out, I had what theater people call a house seat—fifth to twelfth row, center section—to her every mood swing. And in the worst of those moods, I could not avoid being the prime target of her lash-outs and put-downs. Now and then, as I've said, I answered the lash-outs with my own fury. But I didn't always catch the put-downs. Frances could be sly and amusing with them, or so I thought. For example, before *All in the Family* really hit, when we would read something special about me, or I was being honored or receiving an award, Frances would flash me what I read to be a tender smile and say, "Not bad for a little Jew from Hartford." And thinking what I heard was just another way of saying "Look how far you've come, my Norman," I would laugh with her.

As I indicated earlier regarding those years on Mooncrest Drive—and later in Brentwood—I didn't so much live the life we led there as produced it. Or am I just looking at the not-being-where-I-was dissociation phenomenon in a larger framework? Over time, in any number of interviews, I've found myself saying, "I view every day as a production." I now see the difference between a living experience and a production. We are *inside* a living experience and *outside* the production of it. While we may enjoy producing, and I loved it, basically we produce for the pleasure of others. When we live the experience, we are sharing that pleasure with others. It has to be unsettling at the least to live with someone, a father or a husband, who even while producing a special moment stands outside of it looking on. Nor could it have been easy, as I see it now, to have been that someone.

WHEN I STARTED on the screenplay for *Divorce American Style*—ultimately and ironically nominated for an Academy Award—I was suffering from a giant writer's block. "Shit in the head," as I've termed it. I sat at the typewriter for weeks picking at my head and never getting past the first page. I'd cancel evenings when we were supposed to go out to dinner. I'd miss weekend time with my kids. I remember a gala Frances attended without me, coming home after midnight with some friends wearing party hats and carrying favors, intending but failing to cheer me up and cheer me on. I just sat there staring. And picking. There was nothing on the page, but I did have a couple of scars on my head. One day Frances came into my study and threw a little white boating hat on my head to keep me from picking. It worked, and that is how my nearly fifty-year love affair with that white hat began.

Another thing that worked was something a therapist said to me that has stayed with me forever. I went to him specifically seeking help for this problem, and he asked me to imagine myself in a small room with some fifty or so people. Suddenly there is some smoke, someone yells "Fire!" and there is a rush to the single door in the room. Some get out and some, jammed in the doorway, do not.

"Your thoughts are no different from those people who rushed to the door and are crushed there. Let the people out one or two at a time and everyone gets out. If you want them assorted by height or weight or hair color, plenty of time to do that when they are all out and safe. Same thing with your thoughts, Norman."

The first heavyweight writing that came easier for me as a result of adopting that metaphor was my *Divorce American Style* screenplay. The next day I bought a tape recorder and started dictating the entire story, writing some scenes two or more ways, changing my mind and taking unexpected twists and turns, but pushing on to the final scene and the words "FADE OUT" before I had a word transcribed. It was much too long when I finished—more than two hundred pages—but every thought, scene, and sequence was on the page ready to be sorted for the rewrite. I was in heaven at high speed.

After that I dictated the first draft of everything I wrote. It saved my life. My habit was to dictate at home, call an office number connected to a dictating machine, and play my new tape into it. That process might be concluded at, say, two A.M. My secretary would come in early to do the transcription, and the typed manuscript would be ready for me by the time I arrived, at which point I added to it, subtracted from it, or rearranged the content until I had a first draft. As I said, it proved a lifesaver. Over the years, I've passed that advice on to a lot of writers suffering from S.I.T.H., and I've been royally blessed many times for helping to drain it.

The *DAS* story was based on what I'd lived through with Charlotte. Jason Robards, divorced from Jean Simmons, was trying desperately to marry her off to Dick Van Dyke, newly divorced from Debbie Reynolds. What Robards didn't know was that Van Dyke's situation was interchangeable with his. Both men were living on less money with their new families than their ex-wives were getting in their divorce settlements. The movie critic Roger Ebert said of the film, "Who would have thought that a movie starring Dick Van Dyke and Debbie Reynolds would turn out to be a member of that rare species, the Hollywood comedy with teeth in it?"

Those teeth would have been incisors worthy of a wolf had we made the film with the kind of voices and characters I heard in my head as I was writing. They were Stanley Kowalski, Marlon Brando's character in Tennessee Williams's *A Streetcar Named Desire*, in the role played by Dick Van Dyke; and Gittel Mosca, the character Anne Bancroft played opposite Henry Fonda in William Gibson's *Two for the Seesaw*, in the Debbie Reynolds role. Anne, her husband, Mel Brooks, and I were longtime friends, so I sent it over to her as soon as Columbia Pictures and National General said they wished to make the film. Midevening of the day I had it delivered she phoned me and said, "Norman, I'm reading your script and it's good, but I have to ask you not to make me finish it. It's just too painful." As much time as Anne and I spent together in the thirty-some years that followed, "too painful" were the last words between us on the subject of *Divorce American Style*.

Because the voices that motivated me in the writing were those of dramatic actors, it didn't occur to me until sometime later that Dick Van Dyke, a comedian, could handle it, and be a big surprise in the role as well. Especially if he were to perform opposite a gifted dramatic actress. I loved Joan Hackett, a brilliant talent and very beautiful. She was well known but had yet to make a big score. In the right role, on the big screen, lit as they took pains to light leading ladies then, I thought she could make it into the category of a true cinema queen, and I pitched her hard to the studio. But Debbie Reynolds was married to the shoe magnate Harry Karl, a close friend of Irving Levin's, who ran National General, the company cofinancing *DAS* with the distributor, Columbia Pictures. I had no problem with Debbie Reynolds personally, or with the idea of her in the film. It was the phrase "Together at last," the three words that leaped to mind every time I heard or thought "Dick and Debbie." I saw the biting satire I hoped for reduced to fluff.

I had to have Joan Hackett opposite Dick Van Dyke and that became my mission. Thank God Bud agreed and we were united, but that made little difference to Irv Levin or to Mike Frankovich, VP of production for Columbia Studios, under whose reign Columbia made *Lawrence of Arabia, Guess Who's Coming to Dinner, In Cold Blood, A Man for All Seasons,* and *Cat Ballou,* among others. On top of his success running the studio and selecting films, Frankovich had been a Hall of Fame football player at UCLA and was a popular figure, exceedingly well liked. There we were, Bud and I, with our mere TV reputations, tilting against this giant studio head at the peak of his career over our wish to cast a midlevel actress in our film as opposed to his desire to cast the same role with a major star.

We argued Hackett versus Reynolds, a summer romp of a film versus a biting satire, for months. While this went on Columbia made a deal with Van Dyke and had Reynolds, Robards, Simmons, and Van Johnson standing by. The pressure from the studio mounted. It mounted on Tandem's end, too, because Bud and I were basically broke. We had taken an option on *The Night They Raided Minsky's* and I had the screenplay to work on, but that provided no income. Leo Jaffe, president and CEO of Columbia in New York, hoping to mediate the situation, suggested we do a screen test with Hackett and Van Dyke that he hadn't heard Frankovich was resisting. We did it, Joan was wonderful, she made our point, but not one mind was changed on the other side. Finally,

Leo Jaffe flew out from New York, and a knock-down, drag-out meeting was called together. Out of that meeting came a line I could not forget if I lived to be a thousand.

Mike Frankovich, Leo Jaffe, Irving Levin, and Gordon Stuhlberg, Columbia's general counsel, met with Bud and me in Frankovich's office. We went through our spiel, pouring our hearts out as to the film we envisioned: the star it would make of Joan Hackett, what Hackett playing opposite Dick Van Dyke would mean to his performance, and what all of that could mean to the success of the film and to the studio.

As we continued it was clear that Mr. Frankovich, sitting behind his giant desk, was getting more and more riled. He exploded finally: "Hackett, Hackett! For months, fucking months, all I've heard is Hackett. All right, we got Leo here, we got Irving, I'm listening, we're all in the room—once and for all you tell us why Joan Hackett in this part!!" I couldn't believe the man.

"For all these months," I started, "that's all I've been doing: telling you and Leo and Irving, you more than anyone, why Joan Hackett!" My voice was raised now to meet his as I went on. "You know what I'm beginning to think? This is personal. You don't think Debbie Reynolds would be better than Joan Hackett in this film. You have something against Joan Hackett!"

There followed a few "I do not's" and some "You do, too's," during which Frankovich raised himself behind his desk and leaned toward me. We were shouting at each other now, and when I repeated near the top of my voice that he had something against Joan Hackett, he hit me with these deathless lines:

"I have nothing against her, you hear me? Nothing! But if you ever take an ocean voyage with your wife and she is on the ship, you be sure you don't leave your wife alone with Joan Hackett!"

Debbie Reynolds did herself proud in the film, as did Van Dyke. Bud did a great job directing it and I came away loving it, especially one scene. It takes place on a Sunday morning when eight couples in eight cars, caught up in the permutations of their marriages, descend on a suburban house, dropping off and picking up children in the exercise of their visitation rights. We see Debbie picking up a child as we hear a running commentary, i.e., "That's Susie, Fred's second daughter by his first wife, Ethel, picking up her kids—and there's Susie's stepfather, Ed, here to pick up Rosie and Tom, being dropped off by his ex, Monica, whose two kids from her first marriage, Eddie and Sophie, are over there waiting for their dad, Phil, now married to . . ."

In the end, when all the drop-offs and pickups are completed, after all the honking and chasing and door slams, with the last car having driven off, the camera pulls back and up to a high shot of the house, driveway, and front yard, and we see a lone three-year-old coming out from behind a tree, rubbing her blankie to her cheek, totally overlooked in the *DAS* madness.

Film critic Richard Schickel called the scene "a tragic comic gem in a tragic comic gem of a film" that had "something truthful to say about the way we live now and says it with a savagery of tone that runs completely counter to the babbling, socially meaningless flow of our comic mainstream." *New York Times* reviewer Bosley Crowther saw the enterprise differently. He found it "depressing, saddening and annoying, largely because it labors to turn a solemn subject into a great big American joke." There could be no better comment on the two reviews than my grandmother's "Go know."

8

E ARLY IN 1967 BLAKE EDWARDS, who created the hugely successful *Pink Panther,* had a falling-out with his star, Peter Sellers, and both
men bailed out of the third film in the series. United Artists changed the title to
Inspector Clouseau, cast Alan Arkin in the title role, and asked Bud to direct it in
London. Tandem's finances were such, and Arkin in the Sellers role so enticing,
that Bud grabbed it. The timing was good because I was working on a second
draft, from a first draft by Arnold Shulman, of *The Night They Raided Minsky's,*
which I finished in June. Bud and I decided to give our friend Billy Friedkin,
a wunderkind of a young director, his first studio film. Previously he'd done a
few music videos and Sonny and Cher's first foray into independent film, *Good
Times.* A nightmare production about one of the dreamiest corners of the entertainment world had begun.

From day one I wanted Britt Ekland, loveliest of the lovely, a relatively
unknown Swedish actress, to play the innocent Amish girl Rachel Schpiten-
davel, who comes to New York to perform "Bible dances" and, by accident in
an onstage performance, invents what becomes the striptease. And I wanted
one of our most precious clowns, Bert Lahr, who played the Cowardly Lion in
The Wizard of Oz, to play Professor Spats, an older, retired burlesque comic. It
was a smaller role, but key to interpreting the time, the place, and the art.

They were both on board when the concentration on our two lead characters, the comic and the straight man, grew hot. For the straight man my friend Tony Curtis fell into place, excited to be making his first out-and-out comedy since *Some Like It Hot*. Midafternoon the next day, after a studio lunch with Elliott Gould, to whom I offered the role of Billy Minsky, a Tony Curtis near tears phoned me. He'd just been invited by 20th Century Fox to play the title role in *The Boston Strangler*. "I hate to do this to you, Norman," he said. "It isn't like I haven't made a comedy before, but when will I ever get a chance like this again—Tony Curtis as the Boston Strangler?" The nightmare had begun.

Next came the Walter Matthau chapter. The celebrated British comedian Norman Wisdom was available and eager to play opposite Matthau, who lived in New York with his wife, Carol, known on the East Coast as Carol Saroyan because of a prior marriage to the renowned playwright. She was quite a character in her own right and an author as well. I sent Walter the script overnight and made a date to get his reaction in person two days later. I was due to fly to New York the next day for an emergency meeting with Mayor John Lindsay, whose urban renewal team was scheduled to begin tearing down some vacant tenements on two city blocks that we were already at work transforming to look like the Lower East Side circa 1925. There could be no *The Night They Raided Minsky's* without them.

The morning of the meeting with Mayor Lindsay, Walter Matthau's agent called to say Walter loved the script and wanted to play the straight man, Raymond Paine. *Minsky's* finally had its cast—if the city of New York changed its mind about pulling the rug, in this case the streets, out from under it.

In a diary he kept, Mayor Lindsay wrote that the previous year, 1966, might have been the worst year of his life. On his first day in office, New Year's Day, a strike by the Transport Workers Union shut down all buses and subways for twelve days, and the rest of that year saw him forced to raise taxes and water rates to deal with the city's severe economic problems. He was a quite harried Mr. Mayor on the morning that my production manager, Charlie Maguire, and I walked in to see him.

A great-looking man by anyone's standards, Lindsay had been bitten by the showbiz bug before he entered politics and, as it turned out historically, was more of a showman than a politician. A Republican when he ran for mayor, Lindsay was nonetheless endorsed by the Liberal Party, and when he flirted with the idea of running for the presidency he planned to run as a Democrat, which in 1972 he did. As a politician his mistresses were the camera, media attention, and, by extension, showbiz, so of course he and Charlie and I hit it off quickly.

My liberal leanings were of interest to him, and he could deal with the problem we brought to him far more expeditiously than he could a transportation workers' strike. And so he, as mayor of New York City, ordered a halt to the wrecking ball for the time we needed to shoot exteriors. And we gifted him with the feeling, so rare for him at the time, that he could get something done.

The meeting that afternoon with David Picker and Walter Matthau was a lovefest. In the first ten minutes Walter and I learned that we might have flown missions together in World War II. Our 15th Air Force B-17 Flying Fortresses out of Foggia often met up with 8th Air Force B-24 Liberators out of London to bomb the same target. Walter was a B-24 bombardier, and we were quick to bond over the possibility that we had hit targets and caught flak together.

The very next day Walter Matthau, like Tony Curtis, another star who'd become my good friend and who had been so excited about appearing in *Minsky's*, called and told me to find myself another Raymond Paine, "this is goodbye," he was out of the film. It seems that Walter's mother, well known from earlier Matthau mother stories, had gotten angry with Carol on the phone the night before, and told her she was going to kill her. The following morning she called to confirm the threat.

"'I have a gun and give me two days, I'm going to shoot you dead. Dead as a doorknob,'" Walter quoted his mother as saying. We might have laughed, until Walter reported that Carol, no lightweight hysteric herself, was boarding the Super Chief to Los Angeles that afternoon, and under the circumstances he couldn't leave her alone and was flying out a few days later to join her. Many years later I asked Walter why, since he "couldn't leave her alone under the circumstances," he wasn't on the Super Chief with Carol when she skipped town. "Four days cooped up in a train compartment with me wouldn't be good for her," he said with a hint of martyr mischief in his eyes. Another master of mischief and a great actor, Jason Robards, ultimately played the part.

THE TIME IN NEW YORK was as hard on my personal life as making the film was precious. Having their lives totally uprooted was a horror for the kids, but I was handling too many grown-up problems, producing the first musical—and, at $3 million, the most costly film to be made in New York City to that date—to be aware of their problems at the time.

Frances was high on the move to New York initially. She found us a three-bedroom apartment on Fifth Avenue within a few blocks of P.S. 6, considered the best public school in Manhattan. The apartment had the distinction of having been home to the British playwright Harold Pinter, whose play *The Birthday Party*, coincidentally, was set to be directed by Billy Friedkin immediately following his *Minsky's* shoot. Finding and decorating the apartment to satisfy her taste and reconnecting with her old friends was a gas for Frances. For a time it seemed to equate in her mind to what I was up to, and she was in a good mood. That changed in early November when she had less to do and, as photography began on the film, I had more.

Bert Lahr at seventy-two was a bit frail, and we attempted to shoot his scenes first, especially the exteriors, before the deep cold settled in. I can't overstate how deeply I was touched by Lahr's presence, his voice, the way he listened, and the flashes of merriment that occasionally interrupted the ever-present sadness in his eyes. The back of a letter I wrote to Bud in London on November 20, 1967, bears this line in longhand: "Dictated this in the early morning before Bert Lahr came in half dead, unable to work today." Two weeks later, on December 4, Mr. Lahr passed on. The world lost a clown that day, the rarest of the rare.

David Picker suggested we shut down for a few weeks. I knew that Friedkin's and my working relationship couldn't sustain a lull. It was the pull of the next day's shoot that held us together. I sold United Artists, which is to say David Picker, on my rewriting ahead of the camera, hired a well-known comic, Joey Faye, to stand in for Bert Lahr on rear views and long shots, and *Minsky's* plowed ahead.

The resultant publicity following Bert Lahr's death brought a fresh burst of attention to the burlesque musical that was filming in New York City, and to me, its producer. I decided to edit the film in New York so as to be able to shoot or reshoot things as the edit suggested.

A WEEK OR SO AFTER we wrapped principal photography, Billy Friedkin handed me his director's cut of *The Night They Raided Minsky's* and took off for London to start preproduction on *The Birthday Party*. Billy was so tired and unhappy with the project that he went on the British version of *The Tonight Show* and spoke of the difficult time he had with *Minsky's*. But for all the problems we faced together, Billy Friedkin left us with enough well-directed, beautifully photographed footage, sufficiently evocative of the period, to keep alive my passion for fulfilling the promise of *Minsky's*. To that add Pablo Ferro's magical editing of the film, including the two weeks of added footage I shot, and our collaboration was showing lovely results.

Most memorable in the new footage was a two-second shot of Britt Ekland's breasts. Well, actually, they were stand-ins for Ms. Ekland's breasts. When Britt was reluctant to flash hers to the camera the day we were to shoot her accidental striptease, I thought we could get by without it. But as we were editing the dance, it became clear that I was wrong and we needed a body double. Britt was beautifully proportioned but small, and the word went out that *Minsky's* was looking for a pair of diminutive breasts—that is, small but full, and camera-ready. I couldn't bring myself to announce another prerequisite, little areolae, but I knew that's what I would be looking for in the auditions. I never saw Ms. Ekland's chest, just guessed she had small areolae.

I must have auditioned thirty to forty chests before I found the one I thought would match my leading lady's. I was a bit nervous with the procedure, but it was nothing at all for the women involved. It surprised me no end, but when I suggested that my secretary be in the room with us at each bra removal, every woman who auditioned was more embarrassed to do it that way.

In addition to filming some added scenes, Pablo and I played with the footage we had. *Minsky's* was, of course, shot in color. In what might have been a first use of this idea, we shot some new exterior footage in color, printed it in black and white, and distressed the film to look like old stock footage. We then married the new material to the stock footage, cut it into the film, and were able to run what appeared to be historic old film, circa 1925, which, as needed, could spring into living color. The effect would have been a lovely addition to the film even if it hadn't been conceived to solve a problem in the editing.

I brought in Charles Strouse and Lee Adams to do the music, and they wrote a score that deliciously evoked the period, including one song-and-dance number that particularly delighted me, "Take Ten Terrific Girls (But Only Nine Costumes)." Another delightful memory was working with Elliott Gould, whom I'd cast to play Billy Minsky. Elliott was married at the time to a young woman who, four years earlier, had become a sensation on Broadway in a musical called *Funny Girl*. While we were shooting *Minsky's*, the film of *Funny Girl*, in which she also starred, was opening in New York, and Barbra Streisand was on her way to a legendary career as a recording artist, a star of stage and screen, a film producer, and a director.

This comment by Roger Ebert, reviewing *Minsky's* for the *Chicago Sun-Times*, pleased me enormously: "It avoids the phony glamour and romanticism that the movies usually use to smother burlesque and really seems to understand this most American art form." How gratifying that was! *Time* magazine called the film "a valedictory valentine to old time burlesque . . . offering an engaging blend of mockery and melancholy."

THE WORD "MINSKY" was heard in my home many times, day and night, long after the movie was out of our lives. For years it was spoken and shouted by family members, visitors, and household staff alike. I'd come home from the London premiere of the film to learn that Frances had promised Maggie, "When Daddy gets home he's going to take you to the pound to buy a dog," which is exactly what I did. On the way there I asked Mags what kind of dog she was looking for.

"I'll know Minsky when I see him," she said, surprising me with the name she was fixated on.

We looked at thirty or more dogs at the pound before we came across one little guy, white and kind of wet, with matted hair you hoped would be fluffy when dry, but with an angelic face and the most soulful eyes. When those eyes drifted over to Maggie she blurted, "That's him, that's Minsky!" I turned to an attendant who had overheard Maggie and she said that several others had chosen the same dog.

"But I've already named him. Minsky!" Maggie cried out proudly, as if the name made her case for getting the dog. The attendant couldn't have been more sympathetic, but explained that when this happens the dog in question is auctioned off to the highest bidder. This auction had been set for the next morning at nine.

We arrived at the pound at ten minutes to nine. There were about ten groups of people who'd come to bid on our Minsky, among them a few faces I still recall: a boy of about ten and his mother, a thirteen-year-old girl and her granddad, and a woman who looked to be in her forties and her mother—all of them mad for our dog.

When the auction began the little guy could be had for four dollars. Someone said six. Another went to ten. I said, "Twenty." At that, several of the hopefuls moved off, among them the ten-year-old boy, utterly crestfallen. The woman in her forties said, in a voice that sought to close the deal, "Thirty dollars." Those would-be buyers who remained were sadly out of it. They all but gasped when I said, "Fifty," and then did gasp when the woman countered quickly with, "Fifty-five." Maggie read a "Well, that's it" into the moment and couldn't believe what she heard when I said, "One hundred dollars."

I swear I heard the air go out of everyone else. Minsky was ours. But it was an extremely uneasy moment for me. Several kids I hadn't paid attention to were in tears. The woman and her mother, who looked like they'd already centered their lives on taking the little dog home with them, seemed heartbroken. And as happy as I was for my child, I felt like I was in a place where I didn't belong and had taken advantage of people who had every right to be there. When I looked in my wallet for the money I needed to pay for the dog, I was embarrassed by the sight of the hundred-dollar bills I'd received the previous night when I cashed in my British pounds at the airport.

THERE WERE SEVERAL PROJECTS I'd been carrying in my head or working on in bits and pieces over the previous two years, and while editing *Minsky's* I found the time to develop them further. One idea for a film, *Two Times Two*, was the story of two sets of male twins, born in the middle of the night only minutes apart, who in the confusion are mixed at birth. JFK, the president, and RFK, his attorney general, was the image I held for who one set of twins would become. The other set would turn out to be a not-very-talented comedy team, a pair of con men, or circus roustabouts. In the story the two pairs of twins wind up in proximity to each other, another mix-up between them occurs, and the roustabouts are taken to be the real attorney general and president of the United States. Before coming to New York for *Minsky's*, I hired two very funny comedy writers, Fred Freeman and Larry Cohen, to write the screenplay.

Another idea was prompted by my attempts to stop smoking and the tobacco companies' efforts to keep me hooked and seduce new generations to join up. (Remember, it was as late as 1994 that presidents and CEOs of America's top seven tobacco companies testified before Congress and stated their uniform belief that "nicotine is not addictive.")

In my story, a cynical adman talks an elderly tobacco magnate and his board of directors into offering $25 million to any town in America that can give up smoking for thirty days. The bet was that no town could pull it together, or make good on the pledge if they did, and the company would reap the benefit. One down-and-out town in Iowa, led by a driven, celebrity-hungry minister, gets every smoker to sign a written pledge. Halfway through the drive the town's smokers are crazed, but the tobacco company begins to worry that the town could succeed and decides that something must be done to see that this doesn't happen. I brought in a delightful writer from South Carolina, William Price Fox, to write the screenplay with me, but an earlier commitment called him back so I wrote it myself.

Meanwhile, after working on *Two Times Two* for some weeks, Freeman and Cohen came in to suggest that the basic idea of two sets of twins mixed at birth would play funnier as a period piece. We tossed it around and finally agreed to set our story in the French Revolution. The screenplay for what became one of Bud's most memorable directorial successes, *Start the Revolution Without Me*, was on its way. Starring Gene Wilder, Donald Sutherland, Hugh Griffith, and Billie Whitelaw, and shot in France, the picture was so funny and out of the ordinary that it became a cult classic, much to my pleasure as its executive producer. Hugh Griffith's standout line, "I thought this was a costume ball," has been quoted to me dozens of times across the years, usually by strangers, as has been a line ad-libbed by Gene Wilder. In the scene Gene is the roustabout now mistaken for his twin, the count, dressed in finery he could never have imagined, and escorted in one scene around the castle, including the dungeon. There, he walks by a ratty skeleton of a man with a whiplashed back, stretched over a rack, in torn shorts and sandals, and says in passing, "I like your shoes." On elevators, at bars, at rare moments over the years, I have had that line tossed at me, often from a face I didn't know.

9

IN THE LATE SIXTIES I became obsessed with the idea of doing an off-the-wall late-night soap opera to air weekdays Monday through Friday. The only thing that could have interfered with that, and it did, was reading a squib in *TV Guide* about a British show, *Till Death Us Do Part*, that centered on a bigoted father and his liberal son who fought about everything under the sun. "Oh, my God," I thought instantly, "my dad and me." As a kid, when I wasn't moving as fast as he thought I should, H.K. would call me "the laziest white kid he ever met." When I'd accuse him of putting down a whole race of people just to call his son lazy, he'd yell back at me, "That's not what I'm doing, and you're also the dumbest white kid I ever met!" I was flooded with ideas and knew I had to do an American version of this show. In a few days I wrote about seventy pages of notes and asked a well-known, wonderfully peculiar, and very successful New York agent, Sam Cohn, to represent the project.

Between early August and the end of September 1968, we secured the rights to the show from its British rep, Beryl Vertue, ABC commissioned a pilot, and I wrote and cast the episode. It was taped before a live audience with Carroll O'Connor and Jean Stapleton in the leads, but it would take a second pilot, two more years, and another network, CBS, to get it on the air.

Marion Dougherty, a first-class casting agent, worked with me to secure the senior and junior leads. The first time around the show was called *Justice for*

All, and Marion and I read a number of actors in New York for the roles of Archie and Agnes (later changed to Edith) Justice. I'd seen Jean Stapleton in *Damn Yankees* on Broadway and was eager to meet her. She liked the script and loved the role of Agnes, so our meeting was a kick from the start.

Before she auditioned we talked about the thrust of the series should it get on the air, and the odds on that happening. When she heard that my intention, first and foremost, was to entertain, not to raise eyebrows, she was certain we'd get on the air. Jean, more than anyone else involved with the show, always believed it would eventually get on. That positivity, as it happened, was at the core of Edith's character, as were love and faith and empathy. Ms. Stapleton read the role and nailed the part.

Interspersed with auditions for Edith were auditions for Archie. We read an equal number of good actors for that role, too, and Marion Dougherty also scheduled a trip for me to Los Angeles to see actors there. One of our ideas for Archie was the only star on the list, Mickey Rooney, which, if you didn't have Carroll O'Connor so fixed in your head, you might agree was an interesting idea at the time. I knew Mickey's manager, Red Doff, so I called him and asked if Mickey would be interested in doing a series. Go forget this conversation:

"Mickey happens to be in the office now," Red said. "What's the role?"

"Well, it's best we discuss that in person," I replied.

"Okay, I'll put him on," he said. "Tell him in person." Before I could say another word Mickey Rooney was on the phone, calling me "Norm" as if he'd known me for twenty years and speaking of himself in the third person.

"Got something in mind for the Mick, Norm? What's the character?"

"Well, Mickey . . ."

"Call me Mick."

"Mick, I'm coming out there in a couple of days, why don't we meet and . . ."

"Tell me now, Norm," said the Mick. "If it can't be told in a few sentences, it can't be much anyway."

"Well, [deep breath] this guy is a bigot, he calls people spics and spades and kikes . . ."

"Norm," the Mick interrupted me, "they're going to kill you, shoot you dead in the streets. You want to do a TV show with the Mick, listen to this: Vietnam vet. Private eye. Short. Blind. Large dog."

Some years later I worked with Mickey Rooney on another show and loved being around him, but the memory of that conversation remains for me the hallmark of our relationship.

MARIAN REES WAS the first of a series of women who provided the glue that held things together in the most hectic of times and situations. She had Tandem Productions set up in a small office suite on Sunset Boulevard where I auditioned the actors Marion Dougherty had recommended. I'd seen one of them, Carroll O'Connor, in a 1966 Blake Edwards picture, *What Did You Do in the War, Daddy?* I liked his face. It was very important to me that Archie have a likable face, because the point of the character was to show that if bigotry and intolerance didn't exist in the hearts and minds of the good people, the average people, it would not be the endemic problem it is in our society. As the "laziest, dumbest white kid" my father ever met, I rarely saw a bigot I didn't have some reason to like. They were all relatives and friends.

The actors Marion Dougherty brought in for me to meet had all seen the script and had had a chance to think about the role. When Carroll came to audition, he entered as the cultured, New York– and Dublin-trained actor he was. In that mode we discussed the script and the role of Archie quite thoroughly, and I couldn't be sure what he really thought of it. When he turned to the script to read, however, his voice, his eyes, and the attitude of his body shifted, he opened his mouth, and out poured Archie Bunker. Not that I knew exactly what I wanted to hear before Carroll started to read. It was more like Justice Potter Stewart's oft-quoted definition of pornography: "I know it when I see it." Carroll hadn't reached page 3 before I wanted to run into the street shouting for joy. When I told him how I felt, he was pleased, but not about to join me in the street. Yes, he'd be interested in playing the role, but asked if we might meet again before I went back to New York.

Two days later he came to talk further about the script. He'd "done a little work on it," he said, and hoped I liked it. Actually, he had rewritten the first act entirely, the second act to come. And now I had the first of hundreds of difficult moments with Carroll O'Connor, many of them extremely difficult on both sides. At times they were murderously difficult. I was sick to my stomach at the thought of losing him, and that first moment concluded with my telling Carroll that I was committed to my script, as was the network, and that it was the script he had to commit to also. Through his agent, he did.

Marion Dougherty brought in a slew of young actors to read for Gloria and Richard (later changed to Michael), and we found and cast two talented young players, Kelly Jean Peters and Tim McIntire, as the daughter and son-in-law. On September 29, 1968, we shot the *Justice for All* pilot before a live audience that roared at the taping, as did everyone for whom we screened it over the following weeks. My friend Leonard Goldberg, the celebrated film and TV producer, who was a young executive in the ABC program department then, has told me how much the top brass laughed at the show, but they couldn't bring themselves to pick it up. Goldberg convinced them to take more time to think it over by exercising an option to have me make a second pilot. The network sought some script changes to soften Archie, and I politely refused. I did agree that the chemistry between Archie and Edith and the young couple could be improved, so we recast the Gloria and Richard (now Michael) roles with two well-known actors, Candy Azzara and Chip Oliver. We also decided to film Archie and Edith at the piano, singing "Those Were the Days." And that, at the last minute, also became the show's new title.

On February 10, 1969, a little less than five months after making the first pilot, *Those Were the Days* was taped, again before a live audience. This time Bud was back from his *Start the Revolution Without Me* filming, and we directed this taping together. At the end of the opening credits and song, as a measure of the network's concern, they added this line over the shot of Edith and Archie at the piano: "For a Mature Audience Only." Two months later, CBS axed *The Smothers Brothers Comedy Hour,* a brilliant, satirical variety show, for being "too topical" and, as one critic labeled it, "dangerously funny." So ABC passed on Archie and Edith once again. The show was a free ball, and I was out of work once more.

I DIDN'T HAVE TO WAIT long for my next project to materialize. I had learned before we shot the second pilot that United Artists, who appreciated my work on *Minsky's,* loved the *Cold Turkey* script and hoped the film could be shot that summer. The day I told David Picker that ABC had dropped their option on the pilot he told me to start casting the film. When I mentioned whom I had in mind to direct, his reply took my breath away.

"Why don't you direct it?" he asked.

While the thought scared the hell out of me, I confess to having toyed with the idea. Frances, Bud, my girls, everyone in my life, supported my doing it. I asked the advice of just one director, Richard Brooks, whose work on and comments about film I so admired. I told Richard I had never owned a camera, had never taken a lot of pictures, even of my children, and knew nothing about lenses and such. He asked me, in that case, why in hell I had been toying with the idea. I was stumped, and Richard answered his question for me: "Because you know what you want to see, don't you?"

Oh, yes, I had to acknowledge, I knew exactly what I wanted to see.

"Then get yourself a great cinematographer and tell him what you want," Richard Brooks advised.

I had Dick Van Dyke in mind for the minister when I wrote the script, and with UA's okay I sent a copy to him. Having just directed Jean Stapleton, I was eager to work with her again. I liked the idea of casting Bob Newhart against type as the adman who hustles the tobacco magnate, Edward Everett Horton, into his $25 million scheme. Then there was Vincent Gardenia as the mayor of the town I labeled Eagle Rock; Barnard Hughes as the town's only surgeon (and four-pack-a-day smoker); Tom Poston as the town's wealthy inebriate; Pippa Scott as the minister's wife; and arguably the greatest comedy team radio ever produced, Bob and Ray, playing a couple of Walter Cronkite types who descend on Eagle Rock.

Blind to the seduction and cheapening of his congregation and the community by the media frenzy that has the entire town, smokers and nonsmokers alike, gussying up for their fifteen minutes of fame, the Rev. Clayton Brooks is also deaf to the wife who finally cracks and lets him have it. "And finally, Clayton," she demands, "ask yourself, what does it profit a man to gain the world and lose his soul?" To which the reverend draws himself up sharply over her cowering figure and says, "You quote scripture to *me*, Natalie? A *minister*?" Handing her a rolled-up magazine, he adds, "A minister who just made the cover of *Time* magazine?" And indeed that is what we see, indisputable proof of celebrity sainthood, her husband the reverend on the cover of *Time*. The camera cuts sharply to her mind's eye and a shot of Natalie, arms outstretched, shouting from the rooftop of her house, one long, end-of-the-world shriek as we pull back to infinity.

To WRITE the generically American score for *Cold Turkey* I brought in Randy Newman. It was early in Randy's career, his first film, and I think what he composed is one of the most brilliant, underrated film scores ever. Randy also wrote and sang a song over the opening credits, during which you see a lone dog walking down the road that leads into the town, passing signs along the way that advertise stores, businesses, and an air base that have all been closed or shut down. At the end of the road, the dog pauses at the base of a signboard, lifts a hind leg, and the camera pans up to reveal a WELCOME to the twenty-plus churches in the town of Eagle Rock. The song that he plays over that footage, so Randy Newman–like, is "He Gives Us All His Love."

DICK VAN DYKE was as decent and dear and easy to work with as any of his fans might guess. Taking that cue from the star, the entire cast and crew quickly became family. I had determined to quit smoking when I boarded the plane at LAX to fly to Des Moines for the shoot. Two days into it I was directing Barnard Hughes, playing the town surgeon and a heavy smoker. The scene called for him to be taking one last puff of a cigarette in keeping with his pledge as the clock on the town square was striking midnight. I wanted Barney to inhale that last puff and go orgasmic, and instructed him to do so. That's when I learned he had never smoked, never even held a cigarette. I had to show him what I wanted, all but had an orgasm myself with that first puff in three days, and there went my own pledge to quit the habit.

I did quit for good when I boarded the plane back to L.A. after the filming. It is hard for me to believe that I have lived at a time when so many things that seem now to have been there forever were nonexistent. Air travel. The refrigerator. Television. The means to end scarlet fever, polio, and malaria. And this, which used to be the norm but is now so much less usual: rooms full of people smoking, their toxic exhalations sitting in clouds above their heads. That's the way *Cold Turkey* opened. I was attempting to satirize the phenomenon, of course, but what astounds me is that I lived with it. The country lived with it, much in the way we live now, despite some protestations, with climate change, nuclear waste stuffed where we pray it will never surface, and hundreds of products with lies on every label.

My eight weeks in Iowa in the summer of 1969 directing *Cold Turkey* remain a highlight of my life. When I was seeking Richard Brooks's advice about whether to do it, he quoted Alfred Hitchcock as having once said that no man could feel closer to playing God than a director of a film on location. Think about that. You are in Greenfield, Iowa, which you alone have renamed Eagle Rock, to the township's great pleasure. The town is somewhere you—and the 150 or more actors, technicians, and craftsmen accompanying you—have never been. They are all waiting minute by minute for you to determine what they will do next. Your mood each day is their emotional thermometer. You are also the key connection to the host community, whose sense of pride and excitement at your presence among them knows no bounds. Cast, crew, and township— for eight weeks your wish is their command. Go get closer than that.

Frances, Kate, and Maggie visited me several times during the filming of *Cold Turkey*. Nothing made me prouder than to have them with me on the set. The cast adored them. They were there the evening before we started, when Greenfield held a rally for the cast and crew in the town square. With a police escort, we all rode in a pair of fire engines and antique cars through outlying communities, some cornfields, and into town, where everyone in Greenfield and from neighboring Winterset (in which we were also scheduled to shoot) seemed to have turned out.

I adored Iowa and Iowans. Among other things, they taught me not to take for granted that the Program Practices departments of the networks, steeped as they were in research, were correct when they complained of something in the earliest scripts for *All in the Family* and said, "This won't fly in Des Moines." Don't ask me where that came from, but from the very beginning, across the three networks, when Program Practices determined that a moment, a line of dialogue, or a bit of behavior was offensive, "This won't play in the Bible Belt" or "It won't fly in Des Moines" was their informed reason for saying "Take it out."

They played hardball. If not for what I learned in Greenfield, Des Moines, and Winterset (where, by the way, John Wayne came from), I can't be sure I'd have stood up to them as I did. After our writers had their say, and the actors in the rehearsal process weighed in, and I saw two run-throughs and made my comments, I automatically resisted Program Practices' position when they asked for something to be removed from a script. I admit to times when the discussion that followed resulted in a change that bettered the script and solved their problem at the same time, and I thanked them. But those occasions were relatively rare. When they were insistent on a change I could not agree with, they were saying in effect that their research-oriented take on the audience trumped our instinctive understanding. I'd hold my ground. Inevitably I would then hear, "Sorry. It will not fly in Des Moines." The knock-down, drag-outs followed.

BEFORE LEAVING for Iowa and the filming, Frances and I rented a house in Brentwood, our first home out of the valley, on the upscale Westside of L.A. In those years, living in the valley was treated as déclassé. An entertainment industry joke of the time went: "Poor Sammy Davis. Short, black, Jewish, one eye, lives in the valley."

Two blocks away from the house we rented was a house we had hoped to buy. It was owned by Paul Henreid, the Austrian actor famed for playing opposite Humphrey Bogart and Ingrid Bergman in *Casablanca*. He'd also played opposite Bette Davis in *Now, Voyager* in one of the most memorable and alluded-to scenes in American cinema. Amid swelling strings, in a pair of lushly lit, dripping-wet close-ups, Henreid lights two cigarettes before handing one to his steaming costar. No couple in a modern film, even naked between the sheets and pumping away to brass and drums, can stir audience fantasies more than that incandescent black-and-white moment in a movie made seventy years ago.

The word was out that the Henreids were looking for a buyer, but the price they were asking was a bit over-the-top. This was the house Henry Fonda had owned for many years, the home he raised his kids in. It was only a few blocks from the famous Brentwood Country Mart, and Jane used to ride her horse to it. The property was well known and much sought after. I checked with Henreid often to see if he'd lowered his price. We became friendly, and Frances and I were invited to dinner there several times. A time or two we reciprocated. A year or more into our relationship I learned one night that the other two couples at the Henreids' dinner table had met them the way we did. They'd come to see a house for sale. I began to wonder if the elderly Henreids (there were people older than me then) weren't lonely and might not have found the house useful for making friends. While I can't prove it, until the day we finally owned it, and that took a couple of years, everyone I met at dinners there had an interest in acquiring the house of our dreams.

I WAS EDITING *Cold Turkey* on the MGM lot while we kept our eye on the Henreid house. It turns out that the smokers of Eagle Rock do succeed in keeping their thirty-day nonsmoking pledge and win the $25 million award. We see the worldwide media clogging every street, the three network news anchors and their crews on hand, and President Nixon heeding the sweet siren of celebrity and making a last-minute appearance as the clock strikes midnight on that thirtieth day.

The film ends with a wide shot of blue skies, open plains, and farmhouses that we've seen before, Iowa at its most glorious, from which we do a slow dissolve to the same scene some years later. Iowa is now a modern success story and the evidence is everywhere. In the foreground we see community after community of tract homes, and in the background a few large factories with smokestacks belching cones of black smoke that blanket those homes.

In 1969–70 only one studio in town had the effects equipment to deliver that optical, and that is why we were editing at MGM. But there was a wrench in that wheel and it was my old friend Jim Aubrey, the Smiling Cobra. Aubrey had been hired to run MGM and cut costs to the bone. The bone, according to Aubrey, included everything and every department he didn't see as absolutely needed. So, despite the deal we had made to edit *Cold Turkey* there, he was selling the equipment we required out from under us. When I sat with him to plead my case, Jim, in a major rewrite of our history, smiled and said, "You know I'd do anything for you, Norman, but . . ."

It took the threat of a lawsuit to cause Aubrey to hold back on selling the equipment we needed for that last shot in *Cold Turkey*.

BEFORE I'D FINISHED editing the film I sent a rough cut over to David Picker. Within a week he'd screened it for Arthur Krim, the top man at United Artists, and they called to offer me a three-picture deal to produce, write, and direct for them. It was the thrill of thrills. At that time the only filmmakers I knew of who were hired to produce, write, and direct comedy were Blake Edwards and Billy Wilder.

As Tennessee Ernie Ford would say, I was chomping in the tall cotton. My attorney and UA were negotiating a deal when, some weeks later, Bud Yorkin called me from New York, where he'd gone to pitch another Tandem product to CBS's top dog, Mike Dann. Bud didn't know at the time that Mike was leaving CBS and Robert Wood would be replacing him the following week. Old friends, they chatted awhile, and at some point Mike asked him about that pilot we'd made for ABC. "Funny but impossible to air," he'd heard.

Bud disagreed. He'd brought a tape of the pilot east just in case and suggested that Mike see for himself. In those days there were no cassettes so the show was run out of master control thirty floors below.

Mike Dann started laughing from the first lines, and loudly. Fred Silverman, a VP of programming just under the incoming Bob Wood, heard the laughter from his neighboring office and came in. When it was over his excitement was palpable. He and Mike agreed they just had to get it to Bob Wood. "Don't let that tape leave the building" were their last words to Bud.

Within days of my being asked to sign the three-picture deal with United Artists, Bob Wood, newly ensconced in the offices at CBS Television City in Los Angeles, phoned me to say he'd just seen the "Archie pilot" and would I be interested in talking about it going on CBS? Although it would mean I couldn't take the picture deal, I couldn't resist meeting with him after two pilots and more than two years of thinking about it. Wood, an able and agreeable executive, backed up by his talented and driven programming VP, Fred Silverman, had predetermined that the kind of rural comedies that had sustained CBS—

The Beverly Hillbillies, Green Acres, and *Petticoat Junction*—had seen their day, and he hoped to serve up something to change the CBS brand and mark his regime.

My show would do the trick, but he asked me to rewrite the pilot. I said I wouldn't do that. "How about if the show goes on but you make a different first episode?" he suggested. I told him there was a reason I shot the same script for the two pilots I made for ABC. It was deliberately based on the slightest of stories, which gave me the opportunity to present 360 degrees of everyone, but especially Archie—his attitudes on race, religion, politics, sex, and family, holding nothing back. Metaphorically, you can't get wetter than wet, I told Mr. Wood, so we all needed to jump in the pool together and get soaking wet the first time out. The meeting ended with his having to think about it. With United Artists' offer in mind, I left CBS telling myself I was better off not having to choose between the two, yet delighting in the possibility that it could still come to that.

The which-way-to-go discussion started that very evening, just on the chance it could happen, and there wasn't a friend or family member who didn't advise me to take the three-picture deal. First of all, the medium known as broadcast television was the bush leagues compared to motion pictures and the big screen. On top of that, everyone was certain that if the network actually dared to air the show, they wouldn't have the guts to stay with it and it would be off the air in a week or two.

"They'll break your heart with this thing" was the common refrain. Even Carroll O'Connor bet me, and put it in writing, that CBS wouldn't keep the show on the air. He had an apartment in Rome that he would not vacate because he was so sure he'd be back there in six weeks. With all that ringing in my ears I picked up a call from Bob Wood one day.

"Okay," he said, "thirteen weeks, you're on the air."

I think I knew at the time that the film deal presented a far surer career path and income, no small consideration since we were pretty much broke, as opposed to the big question mark *All in the Family* represented in a TV era defined by hillbillies and petticoats. Taking the TV deal was all risk. A show could be absolutely terrific and fail for other reasons, like the night it was on, its time slot, and how well the network was doing overall. Frances and the others were right to be advising against it.

But if anything could keep me from accepting Bob Wood's "thirteen on the air," it wasn't going to be the amount of risk we would be taking, the warnings about the mercurial nature of the ratings-driven TV business, the argument that TV was the bush leagues compared to making movies, or being told "Bury your ego, Norman, the world doesn't need your father on TV." No, there was only one thing that could make me change my mind—and that was CBS itself.

I phoned Carroll in Rome and he couldn't believe we had been picked up. He was still sure he'd be on his way back to Italy in a few weeks, and I agreed to pay for round-trip tickets if he was right. I don't recall whose idea it was, but we changed the title to *All in the Family,* and CBS agreed to auditions to recast the roles of Gloria and Mike. Two years earlier, the first time we'd shot the pilot, Rob Reiner had wanted to play the part but I had thought him too young, emotionally if not chronologically. This time he walked into the audition and out with the role within minutes. Now all we needed was a Gloria to go with Rob's Michael.

John Rich suggested I look at the top of the Smothers Brothers show and check out a young actress for the role of Gloria. There was Sally Struthers, tap-dancing in a pool of light under the opening credits, and oozing comic chops. She auditioned with Rob and it was another bolt of lightning.

While I hired writers Mickey Ross, Bernie West, and Don Nicholl to start on the remaining dozen scripts CBS had ordered, the network decided to do some research and show the earlier pilots to some focus groups. Soon, word floated back to us that the screenings were not going well, and I had to wonder if this was the beginning of the end. Notes from Program Practices followed with suggestions such as these:

"We ask that homosexual terminology be kept to an absolute minimum, and in particular the word 'fag' not be used at all. 'Queer' should be used most sparingly, and less offensive terms like 'pansy,' 'sissy,' or even 'fairy' should be used instead. And again, a term like 'regular fella' would be preferred to 'straight.'"

"Archie refers to the inhabitants of Harlem as a 'bunch of bums.' How about calling them 'a bunch of good for nothings?' Or lose the reference to Harlem."

"'Hells' and 'damns' should be avoided if the episode is not to be grossly offensive to many viewers."

"Archie's comment on the shortness of Gloria's skirt should not be as anatomically personal as, 'Every time you sit down the mystery's over.'"

There were pages of such requests that turned to warnings and occasionally to threats. Over the years and shows they amounted to volumes. Early on I wrote long letters of clarification and reasoning, but rarely was I able to avoid the ultimate confrontation: "Remove that and I go, too."

In this instance, the first of that long line, I called my attorney and asked exactly what I had been contractually guaranteed by CBS. What could they do to me?

They had ordered thirteen episodes and would pay for them, he said. The first episode was guaranteed to air. No absolute guarantees as to the rest.

"But Bob Wood told me 'thirteen on the air,'" I said.

"And he meant it," my attorney replied, "because even they can't believe they would put out all that money and not try to get it back. So the contract keeps his word, but they know if they break it, what are you going to do, sue? They paid for the shows, so go prove damages. You're over a barrel."

I got off the barrel and attended one of the focus groups the network had contracted, hosted by a young guy who sounded like he was a psych major not yet degreed. Some thirty people, likely recruited at a mall, were brought to a screening room and seated before a large TV screen. They were a bused-in midlife group, carrying shopping bags, dressed on a warm day in shorts, sandals, and blowsy short-sleeved shirts, all wearing the "What the hell am I doing here?" expression. Questions from the psych major revealed a few California natives, the rest tourists.

The host explained that they were going to be shown a thirty-minute situation comedy and the network was interested in their reaction to it. At each chair there was a large dial at the end of a cable. They were to hold that dial while watching the show and twist it to the right when they thought something funny or were otherwise enjoying a moment. If they didn't think something was funny, if it offended them or simply bored them, they were to twist their dial to the left. Two big clocklike instruments hung high on the wall over the TV set to register the degree of the likes and dislikes of the group as they twisted their dials.

Those of us monitoring the focus group sat behind them, looking into a one-way glass wall. We saw and heard everything, and it revealed a good deal of what I knew instinctively about human nature. The group howled with laughter, rising up in their chairs and falling forward with each belly laugh. But wait! Despite the sound and the body language, they were dialing left, claiming to dislike much of what they were seeing, and they were *really* unhappy with it. But *really*!

While I can't say I could have predicted this behavior, unlike my friends at CBS I understood and was elated by the audience's reaction. Who, sitting among a group of strangers, with that dial in his or her lap, is going to tell the world that they approve of Archie's hostility and rudeness? And who wants to be seen as having no problem with words such as *spic, kike, spade,* and the like spewing from a bigot's mouth? So our focus group might even have winced as they laughed, but laugh they did, and dialed left. Comedy with something serious on its mind works as a kind of intravenous to the mind and spirit. After he winces and laughs, what the individual makes of the material depends on that individual, but he *has* been reached.

CBS gave me a heads-up a few days before that *All in the Family* would start airing Tuesday, January 12, 1971, at 9:30 P.M. (right after *The Beverly Hillbillies, Green Acres,* and *Hee Haw*). I alerted everyone in my world. There were some who still couldn't believe it was actually happening. Monday morning, the eleventh, Program Practices paid me a visit and—hold everything—asked me to make one trim in our pilot episode.

As taped, this for the third time, our story opens on a Sunday morning with Gloria putting the finishing touches on an anniversary brunch she is planning to surprise Archie and Edith with when they return from church. Michael is helping her, but in a touchy-feely mood. It turns serious. They rarely have the house alone together, he says, and he wants Gloria to go upstairs with him. She demurs. He continues his pursuit, catching her and kissing her. The front door opens and Archie and Edith come in. Archie has caused them to leave church early, and enters complaining about the preacher and the sermon they walked out on. They go into the dining area and encounter Mike and Gloria in a passionate embrace. Archie takes it all in and says, as if he caught them in the act, "Eleven ten on a Sunday morning!" CBS insisted we eliminate that line.

"Why?" I asked Program Practices.

"Because it makes it explicit."

"Makes what explicit?"

"What they were going to do."

"At eleven ten on a Sunday morning."

"Yes."

"So? They're married, aren't they?"

"It doesn't matter. It won't fly in Des Moines."

"And there'll be a knee-jerk reaction in the Bible Belt?"

"Not if you cut the line." I said it didn't make sense, and the line was in.

"Then *we'll* cut it," he said. "Either way it won't be in the broadcast."

That was the first time it occurred to me that the network could have the last word by editing out what we didn't agree to. Fred Silverman called later to mollify me.

"You've got a great show, Norm. What does one line matter?"

I told him the line had to stay in and he said I could talk myself blue in the face but "the boys upstairs" had drawn a line. (I learned later that William Paley, who started and owned the network, had had grave reservations about the show.) Somehow I knew that far more than differing opinions over one line was at stake here. As tiny as this issue was, much of the program content of the series depended on our relationship with Program Practices, and that would be determined right here and now by the way this difference of opinion was resolved.

I knew myself to be reasonable and open-minded, with some fine, experienced writers and a brilliant cast to sift ideas through. And I knew that Program Practices had their people living so much in the fear of offending that the satisfaction of reflecting life realistically, even when it hurts, was anathema to them. Then, too, there were many rungs on their ladder, so no Program Practices executive could think just for himself without worrying for and about those above him. That became my definition of mounting fear, and I was sure I couldn't work that way. The report back to CBS in New York was that the offending line was to remain.

At five P.M. L.A. time, an hour and a half before the show was to go on in New York, Bob Wood called with a breezy "Hi, fella." He had a terrific compromise idea and felt sure I'd have no problem with it.

"Listen, you'll love it, we're gonna run the second episode first," he said. "Then next week we'll run the show intended for tonight. We won't change a word and you've saved your precious line. Done?"

"No," I said. We weren't done, and the rest of the conversation was like drowning in the dark, legs pumping to keep head above water, hands grasping for something, anything, to hold on to. "The point is that we can't keep giving in . . ."

"But we're still talking *one line* . . ." "Yes, but after that, trust me, I know where this is going . . ."

"So, you'd lose an entire series for one stupid line?"

"It isn't the line, it's the decision."

"So you'd lose the series for one stupid decision? Is that what you're telling me? We got twenty-five minutes to airtime, is that what you're telling me?"

"I'm sorry, Bob."

My whole world was flashing before me. Was I being foolish, childish? I certainly wasn't being brave because there was still a three-picture deal sitting out there. And there was Frances, and all my good friends, advising me to take it. The question was all about what was motivating me. Was it a matter of ego, of my having to have my own way? Or was CBS being ridiculously wary? Would Program Practices ever be strong enough to think for itself? Not if you're right, Norman, about understanding the gutless, fear-ridden place they're coming from.

"I'm sorry, Bob," I repeated. "I want the pilot to air first and the line of dialogue to remain as taped."

"And if not?" Bob asked.

"Don't expect me back."

When we hung up it was about 6:10 L.A. time, twenty minutes before the show was about to go on the air in New York. We were working on the script for what would be the fifth episode, preparing to close shop and race home to see our debut with our families. At six-thirty, just as I was about to call a friend in New York and ask what they were showing on CBS, the phone rang. It was Silverman from New York.

"Rest easy," he said. "You won this one."

I wasn't sure whether to laugh or cry, and I was no clearer about that at home three hours later, where a few friends and members of the cast and company who lived nearby were gathered around our TV set with us as the show began in the West and I found out what came with my victory. Before the fade-up on Carroll and Jean at the piano singing "Those Were the Days" (to which Jean had added that crack in her voice on the line "And you knew where you were then"—we did more than four hundred tapings and it never failed to get a laugh), there appeared this advisory:

> The program you are about to see is "All in the Family." It seeks to throw
> a humorous spotlight on our frailties, prejudices and concerns. By mak-
> ing them a source of laughter we hope to show—in a mature fashion—
> just how absurd they are.

The first episode of the nine-season run of *All in the Family* followed. Thirty minutes later America had been introduced to the subversive mind of Norman Lear, and not a single state seceded from the Union.

Despite my being aware that with every episode going forward we would face the same mental masturbation from the network that preceded episode one, I slept well. But I was totally unaware of how much my life would change—and how much the establishment would come to believe that TV and the American culture had been "radicalized" overnight.

Five years later we had seven series on the air and Mike Wallace was introducing me on *60 Minutes* as the man whose shows were viewed by more than 120 million people each week.

PART 3

Joyful Stress

Happiness is the exercise of vital powers,
along lines of excellence, in a life
affording them scope.

—ARISTOTLE

1

O N   T H E   N I G H T *All in the Family* debuted, CBS and its affiliates across the country had hired dozens of additional telephone operators to handle the tsunami of protest the network expected, but they proved unnecessary. The torrent turned out to be more of a trickle. Not that there weren't questions of taste raised, and some severe condemnation, but most of that came from establishment professionals, the people who run research and do focus groups and are paid by the media and academia to tell us at any given hour who we are and what we are thinking.

To me the most telling letter we received was from a woman who had been divorced many years before, when her son was four years old. The boy had never seen his father after that. On the night *All in the Family* debuted, her son was now thirty-two years old and living twelve hundred miles away. The show was on for about ten minutes when the lady ran to the telephone and almost broke her dialing finger phoning her son. When she reached him she screamed across the miles: "You always wanted to know what your father was like—well, hurry up and turn on channel two!"

But while the public seemed to take it in stride, the press expressed a good deal of shock. The reviews were generally poor, which was all it took for the trickle to be judged a torrent. Those in Program Practices particularly were "trickled" to death with the outcome they could claim to have forecast.

In March, *Life* magazine's John Leonard, reviewing the first few shows under his pen name, Cyclops, gave the torrent theory a big boost. *"All in the Family* is a wretched program," he wrote, "and why review a wretched program? Well, why vacuum the living room or fix the septic tank? Every once in a while the reviewer must assume the role of Johnson's No-Roach with the spray applicator: let's clean up this culture."

Neither was Richard Nixon a fan. As he complained to H. R. Haldeman and John Ehrlichman in a critique secretly recorded on the White House tapes, "CBS came on with a movie, one that they made themselves and . . . they were glorifying homosexuality . . . I think the son-in-law obviously, apparently goes both ways, likes the daughter and all the rest . . ."

Still, the show was also reviewed well by some. Jack Gould in the *New York Times* wrote: "Except for 'All in the Family' it is difficult to recall another TV attempt to bring the disease of bigotry and prejudicial epithets out into the open with the aim, one hopes, of applying the test of corrective recollection and humor."

Not long after, seeming to have second thoughts, the *Times* asked the noted novelist Laura Z. Hobson to write an opinion piece that might reexamine the kudos some readers—and possibly an editor or two—viewed as questionably "fit to print" in Jack Gould's official review. There was no better choice to do that than Ms. Hobson, author of *Gentlemen's Agreement,* the bestselling treatise on anti-Semitic bigotry and intolerance, and she did it brilliantly in a lengthy Sunday Arts section piece on September 12, 1971, just as the new season was starting. The *Times* then invited me to respond to Ms. Hobson's critique, which I did three Sundays later. The centerpiece of her criticism was that I'd tried and failed to make a bigot lovable because "you can't be a bigot and be lovable."

My response: "I am 22 years your junior, Madam, and meaning you no disrespect, if you have not known bigots of different stripes and attitudes, and to varying degrees, we are obviously aging in different wine cellars."

While some accused us of reinforcing racism through Archie's attitudes, others gave us credit for exposing the absurdity of prejudice. I don't think either is true. On the one hand, we never received a letter from anyone who agreed with Archie that didn't somewhere say, "Why do you always make Archie such a horse's ass at the end of the show?" It didn't escape the notice of any of those "Right on, Archie!" people that the point of view of the show was that the man was foolish and his attitudes were harmful. And as much as Archie reminded viewers of fathers, uncles, and neighbors, I don't recall a single letter that said, "I see a lot of myself in Archie."

I've never heard that anybody conducted his or her life differently after seeing an episode of *All in the Family*. If two thousand years of the Judeo-Christian ethic hadn't eradicated bigotry and intolerance, I didn't think a half-hour sitcom was going to do it. Still, as my grandfather was fond of saying—and as physicists confirm—when you throw a pebble in a lake the water rises. It's far too infinitesimal a rise for our eyes to register, so all we can see is the ripple. People still say to me, "We watched Archie as a family and I'll never forget the discussions we had after the show." And so that was the ripple of *All in the Family*. Families talked.

Looking back at it, I think Archie's primary identity as an American bigot was much overemphasized because that quality had never before been given to the lead character in an American TV series. But the show dealt with so many other things. Yes, if he was watching a black athlete on television, he'd make an offhand bigoted remark, and Mike would call him out on it. But the episode in which that exchange occurred might have been about Archie losing his job and worrying about how he was going to support his family. While a line or two could reflect Archie's bigotry, the story itself was likely to be a comment on the economics of that moment and the middle-class struggle to get by.

In any event, it wasn't that I thought bigotry per se could be funny, but that a fool on any subject can be funny. It was the state of the man's mind. He was afraid of tomorrow. He was afraid of anything new, and that came through in the theme song: "Gee, our old LaSalle ran great / Those were the days." He was lamenting the passing of time, because it's always easier to stay with what is familiar and not move forward. This wasn't a terrible human being. This was a fearful human being. He wasn't evil, he wasn't a hater—he was just afraid of change.

AITF's initial ratings were anemic and much of the press was dismayed by the sound of television's first off-screen toilet flush. I thought the furor as big an affront to common sense as they thought the flush itself was to common decency. It's likely that the very first joke that passes between every child and parent has to do with a bodily function, 99.9 percent of them in the poop arena. Go make something dirty of that. But many did. That was more than made up for, however, by the occasional critic who found a serious consistency in my work over the years. Vincent Canby, one of the senior critics of his time, wrote in the *New York Times*: "Both *Cold Turkey* and *All in the Family* are commendable for the courageous manner in which each works simultaneously with and against the conventions of its medium. *Their success could even be a metaphor for what is genteelly called peaceful revolution*" (italics mine).

If the show had not begun at midseason, the chances are it would have disappeared after its initial thirteen-week run. But when the other two networks' first-run programming ended, a percentage of their audiences finally tuned in to CBS to see what they'd been hearing and reading about, and our ratings started to climb. By early May the show was red-hot, jumping from fifty-something in the ratings to number fourteen.

And then a miracle occurred. With only two weeks to go before the twenty-third Emmy broadcast, that year's producer called. The show's host, Johnny Carson, had an idea: What if the Emmys opened with America's most talked-about new family, the Bunkers, sitting down together to watch the Emmy broadcast? They do their shtick, Archie hating the whole thing, of course, and Edith loving it, until the Emmys start and cut them off.

We grabbed at the idea and wrote a short scene in which Edith is breathless with excitement as Emmy time approaches. She raves on about "how pretty everyone always looks at the Emmys and how lovely they must all smell," causing Archie to wince. "It makes me feel so good," she adds, "the way they all wave to each other, too. You just know there's so much love in the room." Archie, in the opposite direction, hates "all them Hollywood liberals and Commies" and is watching only in the hope that "Duke Wayne, the only real man in that crowd and a honest to God American, might show up."

Even in that ballroom full of TV professionals, most had never seen the Bunkers before. That was true of the viewing audience as well. Carson was wonderful, the Emmys a smash—we won three: Outstanding New Series, Outstanding Comedy Series, and Outstanding Continued Performance by an Actress in a Leading Role in a Comedy Series—and when Monday arrived the Bunkers entered the category of household names heard around watercoolers everywhere.

WE REHEARSED AND SHOT *All in the Family* before a live audience at CBS Television City in Hollywood. The episodes were written and produced as plays, with people talking and behaving in real time, like a piece of theater. We rarely stopped for a time lapse. The live interaction between our actors and the audience sitting twenty feet away was as palpable to viewers at home as it was for people in the fourth row. Much as a baker sets his dough in the oven, we set down these little plays of ours before an audience of 250, whose laughter, occasional tears, and applause, like heat to bread, caused our play to rise. Watching great comic actors sweep up a live audience and take them to the moon is an indescribable high. There's just nothing like it.

Carroll sat down to every reading worried and unhappy. It seemed to make little difference whether his problems with the script turned out to be few or many, small or large. Most of the time we'd hear, "It just doesn't work." He wasn't always wrong, of course. When he wasn't, his concerns were quickly addressed and the script was better for his input. But much of the time we were facing fear, a fear that could render Carroll impossible to deal with. It was understandable to a degree. He was, after all, at the beginning of a process where he was to shed the gentle Irish intellectual Carroll O'Connor to become the poorly educated full-of-himself blowhard Archie Bunker, spewing a kind of rancid, lights-out conservatism for a television audience that grew quickly to more than 50 million people.

It was a big load that Carroll was carrying, granted, but we couldn't allow his fear to overwhelm the good work that the rest of us churned out in support of him. The best example of the height to which our differences could take us happened early in our nine-season run. It was called "The Elevator Story." Circumstances find Archie on the seventy-eighth floor of an office building. He gets in the elevator reading the hysterical front page of a tabloid. In the car, too, reading his *New York Times,* is a tall, very elegant black man, and a white woman prone to hysteria. Some floors below, the elevator stops and a working-class couple, clearly Latin, get on. They speak both Spanish and English. She is extremely pregnant and nervous. Archie is annoyed with everyone: the classy black guy putting on airs, the emotionally fragile woman, and the pregnant woman yakking unhappily in Spanish. She thought she should go to the hospital, but the doctor said next week would be plenty of time. Between the embarrassing (to Archie) soon-to-give-birth talk, the black man's scorn of his tabloid, and the nervous wreck, Archie can't wait to get out of there. And suddenly the elevator jerks to a stop between floors.

Trapped until maintenance arrives, fear is rampant, but all eyes turn at the moan of the pregnant woman. The emergency has caused her to go into labor and the first act ends with this question: Who will arrive first, the baby or the maintenance team that can get them out of there?

Immediately after the first table reading, which seemed an agony for Carroll, he announced there was no way in the world he would do this show. First of all, five people in an elevator for the whole half hour was impossible to shoot. Director John Rich said he could make it work. Carroll, as agitated as any of us had ever seen him, disagreed. "It would feel cramped on camera," he said, and the ending would be weak as hell. "The elevator gets down, the woman's carried off, and we've taken the audience through all that cramped hell—for what?" I pointed out that that wasn't what he'd read. Maintenance does *not* arrive on time, the woman is *not* carted off, and the baby is born in the elevator.

"But that's a joke! You know you can't do that! A baby born on the floor of a goddamn elevator! What's that all about? I don't want to talk about this anymore!"

I tried to explain that the camera wasn't going to be trained on the birth itself; it was going to be on Archie's face. After all the anguish and irritation between the principals—at one point the Latin father needs some newspaper to lay down and both Archie and the black man offer theirs; the father reaches for the tabloid Archie has thrust in his face, pauses, then chooses the *Times* instead—the birth of this baby, I repeated, would take place on Archie's face.

Speaking of that face, there might never have been a face that would go better with the name O'Connor. It screamed for Archie to be Irish. And Catholic. I heard that on all sides, sometimes in anger from people close to the show. "That face screams 'Irish,' so why fight it, use it!" was all I heard. But I refused to pin the bigot in Archie on any specific ethnicity or religion, so we never went there. Not that the show didn't deal with God and religion, but for eight years we avoided labeling Archie in that regard.

But back to the elevator. As much as Carroll would have no part of it, I was convinced that when the camera witnessed the miracle of the baby's birth on a close-up of Archie, it would be an altogether exquisite and touching moment, and one that only the rarest of actors could pull off. I had to have it.

Carroll walked out of the reading and the rest of the cast was sent home. Several hours later, all hands were gathered in Bob Wood's office at CBS in an emergency session. Carroll, who called us together, was there with his agent and his attorney. And with me, in one of the first of many such meetings we were to have, was my attorney. Carroll said flat out that he thought this week's script was repulsive and unplayable and that in no way was he going to do it. When all the faces turned to me, I said I disagreed with him about the script, and on top of that it was the only one we had ready to shoot.

We were at a standoff. In what became a heated argument, every alternative was discussed. There had to be another script we could get ready. Maybe even one without Archie? Would the network let the show take a week off? Not a chance. Carroll fell to pieces and began to cry. He couldn't go on, hated the show, couldn't bear me, and cried to a point that made me realize that this behavior, this degree of testing, had to end here. If he won this battle, the creative team would be throttled and the show I believed in would die anyway.

Our schedule called for us to work Monday through Friday, do a dress rehearsal without cameras late Friday, take the weekend off, start to put the show on camera the following Monday morning, do an on-camera dress rehearsal Tuesday afternoon, and then shoot two shows before a live audience later, one at five P.M. and the other at eight P.M. It was close to six o'clock on Monday when everything seemed to have been said. The network's position was that they had contracted for a show a week and that's what they expected. I said that we were keeping to our schedule with the current script and would gather again to rehearse in the morning. And Carroll left, saying it was "Good-bye."

The next day, Tuesday, the cast gathered on time, but for Mr. O'Connor. CBS had formally advised Tandem Productions, me personally, and Mr. O'Connor and his advisers that *All in the Family* would be canceled and appropriate legal action taken if they did not have a new episode to air on the expected date. Carroll never showed up that Wednesday, but we learned that he and his team were together all day and that they'd been in touch with Bob Wood and our attorney several times. Sometime that evening I got word that Mr. O'Connor would be at rehearsal on Thursday. I said that would be okay if we could make up for the lost time by working over the weekend.

We worked on Saturday, and when the episode was taped the following Tuesday we got a phenomenal reaction. The audience cheered. Some cried. Everyone agreed it was our best work to date and simply had to win an Emmy. It did. Director John Rich did a brilliant job, Hector Elizondo and the honey-throated Roscoe Lee Browne—the Latin and black man, respectively—were perfect casting, and Carroll O'Connor's Archie was stunning, the scene even better than I imagined. The camera in tight, we see that face reacting to the sounds of the birth taking place below, the mother pushing, grunting, yelping in pain; the father telling her in Spanish to push harder; more grunts, more pushing, more Spanish; Archie's expressions mirroring everything going on— and then, cutting through the commotion, from the center of all life, comes that first cry and Archie melts, simply melts at the wonder, the mystery and beauty of it all. It was a watershed performance.

For the next eight years Carroll would continue to dislike every script at the start. It was nothing but fear, and blind anger was his only defense. Certainly he bettered many a scene with it, but it needn't have taken his belligerence to get there. The marvel of Carroll's performance as Archie Bunker was that at some point each week, deep into the rehearsal process, he seemed to pass through a membrane, on one side of which was the actor Carroll O'Connor and on the other side the character Archie Bunker. Fully into the role of Archie, he was easily the best writer of dialogue we had for the character. He was a full-fledged version of the New York cabdriver he'd patterned himself after, as he'd told me at the beginning. As difficult and often abusive as Carroll could be, his Archie made up for it and I could kiss his feet after every performance. If Carroll O'Connor hadn't played Archie Bunker, jails wouldn't be a "detergent" to crime, New York would not be a "smelting pot," living wouldn't be a question of either "feast or salmon," and there would not be a medical specialty known as "groinocology."

CARROLL COULD NOT HAVE had a grander talent and costar than Jean Stapleton. Unlike the troubled Carroll/Archie kinship, Jean and Edith were spiritually one and the same. Once, after a particularly grueling day, she said of Edith's relationship to Archie, "I know I love him and I have no trouble with that. His dearness hides his foibles for me and I want to take care of him. But when he's saying some of those things you know Edith would never want to hear, what am I thinking? Where is my head?"

"You're tuned out," I said. "You're Patty Andrews, the middle Andrews sister, and you're singing 'Don't Sit Under the Apple Tree.'" Jean remembered the Andrews Sisters—Patty, LaVerne, and Maxene—as I did. They were real sisters and hugely successful on radio, in vaudeville, and in films, singing close harmony in the boogie-woogie era of the midthirties. Jean might have understood intuitively why my response worked for her, and why it mattered a great deal in the way her character handled Archie, but it was reflexive on my part and I'm not sure I did. I think I understand now. The Andrews Sisters represented a freshness and a guileless innocence at a time when America needed just that. The suggestion that she was an Andrews sister evoked something native and totally accessible in Edith. Patty Andrews, singing her heart out, a sister on either side, "sees no evil, hears no evil, and speaks no evil."

While ABC was making up its mind not to pick up our show, I'd cast Jean in *Cold Turkey* and told her about a bit of business that I was injecting into an early breakfast scene, something I saw happen once to my aunt Rose. Sneezing incessantly as she was fixing breakfast, Rose opened the refrigerator and bent way down to get an egg from a lower shelf. Suddenly a breast was sneezed out of her nightgown and was swished back with a wrist flash as if it had happened a thousand times before. Jean smiled at the idea, but she called me from Penn Station a half hour later on her way back to Philadelphia. Unable to tell me she might have thought the bit distasteful, or that it just wasn't something she could do comfortably, she said, "I'm sure your aunt Rose's breast was larger than mine, which is why it would work well, but my breast just isn't right for the scene, but it is such a sweet idea, it really must be in the picture, there are lots of actresses who could do it and I could name a few, but breast size is so personal, you know . . ."

At some point I managed to slow her down and told her I'd already changed my mind about the bit and pleaded with her to understand that it was most important to me that she be in the film. And in my life, too, I thought, as she finally agreed once again to do it. Jean Stapleton was, in life, the very soul of Edith.

To BE ALONE with Rob Reiner is to be in a crowd. His brain and his mouth, like a chain of Chinese firecrackers, are firing constantly. If that sounds like I'm describing a pain in the ass, nothing could be further from the truth. Rob was like that when I fell in love with him as a nine-year-old teaching my daughter Ellen to play jacks. What was great about Rob was that the person, the actor, the director, the friend, the participant, the activist, the star, the husband, and the father all came from the center of his being. If he was talking to you about his entrance to a scene, the importance of washing your hands, whether a line of dialogue would be better this way or that, or the need to do something politically about early education, it all came at you with the same sense of urgency and at the same volume.

On matters political, here is the big difference between Rob Reiner and far too many of the rest of those with deep political leanings and the megaphone that comes with celebrity. Catchphrases and bumper sticker backups often pass for information with many well-known faces. Never with Rob Reiner. He takes the responsibility for knowing the history of his subject, and understanding it as well in a political, social, and economic context. Mike Stivic was his opposite, full of passion absent the facts.

Of the four principals, I knew Sally Struthers least well. I envisioned her character as a Kewpie doll on the outside with an inner strength and street smarts that would be enhanced over the seasons. In her final episode, when she, Mike, and their baby are moving to California, it's clear that Gloria is the head of the family now, and totally in charge. Sally was perfection as Gloria.

There is no way to overstate the good times and laughter the creative and production teams experienced working with Carroll, Jean, Rob, and Sally. Unlike the filmed single-camera TV comedy we see so much of today, each episode was taped with multiple cameras before a live audience. We did not decide where a laugh should come and put it there. Our cast and our writers earned them all, including the wildest and likely the most explosive audience reaction in TV history when Edith escaped an attempted rape by smashing an oven-hot cake into her attacker's face and kicking him in the nuts.

But that cast and the stories we told often evoked more than laughter. Archie opens his front door on a Sunday morning and painted there is a swastika. Gasp. An anti-Semitic group has mistaken the Bunker home for the Blooms' on the next block, and a member of the Jewish Defense League comes to offer Archie violent eye-for-an-eye protection should they return. His family won't let Archie accept the offer and the JDL guy leaves. A moment later we hear a horrendous explosion offstage. All rush to the door, Archie opens it, and the camera cuts to four horrified faces, staring. "Holy Jeez," says Archie. "They blew him up in his car." No musical sting, no applause, just a slow fade to black. The audience was as shocked as the actors, and it was the loudest silence I'd ever heard.

Empathy, like silence, is another sound that can't be measured in decibels. Nothing caused our live audiences to "shout" their empathy more loudly than Edith's reaction to the news that a transvestite who'd become her friend was murdered by a street gang simply for being a man in women's clothes. Grief-stricken and unable to see how a just God could allow that, her faith was threatened. The audience was near tears. I knew that Edith's faith was Archie's tent pole, his tiller. When confounded by Edith's truth and purity, Archie had to see her as a "dingbat." But without that dingbat at his side, he would be lost. He needed a strong Edith, and it was her faith that gave her that strength. In the second episode of this two-part story, Edith saw that her loss of belief had resulted in a bereft and rudderless Archie, and she prayed to regain her faith. And we had what I thought was the best show we'd ever made.

(Someone else to whom religion was very important thought that, too. In September 1978 the cast and I flew to Washington for the installation of Archie's and Edith's chairs into the Smithsonian Institution. President Carter invited us all to the White House, and it was a thrill to stand there in the Oval

Office listening to our president talk about episodes he and Rosalynn had seen and remembered, especially "the one where Edith lost and regained her faith.")

MEANWHILE, our confrontations with CBS's Program Practices department continued. One of the biggest occurred over a story concerning Mike's temporary inability to make love to Gloria. Nearing graduation, he is studying very hard for his exams and worried to death about them. His fear of confessing his anxiety leaves Gloria feeling unloved and unwanted. She confides in Edith, who can't possibly tell Archie, and that was the story we were working on when the network heard about it and panicked.

CBS wanted no part of anything to do with impotence. The subject matter so alarmed them that Bob Wood flew out to California. We met at eight A.M. on a Sunday morning—I was working seven-day weeks—and, with an "Are you fucking kidding?" look on his face, he said, "You're doing a show, a family show, on television, about he can't get it up?" As much as he might have meant that, I wondered if he wasn't fighting to keep a straight face. Also, word had floated our way that it was Mr. Paley himself who found the show "unattractive" and was nervous about its potential for making the network over in its image. I felt sure he would see things differently if CBS's "changed image" continued to be endorsed by the high ratings that translated into higher fees per rating point, so coddling Bob Wood—likable and easy to coddle, by the way—and helping him to handle Mr. Paley was the way to go.

We talked about our ratings and their ascending curve, and about the new shows we had in the hopper, and at one point I asked Bob if he'd like to see the script in question—a first draft the guys were still punching up. We sat there reading the script aloud line by line, he and I playing every character as they came up in "Mike's Problem." We howled, and Bob saw that the big laughs came from the family's inability to discuss sexual matters, however important, and not from Mike and Gloria's attempts to deal with the problem. In the script, when Archie approached a black friend in Kelsey's Bar to ask his advice, because "we all know that you people, the men, I mean, are especially preficient at this," Bob Wood, lost in laughter, had his handkerchief out wiping his eyes. And when the friend told Archie that the secret was hog jowls, and then, pulling him closer, hoarsely whispered, "But tell your friend to be careful, Archie, too many of those jowls and you get this terrible hankerin' to shine shoes," Mr. Wood fell to pieces altogether. So did the audience that came to see it when it was taped a few weeks later with his blessings.

While CBS did hear from a few affiliates, largely in the South, demanding to know what "that madman in California" was up to and why they were allowing it, they also received encouraging words from mainline clergy, from mental health groups, and from numbers of family counseling services. Loud and clear came the message: "The subjects you are touching on are extremely helpful." We heard that sentiment more and more over time from organizations and institutions dealing with everything from rape to drugs, from parenthood to cancer, religion, science, etc.

Possibly the silliest conflict we had with Program Practices—and that's saying something—occurred after Gloria became pregnant. Toy companies came to us and to CBS within days for the rights to Archie and Edith's grandchild. When we delivered the script in which Gloria announced she was carrying a boy, the network pleaded that we make it a girl instead. When I asked why, all I got was a "Come on, you know."

When Gloria delivered a baby boy the network execs knew, as sure as if they were comedy writers themselves, that the time would come when Archie had to diaper his grandson. Two months later, when the script we were about to go into rehearsal with called for Archie to be left alone with the baby, a young man from Program Practices came to see me. He was a fresh face, a Princeton type—you might think him a young physician. He asked me if we contemplated any close-ups of the baby. I told him I had no interest in a close-up of an infant's genitalia, if that was what concerned him. Then I shouldn't mind, he said, if Archie diapered him on his belly. I admit that as the father of three girls

257 Joyful Stress 257

I wondered aloud for a moment if that was the way male babies were diapered. Then I caught a look from one of the writers overhearing this who had a son.

Archie diapering his grandson was as dear as it was funny. For perhaps an instant the child was fully exposed and, assuming they spotted it in the first place, if any of 40 million viewers were offended by the little bugger's doohickey, they never let us know.

2

THE SECOND SERIES Bud and I brought to the little screen, *Sanford and Son*—inspired by the British series *Steptoe and Son*—starred Redd Foxx, whom we'd seen and fallen in love with in Las Vegas. In the history of the medium it was probably the only television show seen and purchased by one network under the roof of another—and there were only three nets at the time. I was producing *All in the Family* at CBS, and we rented a small studio down the hall to rehearse what we hoped would be our pilot episode for *Sanford*. One day Bud and I invited the *AITF* company to come see what Redd and Demond Wilson, playing his son, were up to. We saw the first act of the pilot episode and howled. Redd, a true original, was as fresh and funny as only he could be. For a week or more I asked, ultimately implored, CBS execs just a few floors above us to take a look at what we had. For whatever reasons no one found the time, and so I phoned a programming executive at NBC. A few hours later two of the top guys at the Peacock net stopped by, collars up and hats pulled down like a pair of hoods seeking to go unrecognized. They watched and on the spot offered to purchase *Sanford and Son*, which, for the next seven years under Bud's supervision, was one of their highest-ranking shows.

And next came "that uncompromising, enterprising, anything but tranquilizing" *Maude*. When I was a kid the best family fights took place on holidays, when uncles, aunts, and cousins with long-standing grudges came from everywhere and had just one day to settle old scores. And so, in an episode of *All in the Family* in which we wanted someone to clobber Archie as he'd never been clobbered before, who better than Edith Bunker's cousin, her closest friend and confidante when they were kids, someone who adored her and all those years ago couldn't face losing her to Archie, that "slob of a Nixon lover"? She, Maude, hated him from the minute they'd met and the feeling was mutual. Perfect. We had the character, but what about the casting?

In 1955 I saw an Off-Broadway musical called *Ben Bagley's Shoestring Revue*, which featured a showstopping torch song called "Garbage," written by Sheldon Harnick and sung by a tall, deep-throated woman in her early thirties. She was leaning against a streetlight at night, in a slinky black dress, singing a bluesy torch song about a man she loved who treated her like garbage. Every time she hit the word "garbage" the audience howled. She was altogether hilarious, but with a voice that demanded she be taken seriously at the same time. That was my introduction to Bea Arthur.

Fourteen years before casting her as Maude, I brought Bea to L.A. to make her television debut as a guest on *The George Gobel Show*. The sketch characters she played with Gobel, the woman who sang "Garbage" in *Shoestring Revue*, Vera Charles (the role she played opposite Angela Lansbury on Broadway in *Mame*), and later Dorothy on *Golden Girls*—were all fitted to the tall figure, baritone voice, acid tongue, and totally unique physicality and personality of Beatrice Arthur. That was true, too, of the role of Maude Findlay, which called for her to be both politically and socially 180 degrees from Archie.

Bea Arthur as Maude made me laugh in places in my body I would never have known existed otherwise. She mirrored the most profound understanding of the foolishness of the human condition. It wasn't anything she thought about, it wasn't anything she could talk to you about, it wasn't anything she knew, but her reaction to the bullshit in ordinary life was a gift to the character and contained a degree of truth-seeking madness that got to me and wrung me out. The madness originated in the woman, the actress.

The episode guest-starring Bea aired halfway into *All in the Family*'s second season. As the end credits were running in New York, CBS's programming chief, Fred Silverman, called. "That woman should have her own show," he said, to which I responded, "What a great idea!"

Within weeks producer-writer Rod Parker was at work, Charlie Hauck was hired as his right hand, the team of Bob Schiller and Bob Weiskopf were added soon thereafter, and Hal Cooper signed on to direct.

WITH THREE SHOWS on the air and ideas for several more moving forward, Bud and I realized we didn't have our business base covered adequately. We had a personal attorney, a personal business manager, and an attorney and business manager for our company, Tandem Productions. What we didn't have was a businessman on the inside, a president and CEO. I knew that we, like others before us, could create several TV shows that were basically owned by the network. Paul Henning, who created *Petticoat Junction*, *Green Acres*, and *The Beverly Hillbillies*, was the example that immediately preceded us on CBS. However well paid, he might as well have been an employee of CBS. Ultimately, we wanted to own and distribute what we created, and we knew we didn't have the business savvy to accomplish that.

I had never forgotten A. Jerrold Perenchio, the agent assigned by Lew Wasserman to book an act for us when we wanted Andy Williams to see it in a professional situation. Jerry is Italian and he wears it like a glove, a very fine glove. No one loves and reflects finery better than Jerry. He *is* a piece of finery himself. When they made him they threw away the mold, the room, and the building he came in. Those who work in the creative side of entertainment often feel superior to those who tend to the business, but there is more originality, imagination, and vision in Jerry Perenchio—and a number of other executives I've met who are never considered part of the "creative community"—than there is in a large percentage of that community's bona fide members.

I'd started talking to him about joining us as soon as we got the go-ahead for *Sanford and Son*. Jerry had left MCA by then and started his own company,

Chartwell Associates. He turned me down, but I persisted, almost in the going-after-Frank-Sinatra fashion. It was in the process of his turning me down repeatedly over many months that Jerry and I became good friends.

Finally, after *Maude* went on the air, I went to see Jerry's attorney, Allen Sussman. I talked about it being "How high is up?" time at Tandem, and convinced him that a truly big company could be brewing here with the right promoter and business mind steering it. With Allen's help we turned Perenchio around, and in January 1973 he joined us as Tandem's president and CEO. The following year, for financial reasons, Jerry and I formed the separate company T.A.T. Communications, whose initials came from the Yiddish expression *tuches ahfen tisch*, roughly translated as "enough talk—put your ass on the table."

Our deal with Perenchio dictated that we also bring aboard a young executive he had just hired away from Procter & Gamble. He knew nothing about the entertainment industry, had never considered being in it, but something about him spoke loudly to Jerry, who coaxed Alan Horn to join him nonetheless. I met with Alan at my home one Sunday morning before signing the contract and got the same message. He was considerably younger than Jerry and me, great looking, very smart, and extremely likable. He mentioned coming to California with Charles, spending so much time with Charles, and feeling so good about the way Charles took the trip.

I was sure Alan had come west with a family member, and it was some time before I realized that Charles was his car. You have to know there's something special about a man who would name his car Charles.

Bud and I could not have handled the business matters that were about to hit us when Perenchio and Horn joined the team. When *Maude* came along CBS was becoming short of space, and with another show on the way, Perenchio started negotiating with another studio, Metromedia. When a fifth show in development made even that complex too small, another stage had to be built. More negotiation. More writers. More contracts. More offices. More executives. Jerry and Alan had come aboard in the nick of time.

THE STORY LINE for every episode of every show originated at the conference table in my office. I had instructed our writers to come to work prepared to talk about their marriages, kids, family problems, health problems—their lives in the context of what was going on in their communities and the world. The topicality of our work, the personal nature of so much of it, and the serious subjects we chose to deal with grew out of that.

The audiences themselves taught me that you can get some wonderful laughs on the surface of anything with funny performers and good jokes, but if you want them laughing from the belly, you stand a better chance of achieving it if you can get them caring first. The humor in life doesn't stop when we are in tears, any more than it stops being serious when we are laughing. So we writers were in the game to elicit *both*. My favorite charge to them was "Let's bring the audience to their knees." There was a listening device stationed midtable in my office, and down the hall a writers' aide was transcribing our discussion. By the time our meetings concluded, those notes (or stories, if we'd gotten that far) were typed and ready for the writer or team that had been assigned the task of turning out the script.

If asked what I thought were the five best television episodes of the more than two thousand we produced, the November 10, 1975, episode of *Maude* would certainly be one of them. Maude was on camera alone throughout the entire show, talking to her psychiatrist, who, but for his hand on the arm of his chair, was never seen or heard. The episode was based on one of my most memorable experiences with my dad—the day he promised me his car to take Charlotte to the Westport Playhouse, didn't come home in time, then chased after me to take my jalopy and give me his Hudson Terraplane.

The way I chose to have the story rewritten for a father and daughter was to make H.K.'s late-model car a lovely coat. Just as I longed for the car to take my date to the theater, Maude longed to wear the coat when she accompanied her date to their senior prom.

The episode opened with an overwrought Maude telling her shrink about how upset she was with her father, how he was never there for her when she was growing up, and how their past relationship was affecting her current one with her husband. She hated her father, couldn't think of a single time he'd made her happy. And then, as she wept and searched her past, she suddenly recalled something.

She was graduating from high school and for her graduation her folks bought her the most beautiful coat she'd ever seen, "a pearl-gray coat with a Persian lamb collar." After some minor alterations her father was to have picked it up before the store closed and brought it home in time for Maude to wear to her prom. Maude's heart was so set on it that every time she mentioned "the pearl-gray coat with the Persian lamb collar" the audience seemed ready to cry for her. Of course her father was late, the store had closed, and Maude described how her dad, the H.K. of her life, tracked down the store owner and talked him into coming back downtown to open the store and give him the coat, which he then raced to Maude, arriving just before she was to step into her all-decked-out high school gymnasium.

As she clawed that moment out of her memory Maude burst into tears, and the hate she had expressed for her dad turned into "Oh, no, I loved him, I *loved* him. Oh, God, how I loved my father." The episode was nominated for two Emmys.

BILL MACY AS WALTER FINDLAY, Maude's husband, was ideal casting. I never forgot his performance in an Off-Broadway play by Israel Horovitz in the late sixties, especially a scene in which, sitting at a table eating chicken alone onstage, he begins to choke on a bone. Should he try swallowing it? He starts and his eyes pop. Better to cough it up? He tries, but, uh-uh, no! Falls to his knees, rolls on the floor. Maybe if he coughs with his hands up? Down? He stops, dead still, and just stares out at the audience, possibly praying. They hold their breath and choke down laughter, no small trick. Then, tentatively, like the problem's gone, Macy attempts a slight swallow. His face reads like this is working. Then—*shit!* It starts all over again. Blackout!

There is no way I could have captured the hilarity of that performance for you, but I hope six years of Bill Macy's Walter gives you an inkling of it. Offstage Bill was kind and gentle, and at the same time, surprisingly, an original brand of wild man. No one but Bill Macy would attend a black-tie dinner in honor of the show in which he starred and interrupt a solemn moment in the sold-out proceedings by leaping onstage, grabbing the microphone, tossing his arms out riotously, and shouting, "Cocksuckers of the world, unite!" Have you ever heard fifteen hundred people groan in unison? It was as if the floorboards opened and the evening fell through them.

The next day, in rehearsal, Bill's way of apologizing to his fellow cast members was to suddenly drop his pants. If that sounds more like an "up yours" act of hostility than one of contrition, all I can say is you had to be there. Bill's "I'm sorry" ran so deep as to reach his childhood, where seeking further punishment by the repetition of an offensive act often signals the child's most abject apology.

Rue McClanahan and Conrad Bain, who played the Harmons, the next-door neighbors to the Findlays, were also actors I'd seen in Off-Broadway shows and years later brought to California. Their talents made for hilarious, multifaceted characters and perfect foils for Bea and Bill. Adrienne Barbeau played Maude's daughter, and Esther Rolle as Florida, the maid—better known these days as a housekeeper—filled out the cast. There has never been a closer, more harmonious, and protective-of-one-another cast than the *Maude* ensemble. It all started, of course, with Bea Arthur, who would do anything, try anything, and give her everything to whatever was asked of her.

MAUDE WAS LAUDED or loathed depending on how the reviewers, and viewers as well, felt about the then relatively new feminist movement. The character was a role model and hero to all who cheered the movement on, and was reviled by those who held fast to the idea that "a woman's place is in the home." Men who perceived their male dominance being pissed on all but wanted her dead. On top of that, Frances and I had become close to Betty Friedan, Gloria Steinem, and Eleanor Smeal, the head of the National Organization for Women, so we wound up in the loathed list just behind *Maude*. Those feelings were further ruffled when I elected to have Maude get pregnant and agonize with her family over whether or not to have the child at her age. (She was nearing fifty.) She chose to abort.

As you would expect, Program Practices fought our touching the subject. An abortion was an absolute no-no, still illegal in many states at the time (though not in New York, where Maude lived). William Tankersly, a true gentleman, was the head of the department at the time, and while our business relationship often saw us at odds, we respected and listened to each other. His initial "no way" turned into "go ahead" when I told him we would write in a good friend who had four kids, was pregnant with a fifth that she could not afford emotionally or economically, yet for whom an abortion was out of the question—and who didn't understand how Maude could see it any other way.

Maude's abortion story, written by Susan Harris, took two episodes and went on the air early in the first season. Two Illinois affiliates, in Champaign and Peoria, refused to air the shows—the first time any CBS station had rejected any episode of a continuing series. Things escalated considerably when those episodes were due to be rerun in August. The expanding Religious Right, energized by the Supreme Court's *Roe v. Wade* decision just seven months earlier, went to town. Zealots across the country made thousands of phone calls; seventeen thousand similarly worded letters of protest were received by CBS; hundreds in the South and Midwest picketed their local TV stations; and in New York City protesters lay down in front of William Paley's car as the chairman of CBS was driving into his network's garage. Thirty-nine affiliates declined to air the reruns and, most telling of all, not one corporate sponsor bought commercial time on those broadcasts.

The lesson here, and through the years I've seen it repeated over and over again, is that a relatively small group of agitators, especially when convinced God is on their side, can move corporate America to quake with fear and make decisions in total disregard of the Constitution that protects against such decisions.

The controversy the shows set off—particularly some individual episodes—generated a good deal of criticism of me for what was viewed as editorializing. "If you want to send a message," I was told, "use Western Union." In the early years I would face that accusation by denying it. We weren't sending messages, I'd say, we were doing comedy. If we could not make a story funny we would not do the story. I've always believed that the things that make me laugh will make you laugh, and what makes you cry will make me cry. I have to believe that or I don't have guidelines. But to me, laughter lacks depth if it isn't involved with other emotions. An audience is entertained when it's involved to the point of laughter *or* tears—ideally, both.

At some point my response to the accusation that I was sending a message changed. I came to realize that, as a longtime observer of the culture, now in my fifties, why wouldn't I have a point of view and care to express it in my work? I determined that I need not be apologetic and began saying openly, "Yes, as full-grown human beings who read and think and pay a lot of attention to what is happening in the world our children will inherit, we will write and produce those stories that interest and involve us—and those are usually *about* something. Our humor expresses our concerns."

There then came a moment when—after expressing this for the umpteenth time—I thought: Wait a second. Who said the comedies that preceded *All in the Family* had no point of view? The overwhelming majority of them were about families whose biggest problem was "The roast is ruined and the boss is coming to dinner!" Or "Mother dented the fender and how is she going to tell Father?" Talk about messaging! For twenty years—until *AITF* came along—TV comedy was telling us there was no hunger in America, we had no racial discrimination, there was no unemployment or inflation, no war, no drugs, and the citizenry was happy with whomever happened to be in the White House. Tell me that expressed no point of view!

People also talked about the anger in the shows, and of course there was anger in them. It was social—I was angry at the lunacy that I saw in the world. But for me there was always infinitely more love. I think the shows loved people, and that's why they tried to deal so deeply with the human condition—with all of its suffering, hysteria, foolishness, and sublimity.

It's taken me a lifetime to repeat this, but I think Paddy Chayefsky had it right when he said of me, "Norman Lear took television away from dopey wives and dumb fathers, from the pimps, hookers, hustlers, private eyes, junkies, cowboys and rustlers that constituted television chaos and, in their place, put the American people. He took the audience and he put them on the set." My view is that we made comedy safe for reality.

That reality included black people. As a teenager, I remember taking the train to New York. When we reached the city, we'd slow down for our first stop, 125th Street. We were on an elevated track, quite close to the third- or fourth-floor windows of tenement buildings, and as we slipped past I could see all kinds of activity: family after family—almost all Negroes, as we referred to them then—living their lives. I would imagine their stories; assign a hero here and a villain there; imagine myself one of them; pretend I knew what would happen next. Although there were no black families in my neighborhood, and only one black kid in my high school graduation class, they were a strong presence in my mind.

3

THE CHARACTER OF MAUDE'S MAID, Florida, as played by Esther Rolle, was a standout. In our second season the network and Tandem all thought that with solid support she could carry her own show. From that idea came *Good Times*, our fourth big hit. It was called a spinoff, but I've always considered the term as making too light of a far more thoughtful and innovative approach to birthing a show.

When Esther Rolle was a featured player on *Maude*, I thought of her as performing in the bush leagues while being groomed for the majors. Acting on that, we gave her more to do and her character more background, revealing that she was married and had children. And then, on one episode, we introduced her husband, James, and cast John Amos to play him. Florida and James clicked loudly together and CBS saw as quickly as we did that—add children and stir slowly—we had the potential for another very funny family show.

The story of how *Good Times* went from an idea to a script we felt worthy of presenting—it was, after all, the first full black family on television—just might fall into the "No good deed goes unpunished" department. Mike Evans, the young actor who played Lionel, the son of George Jefferson on *All in the Family*, wanted to write as well as act, and I suggested he take a crack at the *Good Times* pilot script. He brought in Eric Monte, a black writer he wished to team up with. Eric (who later sued me, Jerry Perenchio, Tandem, and CBS for something like $185 million) came from the Cabrini-Green housing project in Chicago, so we settled the James and Florida Evans family there. I was charmed by Eric Monte and, having worked for years with Mike, liked him a lot, too. A number of black writers worked with us through the years, but thus far none had created a show. Mike and Eric now had the opportunity to be the first.

They blew it creatively with a poor copycat of a script. But even though what they wrote was a far cry from what we shot, we did not seek to change their credit as the sole cocreators. I could be confessing to a bit of inverse racism here when I admit that it even pleased me to see them credited and paid. That would not have happened, at least not gratuitously, if they were white.

ALLAN MANINGS, a respected comedy writer Tandem had signed, went to work writing a new story and filling out the family members. The Evanses would have an older teenage son, J.J.; a younger teenage daughter, Thelma; and a second son, Michael, age eleven; plus a neighbor and close friend to Florida named Willona. Manings once recalled that I phoned him at one o'clock in the morning and said, "I want to tell you how much I love your script. So much so that I think we can go right to a table read with it." And then he added, "Fourteen rewrites later we were in rehearsal." We had a good time casting, as indicated, I think, by the actors we wound up with—Jimmie Walker as J.J., Ja'net DuBois as Willona, Bern Nadette Stanis as Thelma, and Ralph Carter as Michael.

The Evans family still lived, as marginally as possible, where Mike and Eric placed them, in the Cabrini-Green project. James held down three jobs if he had to. Still, we were determined that (a) the family would never go on welfare; (b) they would deal with the reality of their world—gangs, drugs, crime, poverty, etc.; and (c) despite that, the kids would not fail to get an education.

By the time we were to go into rehearsal for the pilot episode, CBS had upped their order to thirteen on the air. When we taped that first episode, the cast and audience were aware that history was being made, and the sense of discovery and exhilaration on that stage could not have been higher. The actors all scored in their roles, and when the show aired it was an immediate hit. And not with blacks only, as some predicted would be the case. The viewership was 60 percent white. It was heralded as a breakthrough by the press generally and the black press especially, the actors were proud and excited, and it was a kick sitting down each week to a reading of the new script.

That lasted for about eight weeks. What followed taught me a great deal about a lot of things, including myself. With all the attention being paid, Esther and John began to feel a personal responsibility for every aspect of TV's first black family's behavior. That was quite understandable. The off-camera crew, too, couldn't have cared more about how we portrayed the Evans family. But for the actors, after reading and hearing from all the world about the show—their pastors, their families, their friends, the press, and soon their egos—the weight of believing themselves to be the public image of their race became a bit too much for them, especially when they themselves held different views. The Evans family they thought they should be presenting to the world was becoming too good to be true. In disagreements over a line or a bit of business, Allan and I, their white producers and writers, would often hear from Esther or John, "No, we wouldn't do that." Or, "Uh-uh, I wouldn't say that," or "She would never feel that way."

Some of the cast's input was invaluable and I learned a thousand lessons from John and Esther, not just about black people but about our joint humanity. Still, their hypersensitivity to how they were perceived—by social forces that were not of one mind—cost us all dearly. We were losing some unique subject matter and a degree of reality that made for our show's freshness. This had to stop, and one story line Esther was refusing to consider resulted in a turnaround.

Thelma, the Evanses' mature and beautiful sixteen-year-old, had a boyfriend she cared about who started to hit on her quite seriously. Physically, she had every desire to sleep with him, and a girlfriend was advising her that she should, but Thelma was fighting it and wanted to talk it over with her mom. When Esther heard about it, she refused the script.

"No point in even reading it," she said. "The last thing we want this family to deal with on our show is teenage sex." The fact that Thelma ultimately came to the same conclusion as her mom made no difference to Esther. "It is morally wrong, let's not even discuss it," she said. "There is enough that's morally wrong on TV. Not on my show!"

Maybe it was the "my show" syndrome setting in that did it, but finally I knew I had to do something. At the next rehearsal I asked all the cast members, the writers, and the director to pull up a chair and "Let's talk." I told them that I couldn't be prouder of them and what we'd brought to TV together. I spoke of how much I'd learned in the process about the black culture, for which I held such a deep affection and appreciation. I understood and respected why each of them felt entitled to their feelings about how their race should be represented on TV, reminded them of how many times even they disagreed, and then asked them to consider the problems these mind-sets were presenting to the creative staff, particularly me. Worst of all, I pointed out, this problem had started to affect our work, and we had to put an end to it.

The buck was going to stop with me, I told them. When we couldn't reach an agreement on whatever the issue, I would make the decision as to what route we took. On the matter of "Thelma's Problem," I told Esther, the discussion was over and we were going ahead with that script. But lest they think me arbitrary and dictatorial, I reminded them that we were doing a family show and that I, too, grew up in a family and had made families of my own. I, too, was a father, a son, a husband, an uncle, and a grandson. In the way they all interact and relate, I haven't detected that much difference from one race to another. The difference lies in the patina, the way we may express the same feelings, the way we arrive at similar conclusions. I would continue to defer to them in those matters, but even then, as their executive producer, I'd continue to provide the guideposts.

That didn't go down as well with Esther and John as I would have liked, but it did give them considerable pause. "Thelma's Problem" went well and we got a lot of mail from individuals, schools, and institutions that found the episode helpful in opening up a normally difficult subject for discussion. I shared it all with Esther, but she'd received some mail, too, from her church, her pastor, and a couple of fundamentalist institutions I knew well because I would hear from them all the time. Going forward, I empathized with both John and Esther. Good people and fine actors, their egos were nonetheless bruised from both directions. They couldn't win unless they were sufficiently flexible to open up to another point of view occasionally in the service of the show, maintaining their convictions even when performing something counter to those convictions. Sadly to say, they weren't.

Jimmie Walker, as the older son, J.J., was a big problem to them. It started early in the series when he ad-libbed "Dy-no-mite!" about something that pleased him. It was funny, the audience howled, and he repeated it to the same reaction. A sure laugh, at the next reading the cast found it in the script. John winced and it was clear trouble was brewing.

Let me say that I loved J.J. the character and Jimmie the actor. In reality they were not that far apart. The actor seemed to have shrugged off what was known as "the black man's burden." I believed that was the way he chose to deal with it. Physically, he could have been a cartoonist's vision of Ichabod Crane, a funnyman to the eye, to which he deliberately added the ear. The man, the boy, was just plain funny. "Dy-no-mite!" became a running joke, and the character of J.J., John and Esther began to believe, was running away with the show. It was Mike Evans's idea that the J.J. character be a painter, too, and I thought that could be a great counter to "Dy-no-mite!" I loved the idea. It occurred, coincidentally, at the time I'd taken an interest in contemporary art.

With my older friend (and member of the modern art cognoscenti) Dick Dorso as counselor, I visited galleries and artists' studios and along the way met and collected a number of the modern greats, among them the black artist Ernie Barnes. Ernie cottoned to the notion of his paintings being the on-camera stand-ins for J.J.'s creativity. I'd been learning in my art travels with Dorso that, in appearance, artists were 180 degrees from what I'd ignorantly imagined them to be. They were not Peter Ustinov in a smock and beret. They looked like the guy or gal who came to fix your washer, trim your garden, or unclog your drain. The possibility of an artist lurking in everyone was a point I took special pleasure in making when J.J.'s talent as a painter unfolded.

Ernie Barnes, in his unique style, sketched a few elongated and attenuated athletes to begin with, and J.J.'s artistry was established. Then, to make as big a splash of this as we knew how, and engage in as sensitive and worthwhile a discussion at the same time, we wrote an entire story around J.J.'s latest piece of art. It was a black Jesus, which Ernie Barnes took special pride in. To Esther, who was very devoted to her church, the portrait itself and the dialogue discussion that necessarily followed was blasphemous. Odd that the largely white writing staff of a show about a black family was defending the notion of a black Jesus to a black woman, but to me that was all the proof we needed to know what an interesting and multifaceted topic our story had engaged. Nonetheless, it left Esther Rolle and John Amos entirely on edge. "Dy-no-mite!" was a further and constant irritation. We toned it down and had Jimmie say it less often, but the audience loved it and sometimes burst out with it themselves when they felt it was coming and J.J. had been instructed to hold back.

With all the friction and discontent, the show remained funny and we told some remarkably topical stories (about, among other subjects, VD, drug addiction, and the consequences of having a gun in the house). We'd read that the incidence of high blood pressure was greater in black men than whites and did an episode on the subject that involved John. The next day thousands of black men phoned their doctors and medical centers for more information. Months later, when the episode was rerun, the network attached an advisory for which it was lauded by the medical establishment.

Of course *Good Times* wouldn't have been a Tandem/T.A.T. production without at least one example of inane network censorship. In one episode the grandfather comes to visit and brings a woman with him. Everybody assumes they'd gotten married, and they all make room and give them the bedroom. Then it turns out that they weren't married, and Florida says, "You mean to tell me that you're . . ." and the thirteen-year-old finishes the question: "Shacking up?" After days of wrangling the network said, "We'll let the kid say 'Getting it on.'" They were okay with "getting it on" but not "shacking up."

We shot it the way we wanted to and the line got a warm and dear laugh. Two nights before the broadcast I was saying to Program Practices in New York, "If it's on the air without that moment I'm not going to be here tomorrow or any other day, and you do whatever you want to do . . ."

Their threat when someone stands up to them is always a lawsuit. My response was, "Back up the truck, take the house and the furniture. I know the law prevents you from taking the kids. You can't take the family, and I can always sit down and get another pencil and a piece of paper to start again."

The episode aired with the line intact.

Good Times, while it was rarely out of the top twenty and spent a lot of time in the top ten, became an agony to produce. J.J.'s popularity with the largely black audiences that came to the tapings was a friendly, joyful distraction to the company, but a great annoyance to our stars. Frankly, they hated it. And as sensitive to these fine actors as he was, Jimmie knew how they felt and it tore him up inside. That caused him to be more of what they hated on the outside, to the point where the press began calling him a stereotype.

Had John and Esther thrown their arms around this wild but tender talent and been grateful for what he brought to the show, so hungry for their respect and kindness was Jimmie that they could have owned the lad and helped him to mature, to become more an actor and less a type. The only other adult in the cast, Ja'net DuBois, a comedienne who delivered on everything that was handed her, understood what was going on. Her friendship and respect helped Jimmie keep his sanity.

By the end of the third season John Amos was so glum and dispirited that it seemed impossible to go on, and we decided to write him out of the show. Talk to John and you might as well be dealing with the Sphinx—twenty-five hundred years of silent certainty. I was sure he felt that the work he was doing was beneath him, and that another character, not his, was why the show was on the air. His ego blinded him. Without that family, especially the sturdy, steadfast parents that John Amos and Esther Rolle represented to a fare-thee-well, Jimmie would have been just another loose cannon stand-up comic. It was the family that gave J.J. weight, "Dy-no-mite!" or not.

The fourth season opened with the Evanses preparing to move to Mississippi, where James has gotten a good job, but before that can happen, they receive the tragic news that he's been killed in a car crash. The next season, a new star was born on the show when Janet Jackson made her acting debut in a stunning appearance as a victim of child abuse. Janet's performance and the subject matter captured so much attention that we found a way to keep her on the show for the full season by having Willona seek to adopt her. *Good Times,* which debuted in January 1974, was on the air for six seasons, but with Allan Manings in charge, I was immediately able to devote my time to the development of our fifth show.

EARLY IN THE RUN of *All in the Family,* a black family, the Jeffersons, moved in next door to the Bunkers. For the first couple of years we saw only Lionel Jefferson (Mike Evans) and his mom, Louise (Isobel Sanford), who would be better known as "Weezy" after we cast the role of George, the husband who called her by that name. That occurred in 1973. I had seen Sherman Hemsley in the Broadway musical *Purlie,* and from the moment we considered moving a black family in next door to Archie, I couldn't get Sherman out of my mind. Until he was free of *Purlie,* George was an offstage character and the man of the house was Henry, George's brother. Henry was Archie's counterpart—the same size, same volume, same warped attitudes. As good as the actor (Mel Stewart) was, Henry came off as merely a black Archie, not his nemesis—not someone who could get Archie's goat before he even entered the room. When Sherman came on the scene it was another story. He was a natural irritant—prouder, feistier, more pugnacious, and smaller than Archie—the black bantam cock version of him who could all but literally get under Archie's skin.

We realized early on that being neighbors to the Bunkers was the bush leagues for these talented players and there was another show in *The Jeffersons*. The plan to see them "moving on up to the East Side with a duplex apartment in the sky" came about in a most interesting way. One day three members of the Black Panthers, a militant civil rights group of the sixties and seventies, stormed into my offices at CBS saying they'd "come to see the garbage man"— me. *Good Times* was garbage, they said, and on they ranted: "Show's nothing but a white man's version of a black family . . . Character of J.J. is a fucking put-down . . . Every time you see a black man on the tube he is dirt poor, wears shit clothes, can't afford nothing . . . That's bullshit, we got black men in America doing better than most whites . . ." Hours later, as I was telling my associate Al Burton about the Black Panthers' visit and their view of the Evans family's struggle in *Good Times*, his eyes lit up. I got his meaning—and so did *The Jeffersons*, who were now "Moving on Up."

The show debuted on CBS on January 18, 1975. Sherman Hemsley, already popular as Archie's neighbor, became an instant star on his own show, as did Isobel Sanford as his wife and his equal in the "I give as good as I get" department.

Upstairs lived a mixed-marriage couple played by Roxie Roker, a lovely black actress, and an extremely white comedic actor, Franklin Cover. I describe him as "extremely white" because he had the kind of pure white face that didn't show the slightest sign of assimilation in any direction, at any time over centuries. Roxie was cast first. When I told her she could have the part, I prefaced it by emphasizing several things about her on-screen marriage. Her husband would be seriously white and their marriage would be as real as any other on TV. I cautioned her that television had never seen a mixed couple in a real relationship, never seen them kiss on the lips and sleep in the same bed, and there was no way we could foretell the audience reaction. John J. O'Connor, writing in the *New York Times*, voiced the same concern. Noting that our shows had "a reputation for dealing with the unusual and controversial: breast cancer, menopause, drugs, abortion, rape . . ." he added, "this time, however, whatever the collective psyche of the nation may be at the present moment, Lear is teetering on the explosive."

I told Roxie I thought America was ready for it, but the network's concern exceeded that of Mr. O'Connor's, and if she felt the least bit squeamish about it I would understand. Roxie's answer was to dig into her purse and show me a copy of her marriage photo. "We've been married for nearly fifteen years," she said. "Does this answer your question?" There stood Roxie, the bride, with Seymour Kravitz, her white Jewish groom. A second photo she showed me proudly was of their young son, whom you know as the musician and singer Lenny Kravitz.

Marla Gibbs played the role of Florence, the maid, and everything that fell out of her mouth seemed to be funny. Her reaction to meeting the Jeffersons when she came for her job interview was unforgettable. Given the Park Avenue building she was in, she'd expected to be reporting to a white couple. "Wait a second," she said, pointing to Louise and George. "You mean to tell me you two live here?" And then, pointing to the visiting mixed-marrieds, "And you two live upstairs?" On their nod, she exploded with, "How does it happen we already overcome and nobody told me?"

Paul Benedict, a remarkable comic actor playing a Briton in the next apartment, rounded out the regular cast. In the opening show, after dipping his head in the doorway to call out a "Welcome!" to his new neighbors, he turned back in wonder to exclaim, "Good God, you're black!"

Unlike *Good Times*, *The Jeffersons* ran smoothly and, at eleven seasons, was our longest-running show.

PERHAPS THE FASTEST SOCIAL and civil rights progress America has seen in the past fifty years has been in the area of gay and lesbian recognition.

It raced to the forefront of our culture as a topic of conversation, and was accepted with relative ease by the broad body of Americans and by our justice system as a civil rights and liberties issue, despite its being so bitterly opposed by religious and legal fundamentalists.

There is no doubt as to which direction this civil rights battle is headed and few disagree that the media has led the way. I take great pride in the thirteen-episode run we had on ABC in early 1975—premiering just six days after *The Jeffersons*—of our sixth show, *Hot L Baltimore*, from a play by Lanford Wilson. The title was of course intended to be *Hotel Baltimore*, but the *e* had fallen out of the sign.

I'd fallen in love with a photograph of a mother and her baby lying face-to-face on a bed in a book of photos called *The Family of Man*. I wrote something about the photograph that traveled alongside it to museums across the country. From that moment on, the expression "Family of Man" has rarely left my mind, and that is exactly the way I viewed the characters who resided in the *Hot L Baltimore*. There were a pair of ordinary hookers, not lookers (Conchata Ferrell and Jeannie Linero); a middle-aged pair of straightforward gay men who'd been a couple for twenty years or more (Lee Bergere and Henry Calvert); a dotty old woman (Charlotte Rae) who visited her wacky son "Horse," whom we never saw, and reported on his insane off-camera antics; a well-read spiritual and free-thinking black dude who had the answers to everything (Al Freeman Jr.); the hotel's owner (Richard Masur); and his exhausted desk clerk (James Cromwell). I'll flatter myself—and bless our casting director, Jane Murray—to say the entire cast was brilliant.

ABC wasn't the least bit excited about the series. But for having made the mistake of letting *All in the Family* go, I doubt they would ever have bought it. However, a young Michael Eisner, who had just been named head of programming at ABC, had had no part in that haunting decision, and he liked *Hot L*. I learned quickly that, unlike most of the TV programming executives, Eisner paid real attention, at least to the shows he cared about. His notes were delivered personally because he came to every five P.M. taping and brought with him the excitement of a kid experiencing theater for the first time. Eisner never lost that youthful passion.

After the airing of our fourth episode he had to make a call he didn't like, to tell me that the show would not be picked up. We were to complete our order for thirteen knowing that would be it. It seemed the affiliates and independents across the country were balking at our cast of characters, especially "those two guys who behave like they're married."

Despite knowing *Hot L Baltimore* had no future, Michael Eisner continued to the very end to attend a taping of each episode. He brought the same fervor and dedication to the Walt Disney Studios in 1986 and took it into the next century at the top of the heap.

TANDEM'S SUCCESS—the 1974–75 season ended with *All in the Family* number one in the Nielsens, *Sanford and Son* number two, *The Jeffersons* number four, *Good Times* number seven, and *Maude* number nine—prompted a piece in the *New Yorker* in which critic and social commentator Michael Arlen wrote that "Norman Lear has a feel for what people want to see before they know they want to see it." The way I experienced the wonder we were caught up in was on a number of red-eye flights from L.A. to New York. I would look down anywhere over America and think it just possible that wherever I saw a light there could be someone, maybe an entire family, I'd helped to make laugh. In my dissociated fashion I marveled at this, but it was nothing compared to what I understand now, that I was the architect of all that.

People were forever commenting about how high the stress level must be producing, week in and week out, as many shows as I was involved with. I would inevitably respond, "Well, there is stress, and then there is 'joyful' stress." What I was experiencing was joyful stress. I truly meant that. Certainly there was stress. With all the script conferences, talent to handle and support, rehearsals, tapings, and all the problems native to any effort that strives to keep hundreds of people working constructively together—all while I struggled to maintain my other role as a husband and a father to three—there was *great* stress. But the kick of having an idea one week with the opportunity to convey it to some 40 or so million people not too many weeks later, plus the positive acceptance of our work as evidenced by the size of our devoted audiences, resulted in the kind of high that I believed turned all the strain and pressure into—I've found no better way to put it—joyful stress.

4

M Y POLITICAL LIFE shot into high gear in the mid- to late seventies. The aroma of the dollars in my success led to my being solicited, it seemed, by every liberal, moderate, or progressive who held or ran for office in all fifty states. And calling me, from then to now, have been current leaders of the House and Senate, staff members and political advisers, the heads of political organizations, and a few presidents.

"Basically, you in Hollywood and we in DC are in the same business," they would tell me. "We each seek the affection and approval of the American people and, most important, we seek to communicate with the American people." Clearly I was doing better at that, they said, and oh so humbly they asked for my help. For forty years or so I've spent untold hours in meetings; at breakfasts, lunches, and dinners; and on phone calls offering up my thinking for this campaign and that cause, but—as unbelievable as this is to me even now—no matter how sincerely they seemed to listen, or how grateful they were for suggestions they couldn't wait to put into effect, no one ever acted on a single idea I presented. Not ever. Every bit of contact following versions of that speech had to do with my checkbook and my Rolodex.

In 1973 I was invited to become president of the ACLU Foundation of Southern California, following my friend Stanley Sheinbaum. Because I was so busy, my presidency would be largely ceremonial, to help raise money and such, and I accepted on that basis. My value to the organization increased, however, with the popularity of the TV shows and my resultant celebrity. I admired the ACLU for standing on principle 100 percent of the time, even when they knew a position they had to take on a civil liberties issue would make them terribly unpopular. One such occurred during my presidency. When the National Socialist Party of America (derived from the American Nazi Party) decided to march in Skokie, Illinois—home to neighborhoods of Holocaust survivors—and was denied permission, the ACLU saw this as a free speech issue and interceded on its behalf (*National Socialist Party v. Village of Skokie*).

As an officer of the ACLU my name would likely have found its way into the press in any event, but I was also one of a number who wrote a check to help fund the case, and that became a big deal. One morning the phone rang around six A.M. It was Joan Didion and John Gregory Dunne, who lived up the street and had just passed our house on their early-morning constitutional. They apologized for calling so early but thought I might wish to deal with a problem I didn't know I had. The words "JEW HATER—NAZI SYMPATHIZER" had been printed in large red letters across our white front gate. What the Dunnes didn't know was that a dead pig had been tossed over the fence and lay in our blood-splotched driveway. And it wasn't paint that those hateful red words across our gate were inscribed with.

This was the work of the Jewish Defense League, a vigilante-styled group started by a rabbi, Meir Kahane. Jews did this? Led by a rabbi? The incident taught me everything I needed to know about the universality of all humanity. My bumper sticker reads, JUST ANOTHER VERSION OF YOU.

COMPLAINTS ABOUT SEX and violence on television had for years been a convenient distraction from the real problems facing the nation. If one program can be said to have brought it to a head, it was 1974's *Born Innocent*. Linda Blair had just starred as the possessed teenager in the hugely successful film *The Exorcist*—directed by my old friend Billy Friedkin—and NBC had hired her to headline the cast of a tawdry TV movie set in a girls' detention home. Eager to capitalize on her popularity with America's youth, the network scheduled the movie at eight o'clock on a Tuesday night despite its containing U.S. television's first depiction of a lesbian gang raping a fourteen-year-old (Blair) in the shower with a plunger handle. When a subsequent real-life rape of a nine-year-old with a soda bottle was said to have been inspired by the movie, the notion of the early evening as a sex-and-violence-free zone took hold.

The earliest and most passionate proponent of this noble-sounding concept was Arthur Taylor, then midway through his four-year reign as president of CBS Entertainment. Mr. Taylor had been a top corporate executive at the world's largest pulp and paper company, with no experience in broadcasting, but that didn't stop him from suddenly and unilaterally declaring that the eight to nine P.M. hour (seven to eight in the central time zone) should be a "Family Viewing Hour."

"We want American families to be able to watch television in that time period without ever being embarrassed," read a statement from Taylor's office. This assumed, of course, that there was uniformity in what would embarrass American families, that a significant number of families still gathered to watch television together, and that children who might have an interest in the shows that troubled Mr. Taylor all went to bed by nine o'clock—three premises any single one of which would have earned the man a failing grade in American Family Studies. But the absurdity of these perceptions didn't stop ABC and NBC from joining CBS's Mr. Taylor in his missionary zeal to make the TV screen safe for parents and children.

Of course, the "Family Viewing Hour" was nothing more than the networks' draping themselves in the wholesomeness of the term. When people get upset with the amount of sex and violence on television, they tend to look west to blame Hollywood. Wrong. The content creators—the writers, producers, and directors—are not, and never have been, in control. Television is a business and, as with all businesses, it's governed by supply and demand. If the demand didn't exist at the networks, writers would not be supplying it. The blame lies to the east, on Wall Street and on the giant, often international media entities that answer to its short-term interests.

Nonetheless, sensing that a subject this visceral could provide political advantage, Congress got into the act. The House Appropriations Committee, which funds the Federal Communications Commission, pressured its chairman, Richard E. Wiley, to take action, and the FCC soon made Arthur Taylor's brainstorm into a federal matter. With the three networks on board, the National Association of Broadcasters further demanded that local stations (the majority of them network affiliates) extend the embarrassment-proof programming back into the pre-prime-time hour as well. It was agreed in April 1975 that the Family Viewing Hour—or, as it was officially and more accurately known, the Prime Time Censorship Rule—would commence with the new TV season that September.

I was on vacation in Paris when I first heard how this symbolic attempt to clean up television would affect our company. CBS president Bob Wood called to tell me that *All in the Family* would have to be moved out of its Saturday eight P.M. time slot (from which it had reigned as TV's number one show for four seasons) to a later hour "unless it can conform to Family Viewing time." (Apparently the presence of the very word *Family* in its title was insufficient to inoculate it.) I kidded him and said, "Oh, so now you have a definition of Family Viewing time? Won't you read it to me, Bob?"

"There is nothing to read," he said, "but some of our people went through all of the twenty-four shows you made for this current season, and were you to make those shows next year, under the new Family Viewing concept, you would have to make considerable changes in twenty or twenty-one of them, and you would not be allowed to do two of them at all."

And I said, "So we only made one show this season that was as clean as a whistle?" Bob Wood reiterated that if we were going into the next season with those scripts, that was the way it would be.

I said there was no way I was going to—or would have any idea how to—change America's most popular show to meet the vague standards of decency that the Family Hour demanded. A few days later the fall schedule was announced, with *All in the Family* moved to Monday at nine P.M., where young minds, asleep now of course, could be spared its wicked ways.

Despite the fact that older minds must have found us in greater numbers, since the show remained number one the following season, it was instantly clear that there was a stigma attached to this move. *All in the Family* was virtually devoid of sex and violence, but its propensity for dealing with topical subjects was evidently deemed equally unfit for children, and the tendency of its characters to use the same language that children heard every day in their actual lives earned it banishment to the non-family-approved ghetto.

In addition to the demoralizing effect of being told that this show families had been watching and loving for five years was now considered bad for families, our instincts, confirmed by conversations with others in the industry, told us that there could be a serious economic penalty as well. Since there was now a considerable block of time (seven to nine P.M., counting the affiliates' hour) during which local stations would not be able to run *All in the Family*, its value in the syndication market—where the real money that allowed producers to continue to make new shows was earned—would be significantly decreased. And if the show was not suitable for seven P.M., wouldn't it seem at least as inappropriate for the late-afternoon after-school time slots?

Another by-product of this assault on freedom of speech was that writers of new shows were sanitizing their scripts to minimize potential offensiveness, because no one wanted to cut their chances of getting on the air by a third, which would be the effect if you were precluded from the Family Hour. Additionally, scripts that would have raised four or five objections were now raising dozens, and the intensity of the discussions escalated as well. The creative climate was becoming increasingly oppressive—there was a vapor that snuck under doors and through walls, even on shows ostensibly safe from Family Hour restrictions.

The best example from that season was what Program Practices came to call the "Raspberry to God" show. In the episode, Archie and Mike are arguing about religion, and whether or not Archie's grandson would be brought up to believe in God. Mike's attitude is, "He'll grow up and make up his own mind," and Archie's is, "No, he won't. He is going to go to church. He is going to be a good, God-fearing Christian." Mike restates his opinion, Archie says that if Mike raises his son that way, "God will punish you," and Mike says, "If I did believe in God, he wouldn't be the kind of God you believe in. He wouldn't be a punishing, vengeful God." The argument continues in this vein, and at some point Mike gives Archie a raspberry, and Archie interprets it as his having given a raspberry to God.

Previously the network might, on occasion, have objected to this kind of thing in the script, and I would have said, "Let's wait until you see it on its feet, and if you still have a problem we can talk about it." Now they just decreed, "You can't do it." I suggested that we invite several clergymen from various religious factions to attend the pretaping run-through and said I'd be willing to abide by their decision if they deemed it sacrilegious. A man named Dick Kirschner from Program Practices rejected that idea, saying, "We don't program for clergymen," and assuring me that while *he* understood that the raspberry was not directed at God, others—i.e., our unsophisticated middle-of-the-country viewers—would not.

"There is going to be a knee-jerk reaction," he said, "because they are talking about God and the raspberry comes in the middle of it and they are not going to hear it right. And there is going to be this knee-jerk reaction, and we don't want that."

"So," I said, "you're not programming for the clergy, you're programming for the knee-jerkers."

In the end we shot the show we wanted to shoot, and sometime later we got the word that it had been accepted by the network, so the ultimate result was that dozens of man-hours that could have been creatively spent were instead squandered on useless discussions that produced nothing but needless anxiety and animosity.

The combination of potential financial losses and the climate of unspoken censorship caused by the Family Viewing Hour prompted me to call my friend Geoff Cowan, then the head of UCLA's communications law department, to ask if he thought we had First Amendment grounds for a lawsuit. He did, and a few days later, at Geoff's suggestion, I met with a young attorney, Ron Olson, with the law firm Munger, Tolles—today, Munger, Tolles & Olson. (Charlie Munger is the partner of celebrated investor Warren Buffett.) I liked Olson immediately, and when I learned that he hailed from my adopted home state of Iowa, we linked like a pair of twelve-year-olds.

As I said in my deposition for the lawsuit, "A great deal of what you term excess violence occurs because there is a program department that is asking for action . . . and the euphemism for violence is action . . . In search of ratings, excess violence is coaxed out of writers and production companies by the very networks that bring on from another direction a Family Viewing Hour to lessen it."

The foolishness and perniciousness of the Family Viewing Hour was evidently clear to Los Angeles district court judge Warren J. Ferguson, too. In November 1976 he ruled that the FCC's Family Hour concept, and the NAB's extension of it into pre–prime time, did indeed violate freedom of speech guarantees. "The desirability or undesirability of family viewing is not the issue," Ferguson said, "but censorship by government or privately created review boards cannot be tolerated."

Judge Ferguson's decision was a source of joy and achievement for all the guilds. "One for the good guys," we all felt on the creative end of TV. But little could change materially as long as the business end, the networks in particular, were addicted to and controlled by the numbers.

IN DECEMBER 1975 *One Day at a Time* began its nine-season run. Allan Manings and his wife, Whitney Blake, wanted to do a comedy about a divorced woman raising teenage kids alone. "What happens to Ibsen's Nora after she leaves the Doll's House?" was the question they were asking, and they'd been trying to sell the show for ten years. As the father of three daughters, two of them teenagers, I loved the idea, and over time we developed Ann Romano, her daughters, Julie and Barbara, and a backstory that had them moving to Indianapolis after Ann's divorce into an apartment building with a superintendent, Schneider, as proud of his tool belt as any honored marine is of his medals. Schneider, hilariously played by Pat Harrington Jr., would become a de facto uncle to the girls and would-be suitor to Ann. There was no way I could have guessed that this simple, interesting situation would give rise to one of the fiercest battles with Program Practices we'd ever been through. It was a story involving Julie, the older, more outgoing, and rebellious daughter, that set things off.

When it came to casting the role, Mackenzie Phillips, popular for her part in George Lucas's *American Graffiti* and daughter of John Phillips (leader of the hugely popular sixties band The Mamas and the Papas), was a shoo-in. For the part of the younger daughter, Barbara, fifteen-year-old Valerie Bertinelli came in to audition. Although she had little professional experience, she read the part well and was winning and eager. She also bore a certain resemblance to my youngest daughter, Maggie. I couldn't resist offering her the role.

As to the lead, we read a number of actresses who would have been good in the role, but both Manings and I fell in love with Bonnie Franklin, whose look and personality clashed with the general perception of a divorced woman and mother of teenage daughters. Bonnie was thirty-one at the time, and a young-looking thirty-one at that. There was also a certain spunk and fire to her personality that added to her youthful look. We found her irresistible but didn't think the network unreasonable to advise against casting her as the mother of teenage daughters, one of them sixteen. Still, remembering the lesson we learned when we chose not to play Archie Bunker as Irish despite Carroll O'Connor's indubitably Irish face, I cast Bonnie Franklin as Ann Romano. That, though, wasn't what caused the battle with Program Practices.

The pilot story was about Julie, excited that she'd been invited to go on a weekend camping trip with some new friends in their new surroundings. There would be six of them, three girls and three boys. Ann voiced all the concerns you might imagine, Julie became hysterical and accused her mother of not trusting her, and the dialogue bounced off the subject of boys and girls alone in the wild with raging hormones and sleeping bags with zippers. Allan Manings said of Program Practices, "They had almost as many notes as there were pages in the script." We took some of their notes, made changes, and stood fast on the rest—in particular, a beat where Julie talked about mooning somebody in a car.

There was no moment of mooning on the show. She just talked about it. The line wasn't important to the episode, but I understood that if I allowed this Family Hour victory, the floodgates of such bullshit would be forever open.

After the five o'clock taping, CBS West Coast VP Perry Lafferty reported to New York that the show had been taped without several of the changes they had asked for. We were giving cast notes for the next taping when Perry, accompanied by the Program Practices guy, came down and took me aside to tell me New York was unhappy and demanded that several trims and changes be made. We went over them, accepted a couple of their notes, and said no to the others, including the mooning. Ten minutes later, Mr. Lafferty, a nice man and good friend, returned.

"I just got off the phone with New York," he said. "You make this show with that line in it and not only won't they air it, they won't pay for it." Everything in me ached to say "Screw them" and make the eight o'clock show with only the changes we'd accepted. But this would be taking a huge financial risk, and I had a fiduciary relationship with my partners that made that decision questionable.

My life in TV flashed before me. When I dealt with network executives personally, away from our business together, I found them, for the most part, to be bright, engaging, and able men. But when they retreated into that monolithic conglomerate and became units of the corporation, they suddenly became vague and faceless and tended to view those of us who produced their shows the way they viewed their audience—as "they": *We,* the network executives, moral guardians of the nation—a handful of people sitting around on the thirty-fourth floor of some black building in Manhattan—know what's in the hearts and minds of Americans everywhere. And *we* know what's best for *them*. *We* understand and *they* don't.

But the network executives *didn't* understand. Maybe those of us in the creative community didn't understand perfectly either, but our talents were engaged in dealing with a complex world the way we saw it, albeit comedically, and as honestly as we knew how. And we left the "understanding" of our work confidently to our viewers. It seemed to me that was the more grown-up point of view and it pushed me to tape the eight o'clock show our way.

The following morning Frances, the girls, and I were leaving for Kona Village in Hawaii. We would be gone a week. As we were wrapping up after the taping it concerned me that the network would have that week to mess with the show without me around. Then it occurred to me that it wasn't really their tape, since they'd said up front that they wouldn't pay for it. And so I asked our associate producer, Patricia Palmer, to have the original and backup tapes put in my car, and when we left for Kona the next morning they were locked away in my garage. This happened well before cell phones, and the Kona resort being known for its no-television-or-phones policy, it took Fred Silverman a few days to reach me. Fred, who I always felt came down more on my side than the network's but who was married to that mob, was doing what his position called for. The network wanted the pilot—and now! As its owner, I said, I was well within my rights to keep it. But it was CBS who ordered it and had every right to see it, Fred said. My response: not until they agree to pay for what they ordered. A day later they agreed.

5

B ACK IN 1968, when ABC agreed to fund the original pilot for what became *All in the Family*, I told them about an idea I had for a late-night Monday-through-Friday soap opera and they offered to pay me for the first ten scripts. While active productions kept me from writing, the idea continued to mature in my head. Speeches I made about the media, testimony before congressional committees, interviews I'd given, and articles I'd been asked to write all served to whet my appetite for a show that examined the impact on us of the metastasizing media and consumer culture in which, as Andy Warhol memorably predicted, "everyone will be world-famous for fifteen minutes." How was the average American family affected, I wondered, by commercial products being pounded at them every few minutes from the multiple television sets broadcasting in their homes an average of seven-plus hours a day? The best vehicle for tackling the subject as I saw it was a story that played out on a daily basis, five episodes per week. Preferably, for reasons of content and because it had never been done before, I began to see the soap opera playing in a late-night time slot.

What became *Mary Hartman, Mary Hartman* had been percolating in me for several years when Al Burton, an able and energetic executive, became our director of Creative Affairs. He loved the idea and never let me off that hook. A late-night soap had never been done before, so no network executive was willing to take a chance on such an untested idea without numbers in which to take refuge. Also, it was my intention to satirically comment on the impact on an American family of commercial-driven all-day-and-all-night television, especially on the housewife who was more inclined in those years to be at home with the TV on. By the time I started interviewing writers, I had a few pages of notes that contained all the elements I wanted to see in the pilot episode.

I wanted the mass murder of a family of five, along with their two goats and eight chickens, to take place just down the street from Mary Hartman's home. Inured to such wholesale violence by the unrelenting media, we see it command less of our housewife's attention than the promise of quality on the label of a product she's using, as advertised on the kitchen TV that is never off. At the same time, an elderly flasher who has been exposing himself during milk breaks at the grade school turns out to be her grandfather, and she and her husband, Tom, are having a problem in their sex life. He hasn't exposed himself to her in months.

I must have interviewed a dozen highly talented writers, including Madelyn Pugh and Bob Carroll Jr., who wrote *I Love Lucy* for many years. I could not have respected them more, but we were not on the same page with this one. They asked, as did many others, "Norman, how can we expect laughs after the slaughter of an entire family?" "Plus their goats and chickens," I reminded them. I didn't expect ha-ha laughs, I explained, but there was humor in the deleterious lunacy of our escalating consumer culture, as illustrated here by Mary, so enthralled by the merchandising of a floor-waxing product as to be numb to the most extreme violence in her very own neighborhood. They didn't see it that way. The writer who did, Ann Marcus, eventually came up with this reaction for our title character.

When her next-door neighbor rushes in with news of the killings, Mary, concerned with a "waxy yellow buildup" on her kitchen floor, says: "My, who would want to kill two goats and eight chickens?" (another moment of distraction). "And the people," she adds, never taking her eyes off the label of the product in her hand. "Of course, the people."

Ann Marcus brought in three other writers, Gail Parent, Jerry Adelman, and Ken Hartman. Parent and Adelman, like Marcus, were totally in sync with that off-the-wall part of me Mel Brooks identified as "mad," as was Hartman, who had only recently rechristened himself Daniel Gregory Browne. A dipper into New Age philosophies, including numerology, he was told the letters in his adopted name would be lucky for him. They were certainly lucky for *Mary Hartman*.

The repetition of the name of the title character, by the way, was triggered by my memory of *The Goldbergs*, perhaps the earliest of sitcoms. It began on radio when I was a boy and opened with the sound of Gertrude Berg as Mrs. Goldberg calling out her apartment window to a neighbor, "Yoo-hoo, Mrs. Bloom, Mrs. Bloom!" The melody of that opening never left me, and I was as much a composer as a producer when I cast Dody Goodman to play Mary's mother. Her "Mary Hartman, Mary Hartman" fused melodically in my head with Gertrude Berg's "Mrs. Bloom!"

The casting of Louise Lasser, like that of Carroll O'Connor, took less than a minute. I had sent the script to Charlie Joffe, who called after reading it and said there was only one actress for this part—the former Mrs. Woody Allen. Ms. Lasser refused the role at first, but finally agreed to come in and meet with me. Charlie came with her and told me later that it was the first time he'd been present at the start of a love affair he wasn't a part of. Louise and I hit it off instantly. She was more than a touch of Mary Hartman already. Actually, I supplied the character, but Louise brought with her the persona that fit Mary Hartman like a corset. When she read a bit of the script for me, I all but cried for joy. That reaction won her over completely.

I knew Mary Kay Place was a natural for Mary's young country singer neighbor, Loretta Haggers, married to an older man, Charlie (her "Baby Boy"), played by Graham Jarvis. Mary Kay had been a writer's assistant on one of our earlier shows when I learned that she wanted to act. I loved her country accent, which she never failed to turn up a notch or two in my presence, and cast her in an episode of *All in the Family* as a friend of Gloria's.

Greg Mullavey, who played Mary's husband, Tom, walked into a casting session and was exactly the type I was looking for. That "type" grew out of a dinner I'd held at my home some weeks before. I knew the Hartman family should come from mid-America. I hadn't yet decided where when I read that the United Auto Workers was holding a convention in L.A., and so I called my friend Paul Schrade, then a member of the UAW board and a onetime labor consultant to Bobby Kennedy. (He was, incidentally, accompanying Bobby Kennedy when he was assassinated, and it was Paul who was hit by the first bullet fired.) I asked him to invite a group of autoworkers from a plant in Lordstown, Ohio, to dinner at our home to discuss the idea of the breadwinner in my new show working in a plant such as theirs. It was an exciting and informative evening for me, and as I look around the table in my mind's eye, it was a gas for them, too. Along with the information I drew from that evening was a type for the role of Tom Hartman, and that's what Greg Mullavey walked in with at our casting session. His reading was up to his look, and we had Mary's husband.

While thinking about a director for the show I got a call from a woman named Joan Darling, a cousin so distant we never really figured out how to label it. A good deal younger than me, she had worked in improvisational theater, done some writing and teaching, and now had an idea for a film she wished to pitch me, a biopic on Golda Meir, Israel's first and only woman president. We dropped that subject in minutes and, as we talked and laughed from subject to subject, I began to feel her sensibilities compatible with *Mary Hartman*, certainly with Louise, and I asked her if she ever thought of directing. She hadn't, but asked if she could read the script. Before the day was out, *Mary Hartman, Mary Hartman* had a director.

With Debralee Scott as Mary's sister, Phil Bruns as her father, Claudia Lamb as her daughter, and Victor Kilian as her grandfather/flasher, we went into rehearsal for the pilot. On day one I realized that we had too much material for one episode, and that Louise at her best called for a slower pace. That night I talked to Perenchio and we decided to make the pilot and a second episode. Joan Darling as the director turned out to be a great choice, as did every cast member, and Louise Lasser's Mary Hartman was lethally funny. She was the mirror image of a stretched-beyond-reason reality, to help the viewer see what the media and consumer culture were turning us into. But go explain that to the binary imaginations of TV station programmers. Tandem/T.A.T. was handling its own distribution by then and our sales team tried tirelessly, but *MH2* was not selling well. It was "too off the wall," our salesmen reported.

I knew the show was off the wall, of course, but "*too* off the wall"? As nutty as I can get, I was and am a down-to-earth person and producer, and a commercial one at that, and so I wondered if the independent station guys who didn't know me personally would feel differently if they saw that my feet were on the ground. I decided to use my home and my family to sell my real-life husband and father image in the pursuit of selling a show. Our sales team liked the idea and we invited TV station execs who bought product for some thirty station groups, representing more than one hundred stations across the country, to our home. They were in L.A. for a convention and responded to the invitation well. Out on the grass on a warm August evening, with my wife and young daughters as hostesses and violinists strolling between the tables over dessert, the meal fit the occasion. After dinner we repaired to our screening room, where I told them what I thought and felt about the show, interjecting a few asides to my wife and kids that indicated their appreciation of *Mary Hartman*, too. Now, *this*, it occurs to me, was truly a family hour.

The reaction to the show was tempered but clearly good. I'm sure that many in that fraternity didn't want to be seen liking something they might be fearful of buying for other reasons. There was some reasonable applause, and before I could begin to open up a discussion one of the most conservative and influential TV buyer/programmers in the room, Al Flanagan of Combined Communications, raised his hand and said, "Norman, how soon can I have that for my five stations?" I'll never know what intrigued the most savvy but unlikely guy in the room to behave as he did, but it mattered a lot. The show was on its way. Several other buyers for multiple stations followed Al, and as it began to flourish on those stations, others jumped aboard. During its first six months on the air, *Mary Hartman, Mary Hartman* made the covers of *Newsweek, TV Guide, Rolling Stone, People,* and a number of Sunday supplements, including the *New York Times Magazine.*

In addition to the syndication of *Mary Hartman* being profitable, it established a first-run syndication market that had never existed before. Those independent stations that carried it, for the most part at eleven P.M., became known as affiliates of the Mary Hartman Network. As *Newsweek* reported, "In big cities, where the serial is usually shown in the late nighttime slots, the average station has seen its Nielsen numbers more than double since Mary came aboard; at Cincinnati's WXIX the ratings increased a staggering sevenfold."

In Cleveland, which was a top-ten Nielsen market, the show was on a CBS affiliate, which made the show very important in that area from the start. A new station manager, Bill Flynn, who'd been brought in from Boston, decided to program *Mary Hartman* at seven-thirty P.M. It was programmed even earlier in a few places, but Cleveland was, and I assume still is, the home of a very important archdiocese, and the Catholic bishop there went up the wall and organized twelve-hour-a-day picketing. The city council voted unanimously to condemn the station and its manager for making the move. Bill Flynn, heroically to my mind, preempted an hour of prime time on his station and bought an hour on Telstar, a communications satellite, to have me face the head of the PTA, a critic from the *Cleveland Plain Dealer,* a particularly vicious councilman, and one Episcopalian minister who had flown in from Evanston, Illinois, and was a great *Mary Hartman* fan. The councilman, representing the thirty-one out of thirty-three members of the council who condemned the time change, said that the council just didn't want it on the air at seven-thirty "harming innocent minds."

I reminded the panel that the local news was run at five P.M. on two stations in Cleveland, and on the other two in this four-station market at six P.M. Since the average local TV news show starts with any homicide in the vicinity, any rape, any kidnapping, and every kind of violence, weren't they concerned, I asked, about *that* "harming the innocent minds" of children? The answer given by the woman representing the PTA was stunning. "Yes," she said, "but that's not as real as *Mary Hartman*."

Mary Hartman turned out to be a seminal hit for us and became the subject of numerous sociological studies and phenomenal watercooler conversation. "The nihilistic edge to *Mary Hartman*," wrote James Wolcott in the *Village Voice*, "is that though the characters are trapped in those soap opera rooms, the viewer is always aware of the chaotic world outside." The *New York Review of Books* reported that some viewers "recoiled from its assaults on their cherished ideals and modes of behavior, while devotees would rush home of an evening in time for the latest encounter between the staff psychiatrist of Fernwood Receiving Hospital's mental ward and its celebrated inmate, 'The Number One Typical American Consumer Housewife.'" And as recently as 2010, essayist Claire Barliant wrote, "No program has gone as far as this one in ridiculing the medium, as well as in warning of its power to reduce its habitués to followers of herd philosophies."

MH2 was as personally fulfilling as anything I ever did in the half-hour form on TV. I intend the word *fulfilling* to carry a lot of meaning here. Imagine having *this* kooky little scenario in mind for thirty or so years and finally producing the one show that could handle it. Ever since I started to drive and became obsessed with cars and girls, I loved the role of playing the gentleman— walking on the curbside when with a girl; taking her arm when crossing the street; opening the car door for her, just like Melvyn Douglas, Cary Grant, and Fred Astaire. And so, once, in my twenties, I let a girl into my car, and as I was walking around the rear of the vehicle to get to the driver's seat, I was thunderstruck with this idea: What a wonderful way to have someone disappear from the face of the earth. You let a woman into a car, she sees you crossing to her left in the rearview mirror, loses you in that corner blind spot, expecting you to show a split second later, and you don't. You've disappeared, never to be seen again. I'll bet I pictured that scene and smiled to myself 80 percent of the times

I let a lady into a car, and then, finally, that is what happened to George Shumway, as inimitably described in a courtroom scene by his daughter, Mary Hartman.

Another *MH2* storyline that tickled the hell out of my funny bone had Dabney Coleman playing Merle Jeeter, the father and manager of an eight-year-old superstar televangelist, Jimmy Joe Jeeter. In their last scene together, Jimmy Joe convinces his father to hang a TV above the bathtub so the violence reported on the evening news can give him inspiration for his next sermon while he bathes. He works himself into a frenzy as he watches, and the camera briefly cuts away as we hear a splash and a loud sizzle. At this point, neighbor Loretta Haggers comes in and sees that Jimmy Joe has been electrocuted. "He died for the six-thirty news, Lord," she says. "For the sins of the six-thirty news."

My God, what a good time I had working on *Mary Hartman*! To have a vehicle for one's wildest sense of the outrageous that can be shared with millions is a gift from the heavens and beyond. A prime example: Leroy Fedders, a neighbor, was the football coach at Mary's daughter, Heather's, high school, and for story reasons we needed him dead. We had him coming down with the flu and Mary bringing over a bowl of chicken soup to help cure him. What Mary doesn't know is that he's taken a number of pills for the pain, the cough, the fever, and the need to get some sleep, all the while sipping vodka, too. He doesn't want the soup, but his wife and Mary insist he have it. They leave him alone in the kitchen, his head over the bowl, with the instruction, "Eat!" Because he'd taken so many pills and mixed them with all that booze, and because we were making a soap opera, we could take all the time we needed for the camera to observe Leroy's head sinking slowly, slowly toward the bowl, until—plop!—Coach Fedders drowns in his chicken soup.

Gore Vidal was so struck by *Mary Hartman* that he phoned me from Ravello, Italy, where he lived and to whose villa a friend had been sending VHS tapes of the show. He was coming to L.A. in a few weeks and begged to be written into the script. Because he had no time to memorize lines and no experience at improvisation, we pasted clues to his dialogue on tabletops, doors, lamp shades—in every direction he was required to look. All of us—the writers, cast, director, crew, and especially Louise—were thrilled to have him on the show, and a seven-episode Gore Vidal story line was invented that started with him at Mary's kitchen table telling her he'd like to write a book about her.

"A book about you would be a book about America," he told her. "A book about emptiness, a book about promises not kept—but also, paradoxically, a book about hope, a book about survival"—indicating a stack of magazines and the TV set—"against pretty terrible odds."

Most satisfying of all in the world of *Mary Hartman*, however, was the completion of the arc Vidal was attributing that began with my desire to show the impact of the media on an average American housewife. The penultimate scene of that first season has Mary Hartman on David Susskind's late-night talk show *Open End*, a big deal at the time, and what followed from that appearance is what triggered the *New York Review of Books* article. Mary has just been named Housewife and Mother of the Year by some publication, and is being interviewed—hounded is the truer description—by three smug, self-centered, "intellectual" media types. Attempting to defend her TV-viewing habits and magazine selections, her very lifestyle, Mary is slowly being driven crazy—and then, asked a question about her sex life, she accidentally lets drop that her husband is having a performance problem. Between the panel's salivating reaction to that, her terrible guilt, and the foul questions they start firing at her, Mary goes off, but OFF, her rocker. It is as fine a bit of acting—an eleven-minute scene shot in one take—as I have ever seen.

The next season opened with Mary in the mental home to which she's been sent. One of the most hilariously sad but illuminating moments in the entire series took place there. A nurse is seen wheeling a television set into a common room, where a group of oddball patients, including Mary, are sitting about. As the TV is placed before her, Mary sees a small box attached to its side and exclaims, "Oh, don't tell me! Are we?" This catches the attention of the others as the nurse replies, "Yes, Mary, we are." Mary is carried away with her good fortune. "I can't believe it!" Every unbalanced individual in the room gathers around her as she continues breathlessly, "I can't believe it"—the picture of Mary Hartman surrounded by a half dozen off-their-rocker faces staring at the tube is unforgettable, as she reverentially concludes—"that I, Mary Hartman, am finally a member of a Nielsen family."

6

THE POPULARITY OF *Mary Hartman* raised my public profile enough to attract the interest of Mike Wallace, who profiled me on *60 Minutes*, and, a bit later, Lorne Michaels, who invited me to host *Saturday Night*. This was the show's second season, before the *Live* was added to its title and when the original seven cast members were billed as the Not Ready for Prime Time Players.

I brought only one idea with me from L.A. It was called "Three Brothers," a routine I'd done with my daughter Kate from the time she was five years old. We performed it often before my tapings when I warmed up the audience and Kate was on hand. Lorne liked the bit and scheduled it in the last third of the show. After Friday's dress rehearsal, Kate, her mother, and I were over the moon about it and couldn't wait for the moment we'd be playing to millions.

The show was going well Saturday evening when, coming out of a commercial and just before I was to introduce our routine, Lorne Michaels whispered to me that we were running long. He had to cut "Three Brothers" and asked me to introduce the next thing up instead. My heart stopped. This was not an unusual occurrence in live television. I myself had asked dozens of players to cut things in the middle of a live performance. I stepped into a blinding spotlight to do as I was instructed. There were only a few rows of audience members I could see clearly, and among them sat my darling Kate, looking up at me expectantly, her expression shouting, "I'm here for you, Daddy, cue me!" And of course I did. I cued my daughter as I shamefacedly fucked my producer.

He accepted my apology, at the same time straining to understand. But, then, it was some years before Lorne became a father.

WHEN THERE WERE enough episodes of *AITF*, *Maude*, *Good Times*, and *The Jeffersons*, Jerry Perenchio was able to negotiate with CBS's Bob Daly regarding Tandem/T.A.T.'s ability to sell them into syndication. In short order it was our salesmen handling the sales and/or rejections, and most of what they heard regarding *Maude* was some version of this: "I don't want that ballbuster on my station." Among *Maude*'s hard-core supporters, however, was first lady Betty Ford, who would write to me whenever she missed an episode—long before the DVD and DVR—and ask me to send her a VHS copy, for which she never failed to send a note of thanks. All her letters were signed "Maude's Number One Fan."

When we reached a kind of stalemate in our sales, I phoned *Maude*'s Number One Fan, just out of the White House and living near Palm Springs, where our ex-president was playing golf every day and she was developing the now famous Betty Ford Clinic. I told her that the National Association of Television Production Executives (NATPE) was having its convention soon in L.A., that all of TV would be showing its wares, and that we needed help calling attention to and selling *Maude*.

"Give me three dates that work for you that week and I'll pick one," she replied in an instant.

We decided to have a dinner party on our front lawn, smack in the middle of NATPE's spring convention, and the invitation that went out was from "Mrs. Betty Ford, Beatrice Arthur and Norman Lear." Frances and my three daughters hosted along with the first lady. The evening was a smash. Mrs. Ford was a trouper. She yakked up *Maude* all evening, talked to everyone about the show—at one point grabbing the mike and raving about Bea Arthur—and danced all evening with every station manager in attendance. It was about one A.M. and she was still going strong when I finally suggested to her Secret Service detail that it was time to take Mrs. Ford home.

When I phoned two days later to thank her and told her how well *Maude* was selling now, she was so pleased you would not have known who was more grateful for the evening.

AFTER A SECOND SEASON and a total of 325 episodes, the cast of *Mary Hartman* was exhausted—Louise especially—and we informed our independent stations and affiliates that the show was drawing to a close. Having carried the only first-run syndicated show to attract national attention and reach megahit status, our stations prayed for another show to maintain the franchise. That led us to *Fernwood 2 Night*. What if Fernwood, Ohio, had its own late-night talk show? we wondered. And wouldn't Martin Mull be perfect as its Johnny Carson? Since his wife-beating character on *Mary Hartman* had been impaled on a Christmas tree and was quite dead, we made the host of *Fernwood 2 Night* Garth's twin brother, Barth. We cast the incomparable Fred Willard as his sidekick and announcer, Jerry Hubbard. The last episode of *Mary Hartman* aired on July 1, 1977, and *Fernwood 2 Night* debuted three days later.

The show became a cult hit, about which, to this day, people speak to me reverentially several times a year. The mixture of Barth Gimble's amiable unctuousness and Jerry Hubbard's verbose banality was so unique and hilarious as to be unforgettable to its fans. One of the choicest moments—the guest physicist whose experiments with mice led him to claim that leisure suits cause cancer—added half a day to my life. Make that a full day when I picture him withdrawing a pair of tiny mouse-sized leisure suits from his pocket.

Though its fan base was passionate, it wasn't large enough to keep the show on the air, as was the case with two other shows I was passionate about.

I'd been thinking about a show in which the conservative versus liberal argument, a staple of the Bunker household, was conducted this time by professionals in the political arena. *All's Fair*, starring Richard Crenna and Bernadette Peters, grew out of that. Their political differences provided the troublesome center of a love affair between two very public personalities and political opposites, decades before James Carville and Mary Matalin gave us a real-life version. Our two leads were pitch-perfect, as was Michael Keaton in his first major role, as a fast-talking presidential speechwriter.

As a fancier of melting pots, I was proud and happy to have convinced Irving Kristol, the godfather of neoconservatism (and father of current Fox News contributor William Kristol), to consult with me about our right-wing character's philosophy and its expression. There was more context regarding the issues our characters argued about in *All's Fair* than viewers can find today in their nightly news shows. We felt we were chomping in the intellectual tall cotton. But after twenty-four episodes we learned that CBS wished to chomp in what Nielsen might tell them was more fertile ground.

Another series idea rich with sociopolitical potential, and dear to the heart and mind of my generation, was *Apple Pie*. What if—in the thirties, at the height of the Great Depression—a broke and lonely woman in the Midwest, out of work like everyone else, inherited a farm and some money? And what if, having absolutely no one to share it with, she decided to hire family members by placing ads in local newspapers. More than a funny idea, I sensed this was a great opportunity to compare the New Deal's efforts to raise up the lower and middle classes of that time with the governmental indifference their children and grandchildren were experiencing in the seventies.

Our pilot opened with shots of a farmhouse, the camera moving slowly into its living room and settling on a radio from which FDR's inaugural address was emanating: ". . . And here I assert that we have nothing to fear but fear itself." Listening to it is the woman who has been placing the ads. We learn quickly that she has already hired a grandfather, a daughter, and a son, and is at this moment about to receive a man answering her ad for a husband. Two of the best comic actors I have ever worked with came together—and I will admit to a tear of joy that accompanies the memory—when Rue McClanahan opened the door for her husband-to-be, Dabney Coleman. Of the seventies shows that didn't make it, *Apple Pie* might have been the one I cared for most. ABC dropped it after two episodes because it drew only 22 million viewers. A top-ten show today can draw less than half that.

BY THE END OF 1977, as much as I enjoyed television and the company of those I'd been working with, I felt the need to stretch in other directions, to do a film or a play and devote more time to the causes that interested me. I informed Jerry, and Alan started to think about who might replace me. A writer-producer, someone with my background, seemed the logical go-seek, and I solicited a number of men I knew well, starting with guys in our own shop—Allan Manings, Bob Schiller, Charlie Hauck, and Hal Kantor, among others—all wonderful writers and collaborators, and to a person their response was "Are you kidding?" I reached out to men outside the company—Carl Reiner, Larry Gelbart, Stuart Ostroff, and others—and got the same reaction. What I was doing—seven series on the air—seemed impossible to them and none was interested.

I began to realize that if the situation were reversed, and one of them had my job and asked me to replace him, I'd have thought it impossible, too. I didn't suddenly inherit this forest of shows and actors, scripts and rehearsals, hits and failures. I grew up in that soil. Two shows required me to think and move faster. A third and fourth show required my brain to compartmentalize, a fifth to compartmentalize further, and a sixth saw a broom growing from my butt so I could sweep up the floor, too.

What I needed in a replacement, I came to realize, was an executive with a creative bent, a respect and affection for writers and actors, an eye for incredible detail, and the strength to tell whiners, complainers, and fakers to "Fuck off." It didn't take long before I knew our own Alan Horn, who by then I understood to define the word *decent*, was our man.

Typical of my penchant for acting on impulse, I phoned him the instant I thought of it and asked him to meet me for breakfast at the Beverly Hills Hotel the next morning. Alan was shocked by my proposal but felt he could handle the job as I described it. But did I think to discuss this first with my partner, Jerry Perenchio, the man who actually ran the company businesswise, and from whom I would be stealing Alan in the first place? The question answers itself.

Perenchio was predictably angry. I was predictably sorry. In any event, as angry as he had every right to be, Jerry still agreed my choice was a good one. His opinion was far from unanimous. The creative teams on all the shows we were doing—the writers, producers, and directors—were very unhappy with my decision to replace myself with a Harvard MBA business guy, no matter who he was. They complained for weeks, giving Alan short shrift and finally calling for an all-hands meeting with me. It was set for a weekend morning at our Century City headquarters and I asked Alan to attend. He thought it was wrong for him to be there, and my insistence alternated with his demurrals until, as he recalls, I ended the discussion with: "Alan, I am not 'requesting' this."

At the meeting I listened to everyone's objections, told them I appreciated what I'd heard, pointed to Alan, and said very simply, "My mind is unchanged. This is Alan Horn. He is the man you and your shows report to, and if anyone here can't live with that your resignation will be accepted now." None was forthcoming, and the slow and deliberate transition I'd intended continued. The choice was apparently a good one. Alan Horn went on to cofound Castle Rock Entertainment (with, among others, Rob Reiner), served as president and COO of Warner Bros., and is currently chairman of the Walt Disney Studios.

As I was embarking on my respite from the daily grind of television, an unexpected reward presented itself. I received a call from the China People's Association for Friendship with Foreign Countries in concert with the Chinese delegation at the United Nations. They respected several of my TV shows, thought they showed an appreciation of other cultures, and invited me to put together "a group of like-minded people in the entertainment industry" and lead them on a tour of China.

The invitation came before our countries normalized relations in 1979, which was a pleasant and exciting surprise to everyone I invited on the tour, a group that included Mary Tyler Moore and her husband, Grant Tinker, then president of NBC. In early April we arrived in Canton, the first stop on our tour. We'd heard this would happen, but nothing could prepare us for the novelties we were. A crowd, all in their Chairman Mao suits, would gather just to look at us everywhere we went, and everything about us was of interest: our clothes, our shoes, and anything we took out of our pockets—wallets, family pictures, mints, chewing gum, anything. There was nothing threatening in this, we were simply objects of interest, great interest, like museum pieces.

The arts in China were in ferment at that time. After years and years of radical repression, artists and filmmakers who had been condemned and silenced by the infamous Gang of Four were being celebrated once more. As a consequence, the Ministry of Culture centered our visit on meeting the most successful representatives of the arts, seeing plays and operas, visiting soundstages, and meeting with authors, playwrights, and composers.

Our visit was a feast of unique experiences—everything from shooting film on the Great Wall (the first group to be allowed to do so, we were told) to talks with some of the top figures in the arts and sciences and private flights to communities rarely seen by nonnatives. Toward the end of our visit we spent an afternoon with a class of students about to graduate from college, most of whom spoke English. While we came away from our tour with varying opinions as to what we'd experienced and learned, after our time at the college an opinion we'd held from the beginning was totally affirmed. The Chinese had a self-deprecating sense of humor, as did we Americans. I'm not so sure we haven't lost ours in the new century, but in the 1970s we had the ability to laugh at ourselves, as did the Chinese.

THE DEBATE THEN GOING on in Congress over the proposed Panama Canal Treaty fascinated me. It was finally passed in 2000 when the United States turned control of it over to the Panamanian government, but in the late seventies the issue was red-hot. President Jimmy Carter and Vice President Walter Mondale were pushing it, while in the Senate the strident and powerful Strom Thurmond (who filibustered against the Civil Rights Act) and Jesse Helms were accusing the administration of "surrendering a strategic American asset." Ronald Reagan, former governor of California, then planning his run for the presidency, was staunchly against signing the treaty, and it occurred to me that Mondale and Reagan debating the issue would make good television.

Concurrently with that idea I'd been thinking about political debates in general. Following just about all of them, we'd see or read the next day that one or the other candidate misquoted, misspoke, told a half-truth, or lied altogether, and the opposing candidate didn't have the facts at the ready with which to call him on it. As a consequence, no feathers were ruffled and no one was seen to get under the other guy's skin. I wanted to change that.

I don't know what caused me to think of the bullfight as a metaphor, but I'd seen several of them in Tijuana in the sixties and one in Madrid in the seventies. I was fascinated by the picadors on horseback whose job it was to anger the bull and weaken his neck muscles for the matador, whom they would then help to save should the bull manage to threaten his life. Couldn't that apply as a metaphor for a two-person political debate? The debaters—here considered the matadors—would each be backed by a research professional, performing in this context as their picador. They would be allowed whatever pre-Internet-era materials they required—their opponent's speeches, related articles, history, etc.—to check on the veracity or correctness of any statement. It was a format designed to rattle cages and raise some dust around the debaters, who could no longer feel perfectly safe. It would make, I was sure, great television.

I phoned Ronald Reagan. He took the call with no fuss and as easily accepted an invitation to have lunch to talk about whatever I had in mind. I had met Reagan once or twice at social events, but he made me feel like an old friend on the phone. That was true every time we were in contact over the ensuing years. I invited Geoff Cowan—who'd formerly run Voice of America, was then a board member of the Corporation for Public Broadcasting, and had authored *See No Evil*, a book about the Family Hour lawsuit—to join me for lunch with the governor. We met him at the offices of Michael Deaver, his longtime press representative, who had just partnered with Peter Hannaford. Deaver was present and we talked for just a bit, but when we went to lunch, Geoff and I were alone with Ronnie, which is what he said we might call him. Neither Geoff nor I was able to do that.

The governor could not have been more charming and self-effacing. "It's a thrill to be in this setting with Norman Lear," Geoff recalls him saying as we entered the restaurant. I was sure he thought I wanted to talk to him about a guest shot on one of our shows. (His friend and political ally John Wayne had recently guest-starred on *Maude*.) We talked instead about the Panama Canal Treaty, my debate idea, and the possibility of his taking on Walter Mondale on the issue. The governor was intrigued with the notion of picadors and amused that he would play the role of matador. But his serious side was stirred by the debate itself because he thought the treaty such a bad idea. The United States would be "giving away something it bought and paid for, and should be eternally proud of," he said. All we needed was Walter Mondale and the airtime, and Governor Reagan was a go.

Geoff and I flew to DC for a lunch with the vice president. I found Mondale an affable, friendly sort, though no match in the charm department for Ronald Reagan. The vice president was fascinated by the new debate format and believed firmly in the administration's position. He couldn't commit firmly until he knew the date and the auspices, but he was certainly interested. Geoff and I thought that was as much as we could expect at this point so I turned to securing the airtime and a date.

It didn't take a week to learn that the networks, all three of them, were not interested. "We cover the news," they said, "we don't make it. Tell us where this is taking place and we'll see about getting a camera there." Recalling how we sold Mary Hartman, I called Al Flanagan at Combined Communications, told him I had Vice President Mondale and Ronald Reagan interested in debating the Panama Canal Treaty in a new format, and didn't have to say a lot more before he told me to come back when I had them firmed up and he'd find the time on his stations.

I reported the news to Governor Reagan and got an immediate "Count me in." The vice president was pleased, an aide reported, and would get back to me. With that I asked Tandem/T.A.T.'s production manager, Michael Weisbarth, to locate and put a hold on a proper facility to stage the debate in both L.A. and DC. After several weeks went by with no word from Mondale, I received a call from Governor Reagan, now being talked about everywhere as a possible candidate for the presidency in 1980. The governor had just gotten a call from William F. Buckley Jr. asking if he would be willing to debate the Panama Canal Treaty with someone of his stature on *Firing Line*, Buckley's TV show. Reagan told him he'd like that but had a previous commitment to me on the same subject, and that's why he was calling me now. I told the governor I'd get back to him in just a few days and thanked him for his courtesy.

I immediately phoned the vice president to say that I couldn't wait any longer for an answer. Through an aide he said he'd get back to me in a few minutes, and indeed he did. "I wanted to tell you this directly," he said. "I've been advised not to get in the ring with Ronald Reagan."

That ended my plan for this debate costarring Ronald Reagan, but, unbelievably, not the debate itself. Not long after my effort died on the vine, the governor did get to debate the Panama Canal Treaty, and on *Firing Line*. The "person of equal stature" in the debate turned out to be Buckley himself. The treaty represented one of their rare disagreements. Host and facilitator for the debate was Senator Sam Ervin.

While I'm on the subject of Ronald Reagan, let me flash forward a bit. In December 1979, with Reagan having just entered the race for the GOP presidential nomination, I called him and asked if I could send a reporter and camera crew on the plane with him as he flew around the country raising funds and seeking endorsements.

It was early in the race and George H. W. Bush was in the lead, but I sensed this was Ronald Reagan's moment and, before his campaign caught fire, here was an opportunity to get some real time with Reagan and learn what was driving him. I brought bestselling author and investigative journalist Robert Scheer aboard to grill our presidential hopeful. Scheer, who'd been editor of *Ramparts* and an early force at *Mother Jones*, later created the well-known left-leaning Web site Truthdig. He was and continues to be a tough, outspoken liberal, known for his take-no-prisoners style. Ronald Reagan knew all that about Scheer and had no problem with his joining him on the trip.

The film that resulted was altogether remarkable. They sat side by side in shirtsleeves on a small jet plane over a four-day period, with Scheer in his inimitable hard-ass fashion pressing the governor on every issue. Each time an aide to Reagan looked like he was ready to interrupt the interrogation, Reagan waved him off and took the next question. Nothing Scheer asked seemed to rattle him. He remained cool and open throughout. Many of Scheer's questions demanded a depth that the candidate seemed unprepared for, a situation under which most politicians would take refuge in spewing bullshit, but not Ronald Reagan. He didn't go there because he couldn't go there, yet he never avoided a question. And somehow he made it work. A good example of this occurred when Scheer called Reagan's attention to the increasing use of drugs in America and asked how he proposed to handle it. Reagan, years before his wife uttered the words as first lady, replied that he'd tell drug users to "just say no."

Ronnie (as his kitchen cabinet knew him) had a sly sense of humor, developed and borrowed over years of cocktail party chatter and ringside tables, and it was of no small help to his political career. The film revealed no better example of that than when Scheer asked how the candidate felt about the issue of homosexuality and, not wishing to go there, Reagan said he hadn't thought about it much. Then, with a nod to British actress Beatrice Campbell, he added that he didn't see much cause for concern "so long as they don't do it in the street and frighten the horses."

I presented a ninety-minute edit of the hours-long interview to Nancy Reagan in 2002. Mrs. Reagan, too, thought the interview remarkable and together we dedicated it to the Ronald Reagan Presidential Library, where it can be found today.

I'M NOT SURE which came first, my interest in modern art for its own sake or empty walls in the first nice rooms I thought of as mine, but I started collecting in the early seventies. Mentored by my friend Dick Dorso, my passion for it mounted with my ability to purchase it. In addition to the pleasure of building a collection, it led to as profound an enhancer of the good life as I have known. By 1980 I had come to know a number of other collectors, one of whom invited me to Pasadena one day to see his collection. He had some extraordinary pieces that we were discussing over lunch when his daughter stuck her head in the doorway to say she was going out for a while. "And oh, by the way," she told her dad, "Ken Noland called while you were with Mr. Lear."

Kenneth Noland was a major contemporary artist, variously termed an abstract impressionist, a minimalist, and a Color Field painter. I loved his work and already owned one of his stripes paintings. As we talked about Noland my host wondered whether he'd sold his farm yet. Idly I asked about the farm, and when I heard it was in Vermont and it had belonged to Robert Frost, my heart started to pound. If a baby about to enter the world has feelings, that might be the best way to describe mine at that moment. Not that I'd ever entertained the thought before, but something clicked in me as if it had been a lifelong dream and this kid from New England just knew he was about to own a farm in Vermont, and a Robert Frost farm at that.

I left Pasadena with Kenneth Noland's Vermont phone number and called him the next day. He was a fan of *All in the Family,* welcomed my call, and, *yes,* the farm was still for sale. When was I coming east? I told him I was due in New York the following week and he told me of a small air service that was based at the Bennington airfield—the farm was in the bordering town, Shaftsbury. He suggested they could meet my plane at JFK and fly me to Bennington in fifty minutes, where he would meet me and take me to the farm, which was ten minutes away. The detour would take no more than three to four hours. I took Ken's suggestion, and a week later I stepped out of a prop plane in Bennington into the embrace of a man about my age who oozed something I came to think of as enthusiastic kindness.

Beautiful downtown Shaftsbury was a blinking yellow light at four corners, and a right off Route 7 took us to a delightful wooded area just a minute away. Around a turn, down a light grade, and there on the right was a driveway, at the edge of which was a tree bearing a sign, THE GULLEY, spelled that way because Mr. Frost spelled it that way. It was a bit of a climb to the house, trees to the left, and if a grassy hillside can have a gender, off to the right the most feminine, softly rolling hillside on the planet. That first drive to the farmhouse brought my inner center as close to rapture as it would ever come, and I've experienced a touch of that every one of the hundreds of times I've driven or walked it since.

Ken had purchased the farm from the Frost estate in 1963 and turned a large barn into his studio. Painter friends, including Jules Olitski, Helen Frankenthaler, and Robert Motherwell, and sculptors like David Smith and Tony Caro, loved The Gulley and would often visit Ken there for periods of time and work alongside him. On that first visit a beautiful sculpture garden representing their work sat on flat ground just in front of the house. On the other side of the driveway there was a bronze plaque declaring The Gulley a NATIONAL HISTORIC LANDMARK.

I was awash with a quite bearable lightness of being on entering the home, and later the separate one-room cottage in which Robert Frost wrote his Pulitzer Prize–winning poems. The house was as warm and welcoming as a hug, and as Ken Noland walked ahead, pointing things out, from the mudroom to the kitchen and the short hallway to a library on the right, a bedroom following, and the living room straight ahead, I caught sight of a small blue Noland stripe painting on the living room wall we were walking toward. With his back to me I asked for the first time how much he wanted for the farm. He mentioned a figure and I said, "If you throw in that Noland, you have a deal." Ken turned, we shook hands, and that was the entire negotiation. For the three-plus decades since, it has been a family-and-friends paradise. I think of it always as our Hebrew Hyannisport.

7

I'D BEEN SAYING for years that one of the problems with television was that shows overstayed their welcome, and that they should get out of the way and make room for fresh ideas and fresh talent. By 1978 I thought *All in the Family* had run its course, and when Rob and Sally said they were leaving after the eighth season, it seemed like a natural stopping place.

We prepared to end the series with three episodes that saw Mike getting an offer to teach in California, he and Gloria wrestling with the decision, and then finally deciding to take their leave of Edith and Archie. The farewell scene is a tearjerker to this minute.

After all the other good-byes have been said—with Gloria and little Joey waiting in the cab and Edith having rushed back into the house in tears—Mike and Archie are alone on the front porch. And despite the fact that we'd seen them for eight years disagreeing about everything, there was no way you could miss the love between these two men. Mike understood how much Archie loved his daughter and his wife, and how hard it had been to support a family with the education he'd had. And Archie, whatever else he couldn't really understand about Mike, knew that he loved and would take care of his daughter and grandson. "I know you always thought I hated you, Arch, but I love you," Mike says, embracing him and crying on his shoulder as Archie tentatively and briefly returns the hug.

That was the natural ending to the series, but the relentlessly contrarian Carroll, who had been saying he wanted out for years, changed his mind at the last minute and—with the network's blessing—convinced Jean to do one more season without Rob and Sally.

The best thing that came out of the extra season of *All in the Family* was that it allowed us to do a two-hundredth episode. We produced a two-hour special of which I was particularly proud. We treated it like a broadcast of the Oscars, but instead of a star-studded audience, every chair was filled with a longtime fan from across the country. In two hundred words or less, *AITF* viewers were invited to tell us what the show meant to them and why they wished to come to L.A. for the taping and celebration. There was an avalanche of responses, from which two hundred couples representing all fifty states were selected and flown to L.A., thanks to a participating airline, for a three-day stay at a well-known hotel. The evening of our taping, our guests were brought to the theater by limousine, announced by name at their arrival, and interviewed on the red carpet. I hosted the event, which consisted of clips from across the nine seasons. My narrative provided an inside view of the exhaustingly hard work all of us absolutely relished. It was a blue-collar love story.

AS THE END of the ninth season approached, Carroll still couldn't bring himself to let Archie go. He wanted to continue, even if it meant carrying on alone, and he had an idea. Archie would buy Kelsey's Bar and the show—*Archie Bunker's Place*—would be centered there. The network, believing correctly that the name Archie Bunker attached to a new show would bring ratings, bit hard on the idea. My partners and associates were running a business and could not look a gift horse in the mouth.

Archie as I conceived him was in some but not all respects a version of my dad. When I first started to write about Archie forty-five years ago, I borrowed the pride, vanity, and conviction that he knew it all from H.K., but I substituted Archie's fear of progress for H.K.'s certainty that change meant that he'd reach his pot of gold in ten days to two weeks (even if he had to bend the truth a whole lot to get there).

I ached for both men and loved them at the same time. But while one was all mine, I shared the other with Carroll. Archie's physicality and personality were all Carroll, but his emotional being and belief system came from me. That was the basis of our quarrels and the crux of my problem as I wrestled with the notion of Archie Bunker going on without me.

Before long I received a call from William Paley. "Norman, when are you going to be in New York? Love to see you," he said. Eight years on CBS and I'd never heard from Mr. Paley directly before. I assumed he'd okayed a full-page ad that CBS ran in *Variety* the year before thanking me for providing the network with "a dazzling variety of high comedy enriched with humanity," but that was hardly the same as evincing a desire to meet me. Of course the meeting was all about convincing me that there should be an *Archie Bunker's Place*.

I reminded him of the CBS ad that thanked me for comedy "enriched with humanity," and said that Mr. O'Connor and I held different views as to how that is achieved. Turning control of the character over to him would threaten that, I added. I was a fool to think things like that mattered in a business meeting, although his parting words would give that impression: "Archie belongs to the American people, Norman, and so long as they want him, and I would add *need* him, it's our obligation to serve that need."

Before I'd sign off on it I asked CBS for two concessions. First, I wanted some assurance that Jean Stapleton would appear in a few episodes to help the show get off the ground. Carroll happily agreed, advancing the notion that the first episode of the second season would deal with Edith's death. The other concession was dedicated to seeing that Edith did not die in vain. I asked the network to give $1 million to the National Organization for Women in Edith Bunker's name in support of the ERA. We settled for $500,000, passed through to NOW as a gift from Tandem/T.A.T. to establish the Edith Bunker Memorial Fund for the Equal Rights Amendment.

On November 2, 1980, Edith died off camera of a stroke. In the final scene of the episode, a bereft Archie is seen entering the bedroom they shared. He sits on the bed, touches one of her slippers to his cheek, and tells her how much he loved her. It could not have been a more touching scene, and it played without a laugh to an audience stilled with sorrow. That represented a departure from a dramatic tenet basic to my way of looking at comedy: there is a laugh in every situation; beware of treacle.

In an early *AITF* episode, Archie, about to become a grandfather, visits Gloria at her bedside just after learning she miscarried. He so wanted a grandson and the audience was numbed by his heartbreak. As directed, however, the scene recognized that these two had never faced such an intimate moment before and it was amusing to see how they coped with it. The laugh that was evoked served to enhance the empathy between the characters and their audience, bringing many to tears. Without me, Carroll's Archie didn't reach for such moments. He simply didn't see comedy my way.

Flashing forward for a moment, I received news of Carroll's death in June of 2001. It was not a surprise. He had been ill for some time, and it is inexplicable to me that I had not visited him during his illness. My only excuse, and I do not offer it proudly, is that I felt very strongly that I would not be welcome. His antipathy toward me had increased over the years, to the point where he'd gone on TV to lament that my partners and I had failed to give him a piece of the "empire" we'd created as a result of the impact of his character.

When Carroll died I grieved for what had never been, and for the fact that a talent so rare had, by his own admission, managed to put together so little joy in his life. After his memorial I went to his home to see his wife, Nancy. She and I enjoyed a mutual respect and I always thought she understood my position in relationship to her husband. There were a number of people there when I arrived, and Nancy asked me if I could wait for a while because she wished to show me something. When the crowd thinned out she invited me to follow her into Carroll's study. As she opened the door she told me that nothing had been touched—his desk was exactly the way he had left it. On it were a couple of books and one single paper that I instantly recognized as having come from me.

For his birthday some years before I had written Carroll as much of a love letter as I could. In it I'd explained how, despite our constant disagreements, I so deeply respected him as a talent and so loved the character he created for the character I'd created. Nancy allowed me to read my letter and stood by as I cried. She told me that Carroll had put it on his desk the day it arrived years earlier. And it was there in the same place the day he died.

PART 4

Over and Next

Loneliness is the absence of accepting
the joy of social responsibility.

—NADINE GORDIMER

1

AT ABOUT SIX P.M. one summer evening, Frances drove me out to Van Nuys Airport, walked me up the steps of a small jet, blindfolded me, and off we flew to . . . I didn't know where. We landed a little more than an hour later and, still blinkered, I was ushered to a waiting car. It was my sixtieth birthday so I'd been expecting a surprise, but this was beyond the pale. From our flying time I deduced we were in Las Vegas and wondered who we were driving to meet—likely our daughters and a handful of close friends. Or perhaps, despite the difficult state of our marriage, Frances had arranged for a weekend alone. So maybe we were in Palm Springs.

I was helped out of the car and led indoors. From the voices that suddenly went silent—at the sight, I assumed, of a blindfolded man—I knew we were in a public space. A lobby? We walked a short distance, went down a flight of stairs, walked a few steps more, and suddenly there was the unmistakable sound of a crowd being hushed. It was as if the room itself, and a big one at that, were holding its breath.

The removal of my blindfold was followed by a roar as every family member, every good friend, and dozens of business associates shouted, "Happy Birthday!" in the filled-to-overflowing ballroom of the Beverly Hills Hotel.

Recalling such an event is like rediscovering something long forgotten in an attic somewhere. I cried when Perenchio, in the most tender voice this side of Mel Torme, sang "I've Got a Crush on You." And I cried and laughed and cried some more when Bea Arthur, who had leaped out of a cake moments before, sang "My Man" in her heart-rousing fashion. The Bergmans touched me deeply with their adaptation of a song from *Guys and Dolls:* "We've got the guy right here, his name is Norman Lear . . ." Among the many toasts, the one still pinned to my heart was from daughter Kate, speaking for herself and her sisters and describing me as someone who "walks through life's peaks and valleys with equal wonder."

Frances had clearly gone all out to make my sixtieth a memorable event, but she didn't join the toasters, likely for the same reason I'd wanted to save our daughters from having to salute our steadily deteriorating twenty-five-year marriage several months earlier. We'd been to two silver anniversary celebrations in the preceding year, and at both parties the teenage children toasted their parents as "More in love today than they were twenty-five years ago." As this was definitely not the case with us, for months I'd been dreading our kids having to make syrupy toasts to our blissful marriage. Then, one Sunday night, we were running a James Bond film and suddenly there on the screen was the answer to my problem. It was a mountaintop shot looking down on an exquisite bay and, at anchor, a gorgeous yacht. The plan came to me in an instant. Everyone would understand if the Lears chose to celebrate their twenty-fifth wedding anniversary in the most idyllic fashion—say, a leisurely cruise with good friends on a yacht in the Mediterranean.

Certain that Frances would like my idea, I called out, "Where is that?" Gore Vidal was with us that night and knew the island and the bay, not to mention the boat and its owner. I didn't wind up renting that yacht—we didn't need the helicopter and bowling alley—but ours, *The Paget,* was sufficiently luxurious. With three guest staterooms, we invited nine couples to join us for a week each over the course of the three-week trip. Add to that a wonderful crew tending to our every need as we gently cruised from island to island—Mykonos, Santorini, Corfu, Samos, Rhodes—and there was so much history to visit that Frances and I managed to set our own history aside for the duration.

That history was rife with anguish for Frances. Our Greek idyll served as a miraculous escape from what she experienced much of the rest of the time. "The reasons for me to get well, to smile, to live, were real and fine and all around me," she wrote in her book. "The good life could not bore its way through my illness. I had no alternative." Frances was referring to a suicide attempt that preceded, by several years, our silver anniversary cruise.

We were having a dinner party and our guests of honor were Wynn and Bobbie Handman, who were visiting us from New York. (We'd met the Handmans while working together on the 1968 Eugene McCarthy presidential campaign.) Dinner was called for seven-thirty. Frances had been out all afternoon, and when she wasn't home by seven, I became concerned. A half hour later most of the guests had arrived, and still no Frances. I called her assistant, who, after stumbling and stuttering, finally revealed a total secret. With the approval of the psychiatrist Frances was seeing several times a week, she'd rented an apartment that only he and her assistant knew about. This sad excuse for a shrink had okayed a hideaway that only he and one other person knew about for a patient who had twice before attempted to kill herself. I went nuts.

Fearing the worst, I demanded that the assistant give me the phone number. Frances never gave her one, she said. Well, then, the address? She didn't have that, either. Ready to burst, I hung up and phoned Frances's psychiatrist. A recorded voice offered me an emergency line through which I reached him. When I asked for the address and phone number of his patient's apartment, he wondered why I wanted that information. "Because," I screamed, "I think she could be killing herself there." The good doctor did not have that information. As I smashed the phone down the other line was ringing. It was the assistant. She'd remembered that the apartment was somewhere on Beverly Glen, south of Wilshire.

Within fifteen minutes I was going from building to building. Certain I wouldn't find her name next to a doorbell, I rang each building superintendent, raced through my reason for being there, and described Frances. Well down the block, a super reacted with a troubled look and I demanded he let me in. He couldn't because I didn't have a warrant. I told him to get the owner of the building on the phone. He did, and the owner also refused to let me in. I threatened to call the police. He said, "Go ahead."

"Listen," I said, as loudly as I'd ever said anything, "I think you might have a death on your hands here, and if the corpse is my wife I will sue your sorry ass for every fucking dollar you have and not rest until they lock you up and throw away the key!" I slammed the phone down, imagined the guy on the other end, and held my breath. It was as long a moment as I've ever lived, and then the phone rang. Within seconds the super and I were racing up the stairs.

It was a small apartment, entirely furnished by its owner but for some photographs and a rug I recalled us buying years before in Morocco. Frances was lying on it in a fetal position, a small pool of white liquid at the edge of her parted lips, a near-empty cup of various pills at the tip of one outstretched hand, and a handwritten note on the desk beside her. Choking back a scream, I reached for a pulse I could not detect while the super called 911. In the emergency room at Cedars-Sinai, the first doctor to see her said she was just minutes away from leaving us.

When I left the hospital Frances was in a private room and out of danger. I'd been in touch with Kate and Maggie and knew they were awake. At the sight of them every feeling I'd been holding back broke free and I began sobbing. My children rushed to comfort me. It quickly became clear that they shared only one element of what I was feeling: anger. Their expressions were frozen. Their mother had chosen to leave them—forever. They could never forgive her. At the sight of her suicide note, *they* started crying. When I read it to them, it was clear from the first sentence that they could take no comfort from it. There wasn't a mention of either of them, or of anyone else. It was all about Frances and her need to exit a life that did not allow her to realize herself.

THAT HORROR WAS the last thing on any of our minds that night at the Beverly Hills Hotel. Frances was on a high one would think was permanent, and everyone danced up a storm until the evening's end, when, as expected, I took the stage and had the last word.

I thanked Frances and my office staff, who'd helped her to pull off the surprise of a lifetime, expressed my gratitude for the songs and toasts and the presence of just about everyone I loved—and then expressed something I'd thought about often but had never said out loud. I confessed that even while standing there and thanking everyone, my mind was on the taste of coffee the next morning.

"As much as I've loved it," I said, "as grateful as I am to all of you, this evening is Over and I am on to Next." When something, however great it was, is over, it wants to be OVER without regret, because immediately available is NEXT. Reflecting on this later, I imagined a bulging hammock between Over and Next, and realized: that is where the struggle to live in the moment resides.

My problem—and, of course, my simultaneous good fortune—was that there were so many Nexts I rarely faced one at a time. Sometimes, like those amusement park bumper cars, they thudded and crashed until there was a pileup of Nexts.

2

T HE BIGGEST NEXT after my decade in network television was sociopolitical. It had begun brewing in me years earlier with the proliferation
of fundamentalist TV ministries that perverted the pulpit by mixing politics and religion and spewing the sort of malice that horrified me when I was
nine and came upon Father Coughlin on my crystal set. What they were calling
the Religious Right began with Pat Robertson and his Christian Broadcasting
Network in 1966 and really caught fire in the late 1970s when dozens more
religious radicals added their voices.

"This nation was built upon a Christian foundation, upon a *Bible* foundation," declaimed Rev. James Robison, roaming from the pulpit and brandishing
his Bible like a weapon as he decimated the Constitution in Jesus' name.

On a different channel, Paul Weyrich, a prominent lay leader of the Christian Right and cofounder with Jerry Falwell of the Moral Majority, fumed: "We
don't want everybody to vote. Our leverage in the elections quite candidly goes
up as the voting populace goes down."

"I hope I live to see the day when, as in the early days of our country, we
won't have any public schools," said Rev. Falwell. "The churches will have
taken them over again and Christians will be running them. What a happy day
that will be!"

For all of their virtuous posturing, the morality these power-grabbing men of the cloth were championing was their singular version of it. As their crusades to spread fear and division became more blatant, so did my desire to sabotage their efforts through ridicule. I'd begun making notes for a screenplay titled *Religion*, with the intent to satirize these fundamentalist TV ministries as savagely and commercially as Paddy Chayefsky mocked television itself in the film *Network*.

Mischievously thinking I would take my producer credit as "The Rev. Norman Lear," I sent a twenty-dollar check and became a minister in the Universal Life Church, the largest of the worldwide mail-order ministries. (As a clergyman of the ULC I have yet to baptize a child or offer a wafer, but I have officiated at four weddings, including the first marriage of *South Park* cocreator Trey Parker, which I mention only because I take such pride in our friendship. I think of Trey and his partner Matt Stone's musical comedy *The Book of Mormon* as one of the great gifts of sanity to the world.)

My interest in the ULC was rewarded when I visited its founder, the Rev. Kirby Hensley, at his headquarters in Modesto, California. Hensley was a small, crackly bundle of nervous energy from North Carolina. Speaking with the tangy Southern drawl that I'd learned to love when it issued from the mouth of that left-leaning clodhopper (his term, not mine) John Henry Faulk, Hensley laid out the ULC faith in six words: "Do only that which is right."

One of Hensley's aims for the church was to give the working class a legal opportunity to avail themselves of business-related tax exemptions "just like them fat cats and their teams of accountants do." But didn't it disturb him to see Scripture used for personal gain? I would be surprised, he said, how many ULC ministers "take their holy posts seriously, wrap themselves in their religions, and truly find God." And as for the crafty ones who become reverends only for the write-offs, "Well," said Hensley, grinning, "ain't no one said God was short on patience."

Researching the church ministry for me, an aide came across two best friends whose lives contained the seeds of the kind of story I wanted to develop. In their day jobs they were policemen. As clergymen they held Sunday services in their garages or playrooms, which, for tax purposes, they wrote off as sanctuaries. Their family vacations were claimed as religious retreats. All in all, church-related tax write-offs could allow them four thousand dollars more a year in take-home pay, a considerable sum given the salary of the average cop.

The outline of my story had these good men entering the ministry, motivated entirely by the tax savings it provided them. Both take to their pulpits successfully, but the one with the larger personality outshines his friend and, as the word gets out, finds himself invited to move his Sunday service to a local auditorium, where a TV camera and a vast public soon discover him. Riding on the back of Jesus and seduced by celebrity, big money, and power, he develops a "Feel Good" brand of Christianity that ultimately begets him a megachurch and lands him on the cover of *Time*.

The other cop actually "finds God." His ministry becomes a bastion of help and healing in his community, and his faith grows apace with the results of his commitment. As things play out, the first man gets drunk on his fifteen minutes of fame and becomes a political tool of right-wing billionaires. He gets razor close to running for high office, at which point something unsavory comes to light and, just as he is about to lose everything, he's "saved" by his pal.

Universal Pictures found the story intriguing and ordered a screenplay. I met with two of the funniest comics around, Richard Pryor and Robin Williams, and we couldn't have had a more hilarious time coming up with characters and potential scenes. The more we laughed, the more serious the project became in our minds. Then one day, while working to realize the film we envisioned, my concern reached its peak. I had tuned in to Jimmy Swaggart and caught the reverend, Bible in hand, railing about a constitutional issue that was due to come before the Supreme Court and asking his "godly" viewers to pray for the "removal" of a certain justice. That was the last straw for me—I had to do something. I knew that even if I had a *Religion* script ready to go, it would still take a couple of years to make the film. The need to alert people *immediately* to the danger at hand was pressing and I realized I could create a public service announcement (PSA) and get it on the air in a matter of weeks. That is what I did.

My PSA was on the money. It had a working guy, a hard hat, standing next to a piece of factory equipment, talking straight into the camera, which pushed in from a wide shot to a close-up as he said:

> Hi. I have a problem. I'm religious. We're a religious family, but that don't mean we see things the same way politically. Now, here come certain preachers on radio and TV and in the mail, telling us on a bunch of political issues that there's just one Christian position, and implying if we don't agree we're not good Christians. So, my son is a bad Christian on two issues. My wife is a good Christian on those issues but she's a bad Christian on two others. Lucky me, I'm a hundred percent Christian because I agree with the preacher on all of them. Now, my problem is I know my boy is as good a Christian as me. My wife, she's better. So maybe there's something wrong when people, even preachers, suggest that other people are good Christians or bad Christians depending on their political views. That's not the American way.

The actor was perfect and I couldn't wait to share the spot with my friends and associates. Echoing Mickey Rooney years earlier when I'd described Archie Bunker to him, Robin French, Tandem/T.A.T.'s head of distribution, said, "They're going to kill you, Norman." Everyone felt I was making a big mistake. I was from Hollywood, a Jew, and wealthy, and if that wasn't three strikes against anyone going to war with the Christian Right, my pals couldn't imagine what was.

Realizing that they were correct, and that my TV spot could benefit greatly from the endorsement of mainline church leaders, I reached out to many, first among them Father Theodore Hesburgh, president of Notre Dame. Father Hesburgh was a brilliant and gentle warrior who had served on the board of the United States Civil Rights Commission since its inception. I flew to South

Bend, Indiana, and we discussed my fears about the toxic preachments of the fundamentalist ministers. When I played my PSA he thought it right on target. Most mainline church leaders would agree, he felt, that a voter's political point of view has no bearing on his or her standing as a Christian. Moreover, he shared my concern about the way so many evangelical ministers, as he so unforgettably put it, "torture Scripture."

With Father Hesburgh's endorsement, I traversed the country to visit with other mainline church leaders: in Chicago, Dr. Martin E. Marty, religious historian at the university there; in San Antonio, Rev. Jimmy Allen, president of the Southern Baptist Convention, and the last moderate to serve in that role; in DC, Rev. James Dunn, national spokesman for the SBC, and Charles Bergstrom, spokesman for the Lutheran Church; in New York, William Sloane Coffin, senior minister at Riverside Church (whom I once begged to run for the presidency), Colin Williams, dean of the Yale Divinity School, and minister (and former Republican congressman) John Buchanan; and in Austin, inspirational congresswoman Barbara Jordan.

To a person they approved my PSA and several offered to sign on if I decided to organize around it. After vetting the notion with several friends—Stanley Sheinbaum, a major civil and human rights activist; Rev. George Regas and Rabbi Leonard Beerman, cofounders of Interfaith Communities United for Justice and Peace; and Marge Tabankin, the best-connected civil rights activist in L.A.—I decided to move ahead. "That's not the American way," our hard hat said of the mixture of politics and religion in the PSA, and so People For the American Way was established as a 501(c)(3) nonprofit organization.

We found our first president and CEO when Marge introduced me to Tony Podesta, who had worked on the presidential campaigns of Eugene McCarthy, George McGovern, and Ted Kennedy. He whipped a terrific staff together in what seemed like no time, while I continued to travel, showing the PSA, pitching my heart out in countless homes and hotel ballrooms across America to raise money and awareness.

All of that became easier after we ran the PSA on a local DC station. The national press covered the ad, the nightly news shows played it in its entirety, and I was invited to be interviewed by Tom Brokaw, then on the *Today* show. Brokaw's producers saw the PFAW story as "Hollywood Coming After the Christian Right." To disabuse viewers of that notion I asked former Iowa senator Harold Hughes, himself an evangelical Christian but politically moderate, to appear with me. A single impression on a network news broadcast back when there were only three of them (plus a months-old CNN) was a very big deal, and in a single eight-minute interview—the news had room to breathe then—People For the American Way gained recognition by the establishment and more media attention followed. Our numbers grew and well-known faces became more interested in supporting us.

I wrote several more PSAs, and director Jonathan Demme (later to win an Academy Award for *The Silence of the Lambs*) came aboard to direct them. They featured Carol Burnett, Goldie Hawn, Ned Beatty, and Muhammad Ali, among others, and further emphasized that the right to freely express differing opinions was the American way. Demme's light touch brought humor to each piece, which gave the taglines more punch. It also helped to raise the money required to buy the TV time to run them, and provided me with a degree of pride and satisfaction very similar to what I derived from a hit show. I was reaching people to share my passion. Talk about highs!

Maintaining that high late in 1981, I produced a half-hour documentary about the Moral Majority, narrated by Burt Lancaster, a role-model citizen activist who used every ounce of his smarts and celebrity in pursuit of social justice. *Life and Liberty for All Who Believe* mischievously featured the views of the Moral Majority and its leaders, as expressed in their films, speeches, interviews, and sermons. Giving them the opportunity to reach an audience that didn't already agree with them was tantamount—no surprise—to letting them hang themselves.

AS WELL AS PFAW was doing two years in, it didn't assuage my frustration over the still unfinished script for *Religion*. God, the Bible, and love of country were still, as I saw it, the sole province of the Right. On the Left we were behaving as though we didn't care, and I simply had to do something about that. One morning I awoke with an idea 180 degrees removed from *Religion*—a two-hour, star-studded, nonpartisan salute to America on the occasion of the 250th anniversary of George Washington's birth. I would produce it under the People For the American Way banner "to show that God and the flag belong to all of us, no matter where we stand politically."

By the time I shopped that idea to the networks, I had the title, *I Love Liberty*, and ran the notion by a number of stars who were intrigued by the project. That didn't make it an easy sale. The press had already labeled us "The liberal People For the American Way" and the media could not—and to this day cannot—conceive of a liberal or conservative group engaged in a deliberate nonpartisan effort. Everything requires a label. At the risk of being considered hopelessly naïve or, worse, disingenuous, I say *I Love Liberty* was conceived, written, staged, and produced to be impeccably nonpartisan.

ABC, the network most attracted to it, held back the order until I could offer what they considered proof of its nonpartisan origin. "Get two ex-presidents, one Republican and one Democrat, to cosponsor the show," I thought. The only former Democratic president living then was the recently defeated and still widely unpopular Jimmy Carter, and one of the two living Republican ex-presidents had resigned in disgrace, so I asked ABC if they would be satisfied with a president and a first lady, Gerald Ford and Lady Bird Johnson, as co-chairs of *I Love Liberty*. They said yes.

I phoned Betty Ford, with whom I'd enjoyed a warm friendship based on her fondness for *Maude*. Mrs. Ford said she'd be happy to arrange for me to meet with the president in Palm Springs. They lived by the 13th Fairway at the Thunderbird golf course and I'd be welcome anytime. When Jerry Perenchio, a staunch Republican, heard what I was up to he asked if he might come along. The company had a Learjet at the time, and as we flew down we had a laugh or two at the president's expense. Having bumped his head on a helicopter doorway and fallen down the steps of Air Force One, President Ford's reputation for awkwardness was the subject of sketches and stand-up comedians everywhere. If only he'd do something clumsy for us, we joked.

Mrs. Ford greeted us warmly and escorted us to the president's den, which had a pair of French doors that opened onto the golf course. He would be coming in soon, she said. The room was warm and book-lined, with family pictures cozying the volumes on every shelf, the president's imposing desk opposite the couch Jerry and I were sharing. On a coffee table in front of us sat a very large ashtray with a heap of ashes. It seemed that the president had recently smoked his pipe while receiving someone who enjoyed a good cigar. The feeling in this room was as welcoming as Mrs. Ford's smile.

Minutes later President Ford entered with a cheery "Hello, sorry to keep you waiting." We told him we hadn't been there long and were enjoying all the family photographs. Perenchio, pointing to one of them, asked, "Your grandchildren?"

"Oh, yes," said the president, who hadn't really looked at us yet, "but those are at least a year old. I just got some new ones—let's see here . . ." He rummaged among a desktop of papers and found an envelope. "Here we are. Yes, these were taken just last week." The president came around the desk with the envelope, looking at the photos as he withdrew them. "Here's Hannah, she's the little one, and Sarah. That's Rebekah, second oldest . . . Hannah again," he said, as he flicked each photograph toward us, totally unaware that they were failing to reach us, landing instead among the ashes. Lifting his head after flicking the last photo, the president, perplexed for an instant that we were emptyhanded, looked down into the ashtray. "Oh, no," he said, smiling woefully.

President Ford believed firmly that the government must not favor any one religion over others and that each man's love of God was unique to the individual. The same held true for love of country, and so religion and patriotism, as symbolized by the Bible and the flag, belonged equally to people of all faiths and beliefs. This was the credo our show would seek extravagantly to celebrate, and we left the Ford home, after a very pleasant chat, with the president's agreement to cochair *I Love Liberty*.

A week later my associate Catherine Hand made arrangements for me to meet with Lady Bird at the Lyndon Johnson Presidential Library in Austin. As I was driving home on Sunset Boulevard the evening before I was to fly down there, I was broadsided at a right angle by a car seeking to beat out the cautionary yellow blinker as I was passing through. (Could it have been my fault as well? Not as long as I'm telling the story.) In any event, my mouth hit the steering wheel, I was attended to in the emergency room at UCLA Hospital, and the next morning I flew to Austin with the swollen lip of a Ubangi tribe member. Lady Bird, who in her graciousness reminded me of Betty Ford, made no reference to my aberrant mouth and agreed to cochair the program.

BRINGING *I LOVE LIBERTY* to fruition—before some ten thousand people in person and millions on TV—was the headiest experience of my life. (Up to that point, I should add.) On what other occasion might you see Robin Williams, as touching as he was hilarious, playing the American flag? Or Senator Barry Goldwater—likely the most conservative candidate ever to run for the presidency—introduce the most fantabulous opening this liberal could imagine? Alone in a spotlight, the senator disappointedly explained that he'd hoped to introduce a much bigger and more patriotic opening number but the producer wanted something far smaller. "We argued back and forth," he lamented, "but finally, just as happens in Washington, we had to compromise."

What followed featured some seventeen hundred performers, among them five marching bands, a group of flag-bedecked single-wheel cyclists representing the fifty states, a dozen Uncle Sams on stilts, a reenactment of the raising of the flag at Iwo Jima, singers, dancers, jugglers, acrobats, the dropping of sixteen thousand red-white-and-blue balloons, and the unfurling of a thirty-by-sixty-foot American flag. At the conclusion of this mammoth opening the camera cut back to Goldwater, who, with a straight face, announced somberly, "That was the compromise."

With an introduction by Big Bird, the Muppets were riotous at the Continental Congress that Miss Piggy, dressed first as George Washington, then as Abe Lincoln, kept trying to crash. Kermit the Frog kicked her out because neither had attended that Congress—and besides, women had no place there.

Martin Sheen, who would later star in the hit TV series *The West Wing*, looked to be honing his presidential chops as he strode across the arena floor, fervently proclaiming an open letter to George Washington from the American people, informing our first president of everything they would have to brave to build the America of today—that bellwether of hope, the world's primary bastion of freedom, liberty, and equality.

Burt Lancaster was electrifying as Justice Learned Hand defining the spirit of liberty. Walter Matthau and Christopher Reeve delivered a thrilling reenactment of a debate over religious freedom in eighteenth-century New England; Gregory Hines, a singer and perhaps the greatest tap dancer of his time, led dozens of like performers in a rousing medley of patriotic songs; and Barbra Streisand, backed by the U.S. Air Force Band, sang "America the Beautiful."

The most generically constitutional segment of the evening had a black man, a Hispanic, a Native American, a woman, and a gay man speaking of their frustrations with an America that hadn't as yet delivered on its promise of full equality. Each one concluded by saying, "Right now America isn't working that well for me, but—I love my country."

The *Christian Science Monitor* said: "*I Love Liberty* is an unabashedly patriotic, flag-waving, freedom-loving, electronic paean to America's diversity of people and attitudes. Just about every patriotic song is sung, just about every hero of American history is quoted in this rousing rally, a flag love-in taped at the Los Angeles Sports Arena to celebrate Washington's Birthday."

"A flag love-in." Says it all.

PERHAPS PFAW'S most SATISFYING SUCCESS in the early years, championed on the ground in Texas by our Mike Hudson and backed up by the Tony Podesta crew in DC, was the defeat of the fundamentalist zealots who ran the

Texas School Board Authority. Texas was a primary purchaser of the textbooks (published in New England and Pennsylvania) that were then acquired by school systems across the country, and Texas used that power to control content. As a result of Hudson's tireless effort on behalf of People For, the study of evolution *as science* was returned to textbooks used by schools nationwide. And such classics as *The Catcher in the Rye, The Grapes of Wrath, Anne Frank: The Diary of a Young Girl,* and *Death of a Salesman* were back on library shelves.

While I take great pride in that accomplishment—and the growing influence of PFAW—the fundamentalist Right had its own take. "Norman Lear's new organization will send busloads of Big Labor Bosses in Soviet tanks into your community," warned a fund-raising letter from right-wing direct-mail pioneer Richard Viguerie, "along with homosexual teachers who are trying to stop your children from praying." Pat Robertson threatened me with retribution from no less than the Lord Himself. A letter I received from him read, "Dear Norman, Though I am a former Golden Gloves Boxer I dislike fights. I seldom fight, but when I do I seldom lose . . . I want to warn you with all solemnity . . . 'Your arms are too short to box with God . . .' Sincerely, Pat Robertson." And Jerry Falwell sent out a massive Moral Majority mailing that credited me with bringing "filth and sexual perversion into our living rooms," thus making me "the greatest threat to the American family in our generation."

The most astounding thing to me about these Southern Baptists who flogged me so violently is that the most outspoken public voices against them were also Southern Baptists. It was Bill Moyers, after all, who asked to interview me for *Creativity,* a series he was doing for PBS, and his voice and articulation had the sound of my hero, John Henry Faulk, and of commentator Jim Hightower, journalist Molly Ivins, and future Texas governor Ann Richards. They were the voices that represented the Southern Baptist Convention for me before the establishment of a commission within the Southern Baptist community to "mobilize Christians to be the catalysts for the Biblically-inspired transformation of their families, churches, communities and the nation."

As much as Moyers got me to open up when it came to talking about my father, I could not bring myself to say publicly that he was sent to prison. I did talk about it off camera and that led to the inclusion in his broadcast of a clip between Archie and Mike that said more in six minutes about how Archie became Archie than any other scene or episode we made in nine years.

Archie and Mike find themselves locked in the storeroom of Kelsey's Bar. The bar is closed and this is going to be one long night. They begin to drink, and Archie gets soused. Then, in as open and unguarded a moment as he has ever lived, he tells Mike in a pained reminiscence how his father beat him regularly to teach him right from wrong, and in that way taught him everything he knows. Mike is horrified and saddened; he suggests that maybe, just maybe, Archie's dad was wrong to treat him that way. A tortured Archie explodes.

"What? Your father? The breadwinner of the house, there? The man who goes out and busts his butt to put a roof over your head and clothes on your back? You call your father *wrong*?" Mike, feeling Archie's anguish, moves to embrace him. Archie won't have it, but his expression reveals that a terrible doubt has been placed in him. It's a heart-wrenching moment.

Bill also interviewed Frances, whose views he sought on her husband's creativity. She appeared her usual, very stylish self. That was real, her taste in fashion being totally grounded and impeccable. To match how she looked, though, Frances would have to have been totally at ease and eloquent. Instead, she was squeezing who she wished to be out of a worn tube that she'd polished to a high sheen for the occasion.

THERE WERE A NUMBER of weekends that Frances and I both recognized as once-in-a-lifetime occasions that still took everything she had to get her through them. It all started when I met Cliff Pearlman, who owned Caesars Palace in Las Vegas. He told me that Caesars had two fully staffed five-bedroom villas, one in Palm Springs and the other in La Costa, that they maintained as freebies for their high rollers. I was no high roller, but Cliff liked me and said, "There's no one there half the time. Call my office and if one is open, it's yours."

I did just that and invited four other couples—Carl and Estelle Reiner, Mel Brooks and Anne Bancroft, Dom and Carol DeLuise, and Larry and Pat Gelbart—to join us that first weekend. We all loved the mix, had the time of our lives, and spent two weekends a year together for a number of years thereafter. We called ourselves Yenem Veldt. Translation: The Other World. In the history of fun no group ever had more. We awoke on Saturday morning, had breakfast in our bedclothes, and, from the moment Dom started slicing fruit— you cannot believe how funny Dom DeLuise was slicing fruit—laughed so hard and so continuously that we often stayed in our bedclothes all weekend.

I can bring a laugh to mind with each memory: of Mel Brooks's impersonation of Fred Astaire; or Anne, Mel's Academy Award–winning wife, joining Pat Gelbart and Estelle Reiner (both professional singers when they were younger) to form a trio they called The Mother Sisters; or Dom DeLuise whipping something up on the stove while singing "O Sole Mio"; or his wife, Carol, doing an amazing imitation of Imogene Coca. Honorary emcee Carl Reiner was hilarious telling each of us how funny we were, as was Larry Gelbart, whose highest praise came off like a roast. As for me, I did pratfalls, fell face-first into cakes, and, as an attentive host, offered fists full of whipped cream or mashed potatoes to my guests. And that leaves one.

Frances spent much of her time alone in our room, but once, pressed to perform, gave her impression of a character in a film that was current at the time. The woman became a murder victim and Frances elected to play her after the killing. She lay down on the floor faceup, and as Carl reports in *his* memoir, "Frances seemed not to breathe or move a muscle for a good minute, and her portrayal received at least as much applause as any of the seasoned professionals."

3

NEXT FOR ME in the entertainment arena was the 1982 purchase, with Jerry Perenchio and Bud Yorkin, of AVCO Embassy Pictures. A year or so later Bud elected to be bought out and our three-decade professional association ended. We remained great friends, however, and our personal lives bore a remarkable resemblance. We each divorced, remarried, and had children with considerably younger wives. You who could be reflexively thinking, "Aha, trophy wives!" should know that our marriages preceded that expression, which originated in a 1989 *Fortune* magazine cover story. Besides, you'd have to answer to our brides of nearly thirty years, the lovely Lyn Lear and Cynthia Yorkin, whose every friend will tell you, "Don't go there!"

A-E was a producer and distributor of films that was considered a studio even though it owned no soundstages or real estate. In short order we dropped AVCO, folded in the Tandem and T.A.T. assets, and under our new brand name, Embassy, we were making feature films as well as series television. Among the films we made in the three years we owned the company were *Fanny and Alexander, Saving Grace,* and *A Chorus Line,* but the one I'm proudest of cost the least.

Since *AITF* had gone off the air, Rob Reiner and a few buddies had been trying to get financing for a film he wanted to direct about a fictional British heavy metal band. Every studio and independent investor in town had turned down *This Is Spinal Tap* when Rob learned that our new company was making movies. Since the film—he called it a mockumentary—was to be improvisational, he had no script. His sales pitch was just a bare outline and the force of his personality.

Rob had me from the minute he recited the names of the band members: David St. Hubbins, Derek Smalls, and Nigel Tufnel. (Rob would play the director, Marty DiBergi.) When Rob said he had cast Michael McKean, Harry Shearer, and Christopher Guest to play those roles, respectively, I knew this had to be an Embassy film. As he pitched it, his passion for doing it matched the hilarity and satire in the idea. When he concluded his pitch and left the room, I turned to Alan and Jerry and asked, "Who wants to tell him no?"

"*This Is Spinal Tap* is one of the funniest, most intelligent, most original films of the year," wrote Roger Ebert. "The satire has a deft, wicked touch. *Spinal Tap* is not that much worse than, not that much different from, some successful rock bands." While it wasn't the box office hit we had hoped for, *Spinal Tap* did become a cult classic, and currently enjoys a 95 percent "fresh" rating on the film review Web site Rotten Tomatoes. When the Library of Congress selected it for preservation they deemed it "culturally, historically and aesthetically significant."

One of the great kicks of my life and career has been my relationship with the Reiner clan. Carl, a friend for some sixty years now, is one of a kind. If, no matter how good you may have reason to feel, you aren't feeling just a little bit better for being with him, I would call for a physician right away. Carl always spoke of Rob's having two fathers, and I'm proud to have been selected as Pop II. It was no surprise to me that Rob would be as fine a director as he was a performer, no surprise that everything he touched would be one from the heart. It was also no surprise that Rob would be as important a political activist as he's become. Few things have made me as proud as when Rob has said my social and political activism is what motivated his.

OWNING EMBASSY ALLOWED ME to pick up a property for film or TV far more quickly than having to go to a network or another studio first. My cousin Harold, whose dad made me jealous whistling for him when we were kids, had a massive heart attack in 1973. Months later he underwent a double bypass and was told there was little chance he would fully recover. Harold, a urologist, was married to Martha Weinman, a writer for the *New York Times*, who took detailed notes about his treatment and the doctors providing it.

Harold died in September 1978, and late the next year Martha completed the book that chronicled his battle, *Heartsounds*. It is as relevant now as the day the *New York Times Book Review* called it "an indictment of present day medical care," adding, "One sees not only that there are inadequacies in the health-care system, but occasional acts of callousness that leave one breathless, speechless with rage . . ." Talk about timeless.

The TV movie of the book, starring James Garner and Mary Tyler Moore with a script by the inimitable Fay Kanin, was my final hug of the only family member who understood and often discussed with me our difficult heritage.

THE YEAR AFTER Embassy started I got that Sunday morning phone call telling me that I was to be one of the first inductees into the Television Academy's Hall of Fame. I flew my mother out for the event despite her unenthusiastic response—"Listen, if that's what they want to do, who am I to say?"—when I first gave her the news. I told that story to start my acceptance speech, got a giant laugh—and the camera caught my mother roaring, overjoyed to be the center of attention no matter what it took to get there.

She reigned like a queen from her wheelchair, and, this being a celebratory week, there were a few lunches, cocktail parties, and dinners, where she met the likes of Paul Newman, Burt Lancaster, Loretta Young, and Groucho Marx. Lucille Ball and Shirley MacLaine told her she was beautiful.

At the induction ceremony she met Milton Berle, who was lip and jowl funny all over her. She howled with delight as she looked about to be sure others were seeing this. Cast members from many of our shows were there and they were effusively nice to her.

I don't mean to suggest this wasn't a big night in my life also. My daughters had flown out for the event and could not have made me prouder. Perenchio threw me an after party where I felt as loved and feted as I was able to feel at the time.

When Mother's visit ended and I was driving her to the airport she said she hoped I wouldn't mind if, when she got home, she told the family in Bridgeport "a little white lie." And what might that white lie be?

"It's not important," she said. "We all tell little white lies."

When I pressed her further she finally responded, "I was here ten days. Who has to know I didn't get to Las Vegas?"

AT HOME FRANCES AND I were *empty* empty nesters. Kate and Maggie had graduated from college—Stanford and the University of Oregon, respectively—and were living in New York. Between us there was nothing to hold on to. We continued to host dinners and fund-raisers for any number of political figures, and spent less and less time alone together.

Our last home was in Brentwood, the house we bought from Paul Henreid, built originally by Henry Fonda. It had a screening room in which to view 35mm prints of newly released films that the studios made available to members of the "Bel Air Circuit," and we'd established a Sunday evening tradition known to our friends as Loew's Lear. One Sunday John Dunne brought a print of *My Dinner with Andre*, which he was reviewing for the *New York Review of Books*. The film, set in a restaurant, consists of a single dinner conversation between Wallace Shawn and Andre Gregory. The subject of the conversation was LIFE, as filtered through their personal stories and experiences and passed on to viewers as lessons in how to live. That was it—two men talking, not unpretentiously, for one hour and fifty minutes. You really had to be in the mood for such a film.

The filmgoers at Loew's Lear that evening, among them the Reiners and the Brookses, were in no such mood. Perhaps a half hour into the film, as if on cue, Carl and Mel exchanged a look. I either caught it or sensed it, and in half a minute the three of us were up. A card table and two chairs were set in front of the screen. Carl and Mel were seated and, with a napkin over my arm, I was waiting table. The projectionist in the booth lowered the sound in the screening room, and *My Dinner with Mel* proceeded hilariously alongside the one with Andre.

SUCH FLEETING MOMENTS of pure joy were hardly enough to sustain our marriage, and by 1983 Frances and I decided to spend the Christmas holidays apart. A friend recommended La Samanna to me, a hotel resort on the Caribbean island of St. Martin. Ben Bradlee, famed editor of the *Washington Post*, and his wife, Sally Quinn, were there, and although Ben and I had met before— at the 1976 Muhammad Ali/Ken Norton fight at Yankee Stadium—we didn't really know each other. At La Samanna we became fast friends. Ben is one of those rare guys, a man's man and a lady's man in equal measure.

The Bradlees were scheduled to return to DC for a New Year's Eve party they were throwing, the first of what would turn out to be a thirty-year tradition. I was invited to join them and stay in their sumptuous Georgetown home. I did just that and found myself, as 1983 turned into 1984, chumming with the DC press corps elites and, no fault of theirs, growing sadder by the minute as the New Year approached. As everyone was counting down the last seconds to midnight I looked around the room and saw dozens of couples ready to kiss. It just might have been the loneliest night of my life since H.K. was sent to prison.

Just as the clock struck twelve and all the couples turned to each other, another solo gent I knew slightly but liked quite well sidled up to me. We exchanged a look that said, "Why not?" and kissed. And then one of us cautioned—we each credit the other with saying it—"I hope you realize this isn't going anywhere."

As it turned out, it went *every*where. After some twelve years as head of production at Walt Disney Studios, Dr. Marty Kaplan joined my old friend, Geoffrey Cowan, dean of the Annenberg School of communication at USC. In 2000, as associate dean, Marty conceived of a piece of research that struck at the core of my concerns regarding American media. His research measuring the amount of airtime California TV stations were giving to that year's gubernatorial race, concluded with this statement: "The final imperative to entertain had warped the civic obligation to inform." Only 0.45 percent of local news throughout California had been devoted to covering local politics.

I thought that statistic a most threatening development in our media culture and offered financial support from the Lear Family Trust. My offer of support prompted a suggestion from Geoff and Marty that the Annenberg School establish a Norman Lear Center for the study of the impact of entertainment on the way the American people were informed. Marty's delineation of the center's mission grabbed me:

"Think of entertainment not just as leisure activity, but as the way the messages grab and hold our attention. Think of entertainment not just as a sector of the economy, but as a driving force—maybe *the* driving force—of daily life in this brave New World . . . Today there is scarcely a domain of human existence unaffected by the battle for eyeballs, the imperative to amuse, the need to stimulate and titillate, to tell us stories, to play with us. The stakes for society are enormous. This is the terrain the Norman Lear Center is mapping."

And Norman Lear is mad about its work.

AT THE START of the New Year back home, I agreed to try a kind of trial separation that Frances thought up: we'd live apart during the week and come together on the weekends.

It was then that the USO asked if they could honor me with their Distinguished American Award for my service in World War II. In no mood for a celebration that would include family at its core, I declined their invitation. They persisted, however, and their pitch all but brought a tear to my eye: it was important that the war, and the way Americans had united and sacrificed to win it, not be forgotten. The USO's way of reminding people was by celebrating high-profile figures who had served in battle. They pledged to put no pressure on friends or family to attend, promising to fill the room with no help from my Rolodex.

And that is exactly what they did. The USO avoided soliciting the entertainment industry altogether. The hotel ballroom was jammed with regular folks who'd driven in from as far away as Long Beach and Santa Barbara to see this program: emcee Bob Hope, known for entertaining troops across the globe, introduced comedienne Phyllis Diller, singer Roberta Flack, a huge choir, two splendiferous United States Marine bands, and, to make the presentation, the most decorated airman in World War II, Colonel Frank Kurtz.

Colonel Kurtz flew a plane he named the Swoose Goose. It became so celebrated that when their daughter was born the colonel and Mrs. Kurtz named her with the aircraft in mind. Swoosie Kurtz is one of the finest actresses of her time. The colonel, too, was possessed of great flair and spent the years since the war speaking for the Army Air Forces. By the time I was being honored, Colonel Frank Kurtz had become as brilliant and dramatic an orator as I have ever heard. He told the audience he was going to take them on a mission he and I flew together, describing every moment of it so dramatically it made everyone in that ballroom feel it was *their* life at stake.

By midmorning, while you're having your coffee here at home, Norman has long since donned his flak suit, helmet, and oxygen mask, and headed for the Schweinfurt ball-bearing plant in Berlin. Suddenly the plane's nose lurches upward—then drops a hundred feet. It's ack-ack fire. The Germans are throwing big shells up at us and the sky ahead is solid black with flak. The top turret gunner calls out, "Fighters twelve o'clock high."

Every gunner opens up . . . the entire plane quivers as guns burst from the top, waist, and bottom—while enemy planes fly down right through our formation. Our number three bomber takes a direct hit—he's on fire—peels away—parachutes start to billow out. We lose more bombers, and we're still forty minutes to target . . .

The colonel was electrifying. The crowd in that ballroom was on its feet before he finished. When he called out my name, adding that I flew more than fifty of those missions, it was absolute bedlam—and there wasn't a single person close to me in that audience.

ONE WEEKEND when Frances and I were trying togetherness again we invited our friends the Dorsos to dinner. Richard mentioned that a mutual friend, Dan Melnick, was in town and I suggested he come along. Dan had a blind date that night, and so our foursome became a dinner for six. When I greeted Danny and his date at the front door, little did I know I was meeting the woman who would become my wife of twenty-seven years and mother to my son and twin daughters.

Lyn Davis, a former teacher, had been in training to be a family therapist at the Foundation for Depression and Manic Depression in New York. Born in Whittier, California, and raised in Sacramento, she had just moved back west, settled in L.A., and taken a job with Merv Griffin Productions. A mutual friend had fixed her up with Danny, and they'd known each other for half an hour when they appeared at my front door.

In that time Lyn learned that Frances and I had been separated on and off and that she could expect to see us at each other's throats much of the time. And she did. Melnick and the Dorsos were used to it, as if it were background music, but Lyn never forgot it.

She also recalls my taking her around the house for a tour of the art and being surprised that I was taller than she thought I'd be from the interviews she'd seen on TV. I thought her very beautiful, but in no way a babe. She had all the parts and features that make for a babe, but put together, the hard edges vanished and a gentility and fineness took over—a touch of the noblewoman.

The dinner conversation that night included talk about my work with People For the American Way and Lyn's seeking a PhD in psychology. The subject of her doctoral thesis happened to be a comparison of the attitudes of two church congregations, one conservative fundamentalist, the other liberal Unitarian. To my happy surprise, I received a letter from Lyn a few weeks later, asking for some information about PFAW for her thesis.

In my smart-ass, infant, male chauvinist way I thought this the come-on I didn't dare hope for. A beautiful class act of a woman had made the first move and I was, as the saying went in those years, hot to trot. All I had was a return address and, while there was still a Western Union and it was almost a decade before e-mail, I sent her a telegram and asked her to call me. We met for lunch a few days later. Mark E Pollack, who started to work for me a couple of years before I met Lyn Davis, and my assistant at the time, Jackie Koch, tell me they realized early on that something was different about this relationship. Before I met Lyn they hadn't known me to be unreachable for some hours in the middle of the day, or to leave the office suddenly, tossing an "I'll be back" over my shoulder, only to call in later with a "See you in the morning." At that first lunch we talked about the basis of her thesis, which was right up my alley. There weren't that many subjects that could have maintained my concentration while sitting across from a face as lovely as Lyn's. What she took from our luncheon, as a result of my interest, was a new confidence in her thesis. What I took from it was a strong desire "to be with her," a more genteel way of expressing my desire to bed her.

At our second lunch, I was looking into Lyn's eyes, drinking in her essence as we awaited our appetizers, and heard someone say, "I don't think I can sit through a meal before I know what it feels like to kiss you." When Lyn smiled playfully and started to rise, I realized who'd said that. Within ten minutes we were in her car on a residential street, parked in the driveway of a house for sale, her angel face cupped in my hands, eyes locked, staring down into each other's souls before oh so slowly bringing our lips together.

The spirituality and search for meaning that underlay Lyn's thesis—and her very being—liberated the equivalent in me, and before either of us knew it we were a couple. The twenty-five-year difference in our ages didn't seem to matter at all in that context and hasn't to this day. The only time age came up was when Lyn mentioned that she had to have a child and I questioned whether it was fair to that newborn for a man my age to be his or her parent. But, then, there was little chance of that because, as I told her from the beginning, regardless of the arrangement we might come to, I would never leave Frances.

I believed that without understanding why. I remember Frances trying to convince me that I wasn't really the "nice person, good person" many thought me to be. A need to be loved by everybody, she insisted, prompted what appeared to be a niceness in me, but it wasn't real. In weak moments I wondered if there wasn't some truth in it. But even if there was, so what? The need to be loved is endemic to humans, and earning that love or paying for it with niceness sounds to me like a reasonable transaction.

As for the baggage Lyn was carrying, her father served in the 15th Air Force, as I did, and flew, as I did, out of Foggia, Italy. Unlike me, though, he returned from the war with more than his share of PTSD. Her mother took a job and Lyn, second oldest of four children, the oldest being a boy, was assigned the care of her often abusive father, her younger siblings, and the household. Somehow she managed to get through high school near the top of her class and worked her way through college and graduate school to receive her master's degree at Cal State Northridge. She married her college sweetheart, who suffered a breakdown early in their marriage, and for three years Lyn's income was their sole support. Her husband was her father all over again.

One day on a lunch break a despondent Lyn was wandering through a used-book store and picked one out of a bin. Before she even opened it, she felt a tingle. It was *The Urantia Book*, a 2,097-page volume dealing with religion, science, and philosophy. By the time we met, Lyn Davis, on her way to a doctorate, had read it a dozen times and underlined passages throughout. What I'd been responding to in Lyn was the search she was on—because I was on it also—and also the resounding way our searches clashed. As expressed in *The Urantia Book*, Lyn had found "a faith that willingly carries reason along as far as reason can go and then goes on with wisdom to the full philosophic limit; and then dares to lurch out upon the never-ending universe journey in the sole company of TRUTH."

Here's the clash. Lyn trusted that on her journey she was "in the sole company of Truth." I was determined to spend my life seeking the Truth while, as John Henry would say, praying to be "spared the company of those who have found it."

GEORGE BERNARD SHAW spoke of God as "this wonderful will of the universe." I found that description beautiful, and the GBS words that follow express perfectly how I hope I am acting upon that belief: "If you don't do its work, it won't be done; if you turn away from it, if you sit down and say 'Thy will be done,' you might as well be the most irreligious person on earth. But if you wish to stand by your God, if you will say 'my business is to do your will, my hands are your hands, my tongue is your tongue, my brain is your brain, I am here to do Thy work, and I will do it,' you will get rid of other-worldliness . . ."

In that one phrase, "other-worldliness," Shaw captured what causes me to be one step removed from religion generally. I am a here and now person and what is expected of us in this lifetime Shaw put very clearly. The rest I continue groping to understand. Since I have not joined a synagogue, I suppose you can call me an unaffiliated groper, struggling toward an answer to the eternal question, sublimely posed in the theme song of a famous 1966 film: "What's It All About, Alfie?"

Years after I happened on that Shaw quote that so moved me, I ran across another one: "This is the true joy in life, the being used for a purpose recognized by yourself as a mighty one; the being a force of nature instead of a fever-ish, selfish little clod of ailments and grievances, complaining that the world will not devote itself to making you happy." My God, how those words satisfy me. They make me feel like I had a great meal with everyone I ever loved at the table.

Both quotes appeared in a little-known and extremely rare volume called *The Religious Speeches of George Bernard Shaw*, published by the University of Pennsylvania Press. Eventually we learned that there was a single copy in the University of Pennsylvania Library that they refused to loan out. Since they still had the plates, I made an arrangement many years ago to print one hundred copies to give away to friends who might want one. I have three left today.

THE OPEN MARRIAGE UNDERSTANDING I shared with Frances was be-ginning to feel the consequences of my connection to Lyn. Deep into her own longtime extramarital relationship, Frances had had no problem with my "whoring about," as she put it, but now detected a change in me suggesting that I, too, was in a relationship. While she never referred to it specifically, her "Who was that?" each time I hung up the phone was something new, and to some extent it surprised me.

Halfway through our marriage sex had become something neither of us seemed to require. We would spend the end of most evenings in "our" bed-room, she in bed and I in a chair facing her, often while she was eating a bowl of cold boiled beets—yes, beets. I do remember laughing a lot. The toke we took of a well-rolled joint might have helped in the laughter department. (I've never smoked much pot, but enough to know not to do it when there is any-thing serious that requires attention.) When we said good night at the end of those evenings and I repaired to the single bed just outside my study, my last glimpse of Frances, alone in the big bed, saddened me. Years later, just the memory of her in that moment would make me sad. Now I wonder if I wasn't feeling sorry not for Frances but for myself.

One day she picked up on an idea we had discussed on and off, but this time homing in on it. We should move to New York. Our daughters were in Manhattan, as were some close friends, some new friends, the theater—Frances sold it harder every time she brought it up. She pressed to get me to leave with her immediately after the wedding we had been planning for daughter Kate.

Kate had fallen in love with a young physician who, coincidentally, she might never have met but for her mother and me. In the seventies I had helped a young woman, Corinne LaPook, who was doing her master's thesis on *All in the Family*. In 1983 Frances and I were invited to attend a party in honor of the noted playwright Lillian Hellman, who was very frail and was traveling with a young intern. He introduced himself, clearly expecting a reaction to his name, LaPook, and when he got it he added, "her brother." In the course of the evening Frances mentioned that her daughter Kate lived in New York, and slipped her phone number into Jon's pocket. Weeks later, Jon, uncertain if he wanted to get involved with a Hollywood family, asked Lillian Hellman what to do, and she said, "Call her!"

And so Jon LaPook called Kate Lear. A year later they were deeply in love and Kate wished to be married in the home she grew up in. Kate is as tender a human as exists, and Jon, who becomes family twenty minutes after you meet him, could be brought to tears just talking about her. We were determined to throw them a great wedding, and I think we did. The ceremony, conducted by Rabbi Leonard Beerman, was deeply felt, word proud, and delicious, totally befitting the mood under the tent that covered our tennis court.

Personally, I was a flood of emotions. I could not help thinking of Lyn, how much I wished her to be sharing this moment with me, and how left out she must be feeling. And beside me was Frances, my wife, love, friend, victim, and antagonist of almost thirty years. Around us laughter, sentiment, and joy reigned, and the bride and groom were over the moon, as if they'd just stepped off every wedding cake ever baked.

Among the guests were Carl Reiner and Mel Brooks. When they are together the 2000 Year Old Man can't be far behind, but I couldn't be sure the old guy would make an appearance. Mel turns into him on a dime, but it wasn't clear if he had one with him until Carl got up to make a toast and earned a few laughs. Mel, fidgeting in his seat, suddenly realized he had a pocketful of change. He jumped up and, my God, he was funny. Carl asked Mel what advice he had for these newlyweds. "Ignore each other," the 2000 Year Old Man responded, "and I say that with love and spirit and spirit and love, and in feeling and sentiment, and romance and spirit and love. Because the more you find out about each other, the more disenchanted, the more disgusted, the more you realize you are just plain people like each other, and you'll hate each other because the same hate you feel for yourself you're going to throw on each other. So keep the mystery alive. When Dr. LaPook comes home at night Kate should say, 'Who is it?' and Dr. LaPook should say, 'It's Irving.' Never give your real name in marriage. Never. Once they know who you are in a marriage, you're finished. So seriously, let me be serious. Don't give away too much, you'll be married a long time."

A camera crew filmed the wedding and the party and, of course, that toast. There was but one cutaway as Mel spoke, and it was to a close-up of Kate. This was my middle "darb," named that by me when she was six, the word meant to convey a love beyond expression. Look at her now, a bride. Gorgeous. Lit from the inside, her soul showing. But always my darb.

They are married for almost thirty years now, have two terrific sons, Daniel and Noah, and Jon is the medical correspondent for the *CBS Evening News with Scott Pelley*.

MEANWHILE, the Coca-Cola Company, which had a few years earlier acquired Columbia Pictures, was now showing interest in buying Embassy. While we were not gung ho to sell, Perenchio was not one to dismiss a good deal out of hand, and as the talks continued, a good deal was taking shape.

One of Embassy's films, *The Emerald Forest*, was due to play at the 1985 Cannes Film Festival. I had never been to the festival and could hardly have a better reason to go, especially when I thought of the few days to follow at another exotic European location with Lyn. My friends Stanley and Betty Sheinbaum had a small house on the island of Giglio, off the coast of Tuscany, which they offered to let me have for a week. Not one to dismiss a romantic good deal out of hand, I grabbed the opportunity.

The Cannes experience was thoroughly unmemorable, probably because what I wanted out of the trip was what was coming next. I leased a small jet to fly me to Pisa, from which I would taxi to Porto Santo Stefano for the ferry to Giglio. We were late flying out of Cannes and, to make matters worse, the taxi I'd called ahead for was no longer waiting on the runway when we landed late in Pisa. A replacement was called for, I told the driver I'd pay double his rate, and he sped to Santo Stefano, leaning on his horn all the way.

As we rounded the bend in the approach to the port, there was the ferry, blaring its departure. At the rail on the top deck Lyn was waving frantically, jumping up and down like a little girl. She rushed down the stairs to the first deck as the ferry inched away from the dock. I tossed my bag ahead of me and reached out with both hands to two men at the rail who grabbed them and hauled me aboard. In the history of ferryboat embraces there could not have been another more ecstatic.

Giglio is a small, eight-square-mile rocky island with three villages, lots of hiking trails, and few roads, only one of which, like a ribbon wrapped around the island's edges, winds its way to the walled fortress at the top, the village of Castello. Our cottage was perched on a promontory overlooking the Tyrrhenian Sea, about four hundred feet below Castello. One bedroom with an emperor-sized bed, a kitchen, and a living room, it was a beauty mark on the face of bliss, looking down one thousand feet on the Italian archipelago.

On Giglio Lyn could breathe free. Back home, we were a secret wherever I could be recognized. Our time together had been largely confined to her apartment, hotel rooms we sneaked into, or drives in the dark of night. Here, for the first time, we were in the world. No one on Giglio knew my name or was likely to recognize me. I am stunned to recall the ten to eleven hours of unaided sleep

I got each night on the island. I awoke to the sound of eggs frying, the smell of coffee brewing, and the sight of Lyn in the gauzy late-morning light, hovering over the stove with one thing in mind—to delight me, and me alone.

In the late afternoon we'd drive the narrow winding road to Castello, the top of the world on Giglio, and dined in one of several small cafés that gave us the feeling they were in business only to serve us. I have to believe we took a hike or two, but for the most part we read and talked much of the rest of the time. I opened up to Lyn as much as I could, hiding nothing except that which I hid from myself and have been digging out slowly here.

I've asked myself whether "opening up" on these pages demands that I say more about our lovemaking and concluded that it doesn't. Breathing is a big part of my life, too, but I don't go on about it. I have had a hearty appetite for every physical pleasure available, from a good cry to a great laugh, from anything tasty on the tongue to the afterglow of a terrific dump, from a succulent kiss to the explosive ecstasy of every climax. Suffice it to say, when Lyn was in my arms—well . . . suffice it to say.

THERE WAS A TELEPHONE in the Giglio house. Neither of us made an outgoing call and there was only one incoming. Jerry Perenchio phoned with Alan Horn on the line to tell me that the Embassy deal had just closed. I was officially a very good provider. Jerry's and my split was not a fifty-fifty arrangement. It varied from show to show and entity to entity, and was so complicated that teams of accountants and attorneys representing each of us could have spent weeks haggling over it.

Before I left for Cannes Jerry and I decided instead to make it an inside job and let Alan lead the effort to crunch the numbers along with Daryl Egerstrom, our long-standing chief financial officer. Jerry and I had absolute faith that when Alan Horn said to us, "This is what you get and this is what you get," the numbers would be as correct as they could be and we needn't spend another minute on it. Knowing Alan as he did, my attorney, Deane Johnson, as high-minded and respected a barrister as existed in entertainment law, was totally on board with that decision. And that was the way it went down.

Everyone who held a job at Embassy benefited from the sale. If you were there for only a week or a month you received a little something, a small percentage of the close to $15 million Jerry and I decided to spread among our employees. Alan Horn, of course, worked out the formula, but those who worked for us longest at every level did very well. Some—those who came with us early on—thanked us for the apartments and homes they could afford now, for the things they were able to do for parents in retirement, for college educations and new cars and trips abroad. Amid hugs and tears they came at us from all sides.

WHEN WE RETURNED from Giglio I met with Deane. There were a bottle of vodka, two glasses, and a bowl of ice on his desk when I entered his office, and we had a high old time toasting the sale of Embassy. Deane, of course, had the numbers and pushed them across the desk to me. After taxes I—make that Frances and I—were worth $200 million. Was my half of that really worth one hundred times my father's ten-days-to-two-weeks goal? Deane told me I looked like I didn't know whether to laugh or cry. Then we had this memorable exchange.

"Deane, would you say I'm really rich now?"

"That depends on how you want to use it, Norman."

"Well," I thought aloud, "a group of us are sitting around figuring out how we can raise seventy-five thousand dollars for a cause we believe in. Some say let's do a dinner, some say it should be a screening, others want to do an auction—and finally I get tired of the discussion and I say, 'Forget about it, I'll cover the seventy-five Gs, let's move on.'"

"And how often might you want to do that?" Deane asked.

"As often as I fucking please," I responded.

"You're not really rich," was his answer.

Deane didn't know he'd soon have an accomplice in getting that message across to me. After the Embassy sale I made the *Forbes* list of the four hundred wealthiest Americans. A week or two after it was announced my mother phoned me. Her voice was teary.

"Hello, darling," she said. "I hope you're not upset. It's not the worst thing in the world, you know."

"What, Mother? What are you talking about?"

"Well," she said, "I saw the magazine."

"You mean *Forbes*, Mother?"

"Yes, dear."

"Why would I be upset about that?"

"I didn't want you to feel bad they put you near the bottom of the list."

"Oh, my God!"

"What can I tell you, I'm a mother."

4

A FTER THE COCA-COLA/EMBASSY DEAL was announced, a member of the press phoned me to ask how I felt about the sale—not the deal, but the sale itself. What did it mean to me personally? "I guess you could say the curtain is coming down on act two," I replied, "and going up on act three."

"Oh," her tone was somber, "it's act three already?"

"Hold it," I responded quickly. "We're talking about a Shakespearean piece—there could be five, possibly six acts here." There were so many Nexts—in my personal life, in movies and TV, and in the public arena—that no part of me felt a final curtain coming down.

Just as Coca-Cola was becoming interested in acquiring Embassy, a script was in development for a film based on a Stephen King novella called *The Body*. When the director read a final draft and abandoned the project, it was brought to Rob Reiner. Rob returned to the novella, and between the lines of King's story he discovered what I can best describe as its soul. He pitched us his ideas for a rewrite, and Embassy—which had just released his second feature, *The Sure Thing*—decided to make the film with him. Rob and his associate Andy Scheinman went to work with writers and simultaneously started the preproduction process so he'd be ready to shoot when the script was ready. Cast and crew were in Oregon with a script everyone loved, freshly titled *Stand by Me*, when the deal to sell Embassy closed. Unknown to us at the signing, but quickly learned, was that every project Embassy had in development would now be released (or not) by Columbia Pictures, and Columbia had already turned down *Stand by Me* when it was called *The Body*. Their minds were not changed when they read the new script.

Rob and company were on location ready to go. It was all over for *Stand by Me* unless . . . I felt as if the eyes of everyone on the planet were turned toward me with a big "And . . . ?" hanging in the air. My confidence in Rob and the new script outweighed the advice of the better business heads, and I underwrote the film, budgeted at $7.5 million.

Rob made a tender, sentimental film, and still no studio wanted to pick it up for distribution. Key creative decisions like this one are too often made according to focus groups, the heat on a particular star, the cachet of the director, and how well earlier films on the subject had done. Seldom is the gut reaction of an executive responsible for making or picking up a movie without the support of extensive research. But that is what happened here.

Oddly enough it was Columbia—the studio that twice turned it down—that decided to distribute *Stand by Me*. Over a weekend Columbia hired a new head of production and distribution, Guy McElwaine. Having learned of the appointment, I got the film to him at home on a Sunday morning so he could see it before he was shown the research. The movie brought him to tears, and it had a distributor before McElwaine reported to his new office on Monday morning.

Stand by Me did very well. It appealed to young boys and teenagers and, through them, their families. It solidified Rob's reputation as a director, though not so much that the studios raced to do it when he wanted to make William Goldman's *The Princess Bride*. Goldman had written the screenplay from his own book, published in 1973, and in the history of the written word—I know I've used this phraseology a number of times, but I'm happy to be known as an "in the history of" addict—it has to be one of the most delightful reads. It seemed inconceivable—a word that became celebrated in the mouth of Vizzini, a character in the film—that the script had been circulating for several years and no one at any studio caught a glimmer of the movie that lurked in it. Norman Jewison, Robert Redford, and François Truffaut had all wanted to make it and none of them could find the funding.

Unfuckingconceivable!!

So funny and so rich in character and satire, it was right up Rob's alley, which is where I lived as well. Nobody had to sell me on it. The young lovers, Princess Buttercup and Westley, scaling the Cliffs of Insanity, battling Rodents of Unusual Size, and facing torture in the Pit of Despair, did that. Goldman's script was deliciously faithful to his book and Rob was bringing that story and those characters to life. I was delighted with the opportunity and agreed to fund the film with a $16 million budget.

Rob and his partner, Andy Scheinman, cast the picture brilliantly and turned out one of the most successful cult films ever made. Over time the film sold so well in home video and DVD that it outgrew its cult status and became a bona fide hit. What made *The Princess Bride* so rare was that it appealed to the entire family, to couples on a date, to teenagers of both sexes, and to the kids-only matinee crowd. It found an audience among those who favor fantasy and those who love comedy, and it played to the unsophisticated and highbrow as well. On its twenty-fifth anniversary in 2012 there was a special screening and celebration in New York. Rob and most of his cast were there, and a packed audience of rabid fans who knew the dialogue as if they had played every character themselves shouted out line after line with the actors on the screen.

The Princess Bride has to be one of the most beloved pieces of cinema extant. I was not involved creatively, and but for saying yes to making it I had nothing to do with the business side of it. Mark E Pollack, on and off set, handled that. And yet, if not for me it might never have been a film. Few things have made me more proud. (Another film I helped get off the ground was *Fried Green Tomatoes*. I'd read the script at the request of its brilliant director, Jon Avnet, loved it, and put up the early money to get it started.)

And here's one that got away. Ever since the Jackson 5 made their TV debut on *The Andy Williams Show*—of which Bud Yorkin and I were executive producers—I'd been as big a fan of Michael Jackson as the world of kids who were so visibly crazy about him. One morning I awoke with what I thought was a superb idea for a starring vehicle for him. In Carson McCullers's magnificent novel *The Heart Is a Lonely Hunter*, the three main characters are a deaf-mute, his pal—also mute—and a sixteen-year-old girl. Alan Arkin played the mute in a well-reviewed 1968 film of the novel, directed by Robert Ellis Miller, and I had in mind a remake with Michael in the Arkin role. Given the surprising sound of his normal speaking voice, I felt this very dramatic role was perfect for Michael and would make for a giant surprise and a big hit.

My friend, and today one of the entertainment industry's most powerful attorneys, Skip Brittenham, set up a meeting and attended it with me. It took place in a dressing room just off a soundstage where Jackson had been rehearsing. The room was lit for a squeamish host and Michael was stretched out on a built-in couch along the wall. When we entered he raised up on one elbow and was very pleased to see me again. In a soprano whisper he told me he'd read the two pages I'd sent him, his expression suggesting he liked them, and asked me to tell him more. As I started talking his eyes fluttered to a close. He could have been listening intently or sound asleep. When I finished some minutes later, it had to be twenty seconds or more before he opened his eyes and uttered a very pleasant "Thank you." That was it. We left and I never heard another word about my visit.

OVER THE MONTHS since she first mentioned it, Frances continued to coax me to move to New York. I suspected she had a second and surely more important reason than wanting me with her. I learned from our daughters that she was terribly excited about a new idea that they liked, too, but only she could tell me about. That opportunity arose when I had to be in New York very briefly on other business. I'd flown in on a small jet Perenchio and I owned for a time, and when I was due to go back Frances said she had some things to do in L.A. and asked if she could fly back with me. The trip would also give her time to tell me about an idea she had. That conversation began on the way to the airport.

Correctly assessing a gap in the marketplace, Frances had come up with an idea for a new magazine for women over fifty. She'd met with a number of key publishing heavyweights, received all the encouragement she required, and was ready to make her first move. Just before we boarded the plane Frances said something that assumed I would be the publisher, she the editor in chief. I knew in an instant that this would be a disaster. A half hour later, the Pratt & Whitney engines were settled into that low, sleep-inducing monotone, the sound of a smooth flight, when suddenly the peace was broken and our world at thirty thousand feet combusted. The little jet became home to the first part of the longest, angriest fight we ever had—eleven hours, half in the air and half on the ground. The pilots were sitting just eight to ten feet in front of us in the cockpit, and I wouldn't have blamed them if they'd jumped without chutes.

Frances assured me repeatedly that I would be publisher "in name only." Having bought into the very bullshit that was to her mind making her life impossible, she viewed "Publisher, Norman Lear" as necessary to establish the cachet the project required. In addition to thinking her entirely wrong, I told her that creatively it would send out the opposite message. With my name as publisher, no matter the truth, I would be considered the principal creator of the magazine. But Frances heard nothing I said, and in the course of the flight she grew angrier, as did I. As these kinds of things tend to do, we wandered off and on subject, hurling every kind of invective known to man and wife, each demanding to be heard at a volume and intensity that could fill a stadium.

"How could you not do this for me?" Frances screamed. "I've seen you offer to help every asshole, every fuckup, every stranger who ever wanted anything from you. But when I, your wife of almost thirty years, asks you for *one thing*, something that won't cost you a dime or a minute of your time, what do I get? I get a no! Are you kidding me? *Are you fucking kidding me?* You cruel bastard, you!"

There was a driver waiting for us when we touched down around midnight in Van Nuys. I wouldn't be surprised if he was still talking about what went on in the close quarters of his town car following his amiable "Hi, folks, Hugo here. Have a pleasant flight, did you?"

We were still carrying on when we arrived home, and it continued until around five A.M. It was my habit to run from room to room, slamming doors as Frances chased after me, opening them. If I locked a door, she'd bang on it until I had to throw it open. I had to have heard "cruel bastard" a hundred times that night. And I can see her racked expression as she said it. But is that really Frances? And is that male asshole me? He's telling Frances she's crazy, she should see her doctor—exactly what I wish he wouldn't say, even as I recognize that anything he might say in the situation would be futile.

Then, suddenly, there is silence. I am alone in my study. The clock on my desk reads 6:30 A.M. There is a knock on the door, it opens, and Frances is there. She's in business attire, smart, chic, and collected. Imperiously, as if she's thought about it for days and has just arrived to tell me, she announces that it is over. Here—she places it on the desk—is the ring that has never been off her finger for almost thirty years; she'll send for her personal things in a day or so; and, stopping at the door, she tells me, as a kind of by the way, that I'll be hearing from her attorney, Mickey Rudin, who handled the affairs of Lucille Ball, Frank Sinatra, and Elizabeth Taylor, among other big names. "You know Mickey, Norman"—her eyes narrowed—"the *killer*."

Mickey was a great attorney and tough as hell, but the "killer" moniker grew out of his having had a hernia at one time. The Yiddish word for hernia sounds like "keeler," and when Frances heard a Jewish associate call him that kiddingly one day she grabbed it. Mickey Rudin was as tough as nails, but also as fair and straightforward as could be. He helped us keep our sanity throughout.

I wasn't unhappy splitting everything down the middle, and that's pretty much what we did. We quarreled over only two things. Frances thought splitting everything meant that she should share credit with me retroactively on every episode of every show I produced throughout our marriage. The killer told her that was ridiculous.

The other item was The Gulley. That was a long and emotional struggle. I don't remember what I had to give up by way of art and cash, but Vermont meant more to me than it did to Frances, and over time she recognized that and we worked it out. The divorce settlement—a little more than $100 million—got a lot of press, some sources calling it the largest settlement ever granted (a record that would be shattered soon and often), but it was a tonic to Frances at the time. As for me, I was sure that my obituary, whenever it appeared, would begin with that statistic.

Frances officially filed for divorce in June 1986. Many months later I was sitting over coffee in our home on Chadbourne Avenue with an associate, Rick Mitz, who remembers the moment well. Someone walked in with the mail, and as I looked through it I came across an envelope on the back of which I saw in large print, "Frances Lear." Printed across the front side of the envelope, which contained news of her forthcoming magazine, were these words: "Two years ago, on a brilliantly sunny day in October, I left Los Angeles and a 29-year marriage to the television producer, Norman Lear."

Rick recalls me laughing when I opened the envelope, took out the letter, and continued to read: "I landed in New York, my hometown as a young woman, with two suitcases of the only clothes I really wore and a few sheets of paper on which I had scribbled an idea for a magazine." Talk about funny— maybe she did deserve credit on those scripts.

Though I didn't want to be involved with it, I had no problem with Frances naming her magazine Lear's. It had been her name for more than a quarter of a century. It's the name Kate, Maggie, and Ellen continued to use after their marriages. It belonged to all of us. The word that came back to me as she worked to get Lear's together was mixed. She was difficult, vacillating, demanding, smart as hell, impossible to work with, generally admired, and loved by some. For the first time she was in the position—if she was the woman she wished to be—to live her dream.

I WAS IN A DREAM STATE ALSO, fighting to free myself to be altogether *in* love and to share Lyn fully with my family, friends, and associates. Lyn still talks about what she went through as pockets of my world opened up to her and her days became a series of entrances: "Of course I knew what I was getting into and I was excited because it was what I always wanted. But as they say, 'Be careful what you pray for' . . . it was overwhelming . . . I felt intimidated meeting Joan Didion and John Dunne one night, Barbra Streisand and the Bergmans the next; all the stars from his shows and his political life—it was hard to believe how much he does and who he knows."

In the "how much he does" department, I'd read that on July 4, 1986, there was to be a giant celebration of the centenary of the newly restored Statue of Liberty in New York Harbor. Chief Justice Warren Burger was to conduct a naturalization ceremony and swearing in of a large group of immigrants on Ellis Island, and President Reagan was to speak from the USS *John F. Kennedy* as the largest flotilla ever assembled of "tall ships" (sailing vessels with at least two masts) was passing by. The vessels were to sail upriver before turning and coming back down and around Lady Liberty. The day's events would conclude with twenty-two thousand aerial fireworks launched from thirty barges and other vantage points.

I was as turned on by all the red, white, and blue hoopla as I'd been while holding my granddad's hand at a parade. I was especially moved by the image of dozens of tall ships in New York Harbor, each representing a different country, and I knew in an instant that I had to have one. I had to be in that parade of tall ships, not watching it from a motor yacht, and the cherry on the cake would be the opportunity under those amazing conditions to introduce my bride-to-be to everyone I cared about in the East. I told my world-class secretary, Jackie Koch, and my right- and left-hand associate and friend, Mark E Pollack, to go wherever they had to go, do whatever they had to do, but find me a tall ship.

I had every confidence that Jackie and young Pollack would deliver. Then, and through all the years since, Mark E has been there and has always delivered. MEP is a floater with a purpose. He floats in and out of everything going on around him, sees something—or a thousand and one things—that need to be done, and simply shows up to help. Helping is his purpose in life. He hasn't worked for me formally in decades, but no matter what I've been up to, Mark E has been at my elbow or out in front of me every step of the way.

Mark E came up with the *Galaxy*, a two-mast vessel representing the State of Israel that was on its way to participate in the centennial tall ships parade, now two months away. That gave me time to accept an invitation from Gore Vidal to come to Ravello, on the Amalfi coast of Italy, to discuss a miniseries "based on" Abraham Lincoln. "Lincoln, the man, does not as yet exist in literature," he said, and had intended to write a book about him. But then he fell in love with *Mary Hartman*, appeared on it nightly for a week, and was now convinced that was the way he wished to do Lincoln—a miniseries that would run Monday through Saturday for one week that he would write and I would produce.

I brought Lyn with me, of course, and we had two beautiful days with Gore and his partner, Howard Austen, in their home jutting out over the Mediterranean, motoring the coastline in their small boat, tying up to have lunch at one of the family restaurants dotting the cliff, sipping wine and dining at night at an outdoor café, and in between finding time, Gore and I, to hie off and talk about Lincoln. Gore's mind, historical memory, and verbal acuity dazzled and entertained me. So did his take on the Washington of the time—"a world of gambling clubs and whorehouses that catered to every taste and income." It did not stun Gore, as it did me, that his research into Lincoln unearthed a law partner who claimed the president had confided a concern that he might have syphilis.

It revealed as well that Salmon P. Chase, his chief rival for the presidency, had "an uncommonly close relationship with his daughter." As did Walt Whitman, the research indicated, with a nineteen-year-old boy.

Gore wrote a twenty-four-page outline to pitch the miniseries, which we did some months later. The networks gulped at the Chase and Whitman "revelations" and thought connecting Lincoln to syphilis, even through hearsay, was a joke. Gore sold hard and brilliantly, but I don't think my association with comedy, let alone my being well known, according to Jerry Falwell, for bringing "filth and perversion into America's living rooms," was of much help to him. Eventually Vidal wrote the book he started out to do in the first place, and *then* it was picked up by NBC for a miniseries that starred Sam Waterston and Mary Tyler Moore and won an Emmy for its director, Lamont Johnson.

It was May 11 when we left Ravello. Lyn's birthday was coming up on the fourteenth, and where better to celebrate it than the Hotel San Pietro, one of the most romantic spots I've ever visited. Built into the top of a cliff in the neighboring town of Positano, with an elevator going down some hundreds of feet through the rock to a small Mediterranean beach and a dock below, there could not have been a more perfect location for a proposal of marriage. Not that I brought Lyn there to do that. It just popped into my head like any other idea. What'll I do for her birthday? Ask her to marry me.

On the big day, while she was napping, I spoke with the pastry chef preparing Lyn's birthday cake—and made him smile. Lyn was exquisite at table that night. The dining room at San Pietro is an inside garden with lush, leafy vines along the walls and forming a design on the ceiling. Did I mention that Lyn was exquisite? As we sat over drinks in this magical place, words did not come easily. It was the pauses that spoke volumes.

At dessert the waiter brought a bottle of champagne, two glasses, and a small birthday cake, the frosting styled to make the loveliest of "Lyn." She was teary with sentiment when she started to cut into the cake, and surprised when her knife engaged something hard in the middle. It was a chunk of rolled tinfoil.

Inside was a slip of linen paper folded many times. Unfolded, she found a single sentence on it, in Italian. "Only in Italy," she said, smiling, as she signaled for the waiter. The tux-attired maître d' came over instead. Lyn handed him the paper and asked him to read the sentence to her. Obligingly, he looked at the paper and said, "Will you marry me?"

Lyn looked at the maître d', then at me, and back to him uncomprehendingly. Her puzzlement couldn't have lasted five seconds, but when she "got" it and looked up at me, it was as if the God she always assured me was present had haloed her face and lit a candle in each eye.

THE HEART OF THE CITY on the July Fourth weekend—"Liberty Weekend"—was New York Harbor, and the buzz and excitement equaled the Mardi Gras and Super Bowl combined. The weather was perfect, I was at the top of my game, as happy as I knew how to be, and, as it turned out, as big a horse's ass as had ever existed in the Americas, North or South.

Israel's 160-foot *Galaxy* was the smallest of the thirty vessels gathered, but just perfect for my guest list of about forty people, assuming, as any horse's ass would under the circumstances, that everyone was feeling warm and clubby, especially Lyn and my daughters. I'd phoned the girls just weeks before to tell them, as if they couldn't wait to hear the good news, that I'd just asked that young woman they'd heard about to marry me, adding cheerily, as only an indisputable horse's ass could, that she was coming east with me and I was so excited about their welcoming Lyn into the family on the *Galaxy* in New York Harbor.

What a stranger that Norman is to me now as I tell this part of the story. On the one hand, I know myself to be a terrific host. I've made it my business, and it has given me enormous pleasure, to see that others have a great time. Ninety percent of everyone who has known me would support that claim. Here, I was producing a truly memorable, no-stone-unturned weekend for close friends, family, and associates. When I learned that ABC was covering the entire event—the parade of tall ships; the unveiling of the newly restored Statue of Liberty; President Reagan's speech; the fireworks; and John Williams conducting the Boston Pops with performances by, among others, Johnny Cash, Barry Manilow, José Feliciano, Whitney Houston, and Itzhak Perlman—I told Mark and Jackie I wanted closed-circuit TV on the boat so that my guests could be on the water in the middle of the parade and at the same time see how the media was covering it all. Add three meals a day provided by a fine caterer Pollack found, and all the goodies in between, and could any host be more generous and considerate of his guests?

But what *about* those guests? How removed from his "considerate" self must a man be not to realize that the general mood of those on board did not match his? Four miserable women trump one male cheerleader in any situation. My daughters didn't want to rain on my parade—of tall ships, no less—and suffered in silence, but the pain showed. Lyn, who expressed trepidation about being introduced to them this way, recognized their pain, felt her own, and wanted to run. It was like being stabbed each time a couple introduced themselves as "old, old friends of Frances and Norman." The girls heard this, too, and wanted to scream. It was a dreadful experience for the four people I cared most about.

THE MORNING AFTER the tall ships regatta, Lyn and I flew off for six weeks in Africa, a spectacular trip especially memorable for several once-in-a-lifetime moments. Tanzania is fixed in my mind as the place where, for the first time, I "sensed eternity," which is the best I can do to express a feeling of oneness with the vastness. We were awakened in the middle of the night by some massive stirring. We sat out on a balcony just off our bedroom and watched a large herd of buffalo—somber van-sized presences responding to some internal command—trod heavily by in the otherwise still darkness. The process took an hour, and if I were I to call it moving beyond words, I'd be slighting its magnificence.

In Kenya, after days of hoping to see a leopard, our guide got a furtive message on his shortwave and darted over brush and between trees to a small clearing where, on a low branch of a tree across the patch of ground, one was sitting. I got such a kick out of the spectacle of dozens of vehicles zeroing in from all directions on that lone spotted cat that I didn't really see the animal until I watched the video of our trip some months after we'd returned from our safari.

In the Serengeti National Park, staying in an enclave of individual mud huts that were far nicer than they must sound, I opened the door on the morning of my sixty-fourth birthday—in boxer shorts and a T-shirt—to find a tall, elegant African in a three-piece suit with a sheet of paper in his hand. "Mr. Norman Lear?" he asked. When I said yes he handed me the paper, which said "Happy Birthday," and threw the door open wider. That was the cue for music. Mark E Pollack—I never did find out how he managed it—had sent me a half hour's worth of native African celebratory music and dance. Three groups from different tribes performed as if Lyn and I were royalty. People poured out of the other huts to watch and applaud, and I couldn't have had a more heartwarming birthday if a party planner had worked on it for months.

In Rwanda, we were in search of gorillas. Getting to them was a hard uphill trek through heavy brush. We climbed single file, a guide leading and making a path by swiping away the tall brush ahead of us. Our footing was uneasy, stepping over low brush and branches, and guides behind or beside me often reached out a hand to help this bald sixty-four-year-old with the white sideburns. Reflexively, I motioned them off each time. (The Rwandan people seemed to live to smile and be helpful. It is horrifying to recall that this was just eight years before the genocide that saw the Hutu Rwandans slaughter 800,000 Tutsis living among them.) Toward the end of our first day Lyn and I heard them referring to me as "Majee Kiwanna." When we asked them the meaning, it was "Young old man."

About ninety minutes into our hike, the lead guide whispered something to his colleagues. A moment later, there in a small clearing was a gorilla family: a mother, father, and two little ones. Close to the large male and looking deep into his eyes, I recalled the essence of George Bernard Shaw's quote: "This wonderful will of The Universe, struggling and struggling, and bit by bit making hands and brains for it, feeling that having this will, it must also have material organs with which to grapple with material things. That is the reason we humankind have come into existence . . . and that evolutionary process to me is God." It could have been the Herman K. Lear family, circa twenty thousand years before. I don't think I ever felt more connected, if only sketchily, to the universe's plan for us.

And finally, there was the Seychelles, and an egg-shaped bungalow that rested on a story-high rock above the beach. Inside, a velvety couch followed the curve under a round window. Lying there, the window suggesting God's eye on us—I happily allowed Lyn that—we talked about forever things, made love, and talked about forever things some more. And made love.

A doctor friend had given me a little Ecstasy to take on the trip, with instructions to use it when we were utterly alone and in just the right environment. We knew we'd found it lying in that oval window, and later on a huge rock beside our bungalow that thrust beyond where we sat into the gently lapping waters of the Indian Ocean.

We kissed and, wrapping ourselves in its beams, pulled the moon closer. Not to be outdone, the stars settled on us like a twinkling shawl. At the height of our ecstasy that night in the Seychelles, we were talking about our childhoods. What happened next was mystical and shattering. Looking toward the ocean, the rock on which we were sitting changed shape as it sloped toward the water, and as I tried to tell Lyn what I was seeing, I started to cry. At the water's edge, some distance below us, the rock appeared to take the shape of three fingers extending into the gentle waves that washed over them. Lyn saw them, too, and held me tight.

"My father's fingers," I sobbed, and the dam of memory burst. There was my dad, plucking yet another strumberry from the bowl of berries and cream, plopping it into his mouth with wet fingers, his eyes rolling heavenward with the taste. There he was, driving so contentedly, the thumb and forefinger of either hand diligently at work, depending on which nostril he was picking. There he was at table again, his hands in the air, greasy fingers accenting and punctuating every detail of the point he was making.

At some point I started to laugh at the images tossing about in my head, the laughs and tears running together, and, as Lyn recalls, I asked out loud what my father's hand was doing there. A day or two later we were alone on another island, where she took a video of me that I wrote about in a journal I failed to keep up:

> Yes, oh God, I'm on the beach on one of the islands in the Seychelles where we found not a soul and I come out of the water with my head wrapped in a kind of pirate wrap, and being a pirate . . . Oh, God, it so expressed my zest and exuberance and joy of the moment . . . But with my father's hand around my neck prepared to squeeze at my own invitation.

That last line takes me to my knees like a head-butt to the belly. Only the next Next in my extraordinary life—in this case a week on a yacht in the Mediterranean, just Lyn and me and a crew of six tending to our every want—could allow me to stuff it.

5

S ETTLING DOWN WITH LYN and my newly realized wealth, I thought this was an opportunity to stretch in other directions. When I look at where I went, however, it is hard to believe the person stretching was me. Given my background and known talents, a new direction for me would have been teaching, speaking, writing a play, or authoring a book. It would not have been buying businesses, even ones engaged in publishing, broadcasting, and theaters. That was more like something Jerry Perenchio would do. Or what Herman Lear would attempt to do. An early interview to find an executive to run what I decided to call Act III Productions, Inc., had the H.K. stamp all over it.

Peter Chernin, who had already been president and chief executive officer of two entertainment companies, was considering an offer to join Rupert Murdoch's News Corp in its executive ranks when I invited him to discuss the possibility of his coming with Act III instead. It's so clear to me now that this was my uncannily similar version of H.K. inviting the heads of major manufacturing companies to a hotel room to see a product made by his ragtag company before its inventor had it working. Chernin listened to my pitch—delivered as energetically as kid star Mickey Rooney's "Let's put on a show!" speech in *Babes in Arms*—and just as the general walked out on H.K.'s one-cubic-foot refrigerator pitch, Chernin left our meeting and took the job at News Corp.

There, of course, he served for twenty years as its president and chief operating officer, leading it to become one of the world's largest media conglomerates.

I didn't interview anyone else. At someone's suggestion I split the titles of president and CEO and hired an impressive thirtysomething executive who'd been involved in the Coca-Cola/Embassy negotiations to fill the CEO role. He was, to me, the very model of a modern Harvard MBA: bearded and well tailored, cool and distant, with an acquired jocularity. I would have enjoyed his company at a luncheon, but going into business with him because I wished on some subconscious level to stretch in H.K.'s direction was as misguided as it sounds.

No more misguided, though, than my engagement of a former executive vice president at Disney Studios to be Act III's president. All I remember of his brief time there are two memos and one order for a piece of equipment. The memos both went to my assistant: the first asking for a pair of good seats at the upcoming Oscar ceremonies, the second objecting to the seats she'd procured and "assuring" her that she could do better. The purchase order was for a button to be placed at the side of his desk so that his forty-year-old body didn't have to get up to open or close the door. Within months my original hire was serving as CEO *and* president.

Before long Act III was on its way to building a theater chain of 550 screens, led by a young theater manager we brought on. Another hire came aboard to put together a chain of independent TV stations. Two years later Act III owned eight independent Fox affiliates across the country, and our budding management team included a publishing guru who was on his way to building a miniempire of eleven trade publications. It pulverizes me to remember that I did not make or help to make a single decision about buying a single magazine, theater, or TV station when my company was borrowing vast amounts to make those purchases based on my worth and the assets themselves.

"The greatest burden a child must bear is the unlived life of the parents," psychiatrist Carl Jung famously said. All my life I've swallowed the anger to which my childhood entitled me, while aching for my dad to realize even a fraction of his dream. It never happened. H.K.'s unlived life was my hidden curse, and there was no way I was going to live *his* life, *his* dream, with *my* Act III.

Isaac Newton observed that we stand on the shoulders of giants and see further as a result. Unfortunately, the giants at the beginning of life, our parents, can be emotionally and psychologically handicapped, and our fight as we grow is to separate; to find other shoulders; mentors in persons living or dead. Or stubbornly, to try, against all odds, to make giants of the emotional and psychological pygmies we were born to. Answering to life for our parents' inadequacies can choke that life out of us.

LYN AND I had rented a small house on Mandeville Canyon Road, fully furnished, in a romantically flawless garden setting. Cognizant of the mistake I'd made by throwing everyone together so precipitously on the tall ship, I asked and Lyn agreed to put off the actual wedding for a year. When it took place on September 10, 1987, it was a small family affair at Lyn's sister's home in Belvedere, a San Francisco suburb. My longtime friend Martin Marty, Lutheran minister and religious historian, flew out from Chicago to marry us; Jerry Perenchio was my best man; and Lyn's sister, Diane Cassil, served as her maid of honor. Ellen, Maggie, Kate, and Kate's husband, Jon, came out from New York. Diane's husband, Rob, their son Kevin, Lyn's brothers, Ron and John, and their families, and a few old friends of Lyn's completed the wedding party.

The Norman so woefully responsible for the tall ships saga was convinced that enough time had passed, managed to avoid the remaining hint of anxiety in his bride's and his children's eyes, and saw no reason why the words "I now pronounce you man and wife" wouldn't make for instant kinship in every direction. It took a New Age psychiatrist Lyn met at Esalen in the seventies to help me see my reality when he whispered to Kate, loud enough for all to hear, "I feel your pain."

Once we were married the house we were renting developed the aura of a dreamy honeymoon cottage and I felt wrapped in it with Lyn. When we had our children life became far richer, of course, but for sheer, stripped-down, cloud nine elation, the time on Mandeville was matchless. There were no restraints, no intrusions, and no time limits on the spiritual bond we shared. The one spike in our wheel was daughter Kate's reaction to hearing we were trying to have a child. So upset after two years of struggling to get pregnant, she was sure her father and his young bride would get there first. And sure enough, within a month of our wedding Lyn was pregnant. Kate tried to be happy for us, but had to give up the fight. Lyn understood but was deeply hurt by it. I was of no use to either. Dumbly, I parceled out smiles and assurances to both that this, too, would pass. Both wanted to choke me. My mind was in the vicinity but on a different block. The father to three daughters already, I blithely assumed Lyn was carrying my fourth. Then one day she called and asked, "Are you sitting down?" As it happened I was, but I jumped up when I heard her happily say, "We're going to have a boy."

"Holy shit," I thought. "I'm going to be a seventy-year-old Indian guide!"

Not long after Lyn's news, Alan Horn's wife, Cindy, learned that she, too, was pregnant. The two couples went out for a celebratory dinner, in the course of which we talked about the world our kids would be entering. NASA scientist James Hansen had just testified before the Senate that global warming had begun and was man-made. As soon-to-be mothers, Cindy and Lyn wondered how they might help, and as supporters of the Sierra Club, the National Resources Defense Council, and Greenpeace we recognized that the environmental movement didn't need another organization fighting the good fight so much as it needed a bigger presence in the media. Who better than the four of us, we concluded, to establish that presence? And thus, the Environmental Media Association was born. For a quarter century now it has been responsible for urging the creative community to cover environmental issues in its work, and then providing them with accurate information. For those of us who put more trust in the 97 percent of scientists concerned about climate change than we do in the Tea Party, EMA's work is more urgent with each passing day.

Coinciding with Lyn's pregnancy, I became aware that there was considerable cause for concern on the financial front. Save for our homes, art, and furnishings, our entire personal worth was totally invested in Act III. The company was overleveraged, the economy was starting to slump generally, and the fate of Act III was beginning to concern me. Further, a stock market collapse in October 1987, known historically as Black Monday, resulted in instant panic. That's when I gave two investment teams access to everything they needed to assess Act III's holdings and determine its current net worth and potential. Lyn was about five months pregnant when, late one afternoon, that fateful meeting took place at the Bel Air Hotel with Jerry Perenchio, the Boston Ventures Group, and me. A few minutes of clubby chitchat, and then, with great difficulty, they gave me chapter and verse about my businesses. It was not a pretty picture. Jerry and the teams I'd hired worked exhaustively, and came to their assessments independently. They all concluded that the health of Act III hovered between grave and desperate. When I asked what my combined assets might be worth if I were to sell, Boston Ventures' advice was to take $15 million if it was offered. Perenchio suggested I think hard before holding out for that amount. My investment was more than $100 million.

I left the Bel Air Hotel with a feeling in the pit of my stomach that I hadn't felt since our first days in L.A. when I didn't have a job. When a tire blew back then, I'd scour the city's lots looking for the lowest price on a retread, and shopping for a retread was the taste in my mouth when I came home to Lyn that night. I was compelled to report what I'd heard, but not fully. I couldn't let her in on the depth of my concern, and I couldn't risk her worrying about my sanity if I was to tell her that, flashing across my mind and lightening my concern was the thought "Even *this* I get to experience."

There was still no risk that the word *desperation* would reenter my children's lexicon, but the lifestyle we'd grown used to was severely threatened. What lay ahead was painful and we had to suffer through it, but as 99.999 percent of the world's population understands the word, we would not be "suffering."

As I relate this Act III story and the part I played—and failed to play—in it, I confess to feeling like a fool. But a fool couldn't pull together PFAW, or write and produce a line of hit television shows and films. So what explains my ability to work my ass off and get so much done, yet dissociate so intensely from my personal life as to feel more the clown than the ringmaster? Recently I read of the "parallel play" that occurs when several toddlers are seemingly at play together. While all might be engaged in the same activity, they are actually each playing by themselves. The first twelve years of my life saw me at parallel play, and through my adulthood all that changed in my life were the ages and sizes, talents and personalities, of my fellow toddlers. As much as I've worked in collaboration with others and sought with everything in me to be a good father and husband, my guard against the terrors of my childhood was to dissociate and carry on with my life in parallel play.

I carried on with a cluster of efforts—one might think of them as Overs and Nexts—at any given moment. From my productions across the media, political organizations and causes, and events and festivities prepared for my family, my production skills were in evidence everywhere, but my inner self—my emotions—were on display in my work, not in my being. Pieces of me existed in the characters that inhabited my TV shows and films, most at a considerable volume, all begging to be heard and understood. It is especially painful when I consider the productions that I identify as Mooncrest Drive, Chadbourne Avenue, and Westridge Road. There I see six children in the show that was my life, aching for their dissociated father just to be where he was (but wasn't). Trying not to be too harsh on myself, I think of how easily and sincerely I committed across the board to rational, reasoning, even intimate relationships. But where did I commit to *emotional* intimacy?

ON THE ACT III FRONT I took off my father's hat, put on my own, and decided that I would hold on to the assets and seek out the executive help it required to save rather than sell them. Jerry Perenchio and Alan Horn offered to find someone to take over the management of Act III and to, as I'm sure they spoke of it, "handle Norman." Jerry, thinking long and hard about who was up to this challenge, came up with Hal Gaba, who had worked under him at Embassy. I'd come to know Hal well socially and we'd become good friends. Jerry thought the world of him, said he was smart as hell and had the makings of a first-class executive and entrepreneur, and Alan agreed. Hal, who had been dabbling in real estate, was free to pick up the challenge and he welcomed it.

In short order the execs who'd been running the company were let go, and Hal, bringing on his own right and left hands, set about turning things around. So far so good, but with no money from stock or other investments to rely on, I needed a weekly income. As good fortune would have it yet again, Gary Lieberthal, who had grown up with Hal and under Perenchio in our company, had just been made president of TV production at Columbia Pictures Entertainment. Shortly thereafter, a joint venture that would pay $3 million per year was announced between Columbia and Act III for me to produce at least three pilots in three years for series television. "As quickly as Norman can come up with a program he loves," Lieberthal told the *New York Times*, "there won't be any problem finding a place for it on the networks."

It wasn't that easy, but I already had a good idea and Gary was able to make a six-episode deal with CBS. Inspired by my own life, the pitch went: "A fifty-three-year-old divorced father with daughters in their late twenties falls in love with a young woman about to turn thirty and brings her home to announce their intention to marry. Oh, and she has a strong relationship with God, to whom she tells everything."

The media was taking considerable interest in my return to television, especially the report that the show was based on my third marriage and spiritually inclined new wife. A number of fundamentalist groups organized to demand that CBS withdraw its support of *Sunday Dinner*. Rev. Donald Wildmon, founder of the American Family Association, threatened CBS president Larry Tisch with a boycott of 1 million Christians. But the *Wall Street Journal* decided that Act III's entrance into television production made it a ripe time to do a major business story on me—and to my huge relief they got it all wrong.

On their front page one morning was a headline about Norman Lear's PLANS FOR A SPIRITUAL JOURNEY that referred to me as a CAPITALIST ACTIVIST engaged in ACT III OF HIS LIFE. Accompanied by one of those classic "headcut" drawings, the article read: "Norman Lear has made a fortune, helped acquaint TV with reality, and played a major role in defeating the Supreme Court nomination of Robert H. Bork. Now at an age when people often slow down, the 65-year-old writer-producer-activist is at it again on all fronts: financial, political, even personal . . . Only last fall he married again and now is about to become a father again."

The paragraph that followed could get a laugh from a cadaver: "But most of all, Mr. Lear is proving himself a savvy and unabashed capitalist . . . His business success is so striking because big names like Aaron Spelling, Dino De Laurentiis and others have tried to build multi-faceted public entertainment companies recently only to falter after a year or two in business. Mr. Lear is a sharp contrast . . ." For the sake of the heirs to the Messrs. Spelling and De Laurentiis, I hope the *Journal* reported on their "failing" businesses as loosely as they reported on the "success" of Act III.

SOMETIME AFTER MIDNIGHT on July 10, 1988, the world seemed to hold its breath and Lyn Lear, the first woman ever to give birth in that body, went into labor. Daddies weren't welcome in the delivery room until the sixties so this was my first time there. In an effort to soak up every ounce of the experience, Lyn had us attend a few coaching sessions where we papas-to-be were instructed—talk about bullshit—that this was a team effort. It was one thing in our practice sessions, but quite another with Lyn in labor. There I was, as coached, earnestly directing her breathing with an "Easy does it" here and a "Just relax, darling" there, until a shrill glance from Lyn all but shouted, "Are you fucking kidding?" I relaxed.

Minutes later, there he was, Benjamin Davis Lear, set down in a bevy of going worlds, totally unaware of how difficult it is to be a human being. I had decided against a formal bris, a Jewish tradition that makes a social event of the trimming of the latest penis to appear on the scene. The baby is set before the mohel (the official name for the rabbi/clipper) on a pillow, and the guests—some already into the tea and sponge cake—gather round. He recites a prayer in Hebrew—I've always assumed he prays that he gets this right—then a few clipping sounds followed by a howling baby, and it is over.

Serving as our mohel was the obstetrician who delivered Ben, who asked if I'd like to assist him the next morning with the circumcision. I said okay but felt a twinge. After all, when the San Francisco earthquake hit, how do we know there wasn't a baby on a pillow or a table someplace just about to be cut? Our doctor/mohel performed with great dispatch. I have no memory of what little he asked of me to earn "assisted by" credit, but I recall breathing a big sigh of relief when he said, "That's it," and Ben started to cry instead of shouting, "Oh, my God, what have you done?"

Benjamin Davis Lear and his mother came home that afternoon. Two questions followed me everywhere for some time following. How different does it feel to have a baby at your age? And how does it feel to have a son? I didn't feel the age thing at all, but being father to a son gave me that "Chip off the old block" feeling that can't be experienced as lucidly with daughters. That was good, as was the knowledge that the Lear surname would continue into the next generation. But having grown up without a sports gene, I worried from day one about what I would do if his athletic needs went beyond a game of catch.

SOON AFTER BEN'S BIRTH I went to see my urologist with a complaint about having to get up twice a night to pee. He explained that this was common in men my age, but he examined me anyway. I checked out fine, no problems, but as I was leaving his office, he said he'd like to see me again in three months. I asked what he might do then that he hadn't done today. "A sonogram." I asked if he was awaiting delivery of the necessary equipment. He responded with a laugh and a no, and I stepped back into his office.

The sonogram was clear, the doctor said, but he still wanted to see me in three months. I knew now that he was operating on an instinct, a hunch, which was just fine with me. I asked again what he might do in three months. "A biopsy," he answered. Twenty minutes later, biopsied, I left his office with his promise to call me in a couple of days with the results. Late the following afternoon his nurse phoned. "The doctor wonders if you can come by tomorrow." I told her I could, she set the time, and then, to my dismay, she added, "Oh, and he said it would be good if *Mrs*. Lear could come along."

It was prostate cancer. "Not to worry," said the surgeon, "it was caught early. If you need time . . ." I had everything I could do to keep myself from screaming, "Are you fucking kidding?" I didn't want to live a day longer than I had to with that word on my mind. Although the risk of impotence came with the surgery and that concerned me, the thought of cancer reoccurring and the possibility of its consequences were far worse. Lyn felt the same way and the surgery was scheduled. Ben was only a few months old, it was too soon for Lyn to attempt a second pregnancy, and our understanding had been that we'd have only one child anyway. So why, then, was Lyn suggesting that we collect and save as much of my maleness as we could before the surgery? "Just in case we change our minds," she said, unable to resist a smile, and for the weeks leading up to my surgery we husbanded—love the word in this context—as much of my maleness as we could.

The operation, which son-in-law Jon came out from New York to oversee, went without incident. Actually, my recuperation period was a gas. Taking a page from Norman Cousins about laughter and healing, I called Lorne Michaels. He sent me a bunch of *SNL* tapes, and my ass disappeared with my cancer because I laughed it off.

MY RECUPERATION ALSO GAVE ME the much-needed time to start what turned out to be a lot of work on *Sunday Dinner*, the show based on the Lyn and Norman Lear story. After much struggling to get it right, it went on the air in mid-1991. As I rethink the project, I'm satisfied that the basic idea was solid, up to and including the notion of a young woman who grabs a moment of solitude here and there to talk to God. "Morning, Chief," she greeted Him on the first show. "How can anyone wake up on a morning like this and not believe in you?" I loved that and can't overstate my belief in the project and in the central characters, played by Teri Hatcher and Robert Loggia, yet it was a dud.

Noting that the May-December relationship in *Sunday Dinner* reflected its creator's real-life marriage, Ken Tucker, critic for *Entertainment Weekly*, wrote: "Rooting a show in reality is no guarantee of either truth or quality. *Sunday Dinner* is awful, fascinatingly awful . . . what makes the awfulness fascinating is that Lear has chosen to make TT a deeply spiritual soul who frequently looks up into the studio rafters and talks to God, or, as she calls the Supreme Being, 'Chief.' Loggia's grimace is never more convincing than when he is expressing his discomfort with TT's God talk . . . 'Why can't you talk to Martians, like other people?'"

If I were to do it again—and I'm open to talking about it—I'd make it an hour show and learn more about the daughters, and especially about the effect of TT's devotion on each of them. Also, Loggia's character had a son, and today that son's reaction to TT's physicality, as well as her spirituality, would be something fascinating to deal with.

Just a few weeks after the six-episode run of *Sunday Dinner*, we taped the pilot of *The Powers That Be*, television's first cutting-edge look at the sleazy underside of DC politics. John Forsythe starred as a charming, senseless, utterly pliable senator married to a scheming, castrating, maid-slapping bitch on wheels played by Holland Taylor. Their daughter (Valerie Mahaffey) was a near-hysterical bulimic married to a congressman (David Hyde Pierce) whose one ambition was to kill himself. Joseph Gordon-Levitt made his prime-time debut as their twelve-year-old son.

The show, with a script by Marta Kauffman and David Crane (who next created *Friends*), was as funny and meaningful as any our company ever produced, and with that cast I couldn't resist directing the pilot episode. The same critic who wrote off *Sunday Dinner* credited the new show with "having no problem biting the hand that feeds it," and he welcomed me back with a four-letter word I treasured.

"Who'd have thought that after all these years producer Norman Lear would have enough *bile* left in him to oversee a series as energetically nasty as *The Powers That Be*. This low-down satire of Washington politics (the first on TV) and the American family offers the broad laughs and sly cunning of a first-rate Broadway farce . . . *The Powers That Be* could prove to be an upscale uproarious *All in the Family* for the '90s." Instead, it merely proved to be too soon. The way it savaged the DC political scene of 1992 was too much for NBC. "What would you have us do, root for the bad guys?" one exec asked incredulously. "No," I said, "I'd have you rooting for the next week to pass in two days so you could see the next episode as quickly as possible." The network pulled the plug after just twenty-one episodes.

Another high concept idea, *704 Hauser*, saw a black family move into the Bunkers' old home, thus closing out my career at CBS—at least to date—on the same set it started with. The patriarch of this family tried to raise his grown son, Thurgood, in the image of the acclaimed liberal Justice Thurgood Marshall, but the boy had instead grown into another Clarence Thomas. He was also seriously black, not the light-skinned male most favored in such situations, and in love and smooching with a beautiful young white woman who happened also to be Jewish. The Program Practices team called it "politically disquieting." Although Rush Limbaugh was an unexpected fan and had me on his show to promote it, we came on too fast with too much on this one and made just six episodes. It's possible it would last six years if made today by Judd Apatow.

6

As I report on myself in these pages what surprises and pleases me most is the consistency in my life. In the middle of my financial woes, I began a six-year effort whose roots went back to when I was a junior in high school. I liked reading Walter Lippmann, a columnist for the *New York Herald Tribune* who bemoaned the declining influence of church, family, and community on the values of society, fearing that business—and its obsession with profits—had begun to fill the vacuum and grown to be the fountainhead of values in our society. That read like common sense to me at seventeen and early in my career I thought I saw the signs of it increasing, especially with the explosive impact of television. That's what *Mary Hartman, Mary Hartman* was all about. That's why she was standing there in the very first scene declaring that there couldn't be a waxy yellow buildup on her kitchen floor because the product she was holding promised that there wouldn't be.

The problem crystallized for me when I came across a 1980 article in the *Harvard Business Review*, "Managing Our Way to Economic Decline," by Harvard professors William J. Abernathy and Robert Hayes. This brave and revolutionary essay dealt with what the professors had come to believe was the most rapacious societal disease of our time: short-term thinking. I flew to Boston to meet with Abernathy, a meeting that resulted in a quick kinship and a three-hour lunch in a Cambridge coffee shop in which he provided me with the most striking physical metaphor for that malady.

"You have to understand, Norman, what is coming," he said, sitting across from me and looking straight into my chest. "There will be a time very shortly when young people—*very* young people—will be looking into computer screens like I imagine myself doing now." Unblinking, he continued, "They will be looking directly into screens, not to the side, so there will be no peripheral vision; they won't be looking over the top, so they won't see what's ahead; they'll be staring straight into those screens, blind to everything ahead and around them, and they'll be punching numbers and causing billions of dollars to be transferred in split seconds from London to Tokyo to Hamburg to Zurich to New York. With that narrow focus, like a horse with blinders, they will have more control and hold more power in those split seconds than we can today imagine. And all of it entirely focused on short-term gain."

I told Professor Abernathy that I wanted to help get his message out and that I hoped we could meet again, at which his demeanor abruptly changed. Looking deep into my eyes, he told me he had recently been diagnosed with a terminal cancer and had some six months to live. I held his gaze and cried. He passed on in December 1983, at fifty.

As the world turned, one had only to follow the daily news to see how on the mark the Abernathy vision was. Slowly the values our culture held dear were giving way to numbers. Our political leaders began appealing to their constituencies more as consumers than citizens and the disease of short-term thinking soon infected the government as well. "Advertising," observed historian Stuart Ewen, "has become the primary mode of public address."

What had ripened so vividly for me was the blending of my spiritual groping with what I had taken from my meeting with Professor Abernathy. I addressed these concerns repeatedly in various speeches over the years with the help of David Bollier, as bright and interesting a sociopolitical mind as I'd yet encountered, whom I stole from the staff at People For. He worked with me on a 1986 talk at the Wharton School of Business, and again four years later in my keynote address at a convention of the National Education Association in Kansas City. At both I referred to "a trickle-down value system that breeds in a climate where leadership in the Congress, federal agencies, state legislatures, labor, the universities, leaders everywhere glorify the quick fix and refuse through greed, cowardice, or myopia, to make provisions for the future." The speeches were interrupted frequently with applause, the one in Kansas City ending with a whopping standing ovation. But despite the audiences' reaction, they drew no more media attention than the dropping of a pebble into a Great Lake.

Then one day my experience in the world of entertainment gave me an idea. By honoring their best work with Oscar, Emmy, Grammy, and Tony Awards, and conducting a competition in the process, the motion picture, television, music, and theater communities cause the entire country to focus on them and their function. Why not, then, establish an entity to shine a spotlight on exemplary acts of courage, integrity, and social vision in the world of business? Why not honor instances of bold, creative leadership that combined sound business management with social conscience?

I invited David Bollier to draw up a mission statement, and another spectacular young talent I won away from People For, Betsy Kenny, to assist me in my scheduling and in spreading the word. The first businessman who took an interest in the idea, and he was a titan, was Thornton Bradshaw, a friend and former president of the Atlantic-Richfield Company, and then chairman of RCA. Brad, as he was known, seemed more the Harvard professor he started out as than the tycoon he became. I was thrilled when he agreed to chair what we were now calling the Business Enterprise Trust (BET), but as Fate would have it, some weeks after signing on he took ill and a short time later, to everyone's horror, he passed away. "Thornton Bradshaw," wrote the *New York Times*, "enjoyed a reputation as a corporate statesman who campaigned for the social responsibility of business."

Looking for a replacement, Betsy arranged for me to seek the advice of a

TV pioneer and one of its greatest innovators, Joan Ganz Cooney, creator of the Children's Television Workshop—the home of *Sesame Street*. Of the men Joan knew who set the kind of example the BET required, her first choice was Jim Burke, the former chairman of Johnson & Johnson, known to everyone in the business world as the "Tylenol Hero."

In 1982 seven people in the Chicago area died from arsenic-laced capsules found in a few bottles of Extra-Strength Tylenol. As chairman of J&J, Burke expeditiously yanked 31 million bottles of Tylenol off drugstore shelves countrywide. It was a stunning act of, yes, courage, integrity, and social vision, and when Jim Burke agreed to chair the Business Enterprise Trust, the announcement alone served as a mission statement.

In the course of my friendship with Ben Bradlee and Sally Quinn I had met Kay Graham, president of the Washington Post Company. Now, with Jim Burke as chair of the BET, it wasn't hard to persuade Mrs. Graham to become a trustee. With Burke and Graham on board, the same was true for Warren Buffett. With those heavyweights on board, trolling for other trustees became a relative cinch. One night, I was the guest of honor at one of Katherine Graham's celebrated dinner parties, where Sol Linowitz, adviser to presidents and the man who delivered the Panama Canal Treaty, accepted my invitation to join the BET board.

I was well aware that business executives such as those we would be honoring needed another tribute or cause-oriented hotel dinner like they needed a hole in their budgets, but they just might be up for a breakfast, especially one with all the bells and whistles of a major evening event. And so, in March 1991, at seven-thirty on a weekday morning, in the famed Rainbow Room high up in the GE Building, the first of the Business Enterprise Trust Breakfasts and Award Ceremonies was held. It was attended by, among two hundred of corporate America's top executives, Jack Welch, Larry Tisch, Pete Peterson, and David Rockefeller, and was hosted by Barbara Walters.

Subsequent ceremonies continued in the Rainbow Room and were hosted by Diane Sawyer and Bill Moyers and featured such keynote speakers as President Bill Clinton, first lady Hillary Clinton, Vice President Al Gore, and Senator Bill Bradley.

We honored five companies each year for courageous decisions in the public interest made by their leaders, and established a lifetime achievement award. I produced a group of nine-minute documentaries that told the story behind each of our five corporate honorees, a sixth about the recipient of that year's lifetime achievement award, and they were presented before some two hundred fifty top business executives, the cream of the corporate crop, who viewed the films on a wall of dozens of TV screens.

The stories of the first twenty-five of the companies that received the BET award are featured in David Bollier's book *Aiming Higher* (AMACOM, 1996). The book, the video documentaries, and an extensive array of business education materials developed by BET's inexhaustible president, Kathy Meyer, and her staff were published and sold by the Harvard Business School Publishing Company. More than five hundred business schools, universities, and corporate management training programs have purchased them for use in their curriculums. The materials continue to sell through Harvard Publishing to this day.

The BET caught the attention of Dean Donald Jacobs at Northwestern University's Kellogg School of Business, renowned for its commitment to socially minded business practices. Dean Jacobs's brand of academics and my media acuity seemed a perfect blend, and for a time it seemed the trust would merge with Kellogg. But the air went out of that balloon one day when Dean Jacobs informed me that an illness in his family required him to put a few of his interests on hold, among them the BET. The Kellogg board that had agreed to the merger and its cost lost interest in it before Dean Jacobs could pick up the cudgel again, and the curtain came down on the Business Enterprise Awards. Not a day goes by that something I observe in our culture doesn't make me mourn its passing.

7

THERE WAS ANOTHER passing that should have—but didn't—result in greater mourning. But then, is it possible to lose what you never had? My mother had been ill for a while and passed just a month shy of ninety-one, not too long after an afternoon with her taught me all that remained of what I didn't know about her. I knew she had a way of sucking pleasure out of a good moment, but I tried to think of it, especially her disaffected reactions to my personal triumphs—when I won the Emerson scholarship, the first words out of her mouth were "If I realized it was such a large auditorium I'd have sat closer"—as simply quirky. When, decades later, it was clear that I had "made it," she was heard to rave about me as the subject of all the excitement, but she never talked about how she felt about me, the person, or said anything definitive about my career or my political work. Then came that afternoon.

I'd flown her out to see her newborn grandson, Ben, and my son-in-law Jon, who was also visiting, decided to interview her. She was sitting in the living room in her wheelchair dressed for the occasion and well versed in performing as a model old woman. Was she ready, Jon wanted to know as he raised his camera. So ready, said Mother, that she was shaking and her heart was palpitating. Jon started by asking her a series of questions about her son. I was sixty-six at the time, but from my mother's answers and the stories she told in support of them I was about fifteen.

"Oh, yes, my Norman . . . always, he always made me laugh . . . he didn't walk down stairs, he deliberately fell . . . never gave me a problem . . . what can I tell you, he's Norman . . ." If you didn't pay attention to the actual words, you might have thought you were listening to a mother who was just crazy about her son.

At some point I entered the scene carrying Benjamin, her infant grandson. Since we've long accepted that a picture is worth a thousand words, the next few minutes of Jon's film are equal to a twenty-volume *Encyclopaedia Britannica* on Jeanette Lear and what it must have been like to be her son.

"Oh!" and "Oh!" again, my mother exclaimed, her eyes darting about to see how she was perceived as I presented the baby. "He's beautiful, isn't he?" she said. I offered to let her hold him. "Oh," she exclaimed, but she couldn't. Through distressed sounds and gestures she made it clear that she wanted to, oh, *yes,* she wanted to, but she couldn't. Her hands fluttered about the baby, fingers stabbing in his direction, but they hesitated short of the blanket he was wrapped in. She simply couldn't hold her grandson. How's that for a delayed view of the love available to me when *I* was wrapped in a blanket? But then again, maybe what Mother was able to show wasn't a reflection of how much she cared. After all, she did call me once in my forties, very worried and very relieved when she heard my voice. There had been a terrible plane crash and she wanted to be sure I was okay.

"But, Mother," I said, baffled, "that plane crash was in Canada."

"So?" she responded. "I suppose you don't travel a lot? What do you want from me, I'm a mother."

Mother spent her last month in a hospital bed in Hartford. Her last words to me were that she was ready to go, but it wasn't the soft sound of letting go I heard. It was a sound of annoyance. It annoyed her to be alive. Weeks later I flew in again for her memorial and told the story of her discounting my presence in the adjacent airline seat and asking a stranger to put drops in her eyes.

It elicited a warm laugh from those who had similar memories, now viewed through a sweetened lens with her passing.

BY THE TIME Ben was four, he was bright, thoughtful, and intuitive enough, even at that tender age, to suggest a mensch was on the way. Lyn had not stopped lobbying for another child, and as I watched Ben develop it got to me. I imagined him calling down the hall to a sibling, not having to go to bed alone, growing up with someone besides Lyn and me to talk to. Finally, I told Lyn, "Let's."

And so a call went out to the service that had been keeping fresh the maleness we'd collected before my surgery; then, mixed in a lab with the other half of the equation extracted from Lyn, no two petri cohabiters ever mixed and mashed more prayerfully to generate a pregnancy. After a couple of years with no success, we began to explore the possibility of adoption, but quickly learned how difficult that would be given our ages, and especially mine.

Finally, Lyn's gynecologist told her that if Ben was to have an in vitro sibling it would take two donors and a surrogate. Lyn could not have toiled harder over the next year if donors and surrogates were mined like ore. She pored through the health, education, and family records and photographs of scores of male and female donors and shared that information with me before making those decisions. She also met with a number of potential surrogates. When I heard that the woman she was leaning toward choosing was married, had two sons, and simply "felt a need to do something for someone that no amount of worldly anything could buy," I had to meet her, too.

She and her husband joined us for coffee one afternoon. They were a straightforward middle-class couple, very likable, and it touched me deeply to learn that the idea of a seventy-one-year-old man wishing to do this for a wife twenty-five years his junior was another reason they chose to do this for us. We didn't meet with the faraway egg and sperm donors, but their backgrounds were, as compared to what we knew of our own family histories, peerless. They were from families whose education and levels of success far surpassed ours.

As we were about to tell the world we intended to have another child, we received the joyous news that Kate was expecting. Kate and Jon were over the moon and I was sitting atop it. Since Ben was born, just about every good moment with him made me think of how much I wanted this for her, too, and for Jon, my son-in-law and buddy. Kate's pregnancy with my first grandchild, Daniel, was the root of such excitement in the Lear clan that it freed her to be happy for Lyn as well.

Meanwhile, my efforts to be a buddy to Ben continued apace. When he was four, I gamely assumed the sound and stance of an outdoorsman and asked him if he'd like to camp out. Evidently he knew more about the subject than I thought because he blurted, "Yeah! How about the Grand Canyon?" Maybe the first time should be a little closer, I said, suggesting that we camp out on the lawn just beside our guesthouse. That was fine with him, so we went shopping for supplies. I bought a tent, sleeping bags, and a headlamp so I could read to him in bed. I felt like a horse's ass during the hour it took me to pitch the tent that should have been up in ten minutes, but I struggled to look like I knew what I was doing.

The guesthouse, just a few feet away, had an outside fireplace that "happened" to be set up and ready for a match. Skewers were also at the ready, as were the hot dogs, potato salad, coleslaw, and soft drinks. Finally we crawled into the tent and our sleeping bags, and there ensued as delicious an hour as I've known. With Ben lying beside me and a pinpoint of light from my headlamp directed at the page, I read to him until he fell asleep. I, so content and proud of myself, fell asleep soon after. At about two A.M. Ben awakened me.

"You feel that, Daddy?" he inquired. Pulling one hand out of my sleeping bag, I touched the grass on which we rested; it was soaking wet. A moment later a spray of water passed over us. I had pitched our tent on top of a sprinkler and had forgotten to turn off the system. We spent the rest of the night in the guesthouse that I tried to make seem a logical extension of our camping out. The look on Ben's face said, "Are you kidding?"

As I recall the things I did with him, I can't believe how misguided my attempts were to be the kind of "guy" dad I wasn't. We did the Indian guide thing, which is to say that we sat around on a couple of occasions with other fathers and sons learning what we needed to know about insect bites, tying rope into knots, and building a good fire. Trying to make the best of these evenings, the Lears never told each other how miserable they were.

Then there were the drives deep into the valley to play the extreme sport paintball, as far-fetched an idea for the likes of Norman Lear as the pope serving halvah to his cardinals. And the highlight activity of our time together came when Ben was about ten: we drove to some county airport, got into flight gear, took a class on what we were about to do, then got into a pair of single-engine two-seater planes and took off to do aerial combat.

The pilots, experts at inside loops, rolls, and spins, sat behind us while Ben and I shot at each other with our mock-up 30mm machine guns. The guns were computerized, of course, and we saw our hits and misses on a screen in front of us. Electronically, Ben whipped his dad's ass in the sky.

What I think we both enjoyed doing most, though, was writing, rubbing our imaginations together and following the sparks. We were published twice, first in *Dear Socks,* a book of children's letters to their pets that first lady Hillary Clinton put together, and then in a book of short stories told in one hundred words or less.

We also bonded, happily enough, over comedy. Ben loved *South Park,* and I fell in love with it while watching with him. Since he was such a fan, I called them and brought him to the studio. It turned out that one of the biggest influences on Trey Parker and Matt Stone was *All in the Family*—as they told *60 Minutes,* Eric Cartman was conceived as an eight-year-old Archie Bunker—and a friendship between us quickly developed. They called me when they were preparing their one hundredth episode and asked me to work on it. I spent two days with them and their young writing staff. They used me to voice Ben Franklin and gave me a writing credit for the scene, though I don't remember anything I may have contributed.

As my son grew, I became used to hearing it said of him, "The apple sure doesn't fall far from the tree, does it?" But knowing my son as I did, every time I heard that I thought, "It may not fall far from the tree, but believe me, it rolls . . . and rolls." There is a hint of physical and personality resemblance, of course, but it's been clear to me for a long while that Ben is 100 percent his own person. Whatever came with the territory represented by his parents, he had woven it into an essence that was entirely new in the universe, just as his older half sisters had done.

NOT LONG AFTER the Northridge earthquake—which damaged our Mandeville Canyon home severely enough to displace us to Beverly Hills for a year—we learned that our lives were going to be further shaken up: our surrogate was pregnant and Ben's sibling was on the way. Then an ultrasound revealed that the sibling had gained a sibling. Ben was due to have twin sisters, Lyn was to be the mother of three, and I the father of six, ranging from newborn to forty-eight years of age.

Lyn accompanied the surrogate to every visit with the doctor. On the day before Thanksgiving, November 23, 1994—four weeks before she was due—the doctor shocked both women with the news that our mother-to-be had developed toxemia, and recommended that they consider inducing the birth as early as possible. They decided to induce the next morning, and when the doctor assured them that there was nothing to worry about, they realized the babies would be arriving on Thanksgiving and all but fell to their knees.

That night, a question that had been dancing about in my mind for months now demanded an answer. Would the fact that the twins were not my biological children affect my ability to love them as I did their brother and sisters? I presumed the answer to be that it wouldn't make a particle of difference, but presumptions take place before the fact. Brianna's and Madeline's siblings were, to put it biblically, the fruit of their father's loins. I thought of it in those terms that night, but when it occurred to me that I, too, was the fruit of my father's loins, it more than lost its significance. And as the girls were making their entrance—

and this time it was Lyn who was saying "Push!"—I was as in love as I had ever been.

Madeline preceded Brianna by sixteen minutes, and some hours later the doctor announced that the surrogate and babies were in such good shape that he didn't see why they couldn't go home for Thanksgiving dinner. It was Lyn who led us to this incredible moment, and I thought again how, as a result of her commitment, the entire universe conspired to ensure her success. The surrogate's family had already planned to join us for Thanksgiving dinner and Lyn's family had driven down from Sacramento as well. The babies were the surprise guests for all of them. Our cook came through with a fabulous dinner, and there we sat, with our newborns in their bassinets at the end of the table. Talk about an occasion for thanksgiving!!

As I SAID EARLIER, my bumper sticker reads JUST ANOTHER VERSION OF YOU, but I don't intend that to water down the least bit my appreciation of anyone's uniqueness. Again, like no two thumbprints and no two compacts with the Almighty, we are each one of a kind. And in our kind—human beings—I see us as versions of one another. Since Madeline's and Brianna's arrival we have been gifted with proof of that on a daily basis. From our first weeks together we were aware of their individuality, and not just because they are fraternal as opposed to identical twins. There are wondrous differences between these sisters. To know them is to know that despite their being twins, they are total individuals and could have been born worlds apart.

Though both are beautiful—and I do not use the word idly—you have to know they are sisters before you think to look for the resemblance. When they were very young I recall being conscious of the need to know I was spreading my attention and affection evenly. That had to be true with my older daughters Ellen, Kate, and Maggie as well, but something about the twin factor seemed to raise the ante. Also, as the older father of three, from their infancy through childhood I enjoyed a sharing experience with Kate and Maggie, when they, too, were starting families. And now that my Maddie and Bree are twenty, and Ben twenty-six, I have the pleasure of seeing them share their adult lives with their half sisters and *their* children, Daniel, Noah, Griffin, and Zoe.

I am knocked out by how very modern this layout of family seems, and by the privilege of being the paterfamilias to this glorious bunch. Imagine having five daughters so many years apart—and watching them grow from day one to the twenty- to sixty-seven-year-old women I know and adore today. And, of course, the only male in this brood, son Ben.

Having been a father since I was twenty-four, hungry for connection and dissociated at the same time, I feel like I watched my kids grow from high up in the stands and close up on the field at the same time. Where they played I played, or sought to, anyway. I loved telling them bedtime stories. The older girls recall my asking them to give me five disconnected items—a giraffe, a tractor, a pound of liver, a violin, and a talking snail, for example—and listening to me weave a story that included them all. The younger kids couldn't get enough of one particular story about a little girl who wakes up in the middle of the night with an itch in her belly button, finds a tiny silver screw in there, goes through all kinds of shenanigans before coming across a tiny silver screwdriver with which she is finally able to remove the tiny silver screw, then looks behind her and sees her little ass fall off. Oh, my God, how my girls laughed, and how indescribably happy was my heart.

The older daughters went to public schools and were able to walk to them. The younger ones were in private schools and I drove them until the day they could drive themselves. The littler they were the longer the time together at breakfast, one of the great truths of parenting. Early on there was a variety of ordinary breakfasts I could fix, and so long as I called them Daddy Treats it was a big deal. By the time they were driving I had all I could do to shove a wrapped egg sandwich in the pocket of a fleeing jacket.

I loved waking up to that time with the kids, whatever the length. With Maddie and Brianna, for half of their lives I was engaged in the serious business of reflecting on my own life, in the process learning who I'd come to be, and how. As young ones they had more of that Dad than did Ellen, Kate, and Maggie.

The girls and I bonded best over a love of theater. Among dozens of shows, we saw *Les Misérables* four times. Brianna played top roles in many school musicals, and if there were times in my most intense periods of dissociation that I escaped that prison, it was as a member of the audience at one of those productions. Madeline favored sports for a time in her early teens, and the sight of a Lear running as well as Maddie did in a meet one day is utterly unforgettable for this least athletic of Lears.

BUT I'VE GOTTEN AHEAD of myself. Madeline and Brianna arrived just as things were starting to turn around at Act III. Hal Gaba had trimmed down the staff, one by one sold off the trade publications, and reshaped the management teams running Act III theaters and our group of eight Fox TV affiliates. By the twins' arrival things were really popping at the Fox Network. Starting with *The Simpsons* at the very start of the nineties, Fox began to enjoy ratings it had not known, attracting sponsors at one end of the TV spectrum and show creators at the other. Soon it had *The X-Files; Beverly Hills, 90210; Melrose Place;* and other high-rated shows. Fighting for recognition since its inception in 1986, it wasn't until 1993 that Fox was generally regarded as having achieved "fourth network" status. In 1995, having contracted with the NFL to become its showcase, Fox topped its rivals to become number one in the highly coveted eighteen-to-forty-nine demographic. And in June of that year—talk about good timing, good management, and good fortune—Act III was able to sell its eight Fox affiliates to ABRY Partners for $500 million, which was a big win for the major investors Hal had accrued along the way. My sliver of that made me financially healthy, and I could not have been happier or more grateful to Hal. When he expressed an interest in our continuing to work together, I suggested that we follow his bliss and asked what it was. "Music," he replied.

IN SEPTEMBER 1995 MY SISTER, Claire, and her husband, Richard, celebrated their fiftieth year together. I haven't written much about my only sibling, mainly because until this point in my life I'd not been troubled to really know her.

Claire met Richard Yale Brown when she was fifteen, he sixteen. From that day until and beyond the day he died in his midseventies, he was her "Dickey"—the center of her universe. When Richard—I refused to call him anything else—graduated from high school, Claire couldn't bear his going off to college immediately, so her Dickey went to work for H.K. in whatever H.K. was up to at the time. I don't recall whether Claire didn't know or refused to believe it, but we were in our forties when she learned or accepted that our father had served time in prison. She didn't remember his kiting checks or his broken promises, and she was sure she'd deserved to be slapped around. She simply adored H.K.

The person Claire hated, and she spoke of it often, was our mother, who had very little use for her daughter. When she talked about Claire, it was with the same look she had when describing a bad meal. Monsters raised my sister, but she persevered despite them and built a life and a world for herself just as her brother did. Those worlds could not have been more dissimilar, however. Claire was sixteen when she got married, eighteen when she had her first child, thirty-seven when she became a grandmother, and was a great-grandmother before she turned sixty. She ruled over her family with an iron will of conflicting emotions—a fierce enthusiasm, utter conviction, and bouts of unrestrained disappointment or joy.

It is probably an overstatement to say that Claire never read a newspaper, but what she made of what she occasionally read was a glorious garble, as was her thinking generally. To Claire, being thoughtful was to have a thought. One was as important as the next and all were rendered with the same level of excitement. In 1979 she had an idea that dwarfed all the others, and she dedicated a good portion of the rest of her work life to it. Did I mention that Claire sang? It was her calling. Not that she ever expressed the desire to take voice lessons. I have no idea if she cared to sing better, or even believed it was possible. She was simply a singer. That's the way she was perceived by family and friends—like Doris Day, Dinah Shore, and Lena Horne, she was a singer.

And as a singer, however rarely she performed in public, Claire resented people who smoked, especially when they did it from ringside tables in clubs that featured vocalists. And so she founded an organization to do something about it: SENSE, the Society for the Evolution of Non-Smoking Entertainment. Its mission was to "find and use local talent to entertain our seniors, our handicapped, and everybody bothered by tobacco smoke." Everyone in her life took it seriously except her smart-ass brother in California. Although he never gave her a clue as to how he felt and helped her every way he could—when she needed a portable piano, or a station wagon to haul her crew around, her brother was there—in truth, he thought his sister was a joke.

By 1995 and the occasion of her fiftieth wedding anniversary, something had changed. Not in Claire; in her brother. I couldn't write about it if I didn't have the evidence in a DVD of that event. I had finally grown past the superior attitude I held for so many years about my sister and her extended family. Of course our worlds differed. I caught a different current and gained altitude and distance in my fight to escape the beginnings Claire and I shared. But her escape took no less effort and, in the great scheme of things, was no less successful than mine.

Richard was in on it, but their fiftieth anniversary party was a total surprise to Claire. The camera caught her arrival at a country club where she thought her Dickey was taking her to dinner. We see her enter the big party room and one by one the sixty-some guests pop into view. I have no way of overstating the unbridled joy and accompanying scream that each new face elicited from Claire. It took several sightings, including her children, Diane, Linda, and Robert, before she realized there was a plan here, this was a party, and it was she and Dickey who were being celebrated. And oh, as the camera reveals, how this woman could love and be loved. I was thrilled that Lyn and my three older daughters were there to see this, and to hear my toast.

A fiftyish blind man with a modest voice preceded me to the mike. He sang something he wrote for Claire, and tearfully thanked her for naming him the new president of SENSE, for letting him be a part of the troop that entertained at outlying hospitals, halfway houses, and retirement homes around the state. His was a perfect lead-in to the relatively new understanding I wished to express that night at age seventy-three, and I told them this story:

When I'd suggested once to Claire that she write her councilman about a neighborhood problem, her response was, "A lot of good that'll do. I'm Claire Lear, not Norman." "Claire," I heard myself say, perhaps for the first time, "think about it. You have some sense of the size and scope of the Creator's enterprise here—this earth of ours being one planet among billions that form one single universe of which they tell us there are also billions. Claire, that being the reality, in the great scheme of things you cannot press your fingers close enough to measure the difference in the impact or importance as between any two of us humans."

In a speech some time after Claire's fiftieth I expressed the same idea and a rabbi came up to me afterward to share his Talmudic-style version of what I was attempting to convey: "A man should have a garment with two pockets," he said. "In the first pocket should be a piece of paper on which is written, 'I am but dust and ashes.' In the second should be a piece of paper on which is written, 'For me the world was created.'"

I wish I'd been able to express my thought that exquisitely for Claire, but the way I put it was still central to everything I wished to impart. I spoke of our parents and described—jokingly, of course—the giant fights they used to have. I told how H.K. and our mother, the Saint, talked about the divorce that would come one day, and how they would split the kids. Claire, who carried the Lear blood, would go with our father. I, with the Seicol blood, would go with our mother. No one who knew our history thought that amusing. If there was anything funny there, they didn't get it. But unbelievable as this might seem, until the moment I revisited my toast to Claire and Richard on that DVD, neither did I. The joke was on me. When my father went to prison and the children were split up, which one of her kids did my mother take with her? Lear blood and all, she took my sister.

Claire's fiftieth could not have moved or informed me more. After it I understood her whole life more clearly than I'd understood any single day of it before. I understood myself a good deal better, too. (Presently Claire is in a home for the aged, diagnosed with Alzheimer's disease. She sits in a rocker most of the time, with the sweetest of smiles on her face, and her head somewhere in the clouds, likely with Doris Day.)

IT WASN'T LONG after that event that I got word that Frances was dying of breast cancer. I can't recall being sadder, not simply for her illness but for the torment that had marked her every day. Frances had broken her daughters' hearts when she attempted to leave them with a note that failed to mention them. But when Kate and Maggie talk about their last days, up to the very last minute with her, their faces light up with decades of imprisoned love and respect now free to flow. As her time came, no longer driven by a manic compulsivity, Frances was finally able to express her adoration of her daughters. And loving soul that she was at her deepest, she obviously creamed them.

SADLY, Frances never got to know the man Maggie fell in love with and married—Daniel Katz, the founder of one of the most significant of the environmental groups, the Rainforest Alliance. As a bonus, Dan turned out to be a pal of a son-in-law, too. The wedding took place in June of 1998 at The Gulley in Vermont and had to have been the ultimate in precious family sharing.

Maggie's five-year-old sisters, Madeline and Brianna, were her flower girls, seven-year-old nephew Daniel was the ring bearer, and a miracle played out that had many thinking Frances made it to heaven and had come into her own there. The ceremony was set up to take place at four P.M. in a spot on our property known ever since as Maggie's Meadow. From the main house it was about a ten-minute hike through the woods. The morning was cloudy and in the early afternoon it started to drizzle. No one ever counted on Vermont weather, so an alternative plan called for the ceremony to take place in the tent on the front lawn that had been set up to serve the wedding dinner. The groom was hell-bent on going through with the ceremony in the meadow, however, and every umbrella in the area was on hand. That added up to five at best. At 3:45 most of the guests sat in a light drizzle in the meadow, while a horse and carriage pulled up to the house to pick up the wedding couple.

Everyone looked at the groom, the man who had been calling the shots. He could have ordered all the guests back to the tent and had them there in ten minutes. Or he and his bride could get into the carriage and chance a drizzle that could continue or become a downpour. Dan nodded a definitive "Let's!" to Maggie. In the meadow, when the carriage came into view, everything fell into place. The music started, the bride and groom stepped out, and the maids of honor, flower girls, and others in the procession proceeded slowly down the slight incline to the wedding canopy, where the rabbi waited. By now, in the lush majesty of the meadow, the drizzle seemed a part of the ceremony. The scene, it seemed, could not have been improved upon—until the rabbi, after a few words of welcome, opened her Bible. Miraculously, the clouds parted with the pages—thank you, Frances?—and a wide ray of sunshine cut through the wetness, holding the wedding party in a golden mist.

BEN LEAR TURNED TEN just a month after Maggie and Dan's wedding, and to celebrate that milestone Bill Clinton invited Lyn, Ben, and me to dinner and a sleepover at the White House. I'd known the president since 1982. When he lost his bid for reelection as governor of Arkansas, he accepted my invitation to meet me in New York to discuss the possibility of becoming the honorary chairman of People For. He didn't accept the offer but we had a great time together and remained friends. When Ben was born he was among a number of such friends invited by my staff to record a bedtime story for my son. "Your friend Bill" taped a story he just might have made up on the spot about a sailboat named *George*. Now, on the occasion of Ben's tenth birthday, came this invitation.

To be stay-over guests of the president and first lady and sleep in the Lincoln Bedroom made me feel a full foot taller and practically a Founding Father myself. The dinner on the Truman balcony with the Clintons was more remarkable for its simplicity and hominess. They asked us to address them as Bill and Hillary. Chelsea stopped by on her way to a friend's birthday party, and the Secret Service was out of sight.

Ben recalls the conversation flowing easily and including him. Lyn and I didn't sense the least sign of strain between Bill and Hillary that night. This despite the fact that our evening together fell right between the president's avowal to the world that he "did not have sex with that woman" and the appearance a few weeks later of the stained blue dress that proved otherwise. Hillary and Bill were, first and foremost, it seemed to Lyn and me, friends; dedicated friends of the heart, mind, and spirit. We were convinced, to paraphrase Philippians 4:7: "Their bond surpasseth all understanding."

The president knew our schedule called for us to be at breakfast at seven-thirty the following morning. He was leaving early to give a speech somewhere, and at seven A.M. he was at our door—the Lincoln Bedroom door, if you please—to say good-bye and hoping to have a cup of coffee with us. Leader of the free world or not, Bill Clinton never stopped being a person; and as I see it, his personhood served his presidency—and his distinguished postpresidency—very well.

IT WAS LATE 1999 when Hal Gaba said he'd found the opportunity in the music business that he'd been searching for. Concord Records—the home of John Coltrane, Miles Davis, Thelonious Monk, and Ella Fitzgerald, among other greats—was for sale. A small, Tiffany-like label, Hal had plans for merging Concord with a few other boutique record companies to fashion a major minor. I was game, the deal was made, and not long after that we acquired Fantasy, Inc., owner of the Prestige, Milestone, Riverside, and Stax labels, and formed the Concord Music Group.

Like Perenchio and Horn, everything about Hal and the way he walked in the light told you, his friend, "Count on me." Good attract their like, and so it was no surprise when Hal told me he'd met Howard Schultz and was talking to him about partnering on a new label exclusively for Starbucks. I'd met Howard years before when Starbucks received a Business Enterprise Trust award, and in ten minutes I loved the man. We talked about fathers. Howard's dad fell ill in his sixties and could no longer work. Though he'd worked for the same firm since he was a young man, the company had no insurance or retirement plan and the Schultz family suffered as a result. Howard never forgot that, and determined that if he ever had employees, they would not end up that way. Today Starbucks has more than 150,000 employees around the world who consider themselves partners, and that is indeed what they are called. Even part-time employees have full medical coverage and own a percentage of that piece of the business Howard set aside for them when the company began.

Hal and Howard put Concord and Starbucks together to form the HEAR record label, and the first album to hit the Starbucks counters—Ray Charles's *Genius Loves Company*, a series of duets with other major artists—was a giant success. My personal friendship with Howard Schultz was honored when the TV show *Iconoclasts* invited him to choose a friend to be interviewed with him for an episode about "creative entrepreneurs." We were good together and felt we reflected something more than simple "success." At Howard's invitation I spoke recently at Starbucks' 2014 shareholders' meeting, and our friendship continues to grow.

It wasn't long after acquiring Fantasy that Hal told me he'd been talking about merging Concord with the highly successful Australian company Village Roadshow Pictures, longtime partners with Warner Bros. on such films as *The*

Matrix trilogy and *Charlie and the Chocolate Factory*. The plan under consideration was to merge CMG with the Australian company to form the Village Roadshow Entertainment Group. Hal made the deal and I was with him 100 percent. I liked our Australian partners, largely represented by Graham Burke and Greg Basser, and we got off to a good start with *Happy Feet*, the delicious film that turned the penguin into a dollar sign.

When Hal Gaba took ill in 2008 and passed away the following year, I lost not just a great friend and partner, but also what tethered me most solidly to the Village Roadshow Entertainment Group. The VREG board also grieved Hal's passing and misses him still. His wife, Carole, and their daughters, Lauren and Elizabeth, gave new meaning to the expression "grace under fire." Heartbroken, they still made it possible for Hal to leave us smiling to the end. He was sixty-three, and all who'd known and adored him as far back as the Tandem/ T.A.T. years were shattered, as were those who knew him less well. "I loved Hal like a brother," Howard Schultz told us at Hal's memorial. That, I know, was the way Hal loved Howard, and the way I loved them both. They, I think, loved me like an uncle. Not that their love of me suffered any as a result, but recognition of the age difference showed in them now and then, and it put me at an "ask the wise man" remove. Funny how I get that more as time moves on.

8

I COULDN'T BELIEVE IT!

    In June 2000 I heard that Sotheby's was going to auction off an original copy of the Declaration of Independence on the Internet. I'm unable to express what that stirred in me except to say I couldn't think of another thing until I learned more. It didn't take long. With the coincidental good fortune that has defined so much of my life, I'd only recently met the father of one of my daughter Brianna's classmates, and he ran Sotheby's in Southern California. By the time I got him on the phone I was sure I'd read it wrong because I'd seen the signed copy of the Declaration in Washington and knew there wasn't another. What I did not know was that the Constitutional Convention was disbanded before the handwritten copy could be prepared for signature, and a printer named John Dunlap, down the street from Independence Hall in Philadelphia, ran off a number of copies the night it was ratified, July 4, 1776. Signed only by John Hancock, president of the Continental Congress, these printed copies, known as the Dunlap Broadsides, were the ones dispatched by horseback throughout the thirteen colonies to be read aloud in town squares, declaring the United States independent of the British Crown from that moment forward.

    The copy being auctioned—the only copy in private hands—had just recently been discovered. It had a remarkable history, and it also happened to be on display, I learned, in the Sotheby's showroom just a few minutes from our offices. My associate Lara Bergthold and I practically raced over to Sotheby's. There, on an easel behind a sheet of treated glass, was a near-mint copy of—I was in tears before I could get to it—the Declaration of Independence. Leaping out at me were those soul-massaging words: "We hold these truths to be self-evident, that all men are created equal, that they are endowed by their Creator with certain unalienable Rights, that among these are Life, Liberty and the pursuit of Happiness." Dated: July 4, 1776. "My God," I thought, "it took months to get all the framers to sign the handwritten Declaration that I'd seen on visits to the Library of Congress. *This* copy, printed within hours of its ratification, is my country's birth certificate."

In 1989, a fellow paid four dollars for an old painting at a flea market, largely because he liked the frame. Behind the painting he found a folded document that appeared to be, and later was confirmed as, a copy of the Declaration of Independence, one of the few surviving Dunlap Broadsides. In short order he sold it through Sotheby's for $2.42 million, and now, eleven years later, it was for sale again. As Lara and I walked back to the office I had something as close to a vision as I could ever have. I would buy the DOI, not as a collector to hang it on a wall in my home but as an impresario, a showman, to bring the people's document directly to them in their communities across the country. I loved the romance of sharing it with Americans everywhere and convinced myself that, if I owned it, I'd be able to raise the money necessary to make that happen.

You are likely to be wondering how, after suffering the financial difficulties I've described, I could continue to support the causes that mattered to me and now entertain the notion of participating in this multimillion-dollar auction. The best thing I ever did for myself, quite unconsciously, occurred when Perenchio and I sold Embassy. I'd long admired the idea of the family foundation and held a Norman Rockwell kind of image in my mind of a family, parents and children, sitting around a table choosing their charities and determining the size of their donations together. That image, starring Frances's "little Jew from Hartford" as the Norman Rockwell dad, knocks me out to this day. After we sold Embassy I set up the Lear Family Trust with a donation of $30 million. If you think that generous of me, I want you to know that I view it as equally self-ish. Giving is just plain fun. It tops receiving.

The first live online auction of its scope and significance—from nine A.M. to five P.M. on June 29, 2000—began, we were shocked to learn, with an opening bid of $4 million. Lyn and I in Vermont, and Lara at the Sotheby's offices in New York, were on the phone all day. At $4.8 million the bidding hung tight for several hours. It became clear that we had only a competitor or two. As five P.M. approached, the bidding became extremely intense, quickly passing $6 million, then $7 million, and it became clear that we were down to two bidders. Sotheby's had a policy of extending the deadline some minutes for any bid it received within five minutes of an auction's close, so when we had passed five P.M. the bids came faster. From $7.1 million on, we prayed between each of our $100,000 bids that we would not hear from our competitor again. It became so tense in Vermont, the walls seemed about to crack. At $7.9 million Lyn and I swore that was it and held our breath. Counting down those last seconds—seven, six, five, four, three—and damn it, the other bidder made it $8 million. It was seven minutes after the hour and we were finished as promised, until, inexplicably, Lyn and I shared a tactic and, in one last desperate ploy, like we were a team and there was strength in numbers, we screamed together, "Eight point one!" The competition promptly dropped out and we owned the only copy of the Declaration of Independence in private hands. Minutes later we were in a car on our way to New York.

The next morning I was on the *Today* show with the Declaration, followed by an interview at CNN. As we were leaving CNN a young man on his way to deliver a FedEx envelope leaped off his bicycle when he spotted us. "Holy gee," he exclaimed, in the middle of Midtown Manhattan. "You're the guys who just bought the Declaration of Independence! Can I see it? I *gotta* see it!" I unzipped the thin leather case Sotheby's provided and the boy's eyes popped as he read aloud, "When in the course of human events, it becomes necessary—" and he started to cry, which completely confirmed for me that this document had to travel to the people.

For the record, Lyn and I originally partnered with another couple on this venture. Shortly thereafter, unfortunately, that couple's financial situation took a sad turn and they asked if we'd let them out. By that time my impresario gene had taken hold, I imagined myself the Sol Hurok (he's worth looking up) of America's beginnings, and I was happy to return the money they'd invested and go it alone.

JULY 4, 2001, one year after our purchase—and another indication of the universe conspiring—was the 225th anniversary of the Declaration of Independence. That historic fact helped me to secure presidents Gerald Ford and Jimmy Carter as cochairs of the tour of the document, and to help sell ABC on the idea of a live ninety-minute television special from the steps of the Philadelphia Museum of Art, built around an all-star reading of the Dunlap Broadside. Well over 1 million people gathered in the square for the broadcast that balmy, historic Fourth of July evening and were absolutely awed when the stars Rob Reiner helped me recruit—Michael Douglas, Mel Gibson, Whoopi Goldberg, Kevin Spacey, Renée Zellweger, Benicio Del Toro, Morgan Freeman, Kathy Bates, Edward Norton, and Winona Ryder—stepped onstage, backed by the John Williams orchestra, to read the words that declared them Americans.

At the conclusion of the broadcast it was the Hollywood contingent's turn to be awed. We were bused over to Constitution Hall, where, exactly 225 years before, the document had been drawn and ratified, and where to that moment no cameras had ever been allowed. As staged by Arvin Brown and introduced by Morgan Freeman, Academy Award cinematographer Conrad Hall filmed an impeccable reading of the DOI. By four A.M. on July 5 that iconic rendition was in the can for posterity.

I've talked often of watching my children grow and "fill out their silhouettes." I love the expression as I do the idea behind it, and I've lived the phenomenon six phenomenal times. It is only here, as I contemplate *my* right to the pursuit of happiness, that I think of the DOI purchase and what followed as the filling out of *my* silhouette. Not my father's, but mine, that evening in Philly.

THE BIGGEST CHALLENGE I and our team faced as we began was finding the millions of dollars and other support required to realize the plans we developed for our tour of the DOI to all fifty states. But wait! The good luck—here he goes again!—that lit my path in life one day brought to my Beverly Hills office building a giant of a man, straight out of Gilbert and Sullivan, the very model of a modern major billionaire. As he was leaving whatever meeting brought him there, he saw my name in the lobby, came up to my floor, and thundered, "Norman Lear. I came to see Norman Lear!"

When I stepped out of my office I was grabbed and hugged by this giant, my face head-on against his shoulder, and we heard the sound of my glasses breaking. Ken Langone, a billionaire investor in Home Depot, reacted to seeing my name because his personal physician was my son-in-law, Jon LaPook. Mr. Langone fussed over me as though he'd nearly killed me and insisted he take my broken glasses back to New York, where he had some octogenarian genius of a frame maker who worked no more than three days a week and only for the members of twenty families—or something like that.

Out of all that energy known as Ken Langone has come a ton of charitable giving, including a $200 million endowment that resulted in the NYU Langone Medical Center, from which my son-in-law, CBS medical correspondent Dr. Jon LaPook, now conducts his practice. Of course I thought the Fates had sent Mr. Langone to me to godfather the DOI tour, but when I mentioned that possibility his face lit up with another idea. "You should call Bob Nardelli, the president and CEO of Home Depot," he said. The next day I was on the phone with Mr. Nardelli, who, as it happened, was bringing his sons to California the next weekend to visit a few colleges. We arranged to meet at nine A.M. Sunday in our Concord Music Group conference room.

The meeting with an affable Bob Nardelli and his sons was not a long one.

The DOI reading, viewed at the start of a college tour in closed offices on a Sunday morning with a well-known face speaking every line, was the sneak preview of sneak previews. No one spoke for some seconds when it was over, and Nardelli was still looking at the screen when he asked, "How much did you say you were looking for?"

"Thirty million," I responded.

He looked at me, threw out his hand, and said, "You have half of that." Five minutes later they were gone and I was on the phone like a kid, blubbering over too much good news.

THE GOOD NEWS CONTINUED. I was on my treadmill and watching TV shortly after meeting Nardelli when I happened on a show called *Pinnacle*. The architect David Rockwell was the subject of this episode and I fell in love with him in minutes. I was due in New York a few days later, so I phoned to ask if we could meet. That meeting proved we were destined to know each other, and before it was over he volunteered to create a logo for the Declaration of Independence Road Trip, and to design an exhibit large enough to fill the rotunda at a state capitol yet capable of being broken down for use in smaller venues.

We were looking for a trucking sponsor to transport Rockwell's exhibit from town to town when I remembered our postmaster general, John C. Potter, whom I'd come to know when the post office issued its *All in the Family* postage stamp. A phone call to General Potter and a subsequent meeting resulted in the U.S. Postal Service becoming a proud sponsor and our "official carrier." That resulted in the gift of a sixteen-wheeler and driver for as long as we toured. I don't remember playing with toy trucks, but I've observed other little boys enough to know that our sixteen-wheeler with that Rockwell-designed logo splashed across its length tickled me in just the same way. The memory of its arrival in small-town America—and I witnessed this again and again—is indelible. The procession was led by as many cops and motorcycles as were available locally, followed by two or more high school bands and cheerleaders, elderly veterans in their uniforms, and, finally, the DOI in the emblazoned sixteen-wheeler. Gathered and waiting in front of the venue where the procession stopped were the mayor, the town's high school glee clubs, or a church choir, or some combination thereof.

People stood on line for as long as ninety minutes to spend just a few seconds with the Declaration, often teary-eyed and always grateful. Especially touched were teachers who'd dreamed of taking a class to DC to see such a document. "And now here it is in our hometown!" we heard over and over from teachers reaching for their handkerchiefs. In short order we started adding other elements to travel with the document and fill out the exhibit experience. We learned that one of the signers of the Declaration was John Witherspoon, a great-great-uncle of the actress Reese Witherspoon. Ms. Witherspoon was kind enough to film an introductory welcome to the exhibit and the document. It ran all day in an area designed for it.

In Nashville some fifty country music stars, including Toby Keith, Amy Grant, Lyle Lovett, and Kenny Rogers, gathered at the invitation of music producer James Stroud and Rob Light of CAA to have their pictures taken with the DOI and to be filmed singing a new version of "America the Beautiful." Some iconic footage of America, contributed by famed nature photographer Louis Schwartzberg, was edited into the film, and this rendition drew cheers everywhere.

The Muppets' film of the Constitutional Convention, created for me years before for *I Love Liberty*, was perfect for the thousands of kids being brought to the exhibit, and those who represented the estate of my friend Jim Henson made sure it was part of the Road Trip's portfolio.

As a measure of how all this went down in small-town America, when the tour was on its way to Atlanta, Georgia, I got a call from Jimmy Carter asking me if we could make a stop in his hometown of Plains, population around seven hundred. We accommodated the president, and more than three thousand people showed up, many having driven hours to get there.

ONE OF THE HIGHLIGHT STOPS for me was one of the earliest and among the largest. The 2002 Winter Olympics took place in Salt Lake City, with twenty-four hundred athletes from seventy-seven nations competing. At the invitation of Governor Michael Leavitt and Mitt Romney, president and CEO of the Olympics Organizing Committee, we brought the full exhibit to the giant rotunda at the Utah state capitol, and the crowds were awesome. President George W. Bush, attending the opening, spoke to news cameras so close to our exhibit that he couldn't avoid mentioning the nearby presence of the Declaration. He talked of what it meant to him, and had to acknowledge that it was Norman Lear who'd brought it, adding "Although he and I don't agree on all things political, we certainly agree on the significance of this document." Standing a few feet away, Lyn and I swallowed a chortle.

En route to the stadium in Salt Lake City, the Olympic torch had been passed from runner to runner through forty-five states in sixty-five days, covering some 13,500 miles. As it entered the city proper, someone was dispatched to invite me to come to the street where a runner would hand me the torch so that I could run it to the next bearer. That bearer was not more than thirty yards away, but it was a dizzying experience. I have only to look over my shoulder and see the torch hanging on the wall nearby to remind myself that it really happened.

WHAT I LOVED as much as anything about our DOI tour was its lack of patriotic bullshit. As grand as the exhibition was, especially in major locations, its focus was as direct and humble as these words: "all men are created equal . . . [with the right to] Life, Liberty and the pursuit of Happiness." The tour celebrated the Founding Fathers, who pledged their "lives, fortunes and sacred honor" to make good on those words. Theirs was a start; they didn't have time to make good in terms of the lives they pledged. Would they have delivered had those lives stretched two hundred years further? Likely not, but I've always been knocked out by the pledge of their sacred honor. Where do we hear or sense anything close to that in public life today? We hear a lot of "God bless America," tons of empty praise for "our men and women in uniform," and everywhere the little flag pin offering proof positive of the wearer's love of country.

But, ironically, and God bless America, the last time I witnessed a reference to anything resembling sacred honor was in Francis Coppola's *The Godfather*.

AS THE 2004 elections approached, the tour of the Declaration had proved so winning and impactful, particularly on young people, that we thought of racking focus on the DOI Road Trip. A Princeton Research Associates survey revealed that the percentage of new voters had risen in the midterms, and that suggested the Declaration could have a role to play in the national elections. With the youth vote in mind—along with statistics that showed that youngsters who vote as soon as they are able tend to be consistent lifetime voters—we restructured our approach and named it "Declare Yourself."

Cherie Simon, a vigorous, no-holds-barred, natural leader who had left a government post in DC to head up the DOI tour, stayed on to run the new effort with the help of a brilliant marketer, Christy Salcido, and they brought in such commercial partners as Yahoo!, Clear Channel, American Apparel, and Comedy Central for an all-out drive to get first-time voters and other young people to the polls in just over a year.

Ben Stiller and Vince Vaughn did a twenty-minute short for me called "Let's Go Voting," hilariously showing kids what they have to go through to vote. Traveling with the DOI were some young, inspirational spoken-word artists, and they kicked ass for the college crowds everywhere.

Our hugest, splashiest campaign consisted of several breathtaking short films and still photographs by David LaChapelle. There were stars like Jessica Alba and Christina Aguilera looking hot as hell but for one arresting particular:

their mouths were nailed, spiked, or sewn shut. The magazine world ate it up and the photos were everywhere, including Times Square, where our partner, Clear Channel, controlled several one- and two-story billboards. Imagine turning a corner into Times Square and seeing a twenty-foot Aguilera with her mouth violently sealed, the accompanying legend reading: ONLY YOU CAN SILENCE YOURSELF. REGISTER TO VOTE NOW.

In 2008, the eighteen-to-twenty-four-year-old demographic was the only age group to increase voter turnout, and the Declare Yourself clique basked in the glory of having helped that—and the election of America's first black president—to happen. In the wake of the DOI tour, Declare Yourself, and that living certification of all men having been created equal in the last election—and despite the dismaying number of people, so many of them in government, who have continued to resist that self-evident truth—I was proud of my country and of my role as a citizen activist. It was in that mood that I told myself, "Now, Norman!"

For years I'd been promising to "start on the book," jotting down copious notes, reading the interviews that David Bollier on the East Coast and Digby Diehl on the West Coast conducted with high school and college friends, guys I served with in the war, family members, colleagues and associates, etc. In addition, the remarkable Jean Anderson came aboard to scour through the several hundred boxes of correspondence, scripts, musings, family albums, videos, and other remembrances that my staff had kept in orderly fashion and perfect condition through the years.

As the first decade of the new century was drawing to a close, I determined to finally sit down and tell the stories of my lives. Aiding me as researcher, editor, and all around adviser in chief was the extraordinary Paul Slansky. Other matters would continue to occupy me as well, but the writing at last began.

9

FOR MY BIG NINE-OH IN 2012 there was only one place the family wished to be. We'd been to Europe and to Africa together—all thirteen of us—and both trips were magical, but when we all weighed in on this particular event there seemed to be no place on earth like our own private Camelot, The Gulley in Vermont. My actual birthday is in July, but June worked out better for everyone. It turned out to be the most glorious weekend since Henry Ford in 1926 invented the term when, for the first time, he closed his factories on a Saturday to allow his workers two full days of rest on "the weekend."

The interpersonal mood of everyone gathered matched the weather: a nineteen-part fusion of ages, minds, and spirits that had us all wondering if this wasn't the best family time we'd ever experienced. I was especially pensive about my age and amused myself remembering how young I was when I first started to think about longevity, all the way back before my Bar Mitzvah, actually.

At twelve I had a giant shock of black hair, so black and so thick I had to wash it daily in order to comb and brush it with a hairdressing called Slickum. One day I thought, "What if this is the secret to a long life—washing your hair at the same time every morning?" From that moment to this there have been hundreds, if not thousands, of other odd activities that have caused me to ask myself the same question. Another driver catches me in my car at a stoplight picking my nose. A moment of embarrassment and then I ask myself, "How do you know that picking your nose at a stoplight doesn't add time to your life?" There isn't a single piece of scientific evidence to challenge that possibility. The same is true of a man who at sixty, seventy, eighty, and now ninety frequently finds himself dancing to satellite radio in front of a full-length mirror absolutely and ridiculously naked. There is no guarantee that three minutes of such naked tomfoolery does not add a decade to one's time here. Has anyone, any parent, any professor, any boss, ever proved to you that dancing naked before a mirror can*not* add years to your longevity on this planet? Case closed.

I amuse myself thinking of that and it leads to the recall of other personal idiosyncrasies. For example, every time the door of the elevator I'm riding in opens I pay specific attention, expecting to see a very pretty woman about to enter. *Every* time. Whether or not I was in the mood for it, I have never seen pea soup on the menu and not ordered it. I will be driving along tapping the steering wheel to the music playing on the radio when I imagine Fred Waring— conductor of a celebrated orchestra on the radio when I was a boy—discovering me; next thing I know I am on his radio show, a featured member of his rhythm section playing my steering wheel. As the fabled Jimmy Durante was also fond of saying, "I've got a million of them."

And while I amuse myself, I remember a meal I had with a world religious leader who seemed permanently amused, the Dalai Lama. It was a small luncheon in San Francisco, three tables of ten, and the Dalai Lama was seated at my left. His smile started in his eyes and never left his face. When we took our seats there was a plate of a dozen baby shrimp in a bed of lettuce set before us. We'd all started to eat when I noticed that His Holiness had not raised his fork. Before I could say anything he responded to my attention: "You wish to know why I am not eating. Well, I view these shrimp as twelve sentient beings and— you understand . . ." I understood and we talked about other matters. When the second course was served, a small steak, I was in conversation with the person on my right. I had to turn when I became aware that the Dalai Lama was cutting into it. "Your Holiness," I started. Anticipating me again, he said, "You wish to know about the steak. I have three reasons. First, it represents just one sentient being. Second, I would not wish to disappoint my hostess totally. And third"—oh, that smile—"I just love steak."

OVER THE WEEKEND I received a number of happy birthday phone calls, none more touching to me than Maya Angelou's. (Maya passed away as I was putting the finishing touches on this book. I'd been on the phone with her just a few days earlier and she sounded wonderful. Her son, Guy, spoke with her the evening she died and heard nothing that suggested it could happen.)

I met Maya when we were both invited to address an all-day media conference in New Orleans. She spoke first and I couldn't get over her power and presence. Maya Angelou was tall, elegant, precise, and regal. When she entered a room—robed in her history, her "Hello" a song of promise—one sensed the centuries of struggle from which this indomitable figure emerged triumphant.

Dr. Angelou had followed my work over the years as I'd followed hers. We became fast friends in minutes, and I told her I wanted to do a late-night talk/variety show dedicated to the life of the spirit—a show as upscale as *The Tonight Show*, with a full orchestra and well-known guests who wouldn't come on to hawk their films and books, but rather to talk about what gets them through their days and intoxicates them spiritually. Maya loved the idea. She, too, believed that America was losing touch with the best of its humanity and that our spiritual lives as expressed in words, art, and entertainment were exciting fodder for a talk show and the start of a national conversation. Although circumstances in both our lives dictated that we would never get to do that show, we became family.

Maya was godmother to our youngest and asked to speak to them on her birthday call to me. I enjoyed hearing them address her as Godmother Maya, which Maya insisted on. And I savor the times they dined with Maya in her North Carolina home, where the races mixed without a hint of color line.

Lyn and I were weekend guests at Maya's home when she hosted a party for her friend Toni Morrison, who had recently won the Nobel Prize for Literature. Other guests included Coretta Scott King, Rita Dove, Angela Davis, Oprah Winfrey, Dorothy Height, Jessye Norman, and Rosa Parks. The Court of Saint James comes to mind—not that I know anything about the court—because the words conjure up a sense of nobility similar to what I experienced rubbing elbows with those women and their life stories. In their case the nobility was earned, not inherited, and I felt that so deeply it crowded my insides.

I don't hear it as much these days but black women used to refer to each other as sisters. Lyn felt like she'd made it into the inner sanctum the day that Maya called her Sister Lyn. Long before I was in the Maya Angelou orbit, I had a brother relationship with Alex Haley, Pulitzer Prize–winning author of *Roots*, the story of an eighteenth-century African sold into slavery in the United States and six generations of his descendants. The miniseries based on it became such a cultural phenomenon that it prompted widespread interest among Americans to research their own genealogy. As brothers we collaborated on the only dramatic series with which I was involved.

Our relationship reminded Alex of a deep connection he'd had with a white boy when they were ten years old. In fourth grade they bonded, became inseparable, and, despite their racial differences, spoke of themselves as blood buddies. Their closeness brought their two families together and they believed that this was it, forever. It wasn't. I asked Alex what had interceded.

"Puberty," he said. "Everything changed with puberty."

"There's a series in that," I said. "Three seasons of a boyhood friendship in a culture made uneasy by their relationship, yet managing somehow to transcend the problem—until puberty." Assuming a reasonable run, Alex and I figured we'd be able to cover their early teens, until girls and sex enter their lives. Then the community at large, threatened by the specter of the races mixing, takes to all the racist excesses we've come to know so well. Michael J. Fox, who two years later became a star in Gary Goldberg's *Family Ties*, made his acting debut in *Palmerstown, U.S.A.* It played out more like a miniseries than the seven-season hit we'd hoped for, but it dealt intimately with the race issue in a small southern town in the thirties like no other show.

AS I'VE SAID, we are all versions of each other, but the thought pinches a little when I move from thinking about Alex Haley to Justice Clarence Thomas. Two years after the justice took his seat on the Supreme Court, I was in town to speak at the National Press Club in DC and a mutual friend, the young conservative radio commentator Armstrong Williams, invited me to visit with him in his chambers. Lyn, daughter Maggie, and my associate David Bollier, in town for my talk at the Press Club, accompanied Armstrong and me to our meeting.

It was clear that Justice Thomas wished to be a good host. He took pains to be sure we were all seated well—"You'll be more comfortable here, Mrs. Lear"—and that a clerk brought us the beverage of our choice. People For the American Way had come out strongly against his nomination for many of the reasons it had opposed Robert Bork's, and in consideration of that, I told the justice I thought it quite special of him to wish to meet with us. That was greeted with increased cordiality and I recall thinking he cared a lot that we saw him as a regular guy—and in just those words. It struck a chord in me that touched on my bumper sticker, and that led me to comment on a red leather chair that provided a familiar accent to the somber, dark-paneled elegance of this judicial chamber. It reminded me of my father's red leather chair, I said, and told him briefly about its importance to me.

What followed was, according to Armstrong Williams, some two hours of deep and personal conversation. Maggie, Lyn, and David agree with Armstrong about the time, but they remember it as more of a long recitation than a dialogue. The justice spoke of his childhood with an emphasis on his hero, Booker T. Washington, whose portrait hung on the wall. It was clear that the foundation of Justice Thomas's belief system, as it concerned the historically disenfranchised, was a Booker T. hand-down.

Mr. Washington didn't believe in agitating for equal pay. He favored individual initiative to the exclusion of the collective. He believed in training his people in agriculture and industry, and they would prove themselves worthy of equal pay down the road. He instructed them to forgo the struggle for political and voting rights in order to achieve the economic rights he believed would come. While Justice Thomas may not be a literal copy of Booker T. Washington, I certainly see in that relationship the roots of his ultraconservative bent on the Court. The connection I cannot make is the one between the talkative—make that garrulous—host in his chambers and the quiet—make that altogether taciturn—Justice Clarence Thomas, more than twenty years on the bench emitting rarely a word while the Court was in session.

AT ONE DINNER THAT WEEKEND, one of the kids asked me if there was anything they didn't know about me. I think he was looking for something perhaps a little salacious, so I stopped him cold with, "I saved a man's life once."

The older daughters remembered that in the late seventies I took a few solitary rests where a family vacation might have been. The difference was that, on these rests, there was only me to satisfy. I could sleep, drink, swim, eat, and talk only when *I* wished to. One afternoon in Tahiti I took a long slow walk on the beach, as distanced as I could be from a sign or a sound of another human being, not even of a boat or a plane. And then I thought I heard a distant cry. Looking around, I saw nothing. But there it was again. And again—a woman's voice . . . a *scream*. I looked behind me and saw two dots out in the deep that I'd already passed without noticing.

I tore off my shirt and ran into the water toward them. The tide was out, way out, and it seemed a city block before I was up to my knees. But I made out a woman, arms flailing, her cries for help now directed toward me. Another block and the water was above my waist. I could see more clearly now. The woman, not a swimmer, was chin-deep and beyond her, over his head and unable to swim to her, was her husband. He had experienced a sharp pain on his left side, thought it a heart attack, and panicked. I somehow pulled him to where he could stand and then helped both of them back to the beach. It took more out of me getting to them than actually saving him, but that made me no less a hero to the couple. The woman, crying in relief and joy, couldn't stop thanking and blessing me, as her husband repeatedly gasped, "It's a miracle, a miracle."

If I learned the couple's name on that lonely beach, I didn't remember it by the time I got back to the hotel. And if I told them my name they didn't recognize it or remember it either. And so, when I got home, my heroics, known only to three people, the other two nameless, fell flat in the telling. Frances and the girls wouldn't hurt me by suggesting I made it up, but the possibility lurked in their body language.

Months after my Tahiti trip, Frances, the kids, and I were having a meal at Chasen's when a couple, *that* couple, spotted me on their way out and rushed over to our table. They relived what was for them a harrowing episode, thanked and blessed me again, and now my story about saving a man's life landed solidly. A few weeks later I received a letter from a sitting judge, the man I pulled out of the ocean, expressing his gratitude in writing.

THERE ARE SOME GREAT HIKES in the woods of our Vermont property and I wasn't as up to the longer ones as I was in other years, so reflecting and calling up the past to put my life in perspective is what came naturally when the others were hiking. On one such afternoon, like whiplash, an annoying memory of a long-ago evening snapped into my mind again. It was of a dinner party at the Yorkinses. Frances and I were seated some feet away from another table, at which sat the writer/director Richard Brooks, of *In Cold Blood, Elmer Gantry,* and *Cat on a Hot Tin Roof* fame, with his wife, the British actress Jean Simmons. I had never met Mr. Brooks before and was in awe of him, so over the lively discussions at both our tables it was his voice—quite authoritative and, helpfully, loud—that I was fastened on.

Richard was talking about himself and I hung on every word. I was in my midforties, he about ten years older, and I was startled and turned off to hear him earnestly complain that there was so much he wished to leave behind in this life and so little time to get it done. "Bullshit!" my entire chest would have screamed if a chest could scream. How egotistical can a man get? Over the years each time that incident came to mind I would hold Richard's words just as shamefully self-serving as the night he spoke them.

Even though we became such good friends that I accepted the invitation to direct *Cold Turkey* on his advice and cast his wife in *Divorce American Style,* I always had the feeling that Richard took himself too seriously—until, pondering it in Vermont, it dawned on me that maybe it was I who had the problem. Of course Richard Brooks took himself seriously. And while seriousness is what I've projected all my life—in my work, in my social and political life—it's not what I felt or believed about myself. That's where the dissociation came in, the kid in me seeking subconsciously to make good for my dad.

I had time to walk about The Gulley alone while the others were on their hike, and I drank in what I'd provided for my family. "This is what a father does," I thought proudly as the weight of H.K. slipped away from my being. I liked my past as I thought about it, something I couldn't recall doing earlier. I liked it well enough to reflect on some difficulties that I hadn't wished to face before, such as time's way of thinning out the heady rapids of love and spirit that swept Lyn and me up when we met. "Slowly it turned"—as the old burlesque sketch told it—into a pleasantly hurried stream, then a comfortable steady flow, and finally into a dependable trickle with an occasional series of spurts. We loved one another as deeply as ever, but neither of us was as trouble-free and at peace as we were in the romantic first throes of a loving relationship. Like all couples, we had to come to know each other, and if any couple tells you that process was easy for them you can be sure they were lying in their teeth all the way back to those they lost when they were kids.

Five years earlier, Lyn had turned sixty, and I eighty-five. Maybe the producer in me thought he could produce a turnaround in the marital bliss department, because I'd awoken one morning with the inspired thought of celebrating both birthdays with a single party, calling it our 145th anniversary celebration.

Although sixty of the 145 years we were celebrating were Lyn's, I produced the event unilaterally, with the help of a party planner and old friend, Sharon Sacks, and her young assistant, Brent Miller. I didn't set out to isolate or ignore Lyn in the planning—on the contrary, delighting her and seeing her surprised was very much on my mind—but the only contribution I welcomed from her was her exquisite sense of style. Under the tent that covered our tennis court, the silk tablecloths were antique imports from India, the silverware and plating stunning, and peonies (Lyn's favorite flower) filled your field of vision wherever you looked. The lighting was soft, lush, and romantic, as was the concentration of strings in our sixteen-piece orchestra led by Peter Duchin. (The wood we used in construction was certified through Dan Katz's Rainforest Alliance. Every other ingredient of the physical setup was sustainable and, after the event, was given to Habitat for Humanity.)

Lyn's sister Diane and her husband, and my family—Maggie, Kate, and Ellen and their husbands—were joined by two hundred or so of our friends and the weather partnered perfectly; it was one of those evenings that swept up everyone immediately in affection and good cheer, with one major exception: Lyn. While I felt absolutely selfless in my dissociative desire to make things perfect for her, she felt like a guest at the celebration that was ostensibly *ours*.

At that moment in the culture, no entertainer was hotter than Jennifer Hudson, who had just won an Academy Award for *Dreamgirls*. As dinner began, she walked onstage, sang "And I Am Telling You I'm Not Going," and killed.

Then, as the next course was served, one of the greatest guitarists of all time, Buddy Guy, took the stage. He killed, too. There were no programs on the table so nobody knew who might appear next. That turned out to be Molly Shannon, who hilariously reprised her "Mary Catherine Gallagher" character from *SNL*. After dessert had been served I took the microphone, saluted the great talents that had entertained everyone thus far, explained how Lyn and I arrived at this 145th anniversary celebration, and toasted her, the love of my life. Then I introduced "The one, the only"——Lyn's and my favorite of favorites——"Barbara Cook," who began her set with the song we think of as the anthem of our marriage, "Ain't Love Easy." If the other performers can be said to have "killed," Ms. Cook killed and pillaged!

When everyone thought the evening was over, just before the first person began to leave, I took the microphone again. I told our guests that a few weeks ago I'd been in New York, heard someone sing a certain song, and knew instantly it was the only way this evening could close. Here now was one of our greatest stars and a song that could have been written for this moment——and then, singing "Try to Remember," a song so obviously written for my age, out stepped Harry Belafonte.

"Try to remember the kind of September / When life was slow and oh, so mellow . . ."

Little did I understand how much more those lyrics applied to me at my age than to Lyn.

"Try to remember the kind of September / When you were a tender and callow fellow," the song not just written for my age but clearly for *me*, that still callow fellow.

Nobody could have sung it better than Harry Belafonte. We were all wet-eyed as he concluded, I especially. I took my wife in my arms. She was in tears, too, but felt curiously distant.

Friends who shared that night always recalled it——we hear it to this day——as the best party they'd ever attended. Lyn would shudder when she heard that. "That party was about you, the producer," she'd say. "You didn't intend it that way, but it wasn't *ours*. It was *yours*." We talked often over the ensuing years about the night of our 145th but I never understood what she meant, let alone agreed with her—to my mind, if it was anybody's night it was *hers*. It wasn't until that moment alone at The Gulley, thinking it through and adding it up, that I finally understood her hurt. Daughter Kate had to take the microphone from me to make the only toast that night besides mine. Should Lyn have had to do the same, at *our* party?

I *got* it. Didn't I say somewhere it is hard to be a human being?

MY KIDS AND LYN returned from their walk and as I saw them I recalled a long-ago walk in the same woods with Martin Marty, who officiated at our marriage. I'd asked him for the shortest definition of worship. "One word," he'd replied. "Gratitude."

I drank in my family to the fullest and gratitude owned me. To see my six kids come so lovingly together, despite the different mothers and the years that separate them, then to see another version of it with my younger children, Ben, Madeline, and Brianna, and my fabulous grandchildren, Daniel, Noah, Griffin, and Zoe, and add Lyn, my love of loves to the mix, and there has to be something beyond gratitude.

We sat about raking over our memories—our family vacations at Necker Island in the British Virgin Islands; in the Mediterranean on a lovely yacht; cruising the coast of Turkey and the Greek Islands; on the canals in Venice; on safari in Africa; and of course every minute we've spent together at The Gulley. It was impossible at my age to think about the past without speculating about the future, too, and foremost on my mind as I noodled that future were my son and young daughters and my wonderful grandchildren.

There was my Daniel, whose personality and character lends new meaning to the words *dear* and *true*. I want to be there to see the good he's doing when he's thirty. And his brother, my theater-mad actor/singer/director—look for me sitting in E-101 when you land on Broadway, Noah. And Griffin, who drummed so spectacularly at his Bar Mitzvah and creates electronic dance music—I see him at twenty when Maggie and Dan wheel me into a club where he's leading his own band, the Katz Boys? And his sister, Zoe, the life of the party even when there is no party—at nineteen what corner of the world will I see her lighting up? Then, of course, there were Zoe's step-aunts and -uncle, Maddie, Brianna, and Ben, my noble younger children. How can I avoid wishing to grandfather *their* children?

The stats deem it unlikely but it doesn't seem to stop the possibility from crossing my mind. Recently a friend told me that someone in his family had just died at the age of 104. In the time it took me to express my delight at his relative's longevity, this is what was going through my mind. God, or the minion in charge of such matters, offers me a guarantee that I could live to 104 if I agree to die the next day. I don't take the deal. Is it because I'm a great risk taker? No, it's just that I don't want to miss anything.

MY NINETIETH EXTENDED into the following week, when we all met in DC to visit our nation's capital, explore its historic treasures as a family, and bring the curtain down on my birthday celebration Friday night at the Kennedy Center, where People For the American Way was honoring me.

I have never been in Washington without feeling a half inch taller, my voice deeper, and experiencing a touch of red, white, and blue piety. People For the American Way arranged the tour for us and it was all first class. We started at our offices, which happen to be handsome in a historic way and lovelier than most. I was very proud. We toured the White House, which was thrilling, but unfortunately the first family was traveling. That might sound less presumptuous if you knew that it was Lyn and I who had an event for the president at our home the very first time he came to L.A. when he was running for the U.S. Senate in 2004.

———

THE TWO DC stops I recall most vividly were to the relatively new World War II Memorial and the Library of Congress. Knowing I would be coming, the library filled a long table in a private room with news clippings, government papers, photographs, DVDs, CDs, and other rare items that referred back to my work starting in the fifties. When I saw a tape referencing Bob Hope and me, I was sure it was his appearance at the USO show in my honor. But to my amazement—because I had not the slightest memory of it—there was Hope in front of the curtain at one of his own shows, calling on "the extraordinary Norman Lear" to join him onstage. For some four or more minutes he talked to me quite seriously about how I managed to produce so many shows.

You have to know Bob Hope was a showbiz god to my generation. Although at a 180-degree remove from Charlie Chaplin's art, he was as well known and as highly regarded by his community. I was awed to see myself deemed a peer by Bob Hope.

At the World War II Memorial, what caught my breath was a set of computers set into the brick wall that invited the visitor to type in the name and serial number of any GI who served in any capacity. Surrounded by family, I typed in the info, and in a second there I was—my photo, enlistment date, where I served in the States, the date we flew to Italy, every mission, every target, and the date of our return. The expression "mind-blowing" preceded that moment by a long shot, I know, but was nonetheless created for it, I also know.

The People For thirtieth anniversary event in my honor was an emotional high and a financial bonanza, raising over $1.5 million. The thing that made me proudest, though, was the appearance of several members of our 750-body Young Elected Officials, one serving in the U.S. Congress and the others holding statewide office. They spoke of their difficult beginnings and how they got from there to elected office, and to this moment at the Kennedy Center. Led by the dazzling Andrew Gillum, they could not have been more compelling.

When House Minority Leader Nancy Pelosi introduced me, I spoke of having accepted an invitation some months before from Nancy Reagan and Jerry Perenchio to attend the debate among the candidates for the Republican nomination that was taking place at the Reagan Presidential Library. (In 2004, at the invitation of Mrs. Reagan, I'd also attended her husband's funeral.) That down-to-earth civility, despite our politically contentious relationship, is what I wished to emphasize, especially as compared to its opposite when the seven Republican candidates began another of their truth-bending, screw-the-facts, disdain- and scorn-filled debates—all of which has escalated to the sheer hatred and billion-dollar defamation we are witnessing from the far Right today.

One disgraceful result of the ugliness being spewed is the way the rabid extremists who now define the party have abandoned and discarded one of their own, a giant Republican figure it shames our entire culture to have tossed aside. Not once in all of the debates that culminated with Mitt Romney's nomination for president did any candidate mention the five-star general who commanded our troops to victory in World War II and went on to a two-term presidency of these United States, Dwight David Eisenhower. Maybe it's just my loyalty to the ultimate WWII commander showing, but I can't help but wonder if the denial of General Eisenhower by his party has anything to do with the words he spoke as he left office: "We must guard against the acquisition of unwarranted influence, whether sought or unsought, by the military-industrial complex." (It was "the congressional-military-industrial complex" as originally written.) "Only an alert and knowledgeable citizenry," he continued, "can compel the proper meshing of the huge military and industrial machinery of defense with our peaceful methods and goals, so that security and liberty may prosper together."

I know that Ike was late to come down on Joe McCarthy and failed to take any kind of lead on civil rights, but we have yet to elect the perfect president. And so, well aware of his shortcomings, I have nonetheless recommended to many on the Left that, since the political Right has sought to abort any memory of Ike and the speech that presidential scholars believe to be one of the most significant ever delivered, we should adopt him. No way, they say, and I think Robert Frost had it right: "A liberal is a man who is too broad-minded to take his own side in a quarrel."

THE MAIN THING I took away from Vermont and that celebration of my life was—I know I've touched on it but it's worth amplifying here—the overwhelming part that a four-letter word, *LUCK*, has played in it. My Fates, God, the Creator, Whoever, Whatever, have certainly been generous to me over the years, not least by allowing me so many of them. Unlike an earlier Norman, I'm eager to take the credit and the pleasure my accomplishments have earned me, but not at the cost to my soul of overlooking the consistent aid of a conspiring universe. Yes, I enlisted in World War II, totally committed to serving in battle, but it was good fortune that placed me in the only bomb group of B-17 Flying Fortresses, a faster, more maneuverable plane with a better safety record than the B-24 Liberators that filled out the rest of the 15th Air Force.

I was equally committed to working hard and taking risks, but David Susskind still had to have turned up at Ciro's the night Danny Thomas delivered our routine about Yiddish words, or Simmons and I would not have been in New York three days later writing for Jack Haley. And nothing about how hard Ed and I worked or how well we wrote had anything do with the myriad turns of events in Jerry Lewis's life and career that found him watching Jack Haley one night and then, at the sight of a sketch he thought would work brilliantly for him, moving heaven and earth to have MCA yank us from Haley to work for him and Dean Martin, a team destined to become the toast of the nation.

And through those early years, many of them so financially difficult because of my divorce settlement and remarriage, what else but luck explains why there appeared out of the blue a Mary, the AT&T operator in Boston who so gratuitously saved me tens of thousands of dollars in telephone bills as a result of her most unusual circumstance?

As for the career that followed, while the decisions to cast Carroll O'Connor, Jean Stapleton, Rob Reiner, and Sally Struthers in *All in the Family* were entirely my own, the four-way chemistry that resulted in each player drawing comic strength from the other characters, at the same time brilliantly playing against them to deepen the humor in every direction, was a gift that I can only take credit for nourishing and using well. And then there's the luck of ABC not having picked up the show, which gave Rob time to age into the part of Mike while allowing me to earn the three-picture United Artists deal that emboldened me in my dealings with CBS.

Describing Lyn's and my African safari I mentioned that it ended with a cruise on the Mediterranean. Here's how that came about. Just one day before we were headed east for our tall ships regatta and our prehoneymoon in Africa, I was lunching in a trendy L.A. restaurant and stopped to chat with a friend who happened to be dining with Charles Knapp, founder of a major investment firm. After I told my friend of my plans for the summer, Knapp, who had only just met me, said as casually as if he was handing me a napkin, "If you're flying home through London, as I suspect, and you can tack another week on the trip, hop over to Naples and pick up my boat, why don't you?" No reason why we couldn't or didn't, and that resulted in ten rapturous days cruising the Mediterranean on a gorgeous 110-foot yacht with a most accommodating captain and crew of six—a gift from a total stranger. Go top that for good fortune!

Okay, I will. Given what The Gulley means, has meant, and will continue to mean to the Lear clan, how lucky was I to be sitting in the Pasadena home of that art collector, unknown to me until that very hour, when his daughter informed him that Ken Noland called and left word that his Robert Frost farm in Vermont was still for sale?

THOUGH I CONTINUED my involvement in PFAW, VREG, and other matters, my primary focus was on finishing this book. And then, ironically and dramatically—exactly as you might expect in a life as eventful as mine—just as its completion began to loom on the horizon, my luck changed. I woke up a day or two before Thanksgiving with a deadly blood infection, MRSA. My doctor was on holiday in Mexico, I saw someone else, was misdiagnosed as having pseudo gout, and was put on steroids. The MRSA bug, it turns out, feeds on steroids. A few days later my son-in-law, Jon, who had just arrived in L.A. with his family for the holiday, took one look at my swollen hand and we were off to the emergency room, from which I was quickly taken into surgery. Some weeks later, when he was convinced that I was out of the woods, my surgeon felt free to say that when he first saw me he didn't think I had more than twenty-four to thirty-six hours. Jon had gotten me to the hospital in the nick of time. Son of a bitch! I can't say I wasn't frightened, but again I couldn't help thinking— even *this*!

After surgery I spent a week in the hospital on an IV with a hand that looked like a boy's pitcher's mitt. Then, still requiring a nurse and a daily IV, I returned to Lyn and our lovely home, with all of its glorious modern art, family pictures, and prized belongings. Blotting out all the loveliness, however, and drawing me to it like a giant magnet to a common nail, was the computer in my study that contained among its many icons one labeled "BOOK." I sat there unable to do much more than stare at it for weeks.

In addition to a mind that was having a difficult time getting itself together, I didn't have a right hand or one of the forefingers I required in the application of my two-finger typing technique. And then a second extraordinary event took place, and the bad luck of my MRSA period was trumped by what happened Next.

A quarterly Village Roadshow board meeting was about to take place in Beverly Hills. Attending it was a friend and board member, Rafe Vogel, who'd flown in from New York the day before. He was seated on the plane next to a woman who engaged him in conversation, in the course of which my name came up. The woman caught her breath and said, "Norman Lear! You're seeing him tomorrow? I can't believe it."

She then told him this story. Through the years she had given away hundreds upon hundreds of books, but there were two in her possession that she would never consider parting with. One was her grandfather's Bible, and the other was a book her mother, long gone, had picked up at a fund-raiser in a Jewish temple in Ohio. It was the Bible that Norman Lear held at his Bar Mitzvah. Stunned, Rafe asked if he could have me phone her. She lived in L.A.—a few miles from my home—and the next day I gave her a call. After we'd expressed wonder at the miracle of finding each other, I asked what she intended to do with the book. She said she'd always hoped to give it to me, so I said I'd send someone to pick it up. "But how do I know I'm talking to Norman Lear?" she asked.

I laughed and offered to pick it up personally. She said she wanted to give me my Bible, not take up my time, and then she read me the dedication on the inside cover of the Bible: "Presented to Norman Lear on the occasion of his Bar Mitzvah, July 1935, by the Sisterhood of Temple . . ." She paused. "Temple Shaari Zedek in Brooklyn," I responded eagerly, and had the Bible in my good hand later that day.

I held this weathered volume of sacred text and imagined its history—all the homes it rested in, all the hands that opened it seeking strength and comfort, all the life struggles it witnessed before it was returned to me—and then in the middle of imagining that, it struck me like a bolt of lightning. My Bar Mitzvah Bible, lost to me for seventy-eight years, now back in my hands—and what was *I* doing? I was focusing on where it had been rather than on the staggering miracle of its return to *me*. Could I have a better example of my capacity for dissociation, for not taking my true self seriously? Or is it more a question of how quickly I caught on to myself this time?

I think it is the latter. I've been taking myself more seriously lately, just like Richard Brooks. I may fall off the wagon now and then, but I take seriously the man who countered those religious figures sowing hatred and using God to empower themselves; the man responsible for bringing the Declaration of Independence to all fifty states; who helped to bring 2 million new voters to the polls; and whose proudest associations in adulthood have been with men and women who he believes, for their time, led public lives reflecting an understanding of sacred honor.

I ADMIRE THE MEN AND WOMEN who shared and valued the missions of People For the American Way and the Business Enterprise Trust, including the guy who conceived of them and pulled them together. He's the Norman Lear I feel I own now. H.K. didn't fill out the silhouette I held out for him. I did. It took all these years to get here but it was altogether worth it. I read with new eyes the *Christian Science Monitor*'s description of me as "an attractive man with an expression halfway between a professor and a leprechaun."

And you know what else I keep thinking? Of all the characters I've created and cast, the one who resembles me most is Maude. That's the character who shares my passion, my social concerns, and my politics—not as articulately as the "professor" in me would wish—still, pleading to be heard and understood. Oh, and as important as all the rest combined, it was Maude who dealt best with the foolishness of the human condition because she knew herself to personify it. Oh, my Maude!

Of all the moments in all the shows, nothing touched me more to the core while lifting me to the heavens, nothing in some twenty-six hundred half hours, like a certain scene in *Maude*. Once a year the local TV station in Tuckahoe held a charity telethon that Maude produced. In our third season, on the third telethon, we see Maude step into the spotlight to introduce a surprise guest and a song.

"You've all heard of Paul Anka," she announces provocatively. "Well, performing for you tonight, in person on this very stage, we have Mr. Anka's very own gardener, Mr. Emile Fontazoo."

The orchestra begins to play the intro to "My Way," while Walter, just offstage, furtively motions to her that Fontazoo has not yet arrived and adds, "You sing it, Maude." Maude shoos Walter off as if he were kidding and continues with the introduction.

From the first table reading and at every rehearsal something stirring in me grew more and more emotional and excited as this scene approached, and I wanted to shout and cry with what I was experiencing. Why? Coming up was a great scene, everyone present knew that, but something else had to be going on inside me. As I said, Maude represented my passion, my emotions, my caring, and my giant need to express all of it. If I could accept that part of me reflected in Maude the way I learned to accept the spiritual side of me in Lyn, I would be whole. I'd have filled out my silhouette.

The scene ended with Maude alone onstage. My emotions overflowed at rehearsals because hidden in that fantastic performer was my alter ego. Walter interrupts again and urges her to sing; she sings a few notes and feels it's ridiculous. "I can't, Walter," she says. "Paul Anka sings this song."

"You sing it better than him," Walter responds. That gives Maude a moment's pause.

"But it was written for Sinatra," she protests.

"You sing it better than Sinatra," he replies.

"Oh, please, Walter."

"And better than Fontazoo," Walter adds.

This stops Maude cold. She turns to Walter and, with as much incredulity as anyone can muster in a lifetime, cries out: *"Better than Fontazoo?"* (Oh, my God, that line out of her mouth! *Better than Fontazoo?*) And then she turns to the camera and belts the last half of the song as full-out and with as much soul as Paul Anka, Frank Sinatra, and yes, Norman Lear combined.

> *Yes, there were times, I'm sure you knew*
> *When I bit off more than I could chew*
> *But through it all when there was doubt*
> *I ate it up and spit it out*

I did it all and I stood tall
And did it my way . . .
The record shows I took the blows
And did it my way.

That moment, that woman, that statement will live in my mind to eternity as if it had been shot ten minutes ago. And as I exit this life, however many years from now, I imagine running into Bea Arthur and having this exchange:

"You know, Bea, I think I lived a *better* life than Fontazoo." To which she'll reply: "Better than *Fontazoo*?" BLACKOUT.

Even *that*!

Acknowledgments

IN ADDITION TO THE CHERISHED members of my family, my life has been blessed with friends and associates who qualify as loved ones, and, while I would like to mention them all, as a nonagenarian and an author with a finite number of pages, I have found it impossible. Forgive me all others.

I HAVE SIX CHILDREN: five daughters, one son. I have to believe that you know me well enough by now to know how much I love them, but perhaps not to know why, beyond the fact that I'm their father and love goes with that territory. The fact is, my kids are splendid people. "Splendid"—how seldom we see or hear that word. I have to believe it is because so few things *are* splendid, especially when the word is taken seriously. With all our mistakes as parents—Charlotte and me, Frances and me, Lyn and me—Ellen, Kate, Maggie, Ben, Madeline, and Brianna all grew up with two feet on the ground and their heads on straight. Their personalities are very different, as are their talents, but their desire to live life well, while helping everyone else to do the same, is an evergreen.

I could not feel prouder of these children. As I write this, Ben is producing and directing his first documentary film; Madeline's long-time passion for photography and photojournalism has broadened at Harvard to include Mideast studies and the Arabic language; and Brianna's singing and rich stage presence is alive and well at Vassar (though, if we've been interpreting her phone calls correctly, we may see it compete with a passion for neuroscience).

I talk to their older half sisters several times a week, and to Dan and Jon, husbands of Maggie and Kate, respectively, often as well. That Kate chairs the board of Ballet Hispanico and produces Broadway theater thrills me, as does Maggie's involvement with juvenile justice issues (also the subject of Ben's documentary). And how about this: There are no other couples anywhere with whom Lyn and I would rather spend time.

As for Ellen, the family member I've known and loved longest, she has lived the most independent life of any of us. Married twice and cheerily divorced each time, she elected not to have children of her own but is a terrific grandmother to the triplets of one of her stepsons. Ellen, with a PhD in psychology and a lifelong love of horses, combines the two admirably through the therapeutic riding facility Pal-O-Mine, using the animals to help emotionally and physically troubled young girls fight their demons.

Kate and Jon have selflessly provided me with two glorious grandsons, Daniel and Noah—and Maggie and Dan, with my fabulous Griffin and only granddaughter, the inimitable Zoe. It is they who fill me with my keenest sense of legacy.

JOE TORRENUEVA, "Little Joe," has been cutting my hair for over fifty years, and has spent his life unknowingly giving "How to Be a Human Being" lessons. When my family would assemble in L.A. for the holidays—eventually adding sons-in-law and grandchildren to the mix—we'd all gather in the living room where, sitting on a high stool brought in from the kitchen, Little Joe would cut each one's hair to the music of the others whooping and hollering around them.

I'VE WRITTEN and worked with so many men and women with whom I've laughed, and laughed outrageously. I see each of their happy faces as clearly as the screen in front of me and recall the deep debt I owe to, among so many others, Don Nicholl, Bob Schiller and Bob Weiskopf, Mickey Ross and Bernie West, Alan Thicke, Rick Mitz, Rod Parker, Paul Bogart, Charlie Hauck, Eugenie Ross-Leming, John Rich, Hal Cooper, Susan Harris, Mel Tolkin, Mort Lachman, Hal Collins, Gail Parent, Ann Marcus, Joan Darling, Fred Freeman and Larry Cohen, Hal Kanter, Allan Manings, Charlotte Brown, Phil Mishkin, Ron Burla, John Baskin, Judi Ann Mason, Elliot Schoenman, Larry Rhine, Jack Shea, Jack Ellinson, Herb Kenwith, Frank Tarloff, Saul Turteltaub, Bernie Orenstein, and Ed Simmons.

I can see us all one day at that longest of conference tables where only God, or the gods, or no one at all, will hear us, but that won't keep us—nothing ever did—from "killing" each other.

And, at another table a great many years from now, will be the guys and gals, writers and performers, who have me laughing today—and they know who they are because I tell them at every opportunity.

FOR ALL THE HIT shows we had, there were many others that, for varying reasons, failed. Several of them are discussed in the book, but four that weren't demand mention here: *a.k.a. Pablo*, the first show that centered on an extended Latino family; *All That Glitters*, a late-night soap set in a world where Genesis had been rewritten and man was taken from the rib of a woman; *A Year at the Top*, about a rock band whose members sell their souls to the devil for twelve months of stardom; and *The Nancy Walker Show*, starring the truest female clown of the century. That I let down someone whose comedy added time to my life pains me every time I think of it.

———

THE BUSINESS ENTITIES with which I have been associated over the years could not have succeeded as they did without the help of such key executives as Daryl Egerstrom, Art Warshaw, Kelly Smith, Barbara Brogliatti, Michael Weisbarth, Fran McConnell, Jeanie Bradley, George Sunga, Gary Lieberthal, Jeff Stott, Jess Wittenberg, Fern Field, Andy Kaplan, Viva Knight, Ken Stump, Brooke Buhrman, Glenn Padnick, Helen Hernandez, Stephanie Sills, Martin Shafer, Andy Scheinman, Al Burton, Robin French, and, of course, my long term associates and closest of friends, Bud Yorkin, Jerry Perenchio, Alan Horn, and Hal Gaba.

I'VE NEVER WORKED on a production where a woman wasn't "the glue that held things together." The metaphor stands for an amalgam of personality, strength, and common sense that was a force for uniting disparate individuals and their talents. Among them were Eve Brandstein, Jackie Koch, Marian Rees, Patricia Palmer, Rita Dillon, Brigit Jensen, Madeline Smith, Rita Riggs, Lorraine Sevré, Sylvia Ogilvie, Gloria Vinson, Jadi Joe, Ana Maria Geraldino, Marilyn Pessin, Jackie Jensen, and Cherry Alvarado.

Cherry's daughter, Julie Dyer-Lopez, came to work to assist her mother when she was seventeen, and learned on the job so well that she has worked for me for twenty-eight years now, the past seventeen of them as Act III's CFO. I think of Julie as a tower of trust and the mother of my financial life.

TIME PRESSURES led me to do much of my writing in cars. For thirty years, a series of drivers—young guys who wished to, and more often than not went on to, become writers, directors, producers, set designers, and decorators— allowed me to keep my eyes off the wheel and in my work. I am indebted to Jeff

Shapiro, Todd Waldman, Sean Dwyer, Troy Hutchinson, Sandi Veith, Sam Wendell, Richard Draney, David Hoberman, and Greg Cope White.

AT NINETY-TWO the best thing I have going for me is my predilection for, and working relationships with, young people. A key associate today, Brent Miller, is as talented, charming, and certain-to-make-it a thirty-something as I've ever worked with. Iara Peng and Andrew Gillum, without whom Young People For and Young Elected Officials might not have succeeded, are two more of the young who have inspired me. Among friends I see often are several of the spoken word artists who traveled and performed with the Declaration of Independence—the brilliant and riveting Steve Connell, Sekou Andrews, and Beau Sia.

And then there's Anthony Rich and Mark Johnson. "Ant," as he calls himself, is a young cat—I know, nobody but an antediluvian uses that word anymore—in the music business. When Hal Gaba and I owned Concord Music, award-winning sound engineer Mark Johnson filmed an elderly guy sitting on Santa Monica's Third Street Promenade, playing a guitar and singing his version of "Stand By Me." Johnson then took that footage around the world, put headsets on street singers and musicians, and filmed them singing and playing along to the original track. That became a video that had audiences jumping to their feet. Ant brought it to me, I showed it to Hal, we took it to Howard Schultz, and Starbucks put Playing for Change's *Songs Around the World* CD on the map. The PFC band has produced several CDs since, toured the world, and the PFC Foundation has built six music schools for children in as many African countries.

ADDITIONAL HUGS and kisses to:

David Picker, my longtime friend and the best studio head of his time. Had he not offered me a three-picture deal at United Artists, I might not have had the strength to tell CBS, "I'll walk if you cut that."

Skip Brittenham, the most dynamic and laid back (an extraordinary combination) of entertainment industry attorneys. While executing many of the biggest Hollywood deals you've ever read about, he's found time to sail fish the world.

David Nochimson, a partner of Skip's and the gentleman attorney to whom I most often gratefully turn.

Geri Jewell, who I'm proud to have cast in *The Facts of Life*, and who has been a great inspiration to me. If cerebral palsy couldn't keep this enlightened comedienne down, nothing could.

Virginia Carter, a research physicist at Aerospace who realized that she'd rocketed to the glass ceiling in science and, when I met her in the early '70s, was thinking about work in another field. A vigorous women's rights advocate, she helped Tandem/T.A.T. establish and maintain equity in our hiring and in our scripts. She went on to produce several After School Specials, full-length TV movies on serious subjects produced by the networks specifically for a teenage audience.

will.i.am, as talented an entrepreneur, philanthropist, and citizen as he is a producer and entertainer. He is of that rare breed of stars who sees no risk in spending their public capital fighting for the good of all.

The relative handful of "matinee idols" and "cinema queens" who, through the years, have never ceased to speak their progressive minds. Among those I've known best were and are: Gregory Peck, Paul Newman, Burt Lancaster, Jane Fonda, Harry Belafonte, Barbra Streisand, Martin Sheen, Mary Steenburgen and Ted Danson, Robert Redford, Oprah Winfrey, Leonardo DiCaprio, and George Clooney.

Clooney is perhaps the clearest current illustration of what I find so gutsy and admirable. He doesn't write, produce, direct, or perform—and most remarkably he excels at all four—without reflecting his conscience and his humanity every time out.

I'VE BEEN FORTUNATE to know numbers of philanthropically inclined couples and would wish to salute them all here. Space will not allow, so let me do that by mentioning the first one that leaps to mind, Jon and Lillian Lovelace. Jon and his dad created and ran a giant mutual fund. Giving was as natural to the Lovelaces as their breathing, and since their interests knew no bounds, causes and institutions throughout the culture were the beneficiaries.

HAD I NOT had the advice, encouragement and support of Father Theodore Hesburgh, Andrew Heiskell, Rev. Dr. George Regas, Rabbi Leonard Beerman, Rev. Dr. Martin E. Marty, Rev. Charles Bergstrom, Rev. John Buchanan, Marge Tabankin, and Stanley Sheinbaum, People For the American Way might never have come about.

And it might not have survived and thrived, but for the dedicated and tireless efforts of its leaders, Tony Podesta, Arthur Kropp, Carole Shields, Ralph Neas, and its current brilliant and indefatigable president, Michael Keegan. Also indispensable have been Jim Autry, David Altschul, Carol Blum, Bobbie and Wynn Handman, Peter Montgomery, Melanne Verveer, Elliot Mincberg, Tim McDonald, Nick Ucci, Ricki Seidman, Judy Green, David Kusnet, Jorge Mursuli, Ann Beaudry, Marge Baker, Debbie Liu, Mike Lux, Mary Jean Collins, Carol Keyes, Judith Schaeffer, Nancy Keenan, Ramona Ripston, Bray Creech, Kathleen Turner, Alec Baldwin, Jane Lynch, and Seth MacFarlane. Without them, the organization would not be the bulwark for civil rights and liberties it is today.

I feel as strongly about all those who have been key to the success and cultural impact of the Lear Center at USC: Geoffrey Cowan, former dean of the Annenberg School of Communication, who, with Marty Kaplan, the Center's founding director, brought me the idea; Managing Director Johanna Blakley; Kate Folb, director of the Center's Hollywood Health and Society initiative; and the current dean of the Annenberg School, Ernest Wilson.

A source of great pride, too, is the Business Enterprise Trust: its first director, Kirk Hanson; its longterm director, the indispensible Kathy Meyer; her assistants, Marilyn Turner and Stephanie Weiss; the man largely responsible for editing the documentaries we made, Mark Kornweibel; and my speech-writing confederate—in this and so many other areas—David Bollier. Although he is a much younger man, we've worked together as peers.

THERE ARE ONLY a few cousins named Lear in my life today—the brilliant author and professor of philosophy at the University of Chicago Jonathan Lear; his lovely daughter, Sophia, writing television comedy; and Sharri Lear, granddaughter of the Uncle Jack who flicked me quarters, an executive at Sony Pictures.

LARA BERGTHOLD is the living definition of solidity, smarts, and truth. For the past fifteen years, she has been my close personal associate. Lara was running the Hollywood Women's Political Caucus when I invited her to manage the Lear Family Foundation and consult with Lyn and me in our political, social, and philanthropic involvements. Now partnered in the issue-oriented firm RALLY, Lara represents me in relation to this memoir and chairs the board of PFAW.

MARK E POLLACK has not been in my employ for more than two decades. Surprisingly, remarkably, amazingly, he has nonetheless never been out of my life, my career, my businesses, my causes, or my conscience for a single day. If anyone lived on a practical daily basis with a functioning alter ego, it is NL with MEP.

ADDITIONALLY, I'VE WORKED closely with Catherine Hand, Paul Schaeffer, Bob Burkett, Betsy Kenny, Caty Borum, Andy Spahn, Aviva Rosenthal,

Cherie Simon, Christy Salcido, Marc Morgenstern, and Penny Wright. So much of what I have been into politically and socially over time would not have been possible without them. Their passions matched mine, they interfaced with key people when I wasn't available, and everything we touched was better for their having been a part of it.

I WAS BLESSED at birth with common sense. But common sense, like a tennis player, requires a backboard. This book would have been a considerably lesser effort had I not had a brilliant, exquisitely sensitive professional backboard. Her name is Dr. Maureen Gordon. Many balls—in this case thoughts, memories, ancient reasoning—came back at me in ways that forced me to reach and stretch to pound them back to her. With every stretch came a little more light.

APPROPRIATELY, I DEDICATED this book to my beloved Lyn and my kids, but I am also enormously grateful to those whose encouragement was particularly meaningful to me: William Goldman, Howard Stringer, Bill Moyers, Nora Ephron, A. Scott Berg, Arianna Huffington, Roger Rosenblatt, Phil Rosenthal, Betsy Kenny Lack, Richard Sarnoff, Nancy Friday, Digby Diehl, Byron Katie, and Stephen Mitchell. Stephen went so far as to help me edit the first half of the book as I was writing it.

I sent a draft-in-progress to my friend and book agent Amanda Urban and she happily showed it to Ann Godoff, who purchased this memoir for Penguin Press and is its editor. Ann could not have been more wise, encouraging, or helpful.

ESSENTIAL TO THE gathering of the library of shows, scripts, notes, correspondence, interviews, etc. on which *Even* This . . . depended was the devoted and irreplaceable work of my long-time archivist and dear friend Jean Anderson.

And beyond essential to my actual writing was, as I indicated in the book, Paul Slansky. In addition to his aid and support as researcher, editor, and chief adviser, he was as hard-working and dedicated as he was a delight to work with. If a book can be said to have had a producer, Paul was it on this one.

P.S.: In the course of writing this book I have never picked up my copy of *Roget's Thesaurus* without experiencing the joy and surprise of discovery upon turning to any page. How the man got all that together in a single lifetime is one of the most delightful of mysteries. Thank you, Mr. Roget.